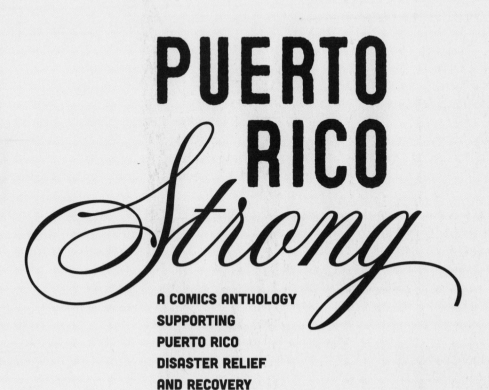

# PUERTO RICO *Strong*

## A COMICS ANTHOLOGY SUPPORTING PUERTO RICO DISASTER RELIEF AND RECOVERY

EDITED BY MARCO LOPEZ, DESIREE RODRIGUEZ,
HAZEL NEWLEVANT, DEREK RUIZ, AND NEIL SCHWARTZ

Cover illustration by Naomi Franquiz
Back cover illustration by Kristen Van Dam

ISBN: 978-1-941302-90-3

Library of Congress Control Number: 2018931321

Why did I do this? It's obvious, isn't it? Two hurricanes hit Puerto Rico. How could I not do anything? As I was sitting there in my home, comfortably watching the news online, all I could say to myself was, "I've got to do something." But what? Outside of writing (and working on film projects rarely), I don't have any other skills. I stopped drawing almost twenty years ago. So, what do I do? There's that old saying, "write what you know." I know how to make comics. So, in this case, it was "make what you know." And that's when I messaged Derek, and then Desiree.

I asked them if they wanted to do something for Puerto Rico. An anthology bringing together the best of the best in Puerto Rican and Latinx creators, and friends, to raise money for an island full of Americans that were about to be struck by a monumental disaster. We'd later find out it was far worse than any of us could imagine. And they said yes. Of course, they said yes. Because that's how they roll. Derek brought in Neil (whom I can never say enough good things about), and I went off messaging and e-mailing individual writers and artists. I was hitting up a lot of the bigger names in this business. Desiree was thinking outside the box when it came to talent. She's good at that.

There was, of course, the obvious discussion. Do we raise the money ourselves to print this book? Or do we get a publisher? I used to write for Lion Forge. They're only one of the best publishers in this business. An African-American owned juggernaut. Why not? Worst that could happen is they say no. Thankfully, that didn't happen. I owe you big, Carl. Not only did you give me my first actual writing gig in this business, but you always respond to my e-mails. That says a lot about an individual.

With Lion Forge on board, Hazel Newlevant joined the editing team. You know that phrase awesomesauce? That's Hazel.

I sometimes look back and can't believe this actually came together. That this is in your hands and that you're reading it right now. Just one random thought, amongst a myriad, of what could I do to help my people. And it blossomed into something very powerful. Or at least, I hope that's what's happened by the time you head to your comic shop to buy a copy.

This is probably the part where I should wrap things up. But know when you say the title, that's because of Derek. The stories we cover? That's because of Desiree. But all of this is the heart and soul and sweat and tears and perseverance of an amazing group of editors, writers, artists, colorists, letters, and more who came together to help an island of Americans.

I only did what I knew was right and what I knew was needed. Comics have power, and with this anthology, we've shown that. Always proud to be Boricua.

**MARCO LOPEZ,** *Co-Editor*

There's a song I've been listening to a lot recently, "Vivir Mi Vida," specifically an acoustic cover by Jennifer Lopez, though the original is sung by Marc Anthony. Even in the States it's a well-known song; the upbeat salsa rhythms have been played on the radio, movies, and television countless times. But the lyrics are actually very poignant. The line, "Si así es la vida, hay que vivirla, la la lé" can be translated to, "If this is life, you must live it."

In this anthology our contributors share their personal stories about Puerto Rico, they share our history, our struggles and strife, the beauty of our island, and the resilience of our people. The history of Puerto Rico and the Puerto Rican community is a complicated one, but one of the goals of this anthology was to educate others on those complications. My only hope is that we have accomplished that in whatever small way.

I am grateful to Marco Lopez for pulling me in on this project. I am grateful to my co-editors who worked so hard in making this a reality. I am grateful to each and every contributor who put their valuable and irreplaceable time into making *Puerto Rico Strong* what it is. I am grateful to Lion Forge for believing in this project and in wanting to help my community. I am grateful to each and every person who tweeted about this project, or posted on Facebook, or shared the news with friends. I am grateful to every single reader who now holds this book in their hands.

If this is to be our lives, we must live them, with compassion and pride. Yo soy puertoriquena con mucho orgullo.

**DESIREE RODRIGUEZ,** *Co-Editor*

It has been my great honor to work with the contributing artists and writers, and the other editors of *Puerto Rico Strong*, to help bring these stories to fruition. The devastation of Hurricane Maria, and the federal government's unconscionable lack of rebuilding efforts, revealed the deep ignorance that so many mainland, white, non-Latinx Americans had about Puerto Rico's history, culture, and status as part of the United States. I include my past self in this ignorance.

The comics in *Puerto Rico Strong* weave together a prismatic tapestry of Puerto Rican identities and experiences. They range from intimate family traditions to uncovered histories; the direness of the present moment to the luminous possible futures we can strive for. I am so grateful to all the creators who have bared their souls and flexed their talents within this anthology. Everyone should read this book, and then commit to working toward a future of dignity and self-determination for Puerto Rico, in big ways or small.

Tackling any of the world's serious, life-threatening problems feels overwhelming. We can't all be aid workers, but many of us can use the abilities we do have to raise money for the people who are able to help on the front lines, or uplift voices that need to be heard. For me, I can use my abilities to edit and publish comics anthologies that matter.

**HAZEL NEWLEVANT,** *Co-Editor*

You know that scene in *Step Brothers* where Will Ferrell says to John C. Reilly "Did we just become best friends?" after they find out how much alike they are? Well, that's basically how Marco Lopez, my fellow editor on *Puerto Rico Strong*, and I became friends. We had been talking about comics for a couple of months, and besides us both being Puerto Rican, we had a lot of the same fanboy tendencies.

When Hurricane Irma happened, we talked a lot about how we both had family in Puerto Rico, how close that one got to the Island, and how we should be working together on comics. I think that's about the time I sent him the "Did we just become best friends" gif. At around the same time, I introduced Marco to Neil Schwartz, who is also an editor on *Puerto Rico Strong* (and my brother from another mother). We started a Facebook Messenger chat where we discussed many, many, many comic nerd things, and that's where *Puerto Rico Strong* came to life.

Maybe a week after Irma hit, we were talking about Hurricane Maria and how close this one seemed to be getting to our beloved Puerto Rico. Then September 20 came around and Maria hit Puerto Rico, and as days started to go by, Marco and I got angrier and sadder as it seemed nothing was being done to help our friends and family. Marco in his frustration shot me a message that was something along the lines of, "We need to use what we are best at to help Puerto Rico!" My first thought was, "How is being a weirdly awkward nerd going to help PR?", but he explained he meant using our skills as comic creators and doing an anthology.

From there, the book came together relatively fast. Desiree Rodriguez signed up the same day as me, and I asked Neil shortly after that. I jokingly started to refer to us as Team Voltron and am pretty sure I sent Marco and Neil a whole bunch of Voltron gifs—which maybe was the universe using my humor to tell us to ask Lion Forge to be the publisher of this amazing project called *Puerto Rico Strong*. So, Marco and Desiree did that, and Lion Forge said yes based purely on Marco's and Desiree's pitch. Which lead us getting our pilot for the Black Lion, Hazel Newlevant, who has made sure we have stayed on course this whole time and made sure we acted as a team. So, Team Voltron became Team *Puerto Rico Strong*, and now we have the book you are holding in your hands.

This book would not exist if it wasn't for Marco. I've known him less than a year, and that guy is already family to me. I will always be there for him in the same way he has been there for Puerto Rico.

Marco made me remember something my parents always told me about being Puerto Rican: we are all one big family, and even if we are not on the Island, it is our home. If one of us is hurting, we all hurt, so we help no matter what.

So, take a bow, Brother Marco.

**DEREK RUIZ,** *Co-Editor, Proud Puerto Rican*

I have no words...OK, that's a bit of a lie. I actually have a lot of words, but the problem is getting them out. I mean, how do you sum up months of working on a project with an amazing group of people in a few short paragraphs? Let me tell you, it isn't easy.

Now, you may be asking yourself, why start with "I have no words"? Well, I have a good reason for that, but I will get to that in a moment, so bear with me, as this requires some setup. On the first page of my story, "Hope"—featured in this anthology—the main character, Adrian, says, "I have no words," while standing on a jetty in Puerto Rico. For him, this comes from all the emotions he's been feeling, from the moment the hurricanes first hit to physically seeing his family after traveling through a devastated Puerto Rico. Adrian simply doesn't know what to say after the journey that has shaken him to his very core, or to be more exact, his Puerto Rican spirit. He's tired and ready to falter, but he doesn't, because if I've learned one thing over the course of this anthology, it's that the Puerto Rican spirit is strong. Puerto Ricans have a sense of unity and determination to do something for their brothers and sisters in need. It is an extremely powerful thing to watch and be part of. So, I have no words because humans never cease to amaze me.

From the moment I was brought on to this project, I have been in awe of the fire burning within not only my co-editors, but in the writers, artists, inkers, colorists, letterers, and everyone else whose hands touched this project. Without hesitation, everyone came together to help those in dire need of aid, and it has been one of those moments where my faith in humanity has been restored. I also have learned more about Puerto Rico than I have ever known, and I find that to be both wonderful and sad. Wonderful because of the amazing culture that began with the Taíno and has continued to thrive, despite what they've been through. What's sad is that I didn't learn about Puerto Rico or its history in school. While not an official state, Puerto Rico is America, and their history should be just as important as the "mainland." I'm not going to get political here, but I hope/know you will all learn and take something magical away when reading this book. I envy those who will read these stories for the first time, because the stories in this book are filled with emotion, making them powerful.

I can't begin to express how honored and privileged I am to have been a part of an anthology with so much heart behind it. Without Marco Lopez, we wouldn't be here today. Not only was he the brains behind this operation, but he poured more blood, sweat, and tears into *Puerto Rico Strong* than anyone else. Thank you for letting all of us be part of your vision. I also have to thank Derek Ruiz for getting me involved in this anthology and always looking out for me, as any brother would. Desiree Rodriguez and Hazel Newlevant, thank you for keeping us on task and your part in making this vision a reality—I know this wasn't easy, but it was a pleasure working with you. A big thank-you to Lion Forge for backing this project, and to all my fellow writers, artists, inkers, colorists, and letterers for your time, energy, and unwavering spirit.

Last, but certainly not least, I want to thank my amazing wife, Delilah, for always being by my side and encouraging me to follow my passions. I love you always and forever.

Now, turn the page and enjoy this anthology.

**NEIL SCHWARTZ,** *Co-Editor*

# CONTENTS

**INTRODUCTION** 3

**HERE** *by Ronnie Garcia* 10

**MADRE DE DIOS** *by Daniel Irizarri Oquendo* 16

**HELPING HANDS** *Written by Alan Medina, Art by Ariela Kristantina* 18

**PASITOS GRANDES** *Written by Tristan J. Tarwater, Art by Cynthia Santos* 21

**AREYTOS** *Written by Vita Ayala, Art by Jamie Jones* 41

**GODS OF BORIKÉN** *by Sabrina Cintron* 51

**STORIES FROM MY FATHER**
*Written by Adam Lance Garcia, Art by Heidi Black* 52

**RESILIANCE BY LAMPLIGHT** *Written by Aldo Álvarez, Art by Sofía Dávila* 58

**FROM WITHIN** *by Nicole Goux* 62

**A BROKEN P.R.O.M.E.S.A.** *by Rosa Colón* 63

**THANKS FOR NOTHING** *by Tom Beland* 68

**LA CASITA OF AMERICAN HEROES**
*Written by Anthony Otero, Art by Charles "Ooge" Ugas* 70

**YÚCAHU AND THE CREATION OF THE FIRST MAN** *by Little Corvus* 79

**A TAÍNO'S TALE** *Art by Alejandro Rosado, Words by Shariff Musallam* 80

**OF MYTH & MONSTERS**
*Written by Marco Lopez & Derek Ruiz, Art by Jamie Jones* 86

**EL VAMPIRO DE MOCA** *by Leonardo Gonzalez* 95

**FAMILY ENDS WITH ME** *Written by Lilliam Rivera, Art by Allison Strejlau* 96

**LA OPERACIÓN** *by Ally Shwed* 102

**THE PUERTO RICAN BIRTH CONTROL TRIALS** *by Ally Shwed* 104

**BREAKING BREAD** *Written by Tara Martinez, Art by Rod Espinosa* 106

**THE DRAGON OF BAYAMÓN**
*Written by Jeff Gomez & Fabian Nicieza, Art by Adriana Melo* 114

**ON TRADITIONS & BEING HOMESICK** *by Jesenia Santana*  120

**CON AMOR, L.E.S.** *by Kat Fajardo*  125

**COCINAR** *Written by Vito Delsante, Art by Yehudi Mercado*  126

**FAMILY** *Written by Grant Alter, Art by Manuel Preitano*  130

**DREAMER** *by Kristen Van Dam*  139

**TAÍNO ONLINE** *by Joamette Gil*  140

**KNOWLEDGE OF SELF** *by Javier Cruz Winnik*  143

**BLAME IT ON 'RICO** *by Alberto "Tito" Serrano*  148

**MACONDO, PUERTO RICO**
*Written by Javier Morillo, Art by Dan Méndez Moore*  155

**FACELESS** *by Matt Bellisle*  163

**I DREAM OF HOME** *Written by Greg Anderson-Elysee, Art by Dennis Calero*  164

**HOPE** *Written by Neil Schwartz, Art by Ramón J. Sierra Santiago*  167

**PUERTO RICO STRONG** *by Alejandra Quintas*  177

**REALITY CHECK** *Written by Tony Bedard, Art by John R. Holmes*  178

**HEROES OF OUR OWN**
*Words by Marco Lopez & Derek Ruiz, Art by Brett Booth*  181

**THE LAST PIRATE IN THE CARIBBEAN**
*Written by Mina Elwell, Art by T.E. Lawrence*  182

**TODAVIA TENGO PUERTO RICO EN MI CORAZON**
*Written by Eugene Selassie, Art by Orlando Baez*  186

**THE HEART OF PUERTO RICO** *Written by Alexis Sergio, Art by Jules Rivera*  192

**OJALA** *by Mike Hawthorne*  197

**WHAT REMAINS IN THE DARK**
*Written by Amparo Ortíz, Art by Eliana Falcón-Dvorsky*  198

**CONTRIBUTOR QUOTES**  202

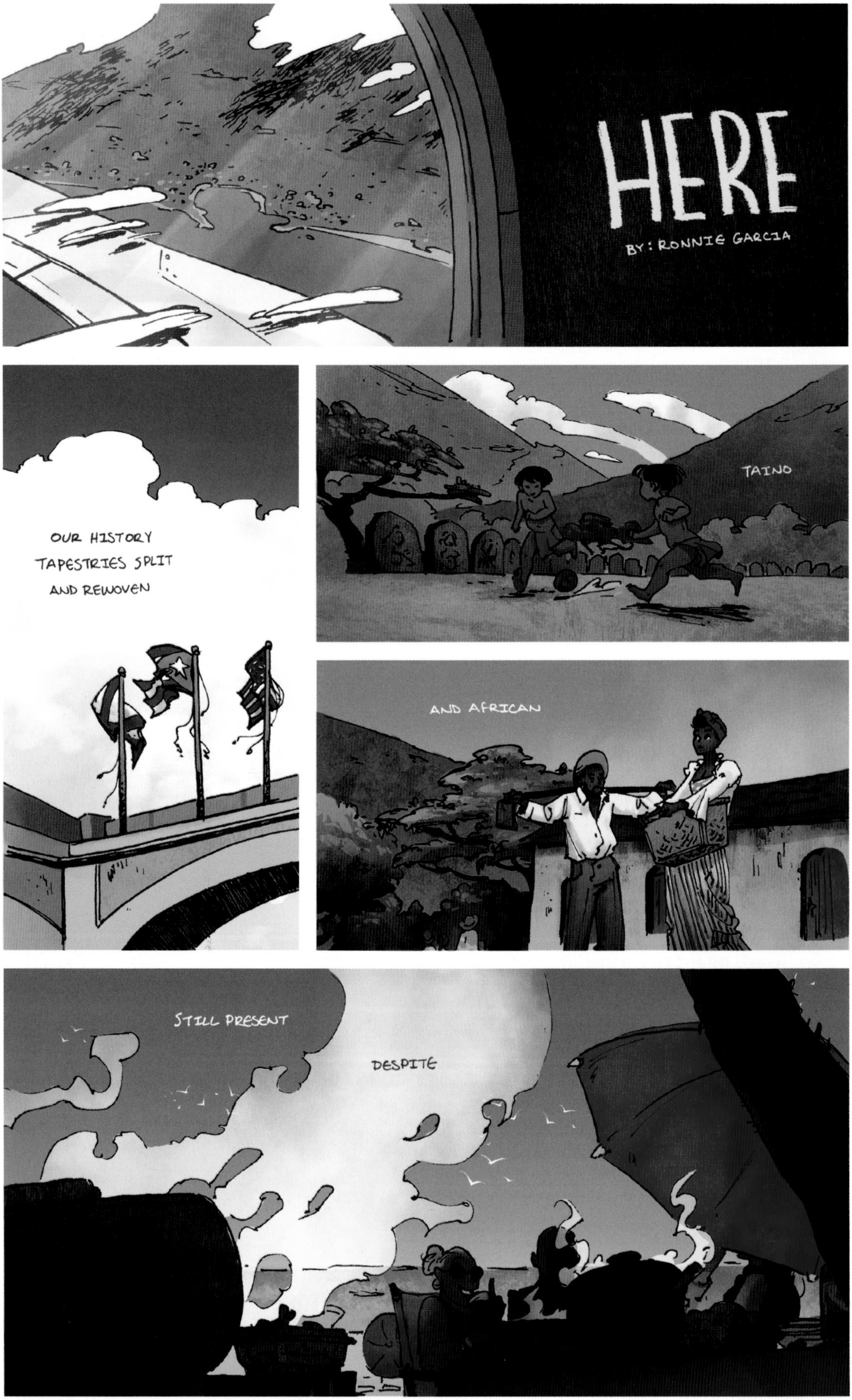
HERE
BY: RONNIE GARCIA
OUR HISTORY
TAPESTRIES SPLIT
AND REWOVEN
TAINO
AND AFRICAN
STILL PRESENT
DESPITE

CENTURIES OF
COLONIZATION

LIKE WAVES
ON STONE

CRASHING

BEATING

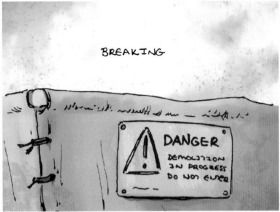

BREAKING

**DANGER**
DEMOLITION
IN PROGRESS
DO NOT ENTER

OUR PEOPLE

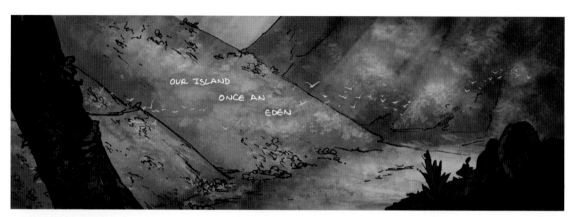

OUR ISLAND
ONCE AN
EDEN

UPROOTED

OVERNIGHT

THE FORESTS OF EL YUNQUÉ

DECIMATED

THE SONGS OF COQUIS
TURNED TO

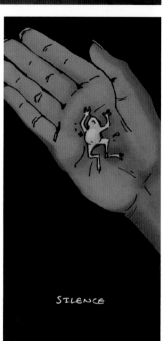

SILENCE

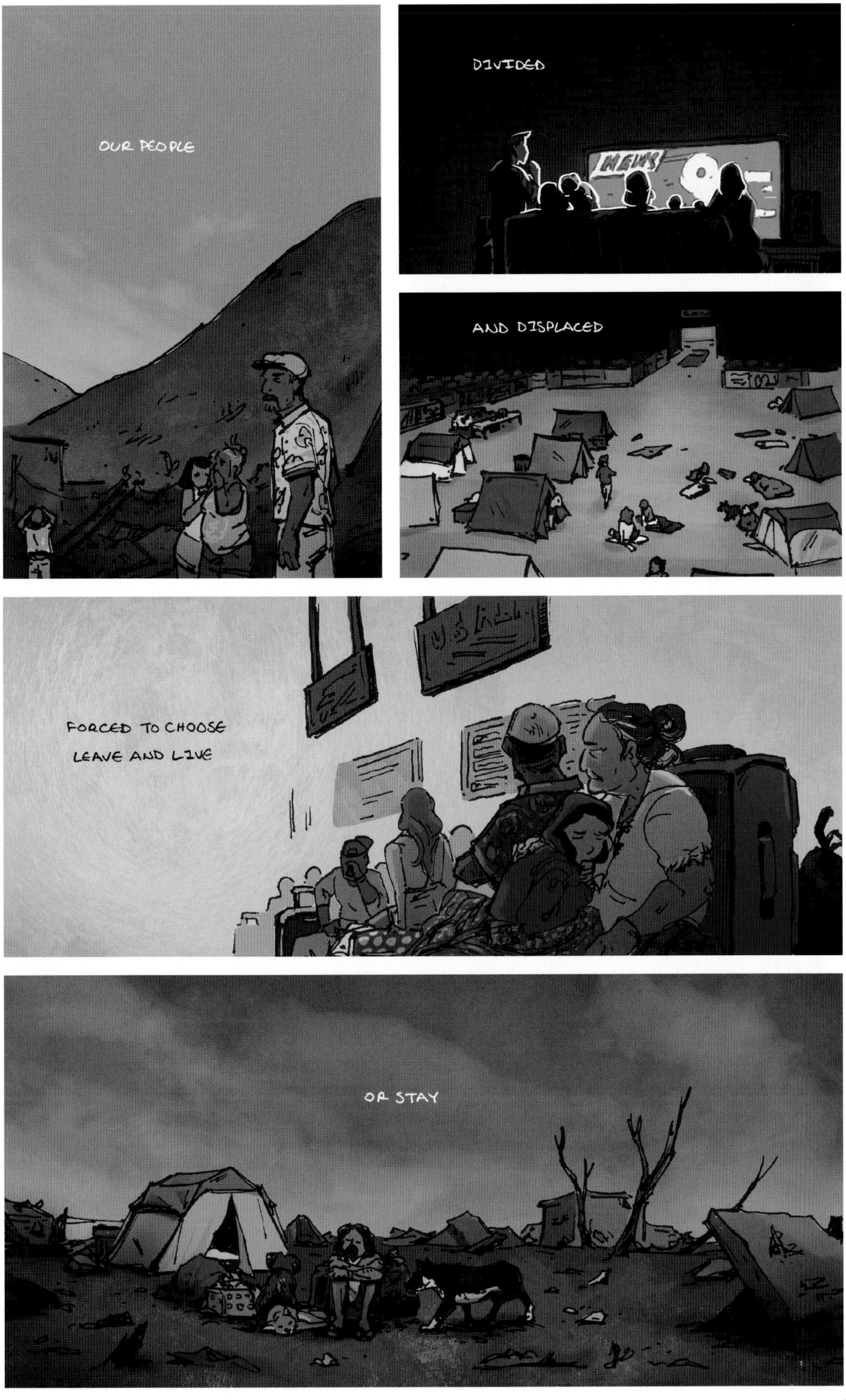
OUR PEOPLE
DIVIDED
NEWS
AND DISPLACED
FORCED TO CHOOSE
LEAVE AND LIVE
OR STAY

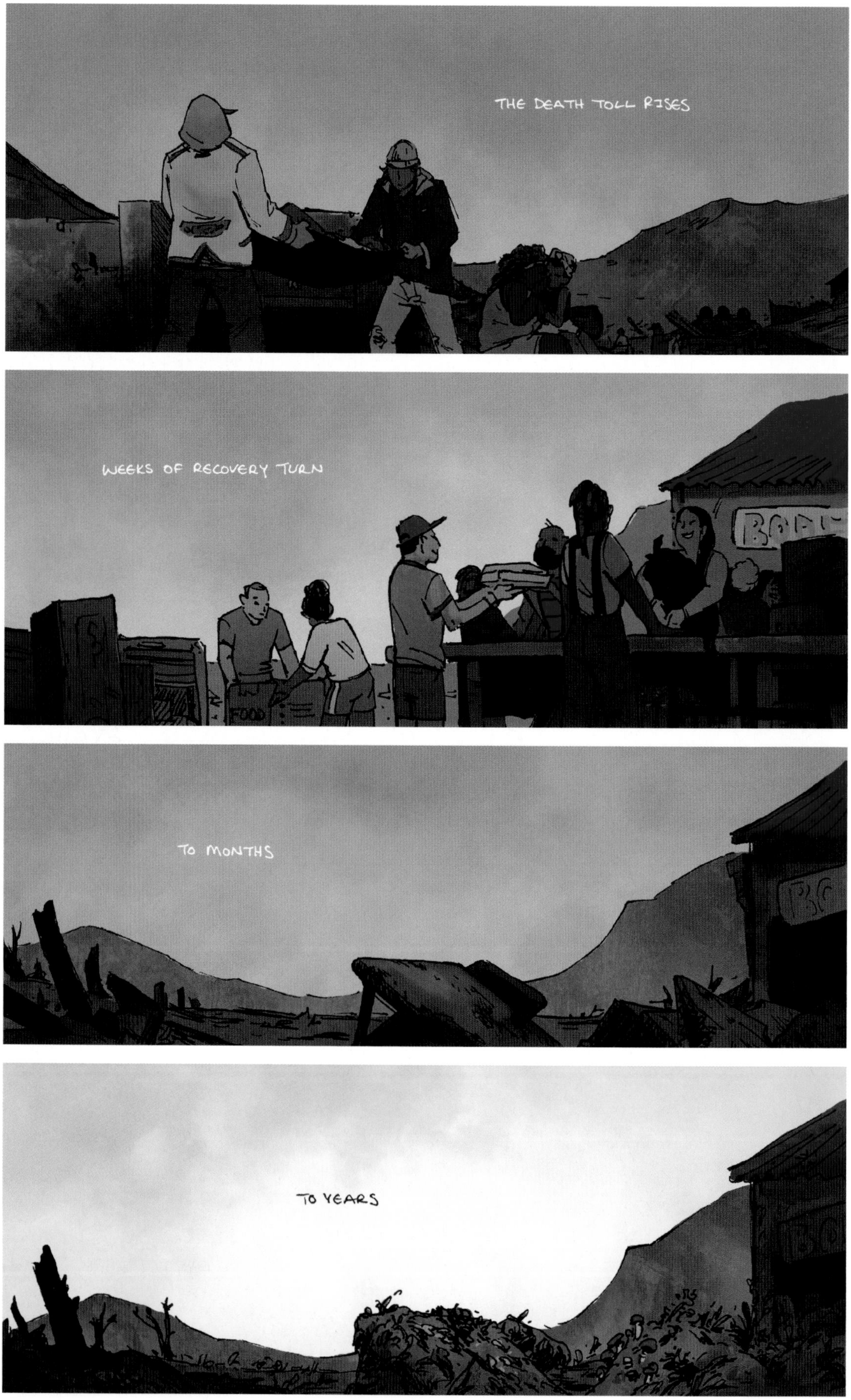
THE DEATH TOLL RISES
WEEKS OF RECOVERY TURN
FOOD
TO MONTHS
TO YEARS

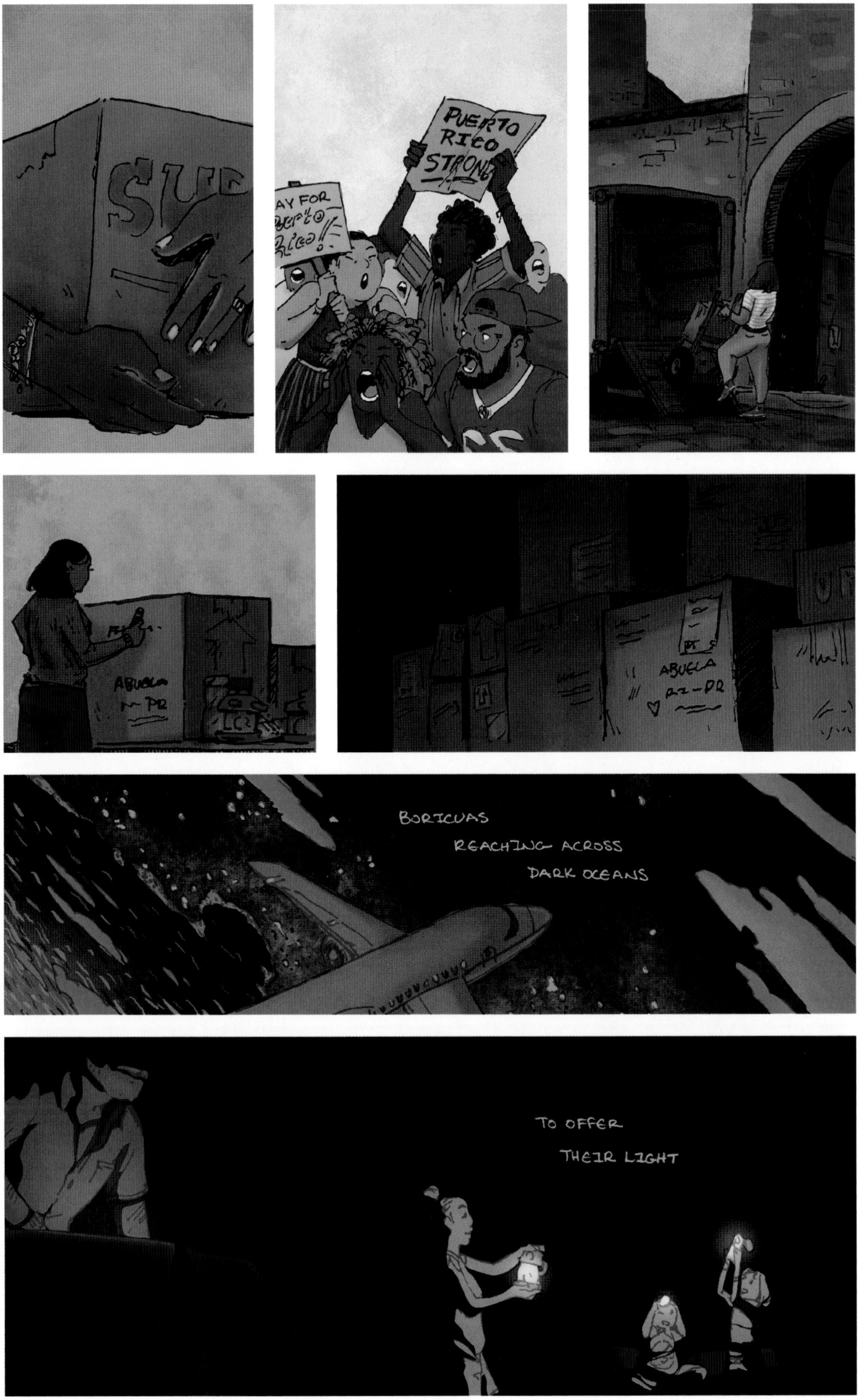
PUERTO RICO STRONG
ABUELA
BORICUAS
REACHING ACROSS
DARK OCEANS
TO OFFER
THEIR LIGHT

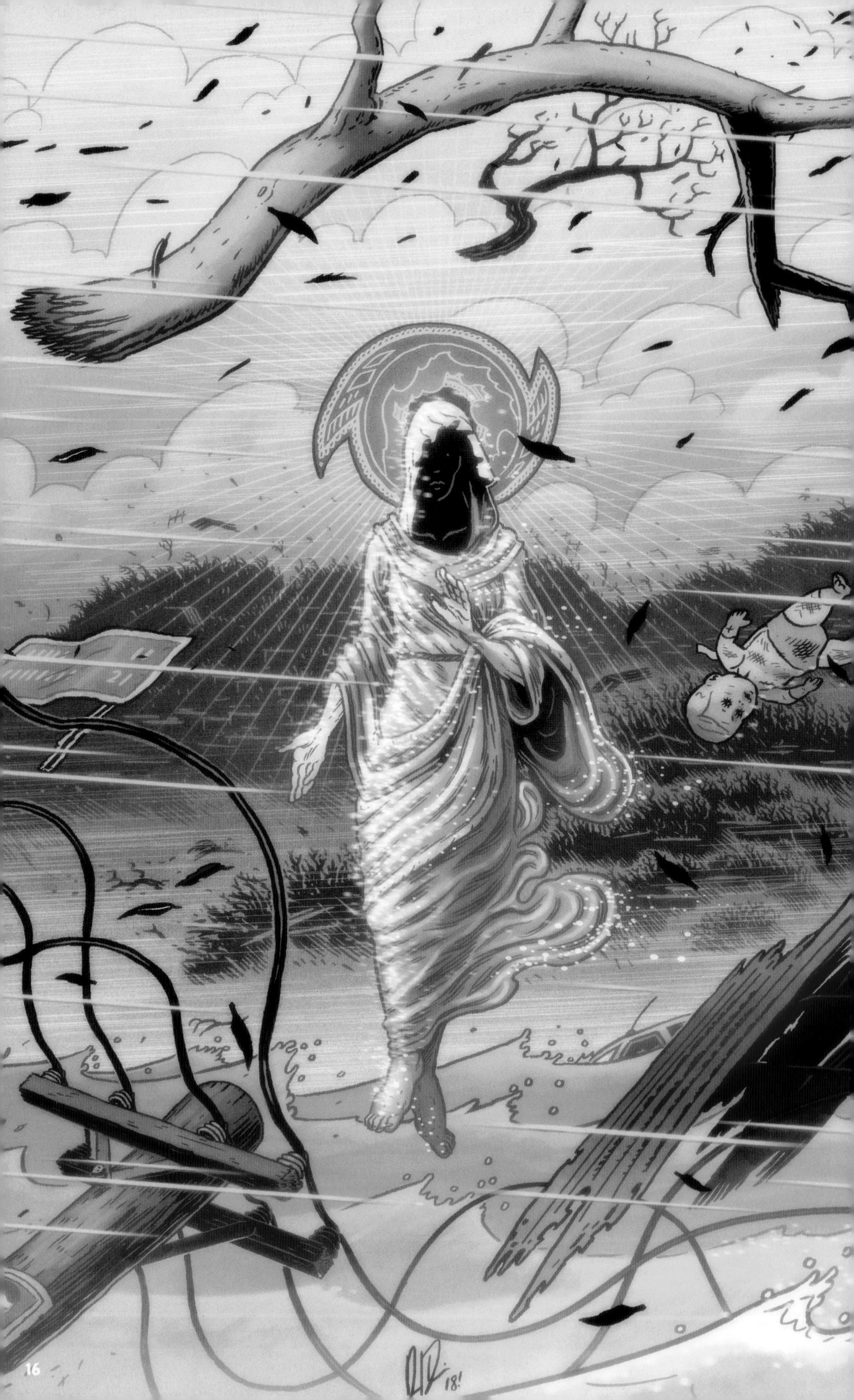
21

# MADRE DE DIOS

+

On September 20th 2017, Puerto Ricans became reacquainted with the old gods. Juracán was a Taíno god of chaos, the controller of the weather. Hurricanes are called hurricanes based on that old god. A taíno word is part of the entire world's lexicon and that always brings a little smile to my face. When that old god finally came back, it spared no irony in being named Maria.

Puerto Rico was predominantly Catholic as it was colonized by the Spanish with Protestantism being brought into the island after it was traded off to the US in 1898 as payment for the Spanish American War. That original Catholicism blended well with island beliefs. Catholic saints began standing in for all the previous attributes of the old gods, Taíno and African.

When me and my friends talk about our time without water, without power, we refer to it as "during the hurricane." The hurricane didn't end on september 22nd, the hurricane ended when we finally had our basic human needs met and we could continue our lives. Until then, we were in the hurricane. We were in the dark, disconnected, restless, desperate and hopeless.

To this day, there are still Puerto Ricans in the hurricane. The category 5 hurricane has not ended because their basic human needs have yet to be met. What Huricane Maria did was remind us of what true power looks like, what begging for mercy looks like and how little we are. All we can do now is pray to the Mother of God for more time. Maybe we can climb our way out of this if she has mercy.

Daniel Irizarri Oquendo
January 11, 2018

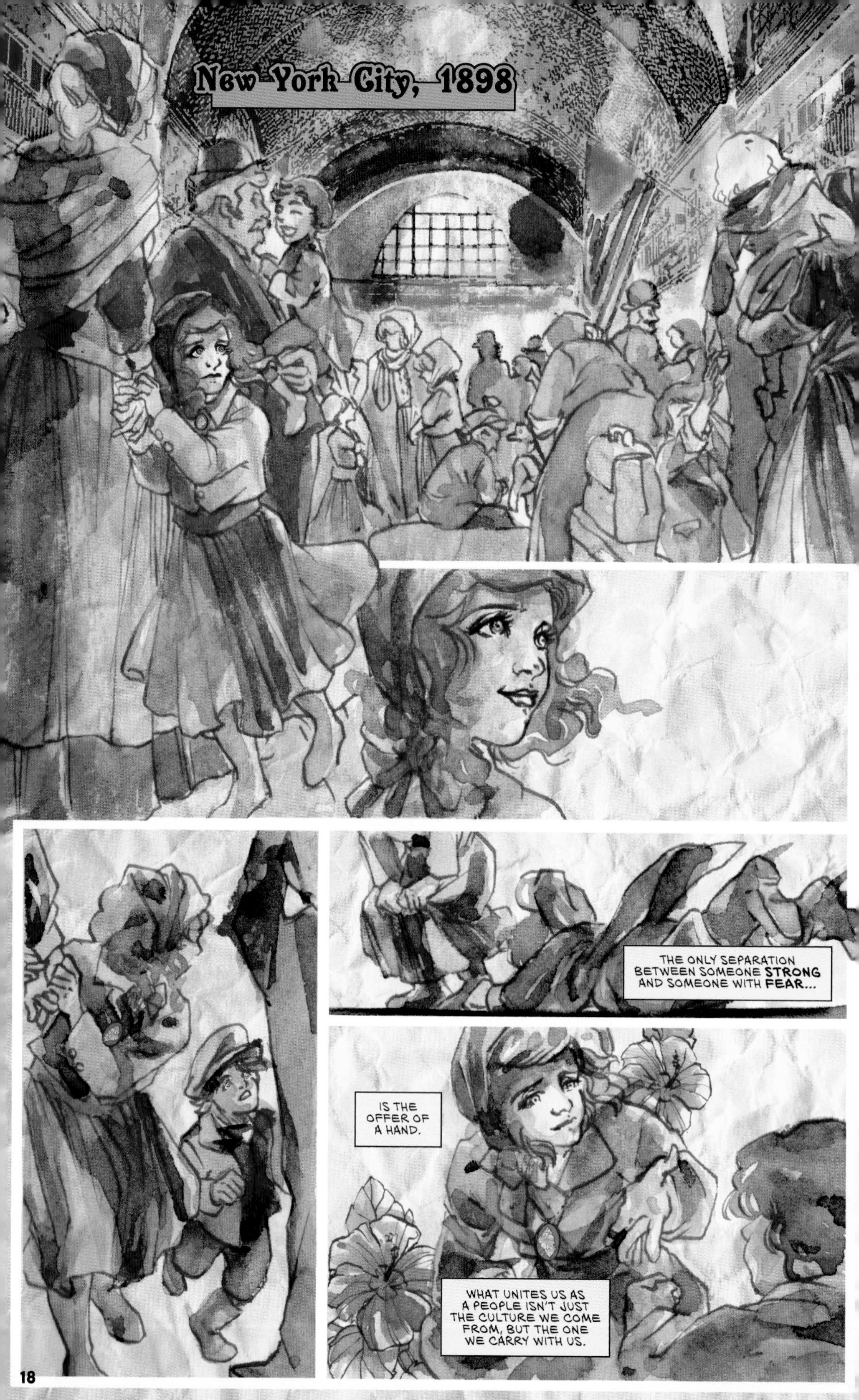
New York City, 1898
THE ONLY SEPARATION BETWEEN SOMEONE STRONG AND SOMEONE WITH FEAR...
IS THE OFFER OF A HAND.
WHAT UNITES US AS A PEOPLE ISN'T JUST THE CULTURE WE COME FROM, BUT THE ONE WE CARRY WITH US.

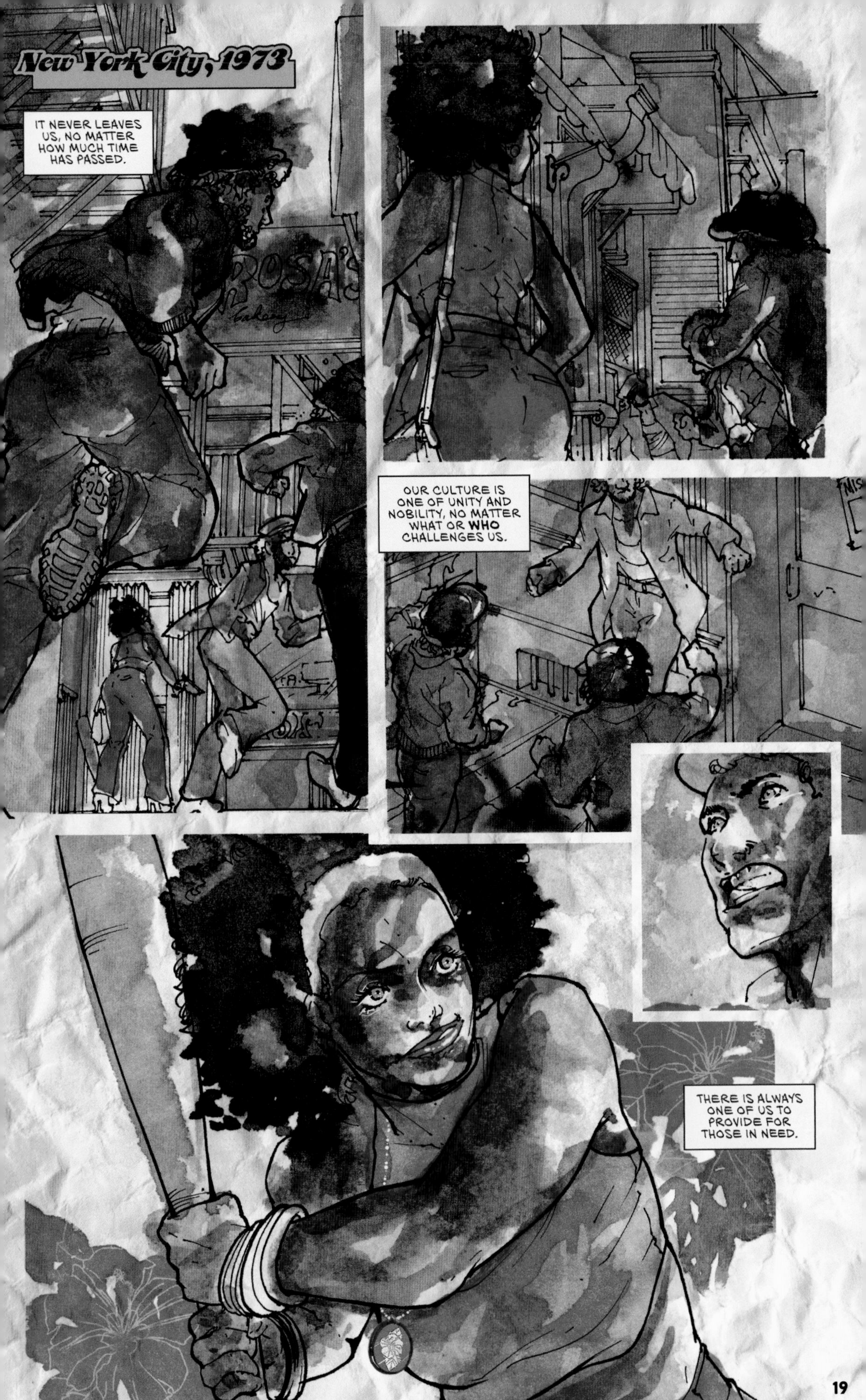
New York City, 1973
IT NEVER LEAVES US, NO MATTER HOW MUCH TIME HAS PASSED.
ROSA'S
OUR CULTURE IS ONE OF UNITY AND NOBILITY, NO MATTER WHAT OR **WHO** CHALLENGES US.
THERE IS ALWAYS ONE OF US TO PROVIDE FOR THOSE IN NEED.

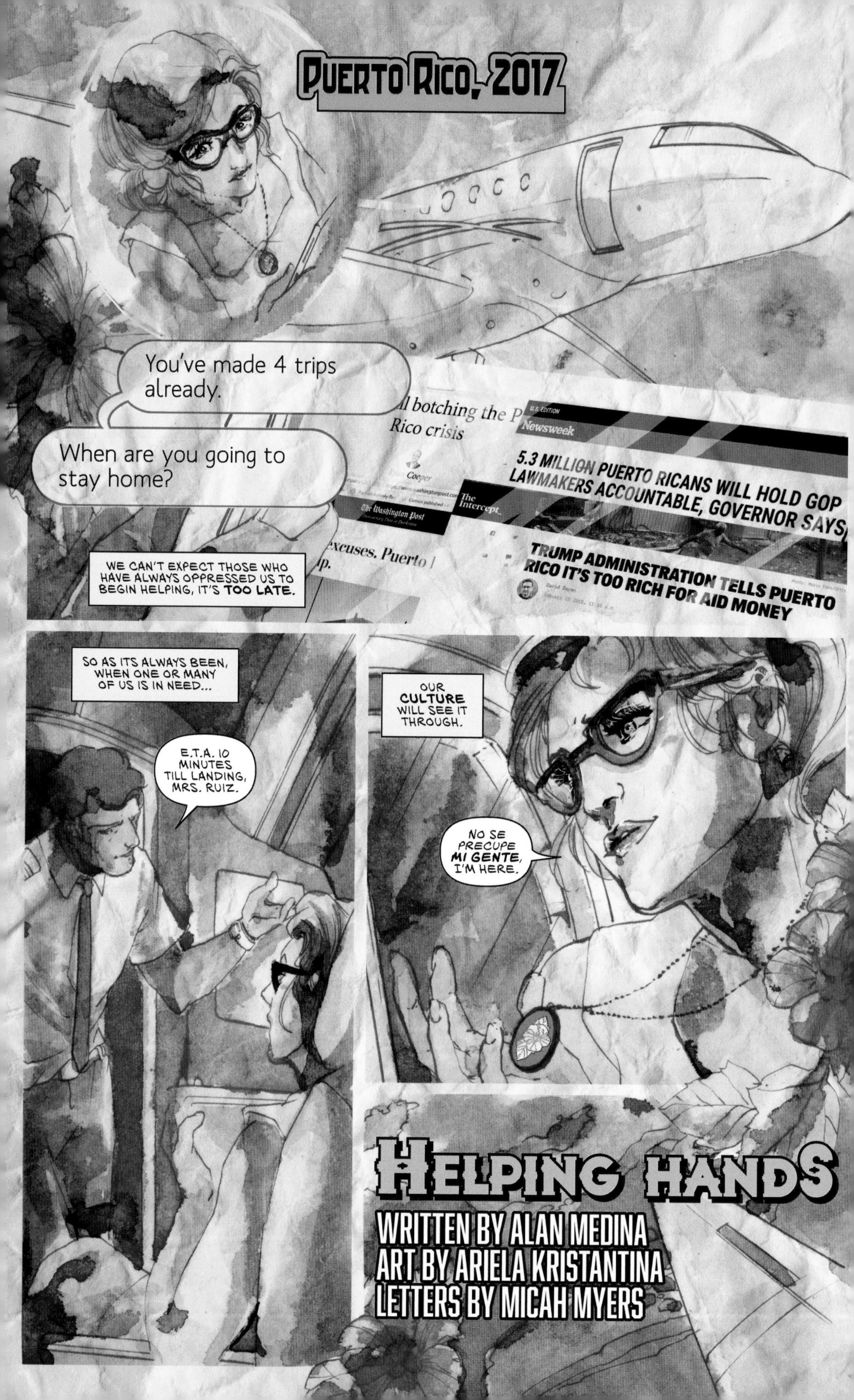
PUERTO RICO, 2017
You've made 4 trips already.
When are you going to stay home?
Rico crisis
Newsweek
5.3 MILLION PUERTO RICANS WILL HOLD GOP LAWMAKERS ACCOUNTABLE, GOVERNOR SAYS
The Washington Post
The Intercept
TRUMP ADMINISTRATION TELLS PUERTO RICO IT'S TOO RICH FOR AID MONEY
WE CAN'T EXPECT THOSE WHO HAVE ALWAYS OPPRESSED US TO BEGIN HELPING, IT'S TOO LATE.
SO AS ITS ALWAYS BEEN, WHEN ONE OR MANY OF US IS IN NEED...
E.T.A. 10 MINUTES TILL LANDING, MRS. RUIZ.
OUR CULTURE WILL SEE IT THROUGH.
NO SE PRECUPE MI GENTE, I'M HERE.
HELPING HANDS
WRITTEN BY ALAN MEDINA
ART BY ARIELA KRISTANTINA
LETTERS BY MICAH MYERS

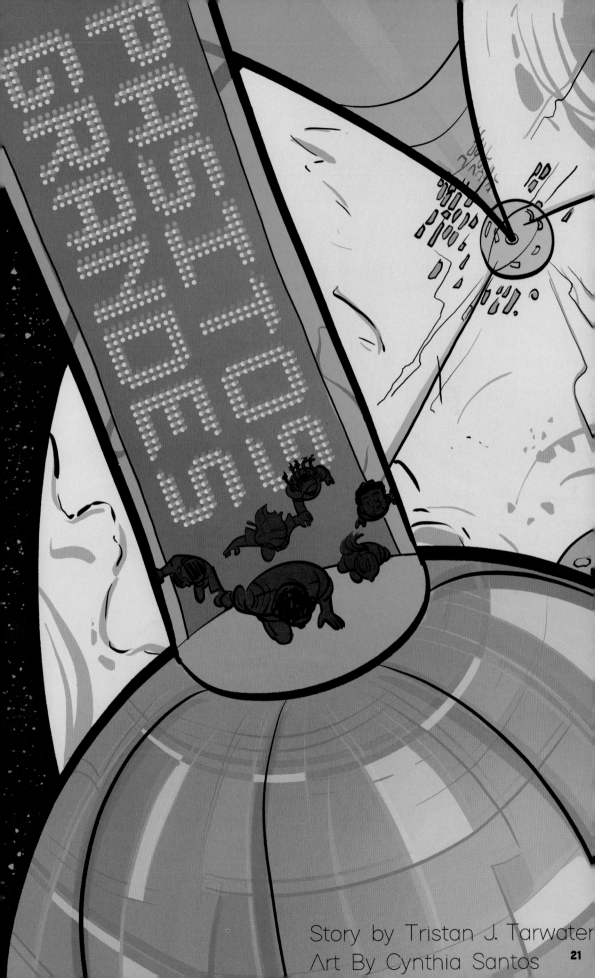

Story by Tristan J. Tarwater
Art By Cynthia Santos

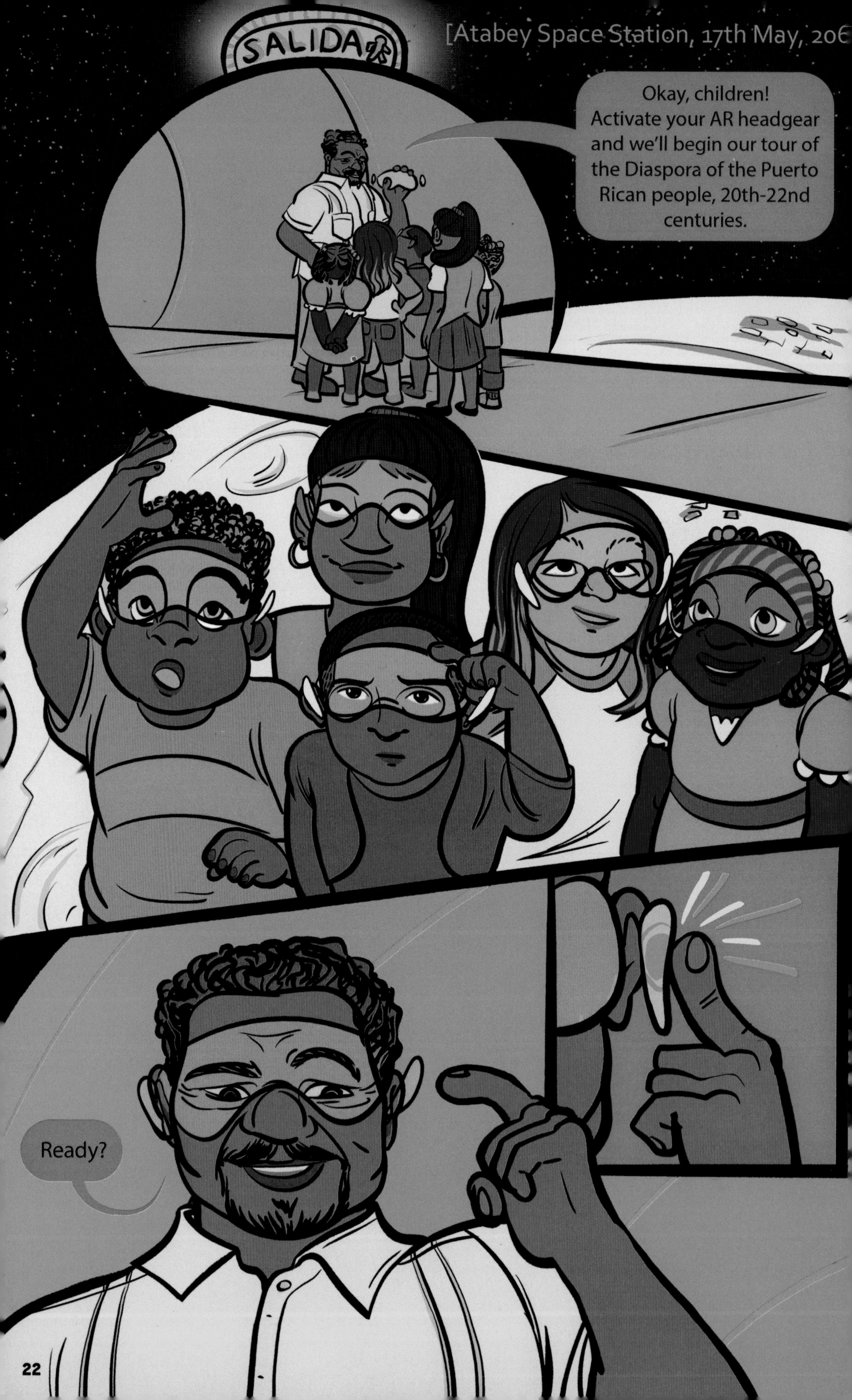
SALIDA
[Atabey Space Station, 17th May, 206
Okay, children! Activate your AR headgear and we'll begin our tour of the Diaspora of the Puerto Rican people, 20th-22nd centuries.
Ready?

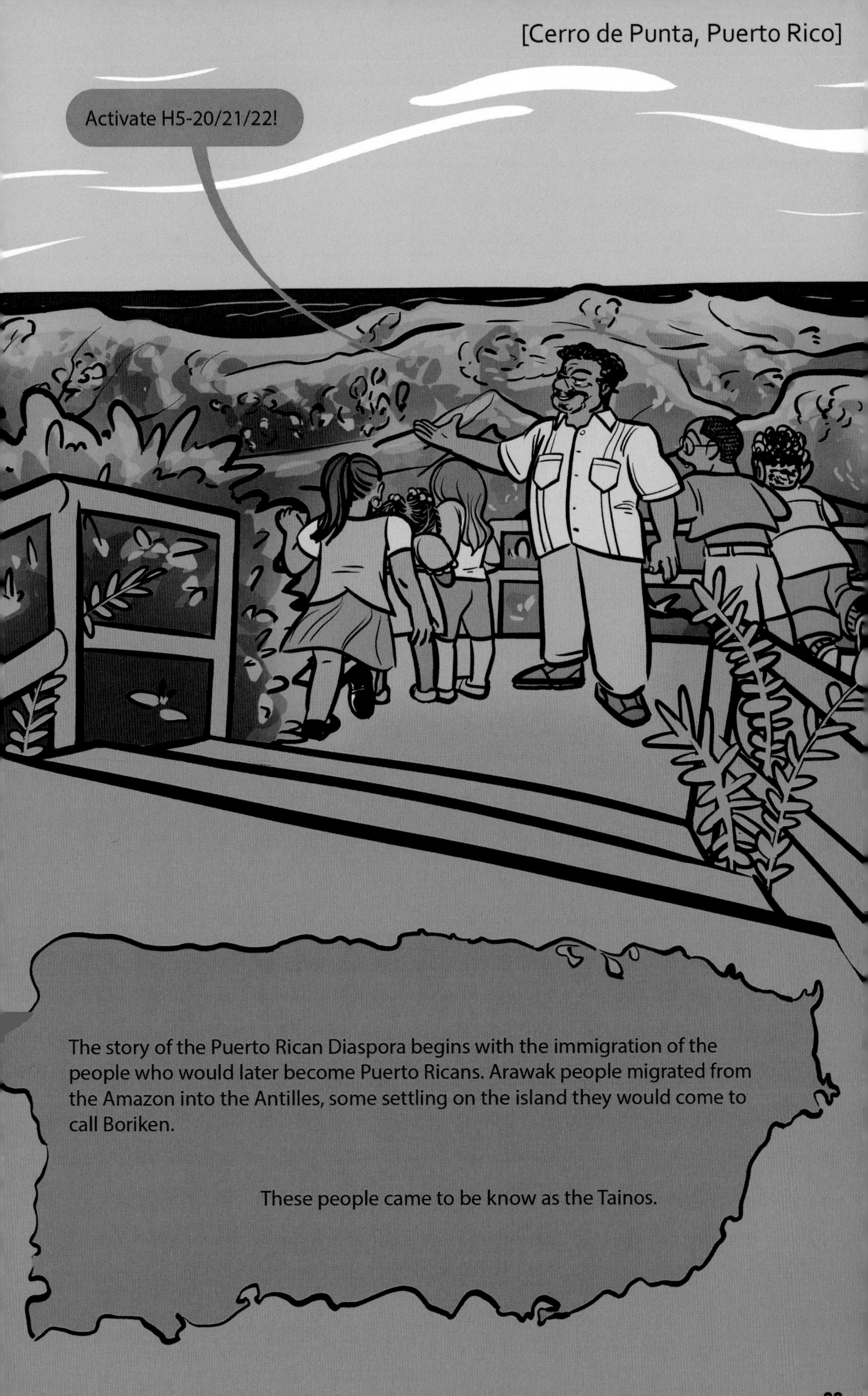
[Cerro de Punta, Puerto Rico]
Activate H5-20/21/22!
The story of the Puerto Rican Diaspora begins with the immigration of the people who would later become Puerto Ricans. Arawak people migrated from the Amazon into the Antilles, some settling on the island they would come to call Boriken.
These people came to be know as the Tainos.

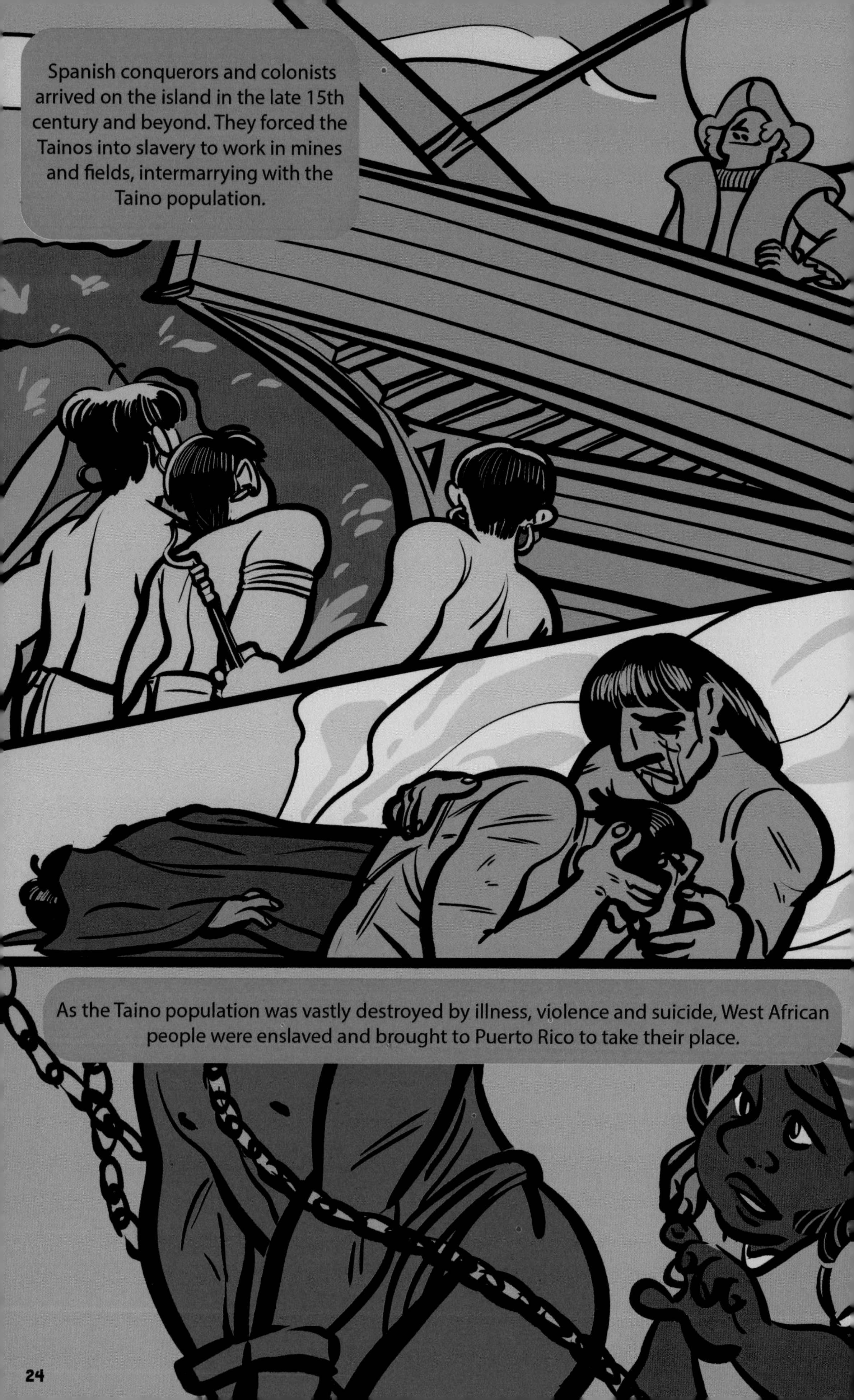
Spanish conquerors and colonists arrived on the island in the late 15th century and beyond. They forced the Tainos into slavery to work in mines and fields, intermarrying with the Taino population.
As the Taino population was vastly destroyed by illness, violence and suicide, West African people were enslaved and brought to Puerto Rico to take their place.

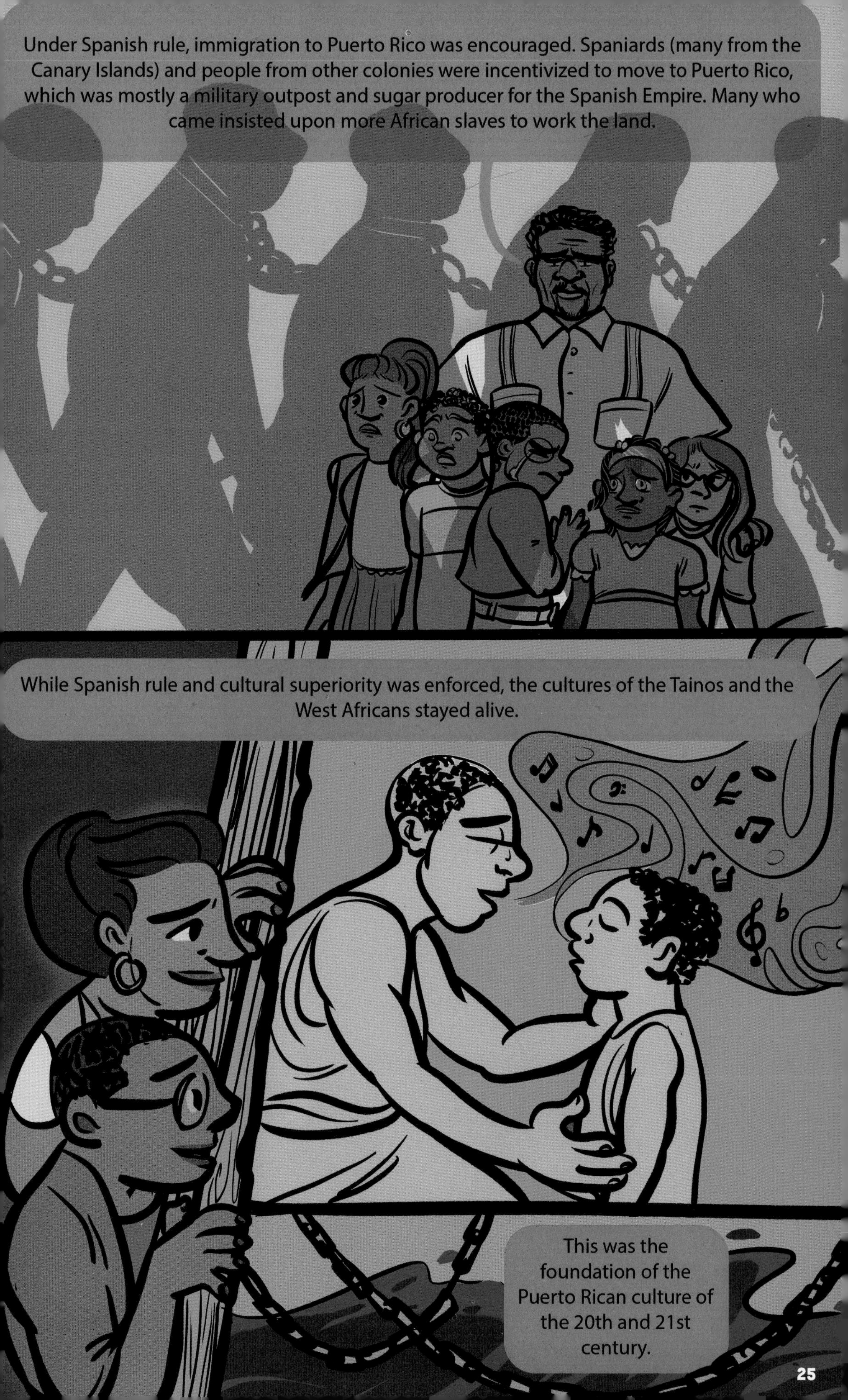
Under Spanish rule, immigration to Puerto Rico was encouraged. Spaniards (many from the Canary Islands) and people from other colonies were incentivized to move to Puerto Rico, which was mostly a military outpost and sugar producer for the Spanish Empire. Many who came insisted upon more African slaves to work the land.
While Spanish rule and cultural superiority was enforced, the cultures of the Tainos and the West Africans stayed alive.
This was the foundation of the Puerto Rican culture of the 20th and 21st century.

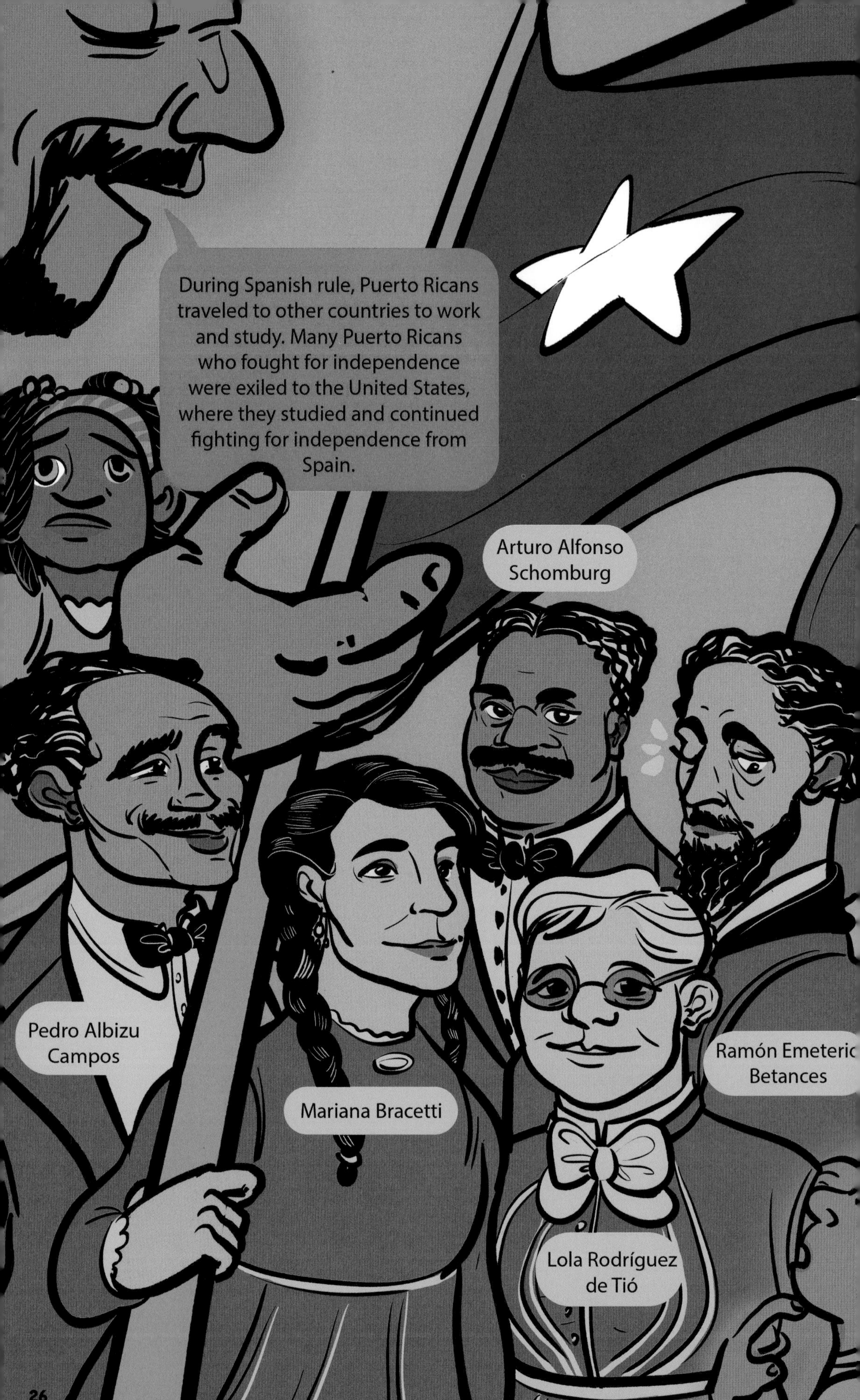
During Spanish rule, Puerto Ricans traveled to other countries to work and study. Many Puerto Ricans who fought for independence were exiled to the United States, where they studied and continued fighting for independence from Spain.
Arturo Alfonso Schomburg
Pedro Albizu Campos
Ramón Emeteric Betances
Mariana Bracetti
Lola Rodríguez de Tió

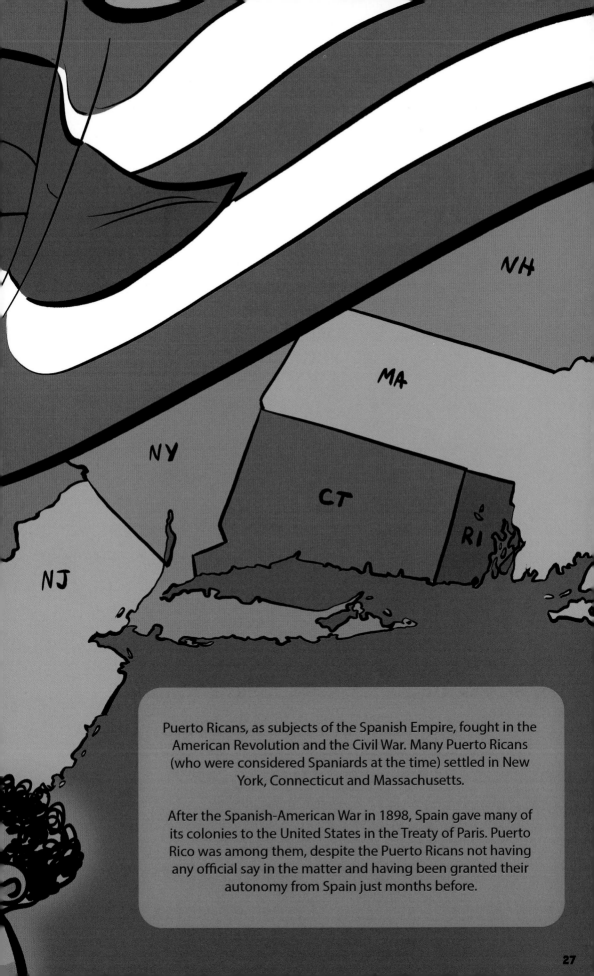

NH

MA

NY

CT

RI

NJ

Puerto Ricans, as subjects of the Spanish Empire, fought in the American Revolution and the Civil War. Many Puerto Ricans (who were considered Spaniards at the time) settled in New York, Connecticut and Massachusetts.

After the Spanish-American War in 1898, Spain gave many of its colonies to the United States in the Treaty of Paris. Puerto Rico was among them, despite the Puerto Ricans not having any official say in the matter and having been granted their autonomy from Spain just months before.

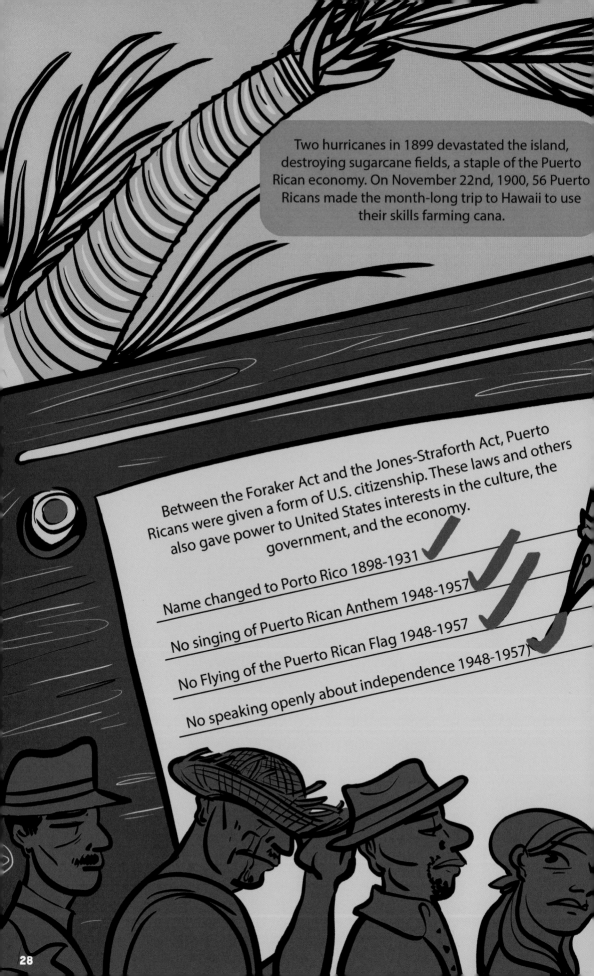

Two hurricanes in 1899 devastated the island, destroying sugarcane fields, a staple of the Puerto Rican economy. On November 22nd, 1900, 56 Puerto Ricans made the month-long trip to Hawaii to use their skills farming cana.

Between the Foraker Act and the Jones-Straforth Act, Puerto Ricans were given a form of U.S. citizenship. These laws and others also gave power to United States interests in the culture, the government, and the economy.

Name changed to Porto Rico 1898-1931

No singing of Puerto Rican Anthem 1948-1957

No Flying of the Puerto Rican Flag 1948-1957

No speaking openly about independence 1948-1957)

Tied to the economy of the United States, Puerto Rico was industrialized to meet with US interests. Some of these changes caused farmers to lose their land to larger companies. The government and businesses recruited Puerto Ricans to work in the United States, especially after the labor shortage during World War 2.

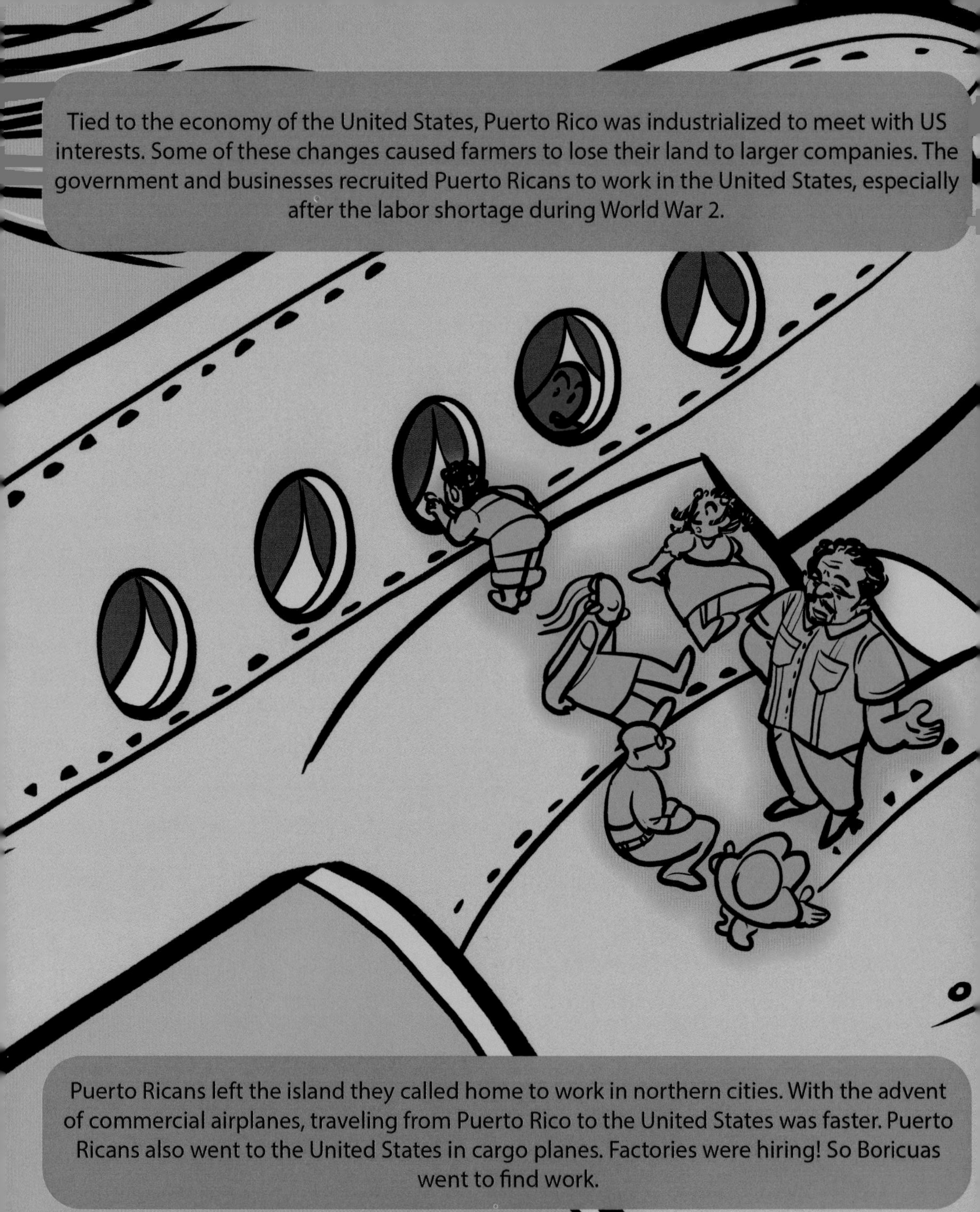

Puerto Ricans left the island they called home to work in northern cities. With the advent of commercial airplanes, traveling from Puerto Rico to the United States was faster. Puerto Ricans also went to the United States in cargo planes. Factories were hiring! So Boricuas went to find work.

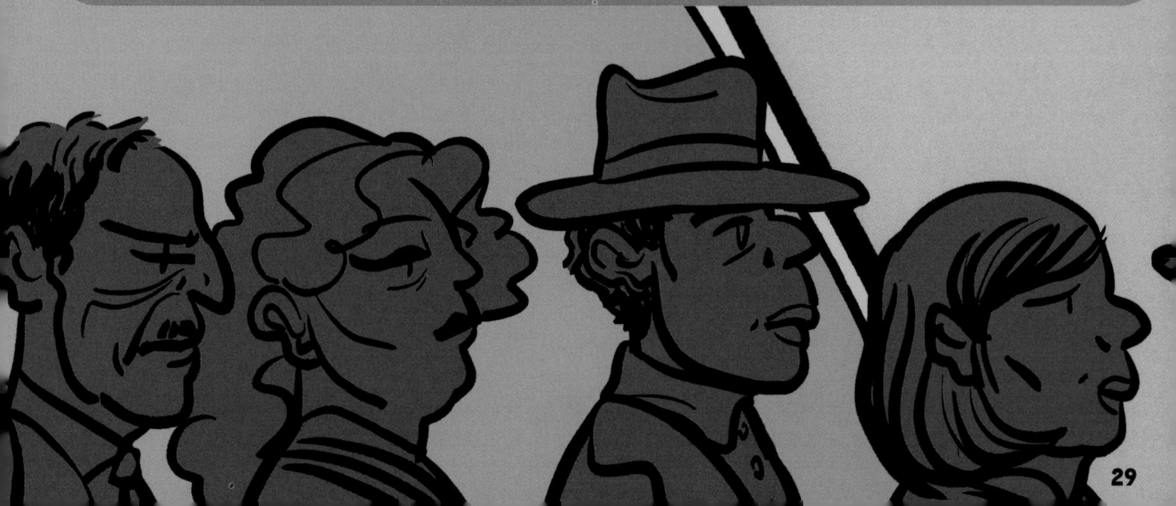

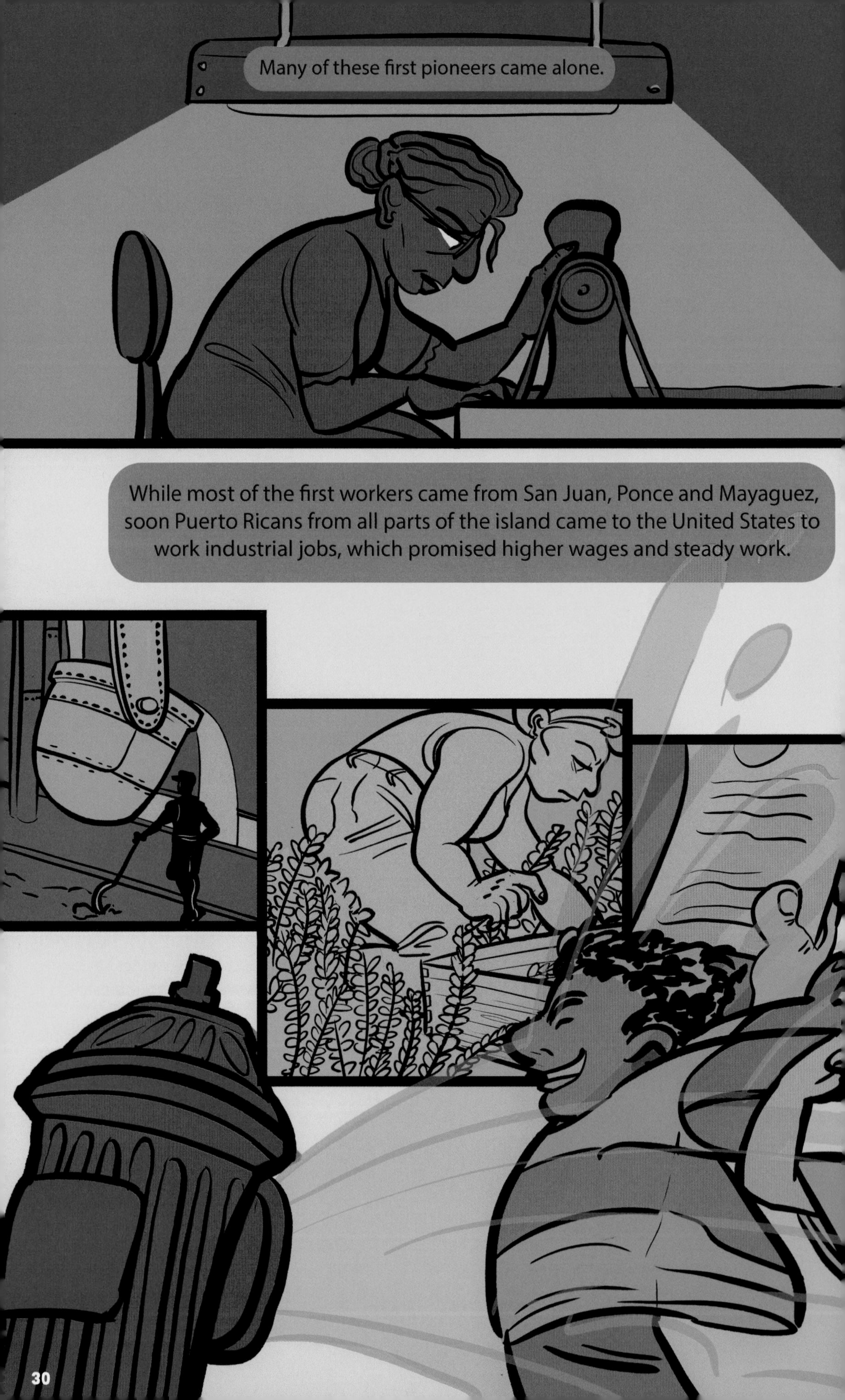
Many of these first pioneers came alone.
While most of the first workers came from San Juan, Ponce and Mayaguez, soon Puerto Ricans from all parts of the island came to the United States to work industrial jobs, which promised higher wages and steady work.

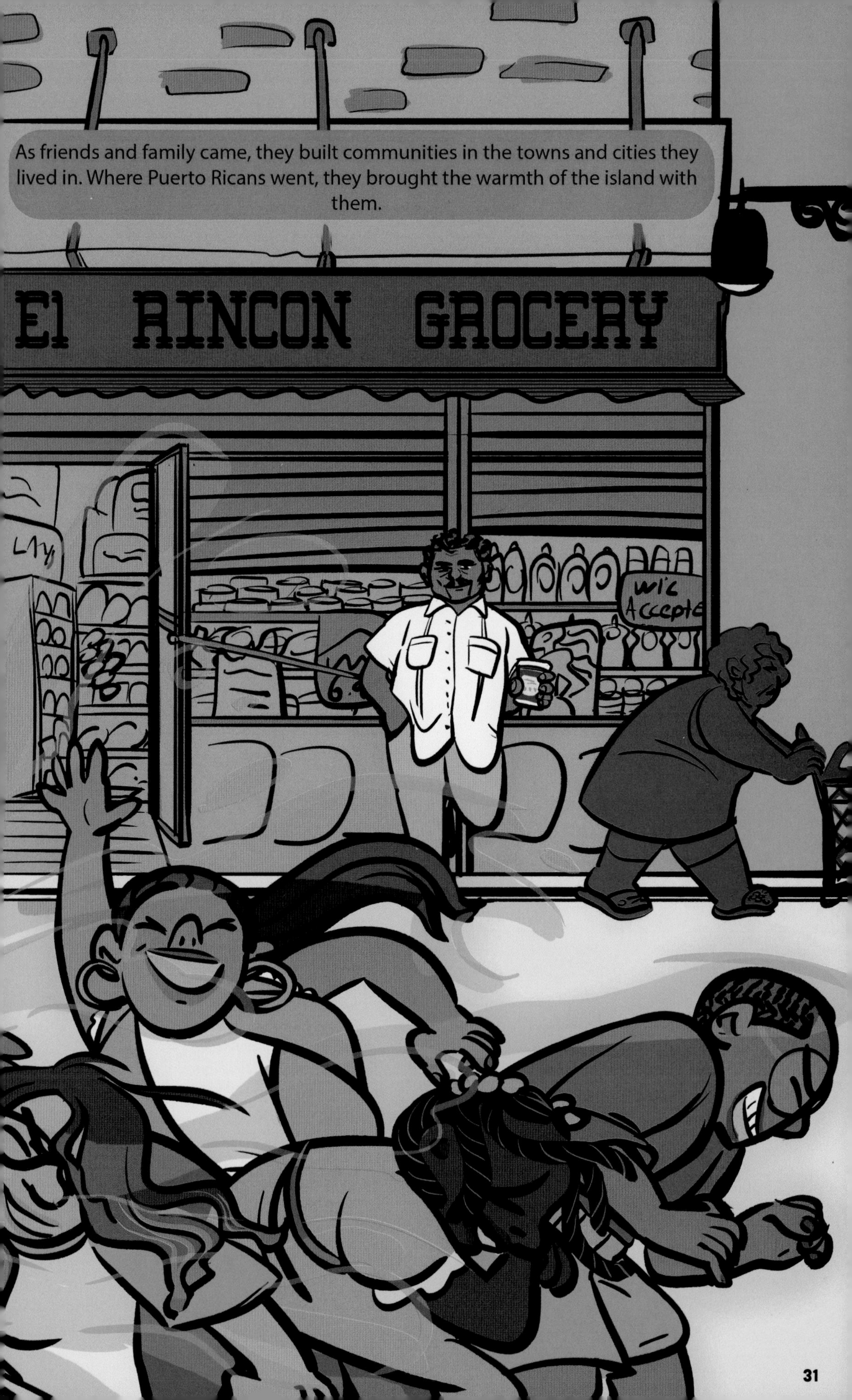
As friends and family came, they built communities in the towns and cities they lived in. Where Puerto Ricans went, they brought the warmth of the island with them.
El RINCON GROCERY
WIC Accepte

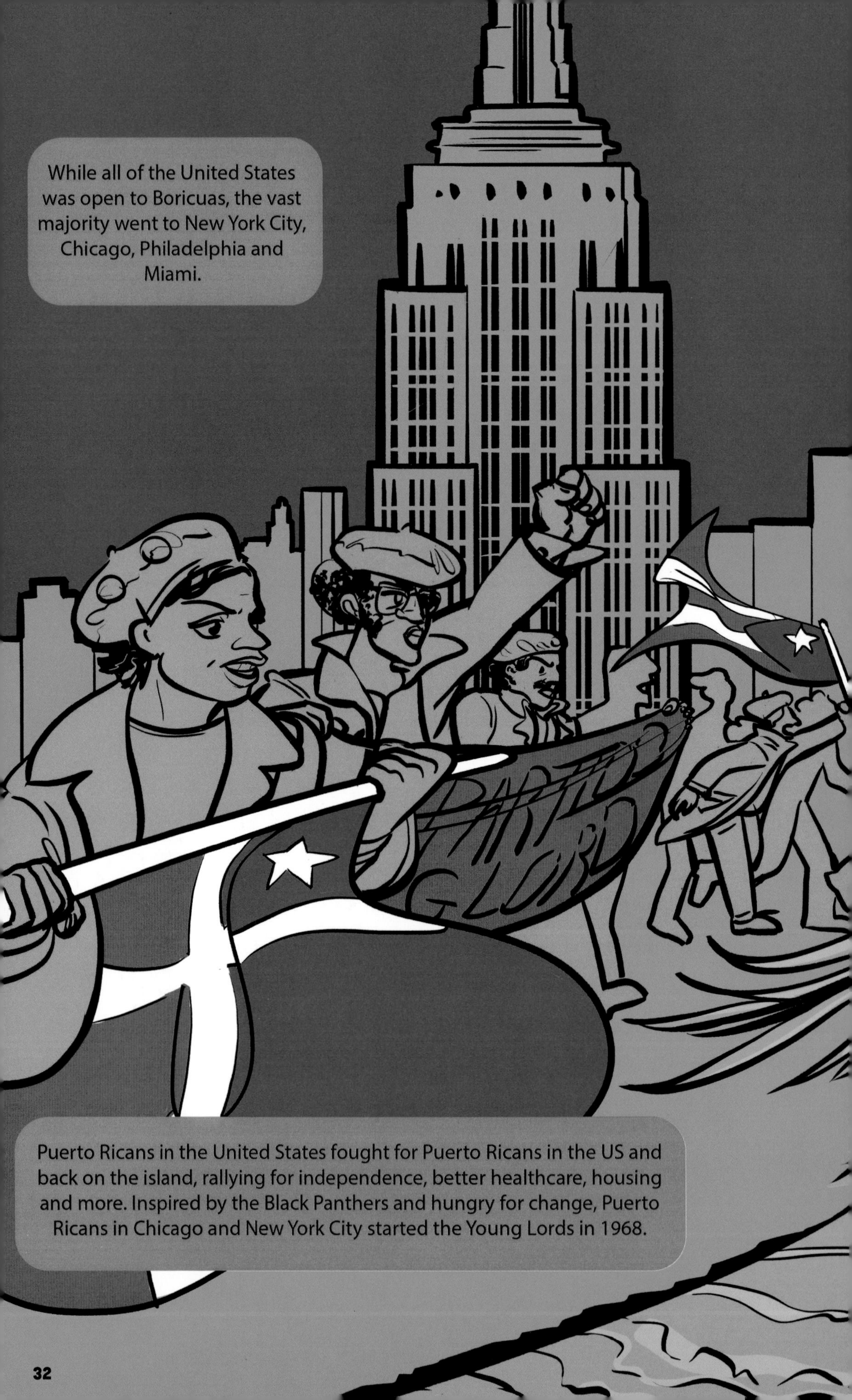
While all of the United States was open to Boricuas, the vast majority went to New York City, Chicago, Philadelphia and Miami.
Puerto Ricans in the United States fought for Puerto Ricans in the US and back on the island, rallying for independence, better healthcare, housing and more. Inspired by the Black Panthers and hungry for change, Puerto Ricans in Chicago and New York City started the Young Lords in 1968.

While Puerto Ricans worked and built families in the United States, some moved back to the island, free to do so with the version of citizenship the United States government had allowed them. Work, family and education kept the emigration of Puerto Ricans moving in a circle.

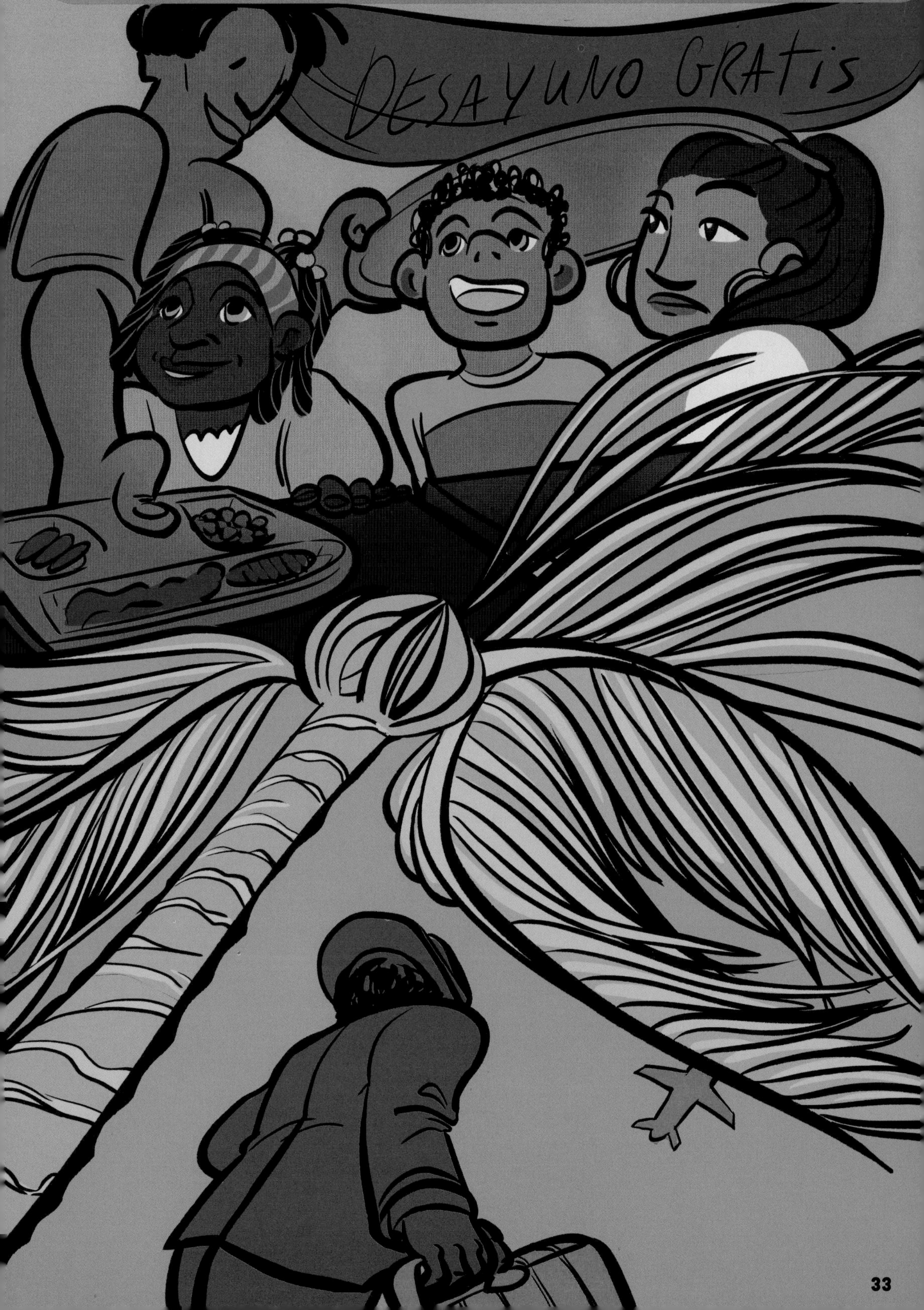
DESAYUNO GRATIS

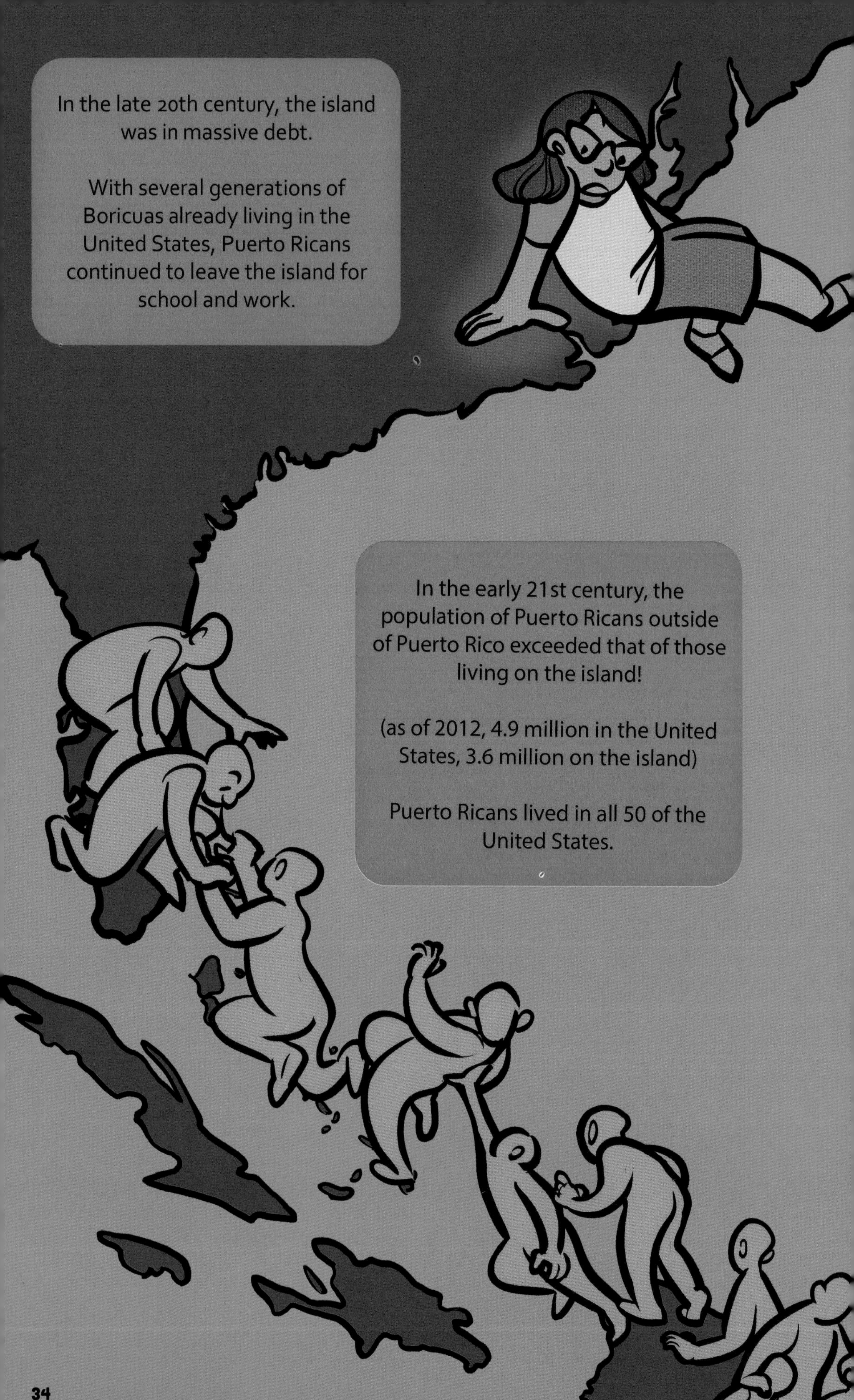

In the late 20th century, the island was in massive debt.
With several generations of Boricuas already living in the United States, Puerto Ricans continued to leave the island for school and work.
In the early 21st century, the population of Puerto Ricans outside of Puerto Rico exceeded that of those living on the island!
(as of 2012, 4.9 million in the United States, 3.6 million on the island)
Puerto Ricans lived in all 50 of the United States.

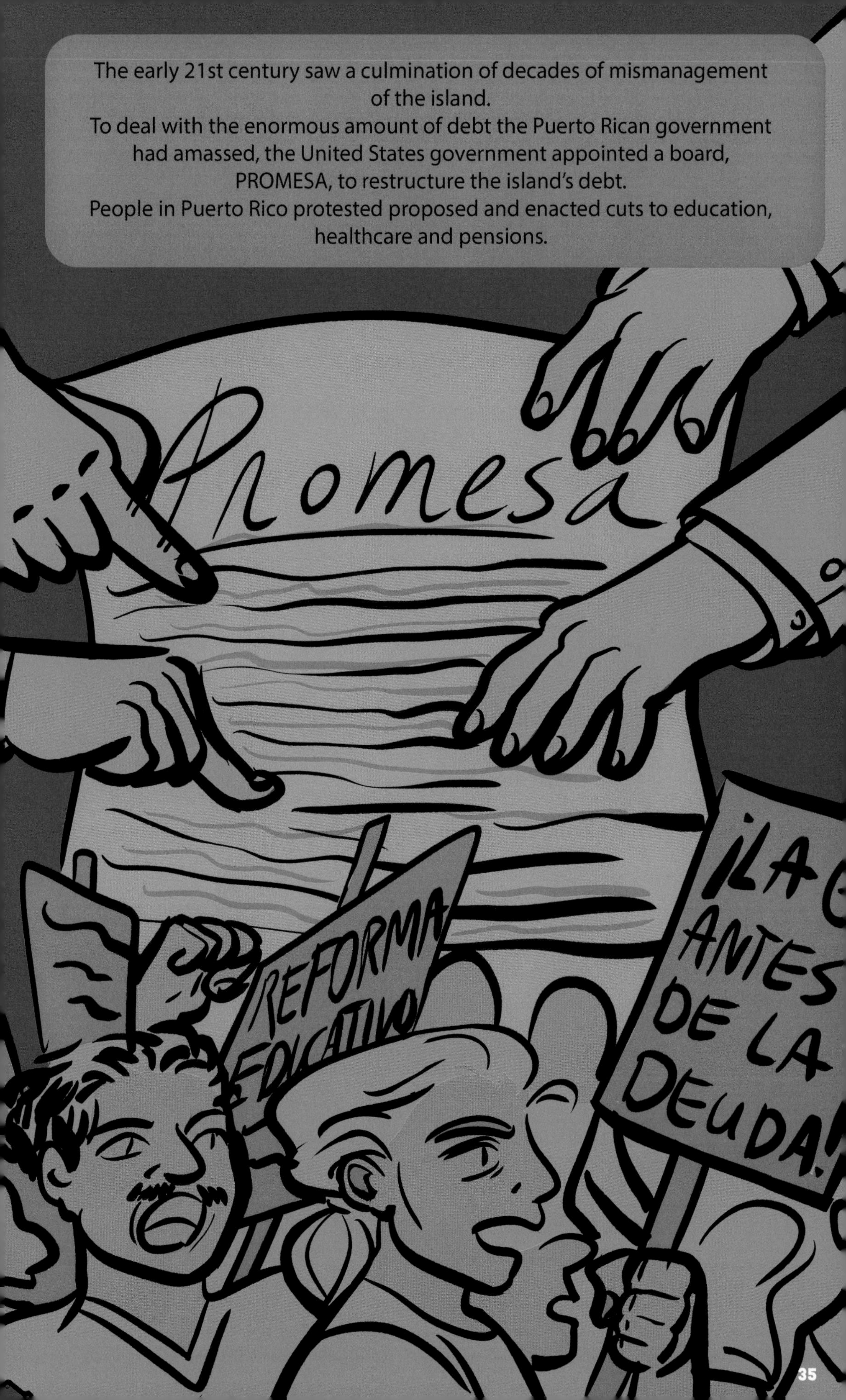
The early 21st century saw a culmination of decades of mismanagement of the island.
To deal with the enormous amount of debt the Puerto Rican government had amassed, the United States government appointed a board, PROMESA, to restructure the island's debt.
People in Puerto Rico protested proposed and enacted cuts to education, healthcare and pensions.
Promesa
REFORMA
ANTES DE LA DEUDA!

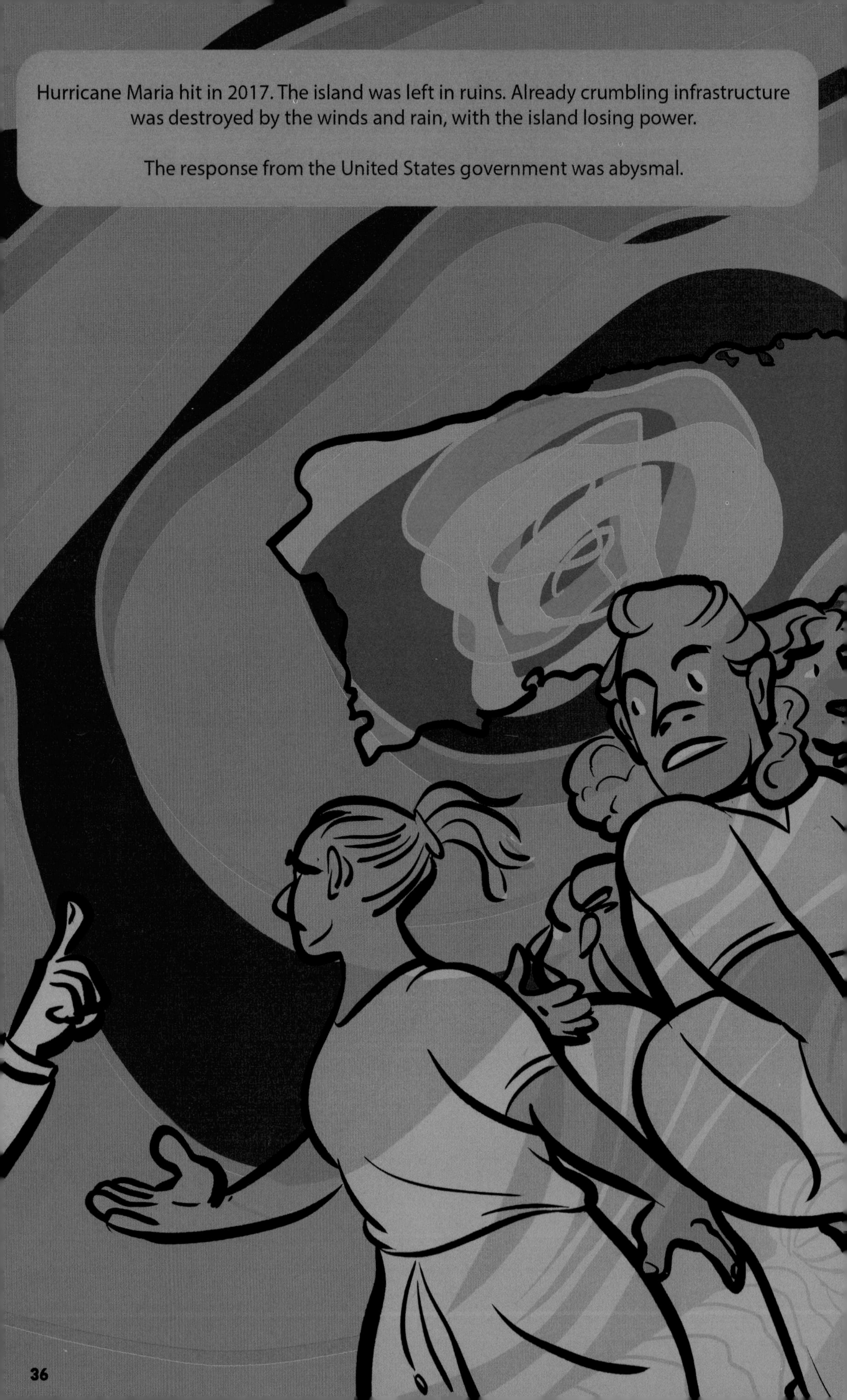
Hurricane Maria hit in 2017. The island was left in ruins. Already crumbling infrastructure was destroyed by the winds and rain, with the island losing power.
The response from the United States government was abysmal.

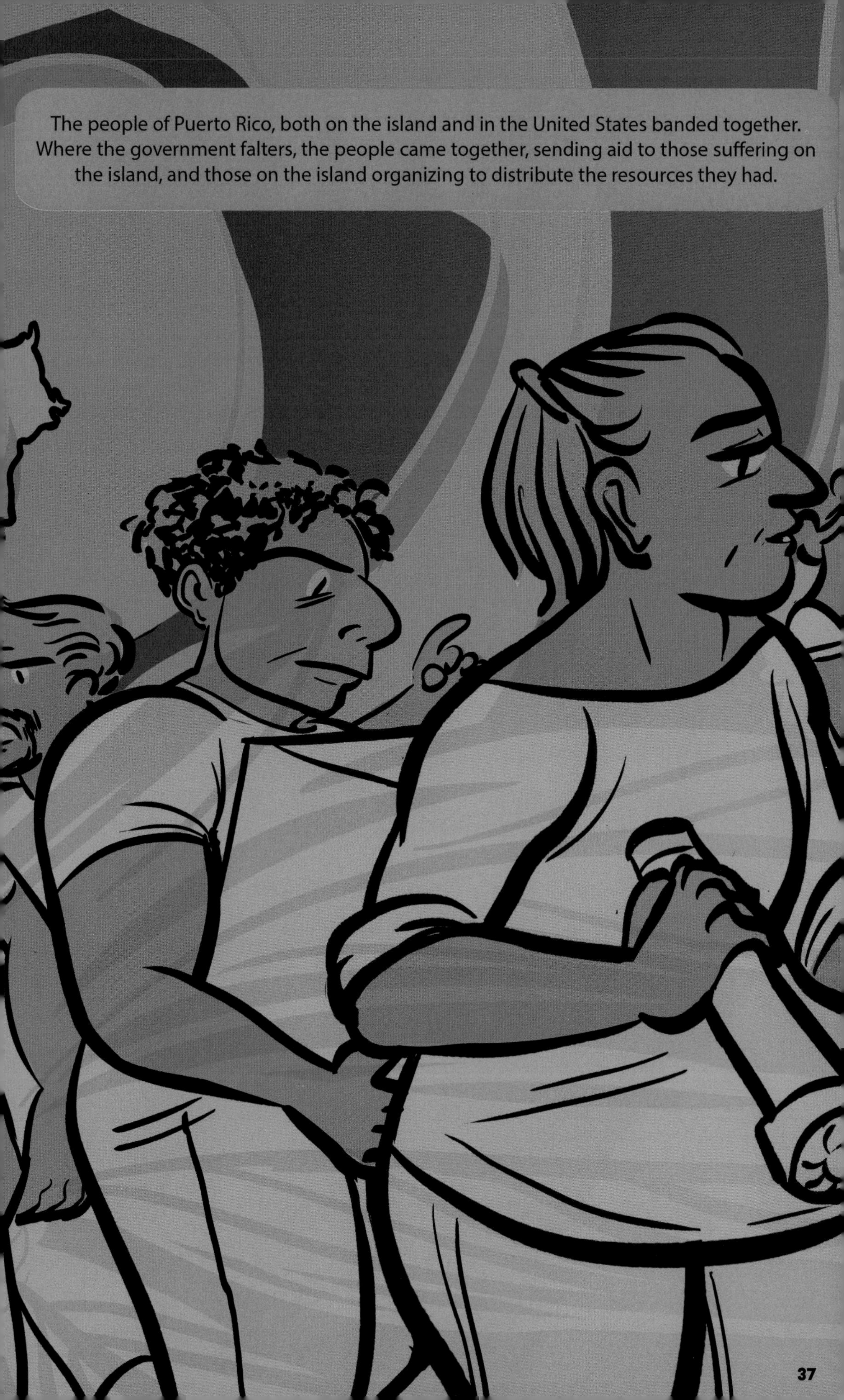
The people of Puerto Rico, both on the island and in the United States banded together. Where the government falters, the people came together, sending aid to those suffering on the island, and those on the island organizing to distribute the resources they had.

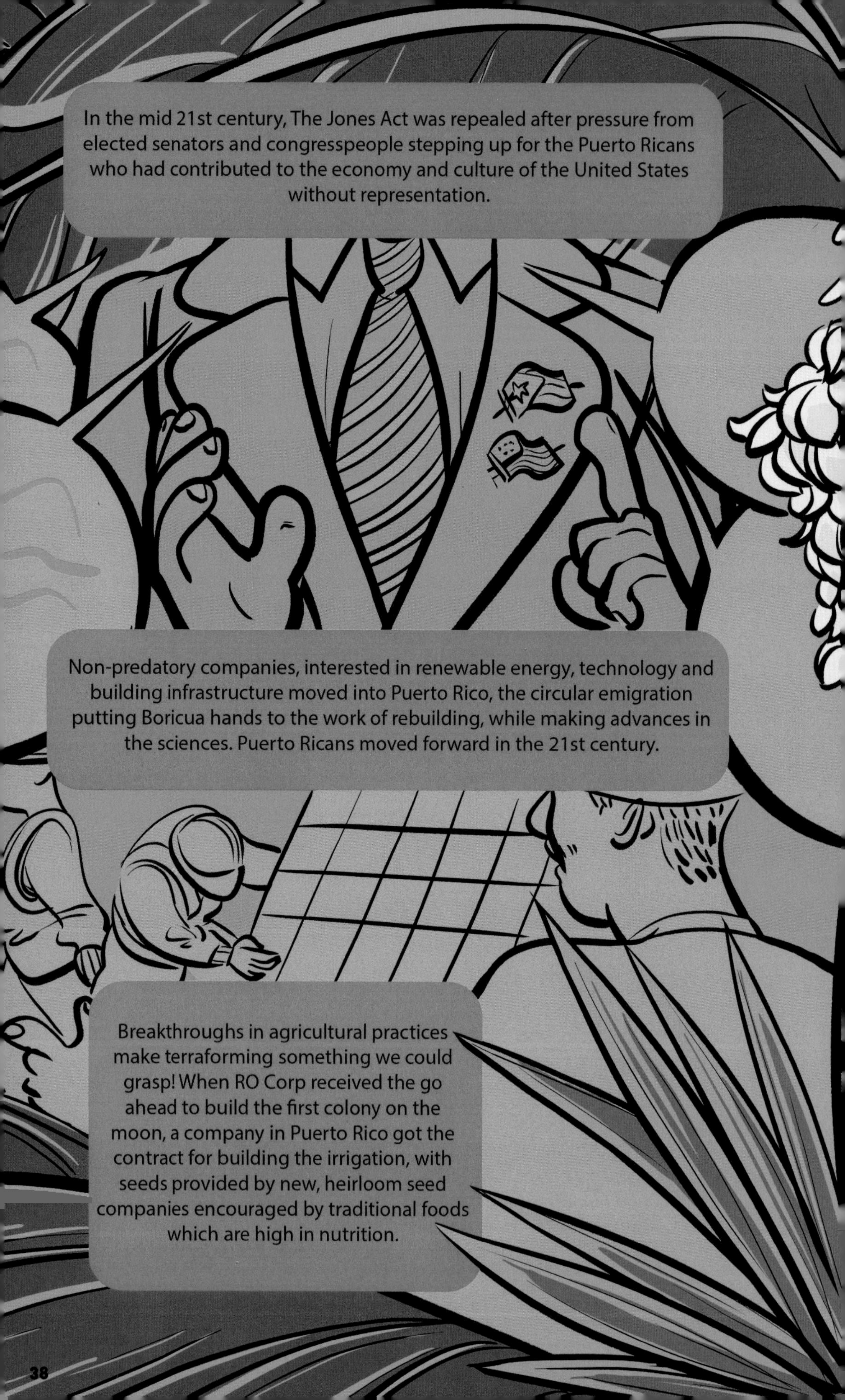
In the mid 21st century, The Jones Act was repealed after pressure from elected senators and congresspeople stepping up for the Puerto Ricans who had contributed to the economy and culture of the United States without representation.
Non-predatory companies, interested in renewable energy, technology and building infrastructure moved into Puerto Rico, the circular emigration putting Boricua hands to the work of rebuilding, while making advances in the sciences. Puerto Ricans moved forward in the 21st century.
Breakthroughs in agricultural practices make terraforming something we could grasp! When RO Corp received the go ahead to build the first colony on the moon, a company in Puerto Rico got the contract for building the irrigation, with seeds provided by new, heirloom seed companies encouraged by traditional foods which are high in nutrition.

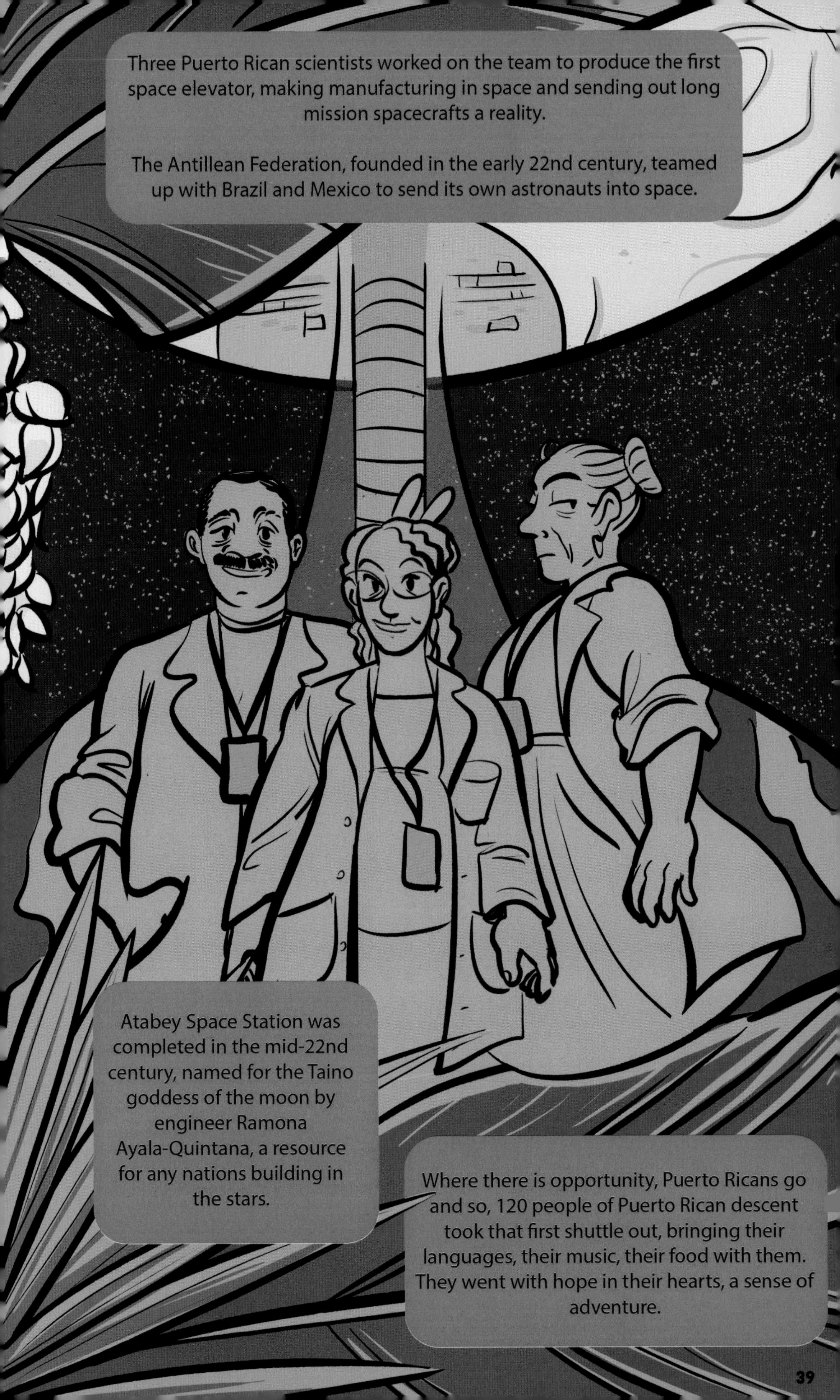
Three Puerto Rican scientists worked on the team to produce the first space elevator, making manufacturing in space and sending out long mission spacecrafts a reality.
The Antillean Federation, founded in the early 22nd century, teamed up with Brazil and Mexico to send its own astronauts into space.
Atabey Space Station was completed in the mid-22nd century, named for the Taino goddess of the moon by engineer Ramona Ayala-Quintana, a resource for any nations building in the stars.
Where there is opportunity, Puerto Ricans go and so, 120 people of Puerto Rican descent took that first shuttle out, bringing their languages, their music, their food with them. They went with hope in their hearts, a sense of adventure.

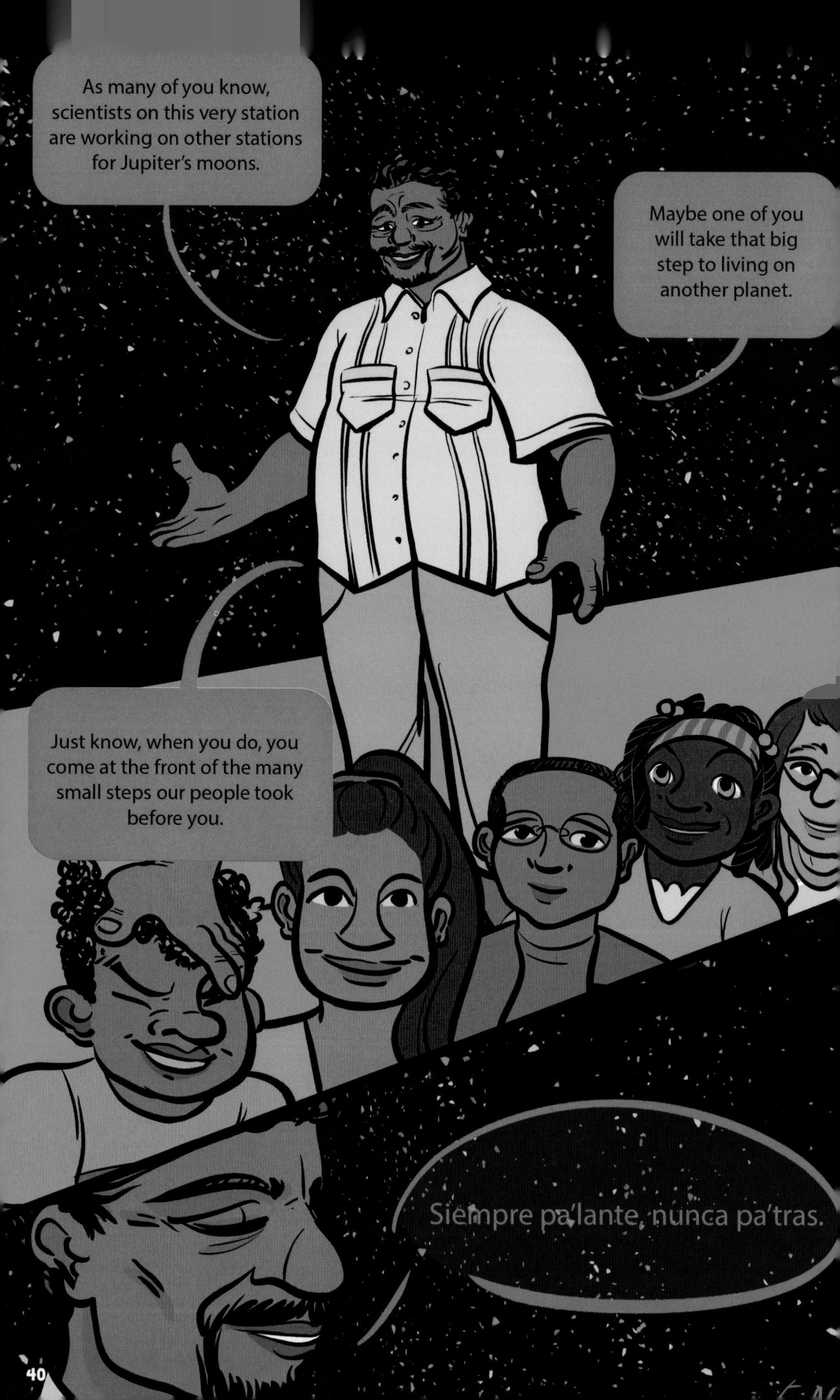
As many of you know, scientists on this very station are working on other stations for Jupiter's moons.
Maybe one of you will take that big step to living on another planet.
Just know, when you do, you come at the front of the many small steps our people took before you.
Siempre pa'lante, nunca pa'tras.

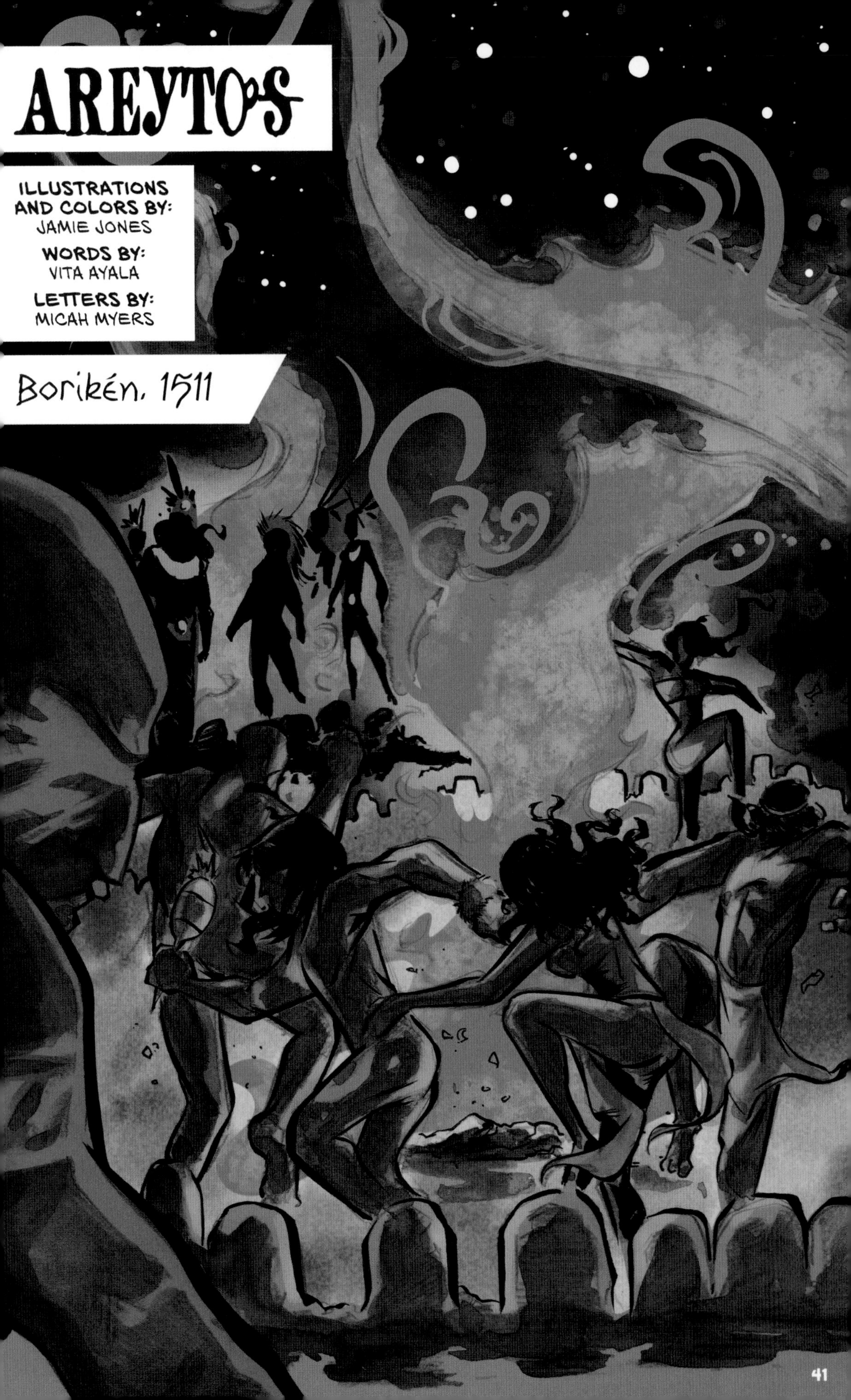
AREYTO'S
ILLUSTRATIONS AND COLORS BY:
JAMIE JONES
WORDS BY:
VITA AYALA
LETTERS BY:
MICAH MYERS
Borikén, 1511

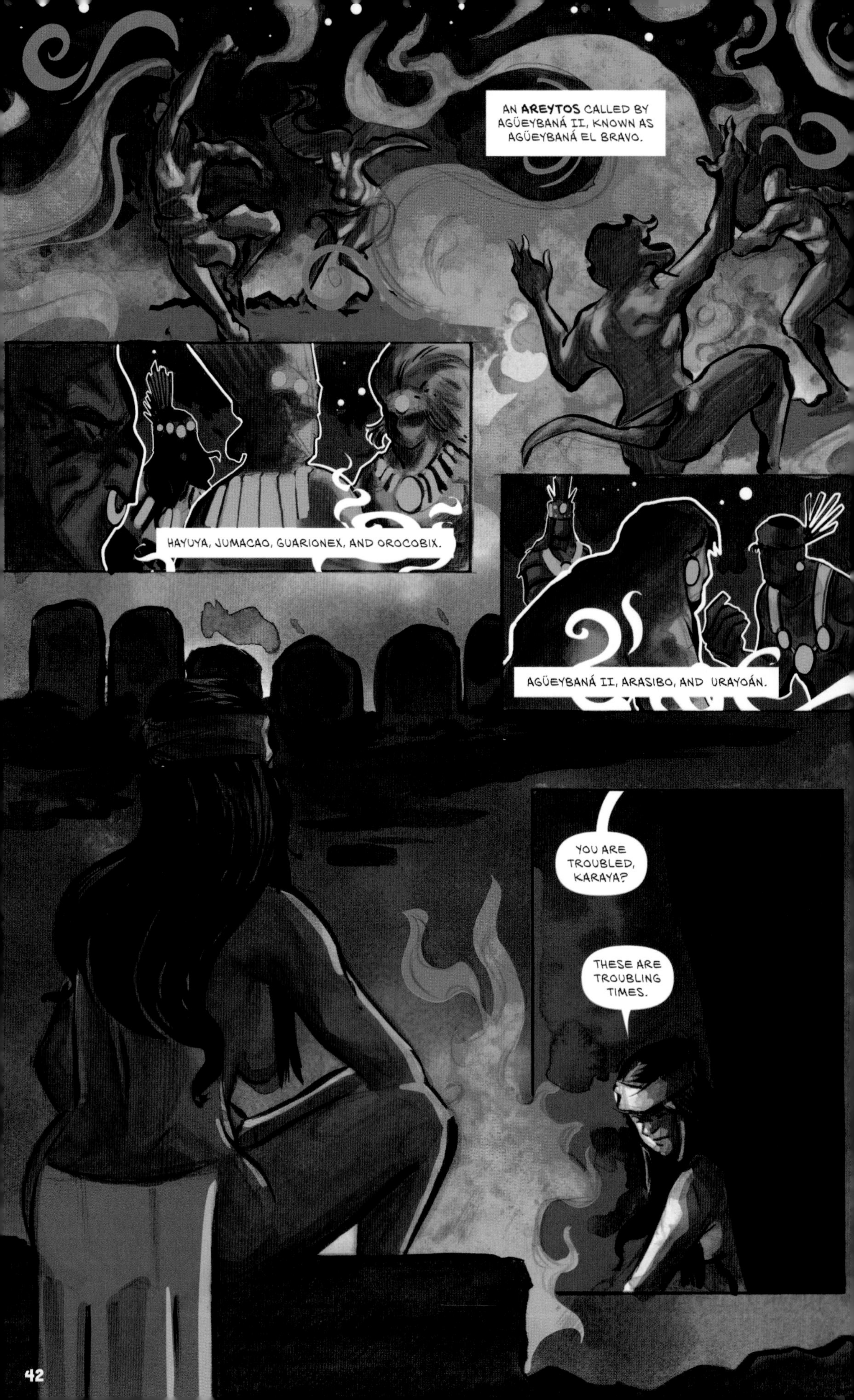
AN AREYTOS CALLED BY AGÜEYBANÁ II, KNOWN AS AGÜEYBANÁ EL BRAVO.
HAYUYA, JUMACAO, GUARIONEX, AND OROCOBIX.
AGÜEYBANÁ II, ARASIBO, AND URAYOÁN.
YOU ARE TROUBLED, KARAYA?
THESE ARE TROUBLING TIMES.

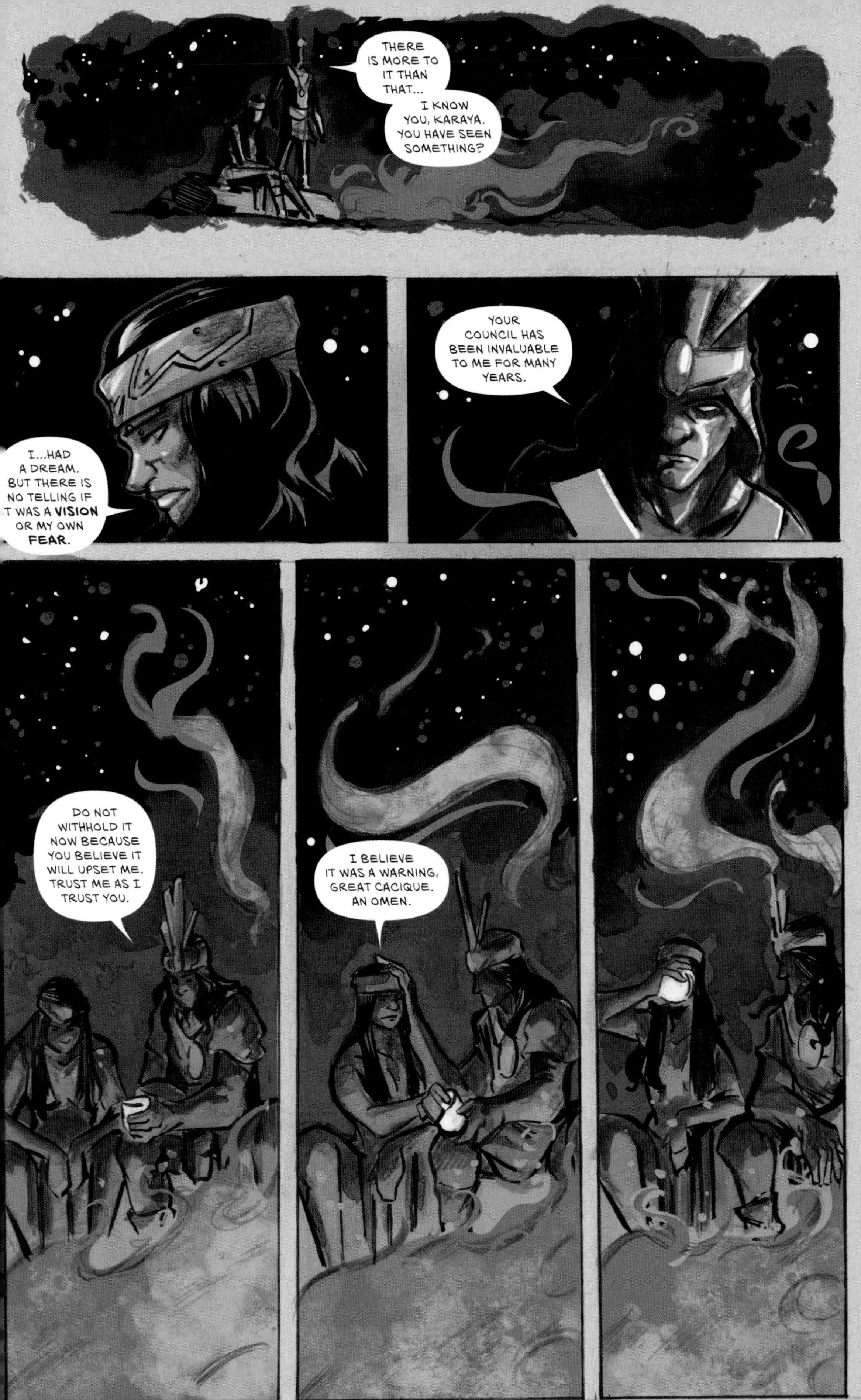
THERE IS MORE TO IT THAN THAT...
I KNOW YOU, KARAYA. YOU HAVE SEEN SOMETHING?
I...HAD A DREAM. BUT THERE IS NO TELLING IF IT WAS A **VISION** OR MY OWN **FEAR.**
YOUR COUNCIL HAS BEEN INVALUABLE TO ME FOR MANY YEARS.
DO NOT WITHHOLD IT NOW BECAUSE YOU BELIEVE IT WILL UPSET ME. TRUST ME AS I TRUST YOU.
I BELIEVE IT WAS A WARNING, GREAT CACIQUE. AN OMEN.

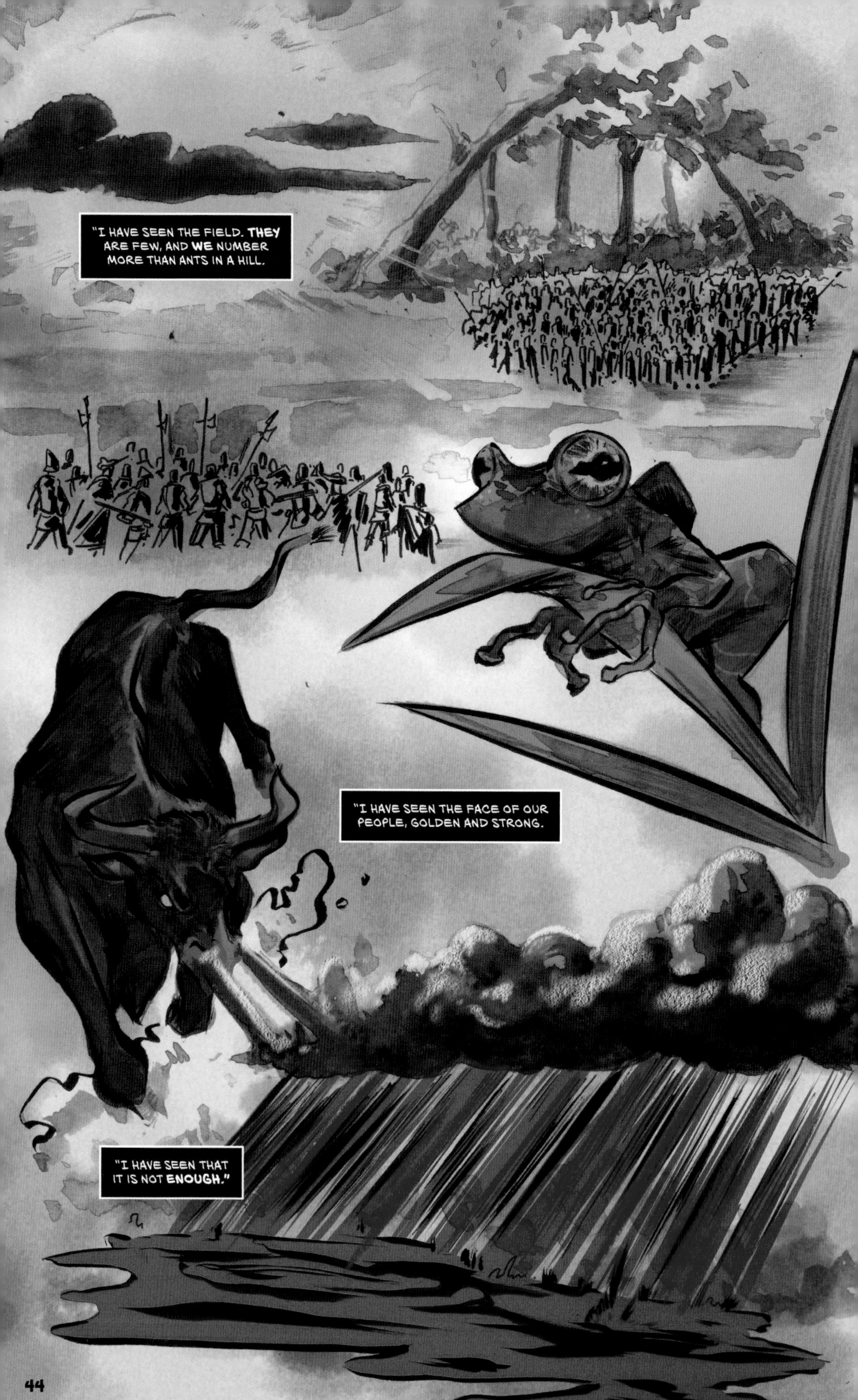
"I HAVE SEEN THE FIELD. **THEY** ARE FEW, AND **WE** NUMBER MORE THAN ANTS IN A HILL.
"I HAVE SEEN THE FACE OF OUR PEOPLE, GOLDEN AND STRONG.
"I HAVE SEEN THAT IT IS NOT **ENOUGH.**"

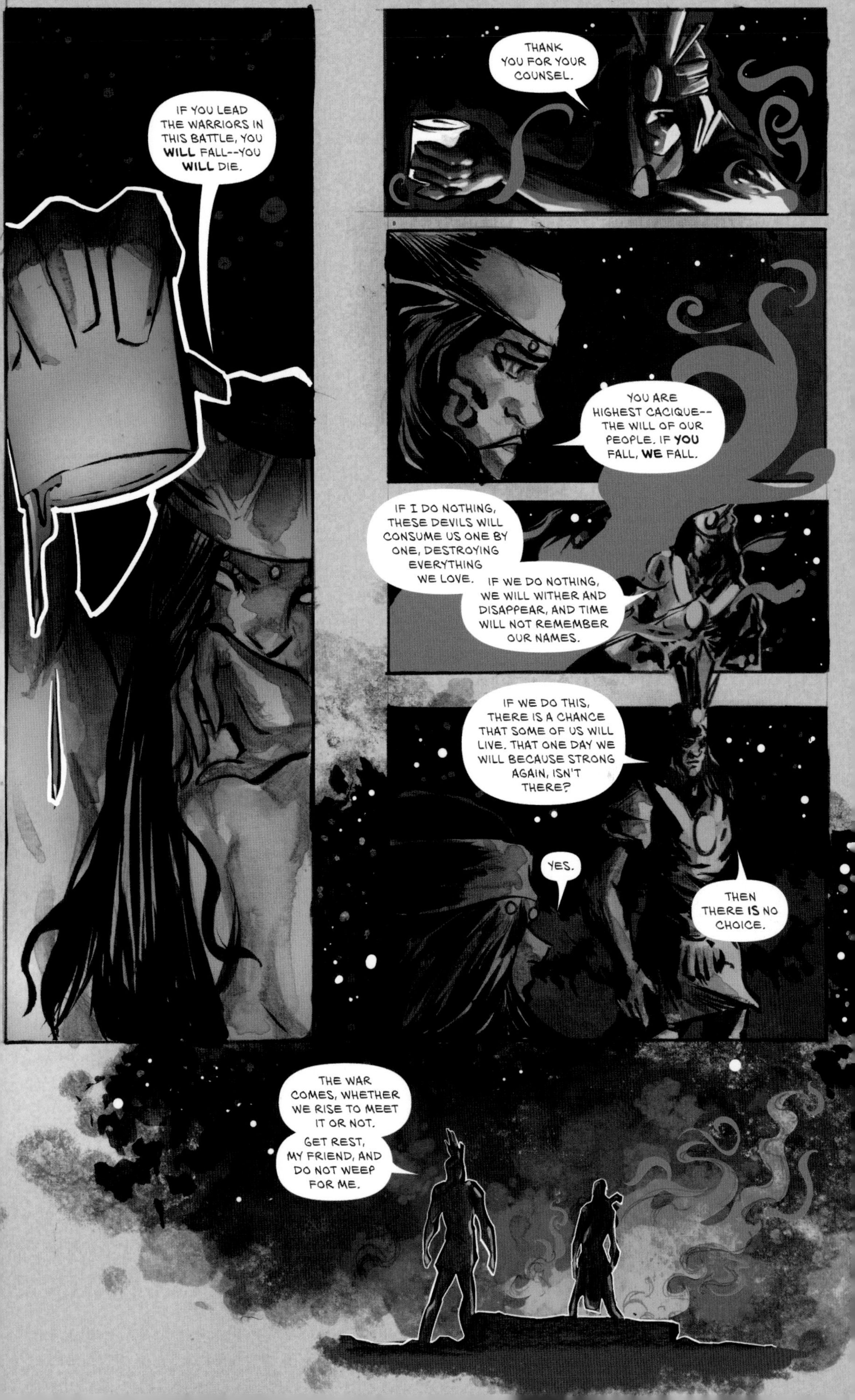

IF YOU LEAD THE WARRIORS IN THIS BATTLE, YOU **WILL** FALL--YOU **WILL** DIE.
THANK YOU FOR YOUR COUNSEL.
YOU ARE HIGHEST CACIQUE-- THE WILL OF OUR PEOPLE. IF **YOU** FALL, **WE** FALL.
IF I DO NOTHING, THESE DEVILS WILL CONSUME US ONE BY ONE, DESTROYING EVERYTHING WE LOVE.
IF WE DO NOTHING, WE WILL WITHER AND DISAPPEAR, AND TIME WILL NOT REMEMBER OUR NAMES.
IF WE DO THIS, THERE IS A CHANCE THAT SOME OF US WILL LIVE. THAT ONE DAY WE WILL BECAUSE STRONG AGAIN, ISN'T THERE?
YES.
THEN THERE **IS** NO CHOICE.
THE WAR COMES, WHETHER WE RISE TO MEET IT OR NOT.
GET REST, MY FRIEND, AND DO NOT WEEP FOR ME.

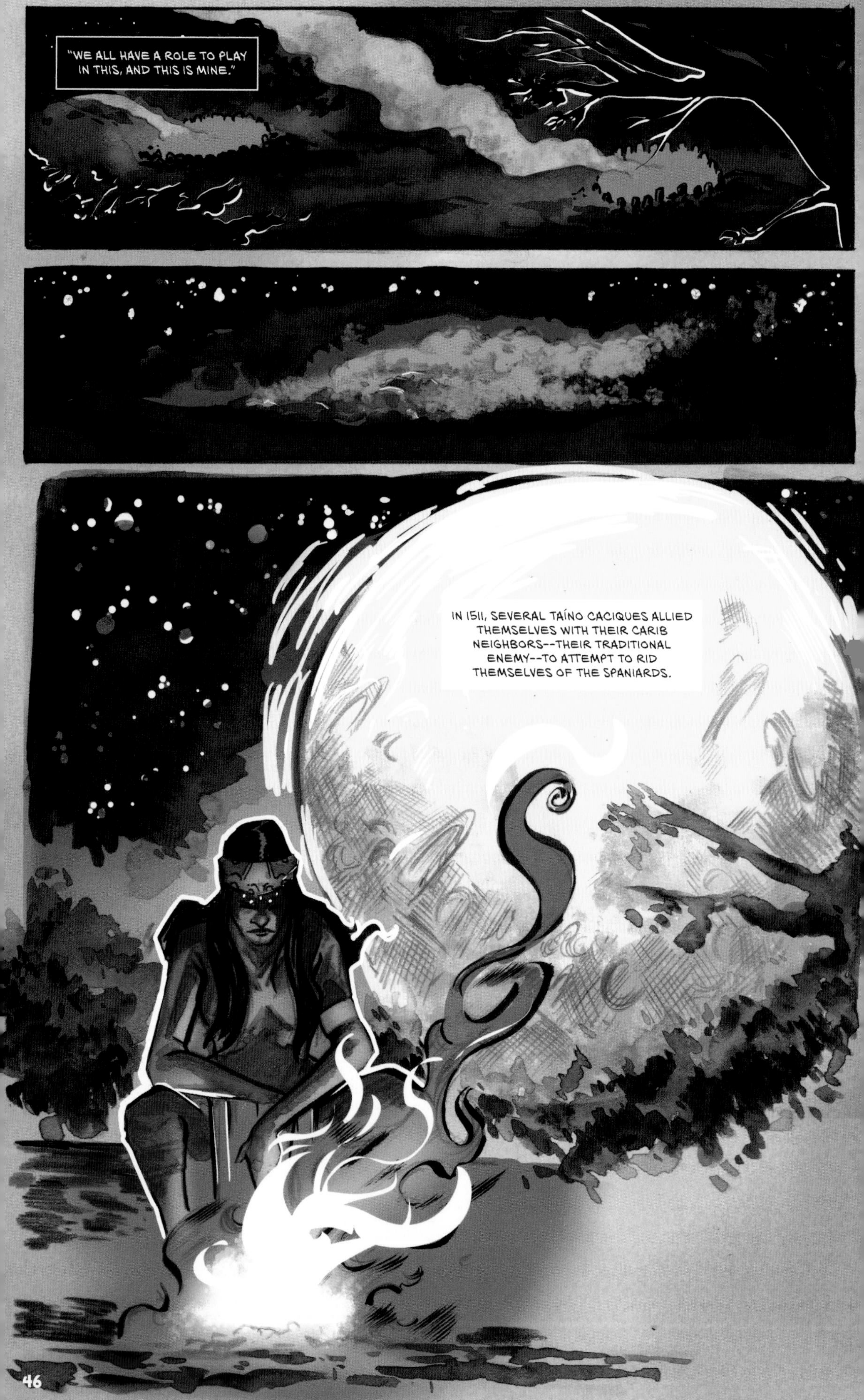
"WE ALL HAVE A ROLE TO PLAY IN THIS, AND THIS IS MINE."
IN 1511, SEVERAL TAÍNO CACIQUES ALLIED THEMSELVES WITH THEIR CARIB NEIGHBORS--THEIR TRADITIONAL ENEMY--TO ATTEMPT TO RID THEMSELVES OF THE SPANIARDS.

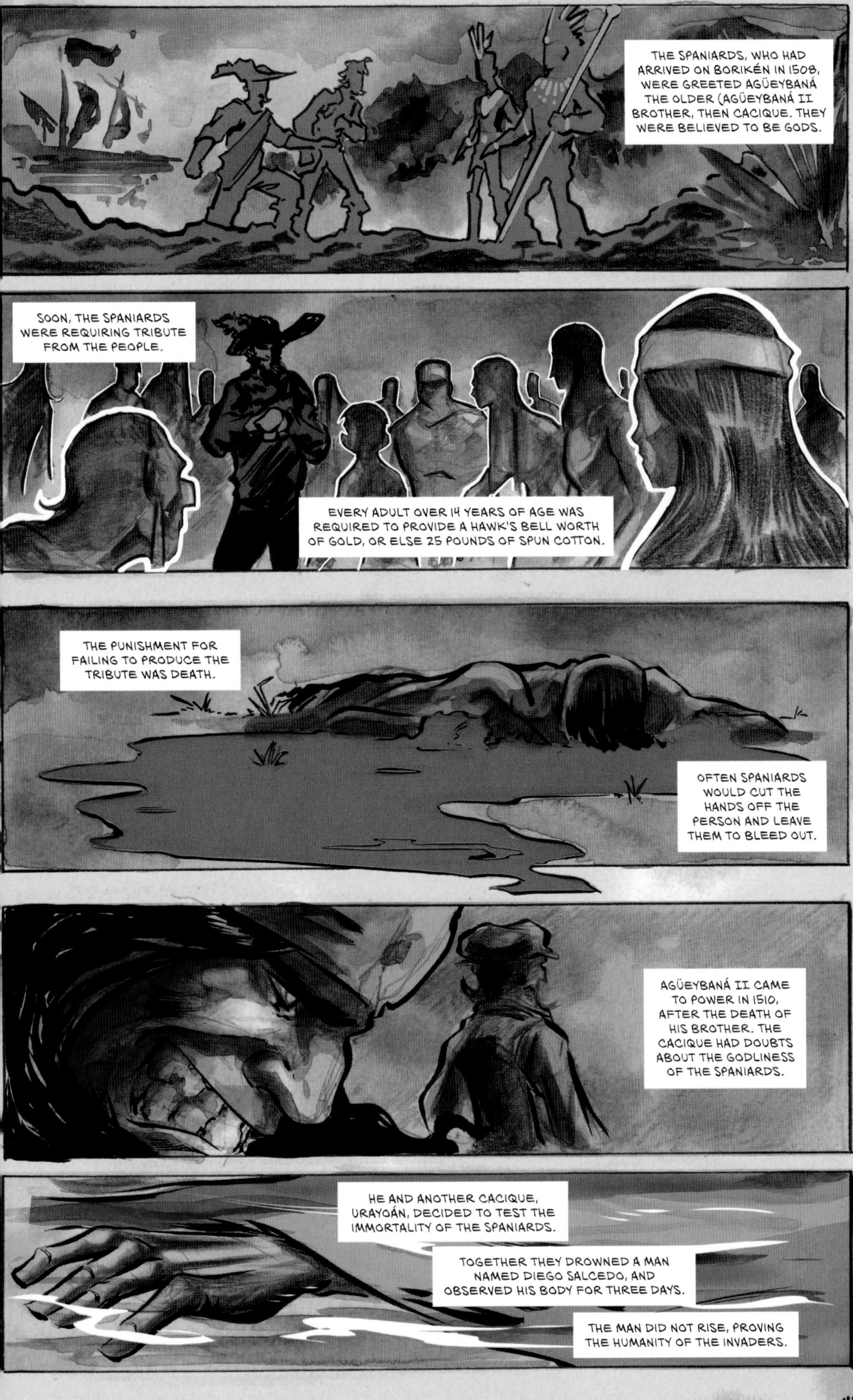
THE SPANIARDS, WHO HAD ARRIVED ON BORIKÉN IN 1508, WERE GREETED AGÜEYBANÁ THE OLDER (AGÜEYBANÁ II BROTHER, THEN CACIQUE. THEY WERE BELIEVED TO BE GODS.
SOON, THE SPANIARDS WERE REQUIRING TRIBUTE FROM THE PEOPLE.
EVERY ADULT OVER 14 YEARS OF AGE WAS REQUIRED TO PROVIDE A HAWK'S BELL WORTH OF GOLD, OR ELSE 25 POUNDS OF SPUN COTTON.
THE PUNISHMENT FOR FAILING TO PRODUCE THE TRIBUTE WAS DEATH.
OFTEN SPANIARDS WOULD CUT THE HANDS OFF THE PERSON AND LEAVE THEM TO BLEED OUT.
AGÜEYBANÁ II CAME TO POWER IN 1510, AFTER THE DEATH OF HIS BROTHER. THE CACIQUE HAD DOUBTS ABOUT THE GODLINESS OF THE SPANIARDS.
HE AND ANOTHER CACIQUE, URAYOÁN, DECIDED TO TEST THE IMMORTALITY OF THE SPANIARDS.
TOGETHER THEY DROWNED A MAN NAMED DIEGO SALCEDO, AND OBSERVED HIS BODY FOR THREE DAYS.
THE MAN DID NOT RISE, PROVING THE HUMANITY OF THE INVADERS.

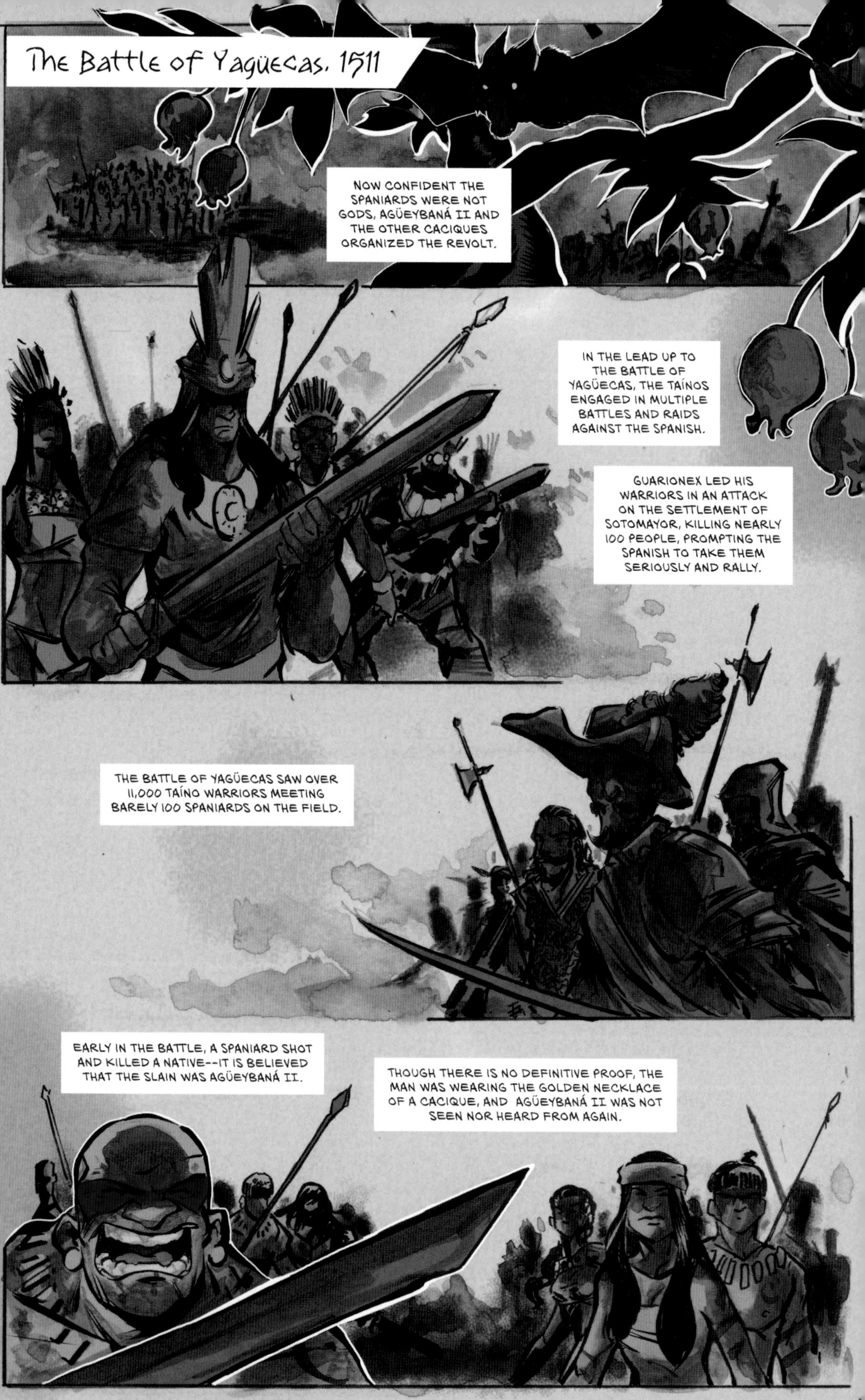
The Battle of Yagüecas, 1511
NOW CONFIDENT THE SPANIARDS WERE NOT GODS, AGÜEYBANÁ II AND THE OTHER CACIQUES ORGANIZED THE REVOLT.
IN THE LEAD UP TO THE BATTLE OF YAGÜECAS, THE TAÍNOS ENGAGED IN MULTIPLE BATTLES AND RAIDS AGAINST THE SPANISH.
GUARIONEX LED HIS WARRIORS IN AN ATTACK ON THE SETTLEMENT OF SOTOMAYOR, KILLING NEARLY 100 PEOPLE, PROMPTING THE SPANISH TO TAKE THEM SERIOUSLY AND RALLY.
THE BATTLE OF YAGÜECAS SAW OVER 11,000 TAÍNO WARRIORS MEETING BARELY 100 SPANIARDS ON THE FIELD.
EARLY IN THE BATTLE, A SPANIARD SHOT AND KILLED A NATIVE--IT IS BELIEVED THAT THE SLAIN WAS AGÜEYBANÁ II.
THOUGH THERE IS NO DEFINITIVE PROOF, THE MAN WAS WEARING THE GOLDEN NECKLACE OF A CACIQUE, AND AGÜEYBANÁ II WAS NOT SEEN NOR HEARD FROM AGAIN.

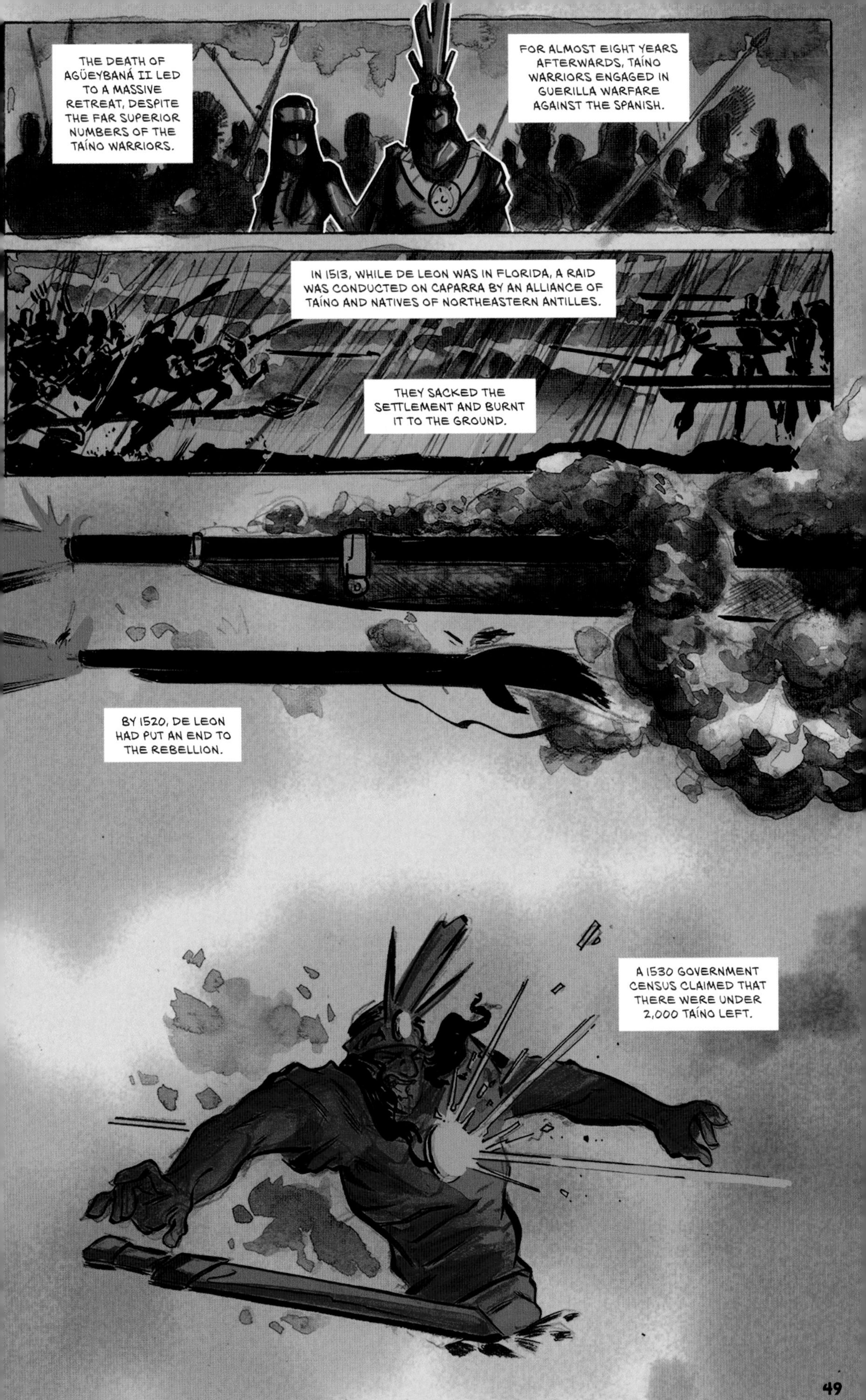
THE DEATH OF AGÜEYBANÁ II LED TO A MASSIVE RETREAT, DESPITE THE FAR SUPERIOR NUMBERS OF THE TAÍNO WARRIORS.
FOR ALMOST EIGHT YEARS AFTERWARDS, TAÍNO WARRIORS ENGAGED IN GUERILLA WARFARE AGAINST THE SPANISH.
IN 1513, WHILE DE LEON WAS IN FLORIDA, A RAID WAS CONDUCTED ON CAPARRA BY AN ALLIANCE OF TAÍNO AND NATIVES OF NORTHEASTERN ANTILLES.
THEY SACKED THE SETTLEMENT AND BURNT IT TO THE GROUND.
BY 1520, DE LEON HAD PUT AN END TO THE REBELLION.
A 1530 GOVERNMENT CENSUS CLAIMED THAT THERE WERE UNDER 2,000 TAÍNO LEFT.

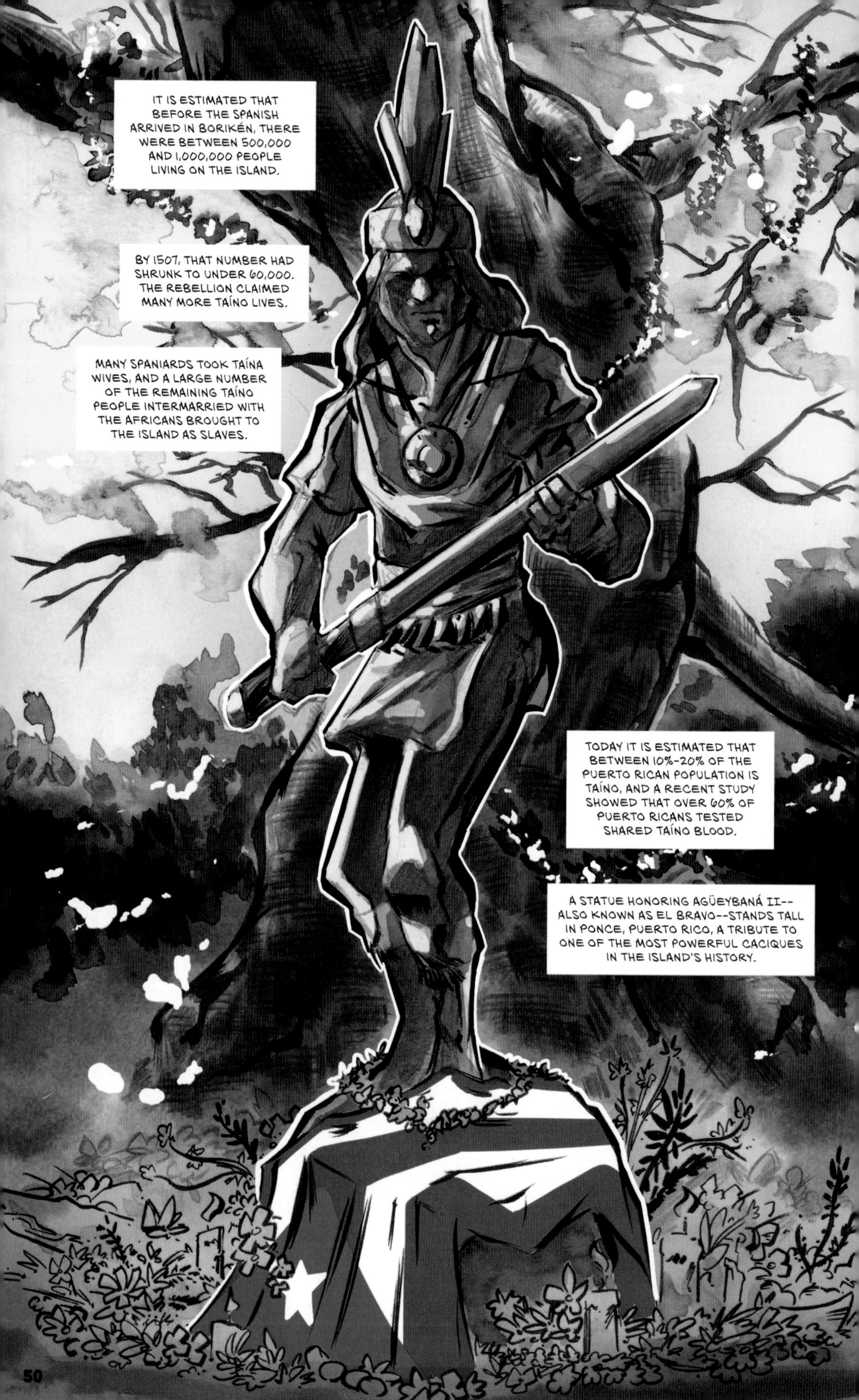
IT IS ESTIMATED THAT BEFORE THE SPANISH ARRIVED IN BORIKÉN, THERE WERE BETWEEN 500,000 AND 1,000,000 PEOPLE LIVING ON THE ISLAND.
BY 1507, THAT NUMBER HAD SHRUNK TO UNDER 60,000. THE REBELLION CLAIMED MANY MORE TAÍNO LIVES.
MANY SPANIARDS TOOK TAÍNA WIVES, AND A LARGE NUMBER OF THE REMAINING TAÍNO PEOPLE INTERMARRIED WITH THE AFRICANS BROUGHT TO THE ISLAND AS SLAVES.
TODAY IT IS ESTIMATED THAT BETWEEN 10%-20% OF THE PUERTO RICAN POPULATION IS TAÍNO, AND A RECENT STUDY SHOWED THAT OVER 60% OF PUERTO RICANS TESTED SHARED TAÍNO BLOOD.
A STATUE HONORING AGÜEYBANÁ II--ALSO KNOWN AS EL BRAVO--STANDS TALL IN PONCE, PUERTO RICO, A TRIBUTE TO ONE OF THE MOST POWERFUL CACIQUES IN THE ISLAND'S HISTORY.

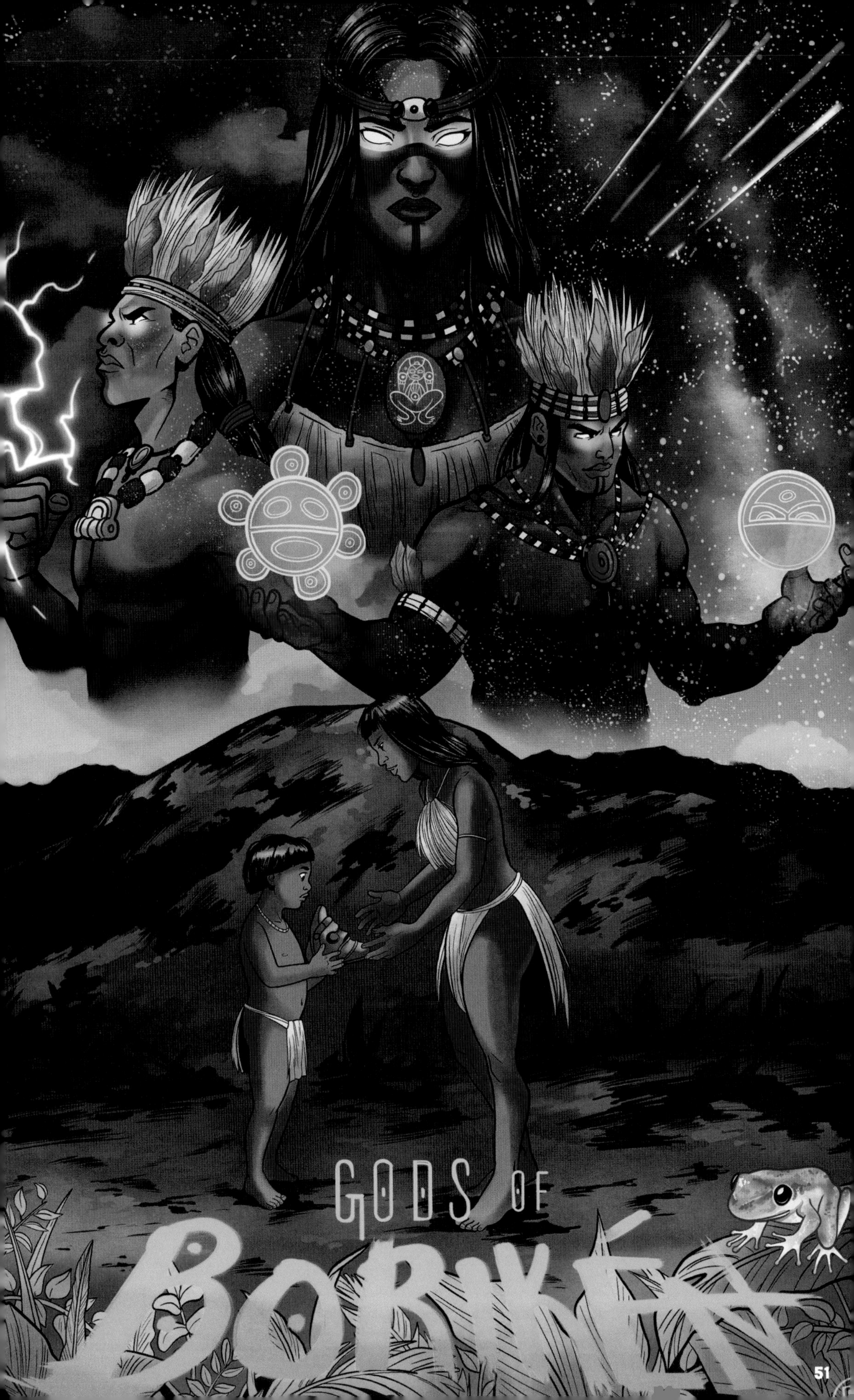
GODS OF
BORIKÉN

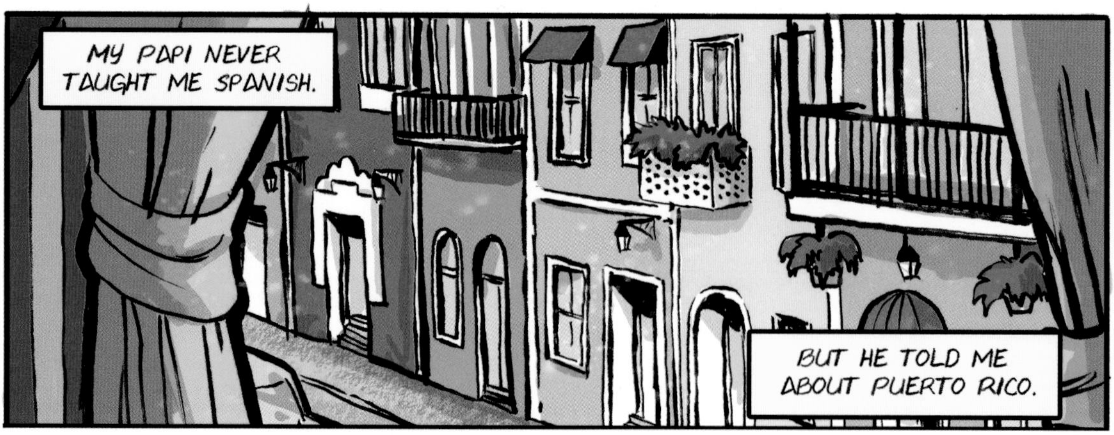
MY PAPI NEVER TAUGHT ME SPANISH.
BUT HE TOLD ME ABOUT PUERTO RICO.

# STORIES FROM MY FATHER

STORY BY ADAM LANCE GARCIA
ART BY HEIDI BLACK

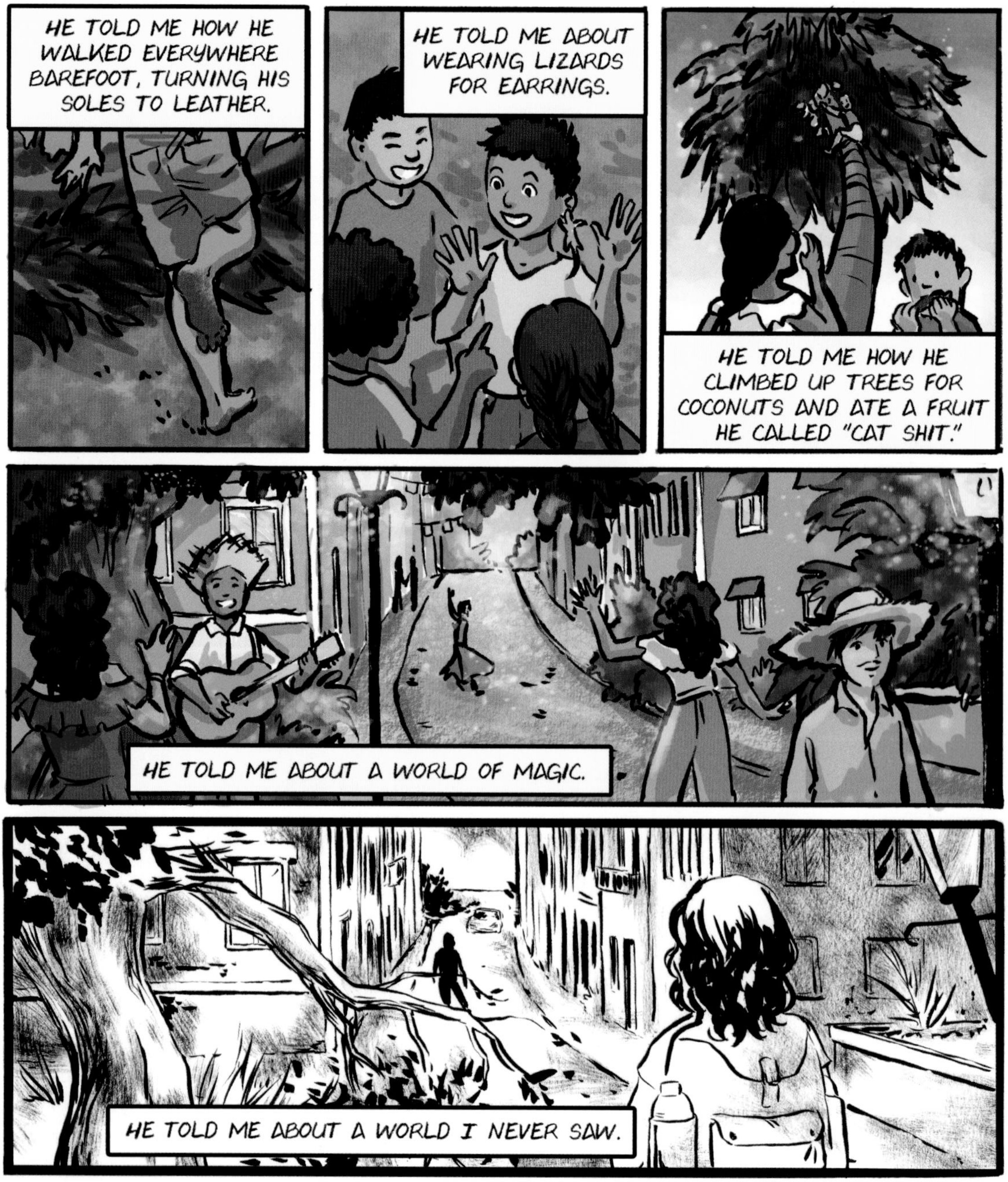
HE TOLD ME HOW HE WALKED EVERYWHERE BAREFOOT, TURNING HIS SOLES TO LEATHER.
HE TOLD ME ABOUT WEARING LIZARDS FOR EARRINGS.
HE TOLD ME HOW HE CLIMBED UP TREES FOR COCONUTS AND ATE A FRUIT HE CALLED "CAT SHIT."
HE TOLD ME ABOUT A WORLD OF MAGIC.
HE TOLD ME ABOUT A WORLD I NEVER SAW.

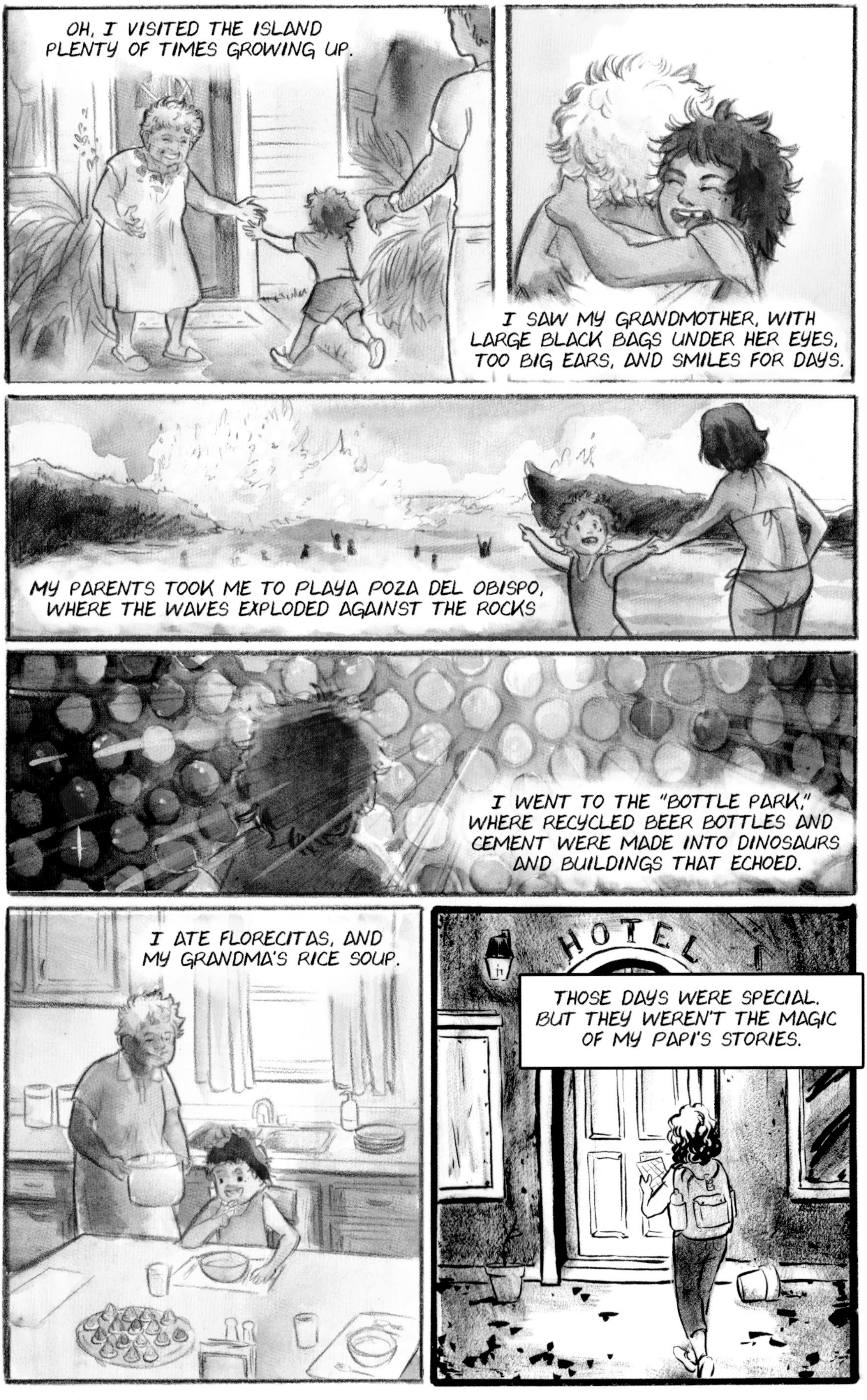
OH, I VISITED THE ISLAND PLENTY OF TIMES GROWING UP.
I SAW MY GRANDMOTHER, WITH LARGE BLACK BAGS UNDER HER EYES, TOO BIG EARS, AND SMILES FOR DAYS.
MY PARENTS TOOK ME TO PLAYA POZA DEL OBISPO, WHERE THE WAVES EXPLODED AGAINST THE ROCKS
I WENT TO THE "BOTTLE PARK," WHERE RECYCLED BEER BOTTLES AND CEMENT WERE MADE INTO DINOSAURS AND BUILDINGS THAT ECHOED.
I ATE FLORECITAS, AND MY GRANDMA'S RICE SOUP.
HOTEL
THOSE DAYS WERE SPECIAL. BUT THEY WEREN'T THE MAGIC OF MY PAPI'S STORIES.

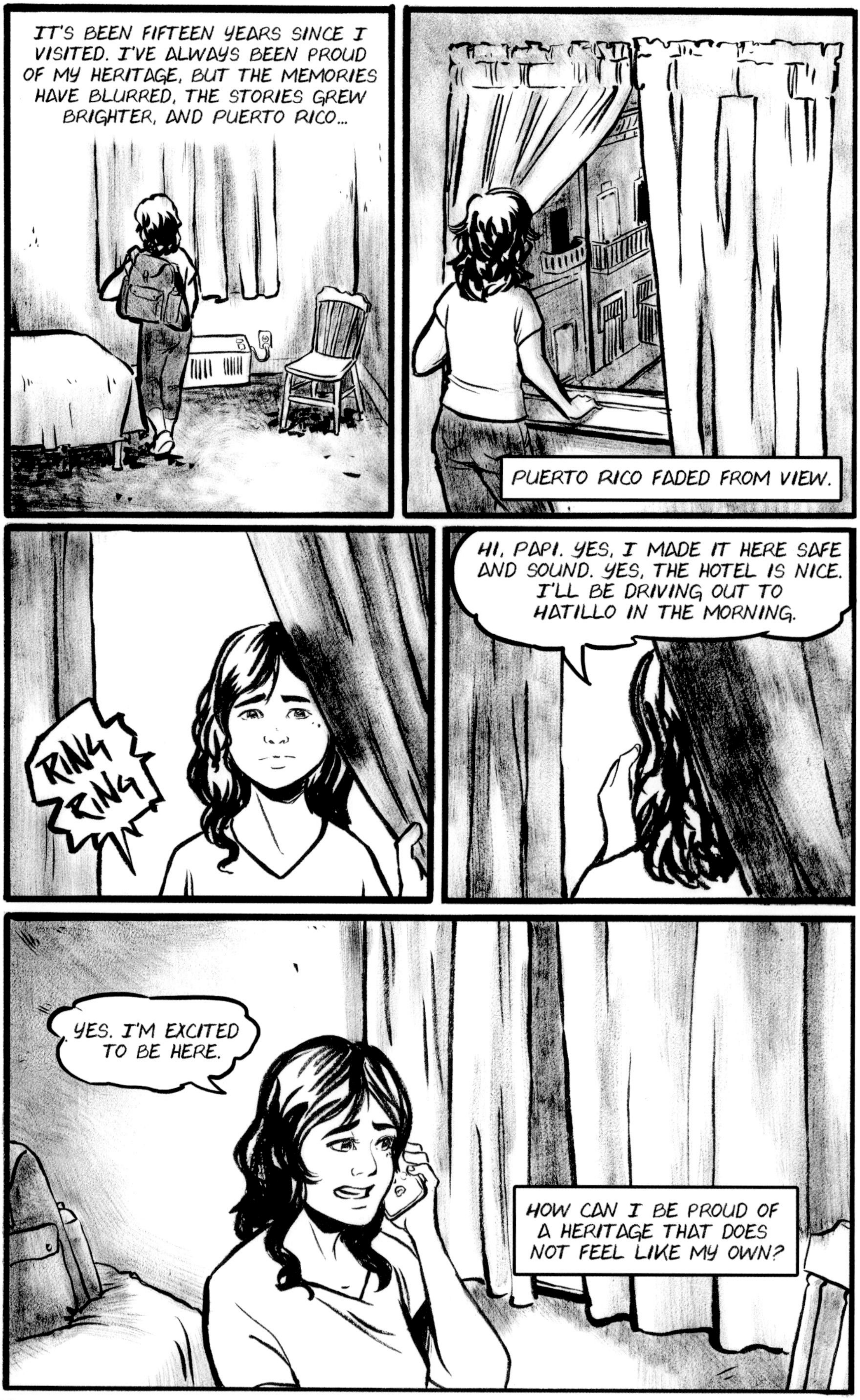
IT'S BEEN FIFTEEN YEARS SINCE I VISITED. I'VE ALWAYS BEEN PROUD OF MY HERITAGE, BUT THE MEMORIES HAVE BLURRED, THE STORIES GREW BRIGHTER, AND PUERTO RICO...
PUERTO RICO FADED FROM VIEW.
RING RING
HI, PAPI. YES, I MADE IT HERE SAFE AND SOUND. YES, THE HOTEL IS NICE. I'LL BE DRIVING OUT TO HATILLO IN THE MORNING.
YES. I'M EXCITED TO BE HERE.
HOW CAN I BE PROUD OF A HERITAGE THAT DOES NOT FEEL LIKE MY OWN?

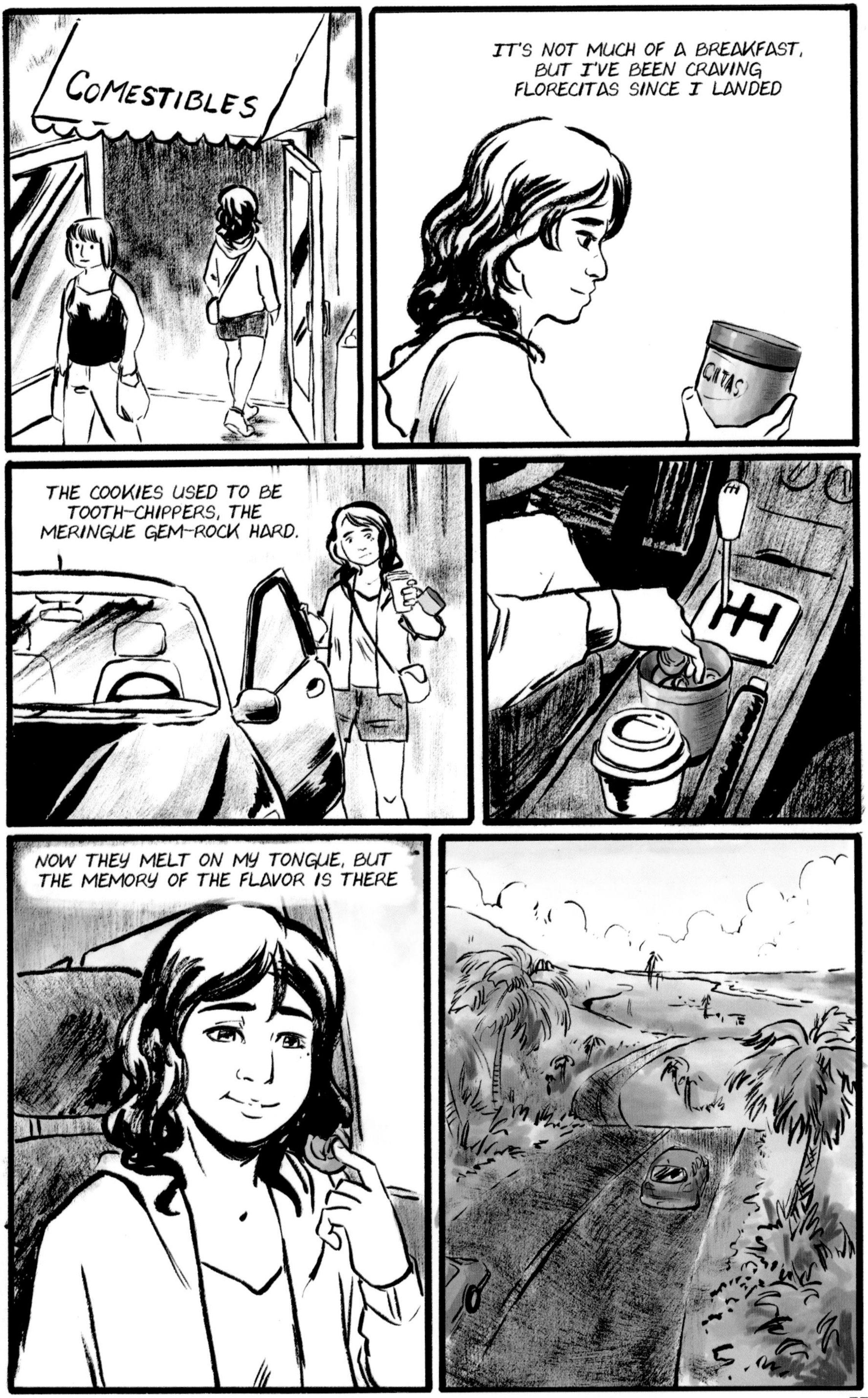
COMESTIBLES
IT'S NOT MUCH OF A BREAKFAST, BUT I'VE BEEN CRAVING FLORECITAS SINCE I LANDED
CITAS
THE COOKIES USED TO BE TOOTH-CHIPPERS, THE MERINGUE GEM-ROCK HARD.
NOW THEY MELT ON MY TONGUE, BUT THE MEMORY OF THE FLAVOR IS THERE

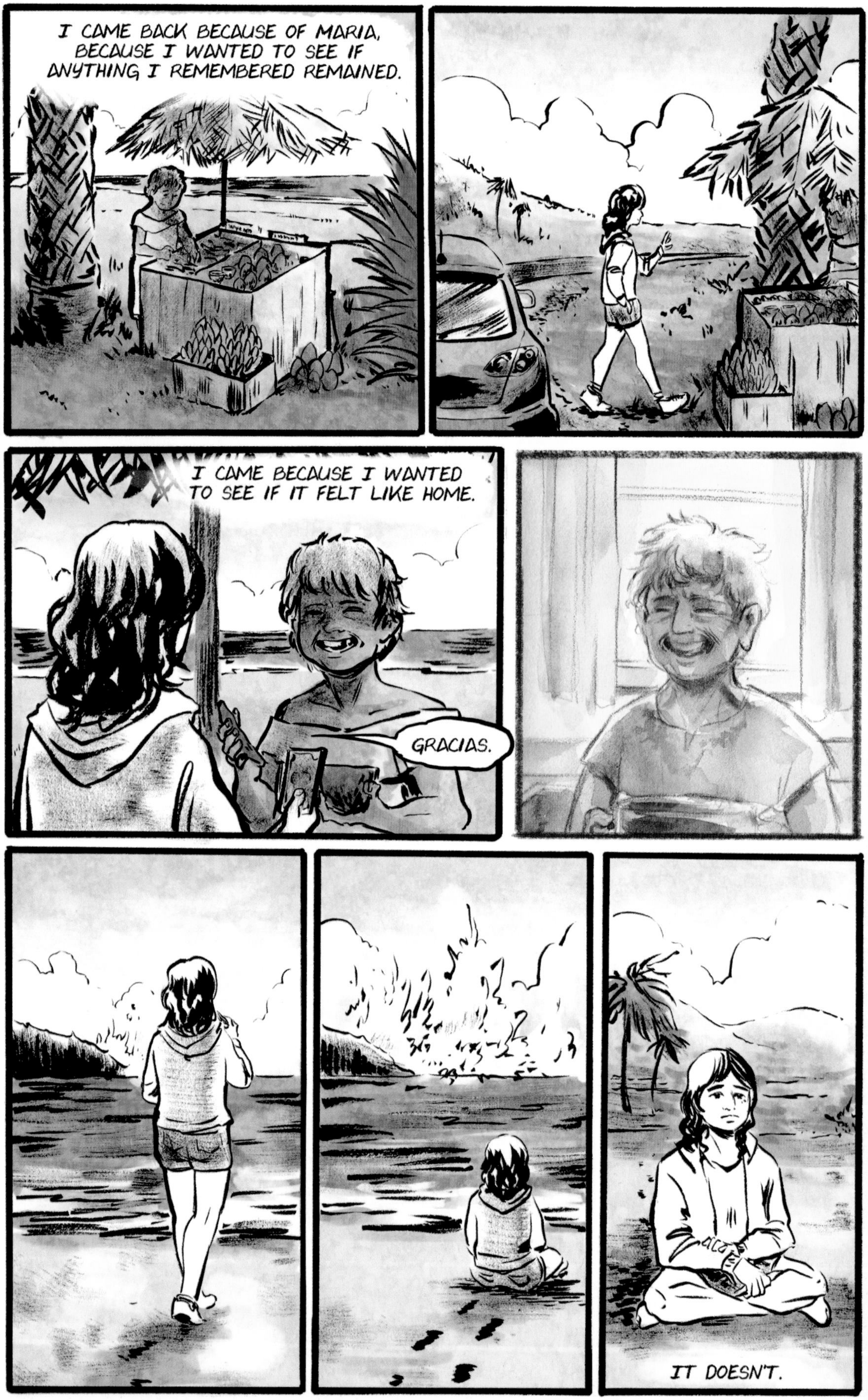
I CAME BACK BECAUSE OF MARIA, BECAUSE I WANTED TO SEE IF ANYTHING I REMEMBERED REMAINED.
I CAME BECAUSE I WANTED TO SEE IF IT FELT LIKE HOME.
GRACIAS.
IT DOESN'T.

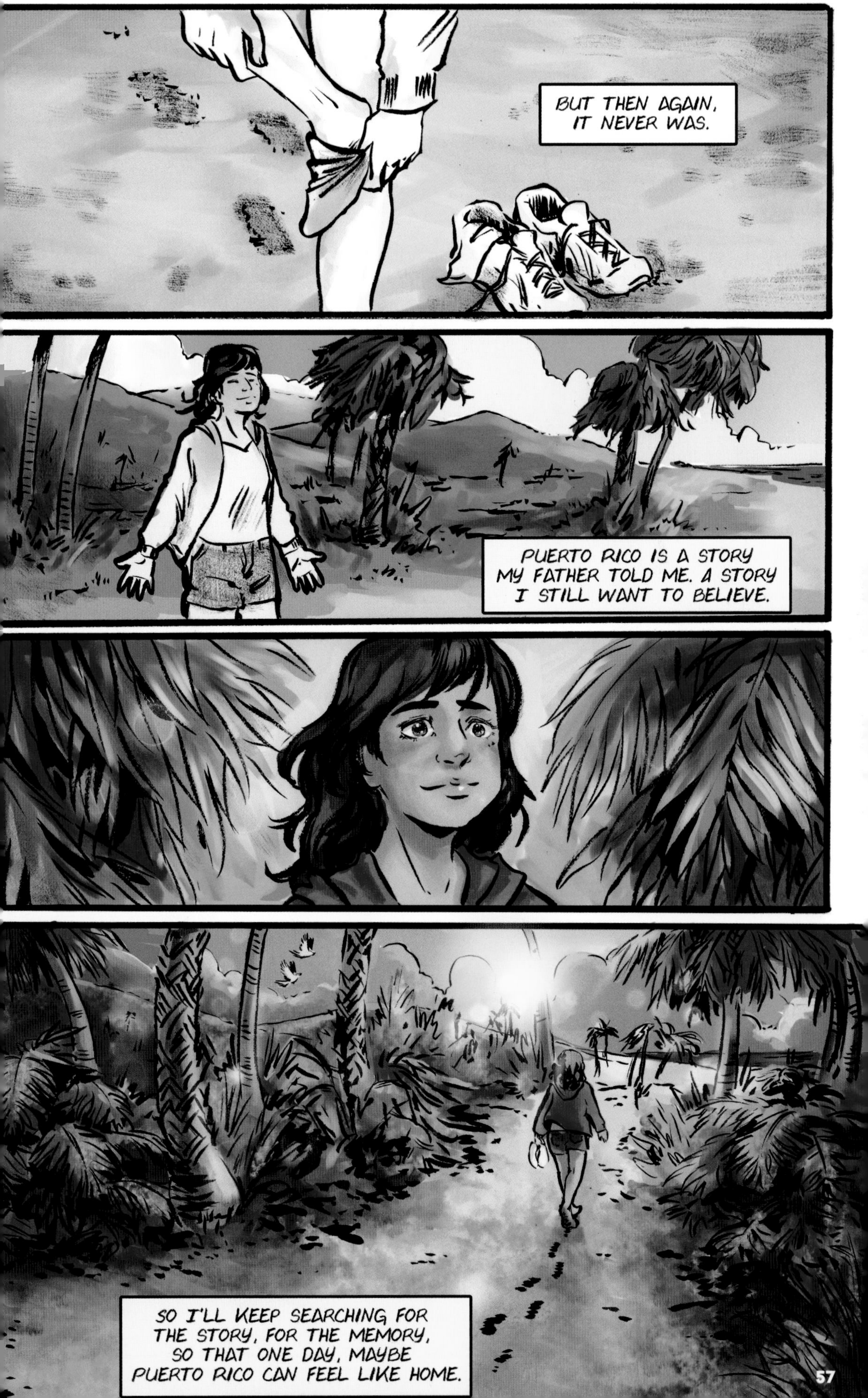
BUT THEN AGAIN, IT NEVER WAS.
PUERTO RICO IS A STORY MY FATHER TOLD ME. A STORY I STILL WANT TO BELIEVE.
SO I'LL KEEP SEARCHING FOR THE STORY, FOR THE MEMORY, SO THAT ONE DAY, MAYBE PUERTO RICO CAN FEEL LIKE HOME.

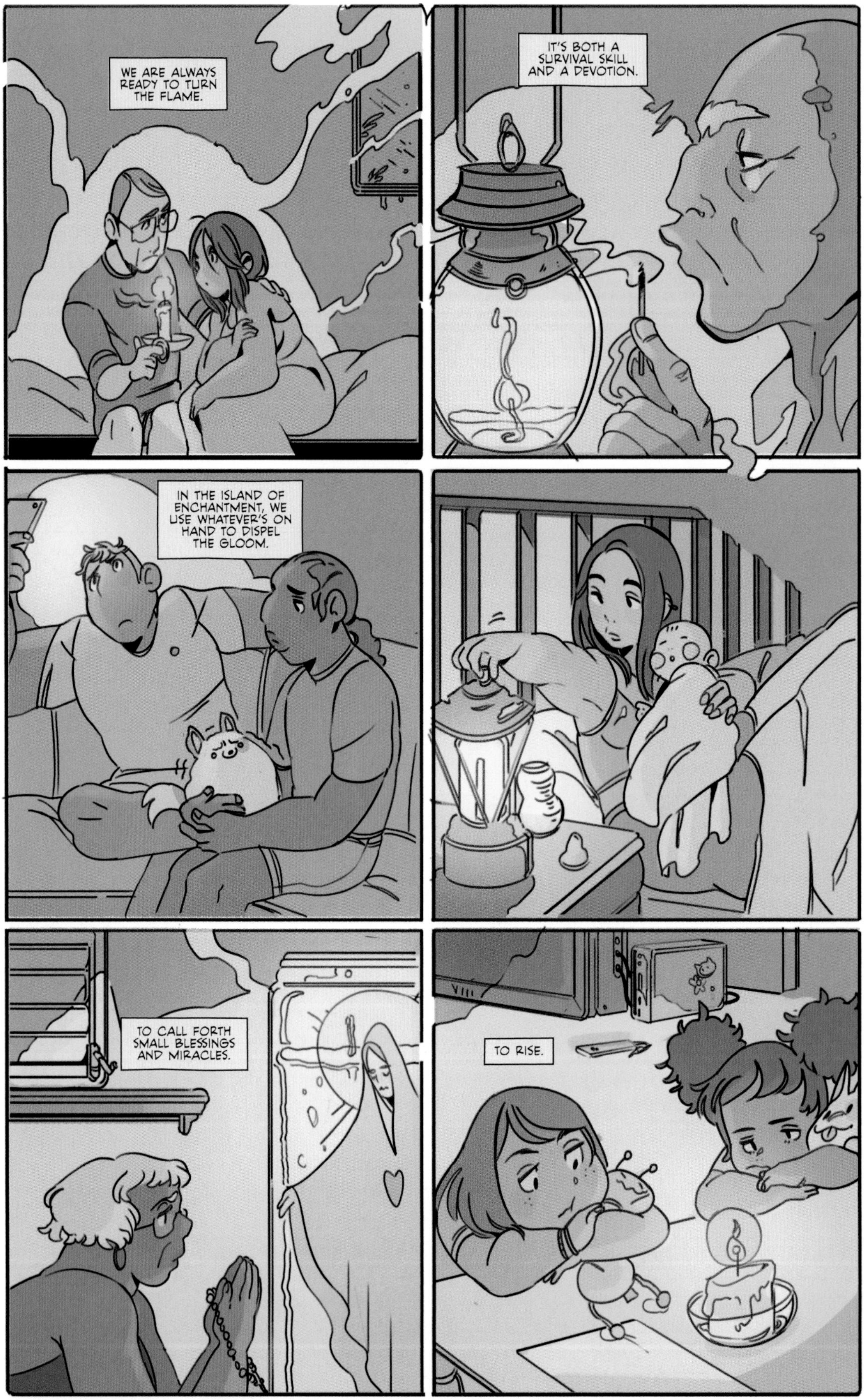
WE ARE ALWAYS READY TO TURN THE FLAME.
IT'S BOTH A SURVIVAL SKILL AND A DEVOTION.
IN THE ISLAND OF ENCHANTMENT, WE USE WHATEVER'S ON HAND TO DISPEL THE GLOOM.
TO CALL FORTH SMALL BLESSINGS AND MIRACLES.
TO RISE.

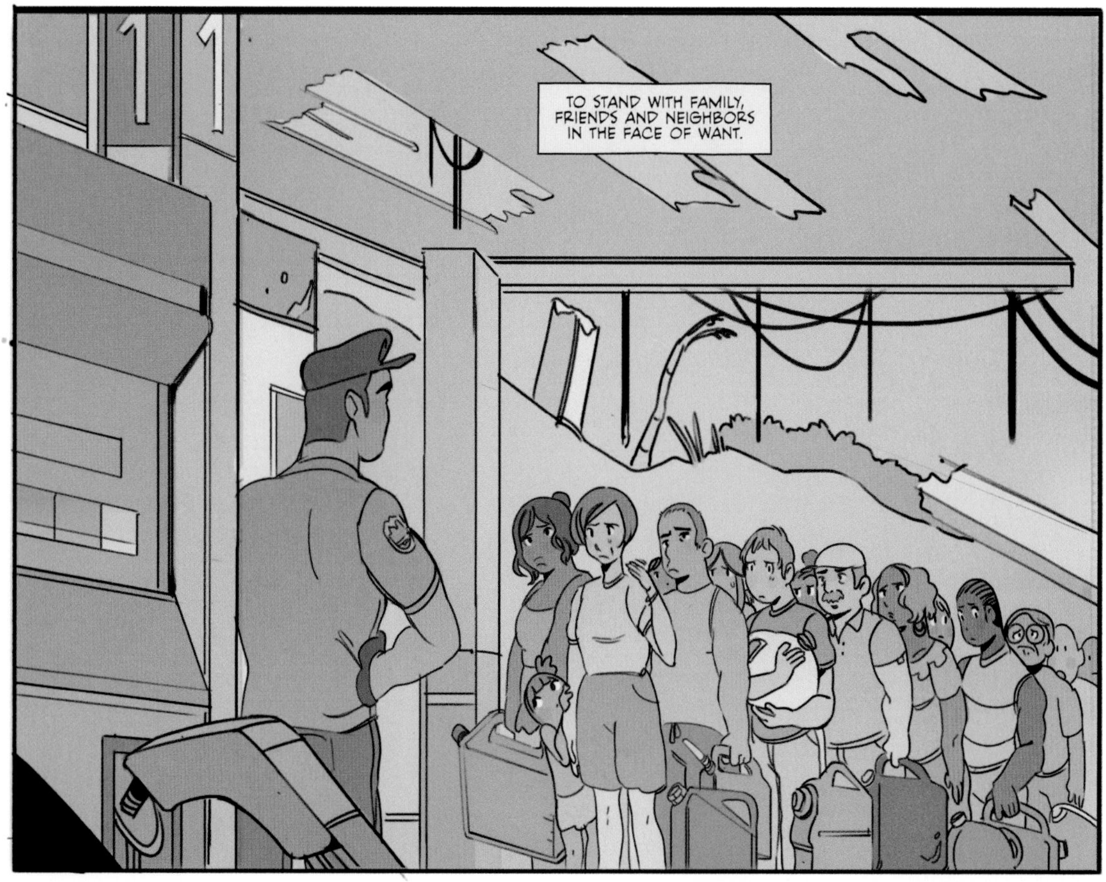
TO STAND WITH FAMILY, FRIENDS AND NEIGHBORS IN THE FACE OF WANT.

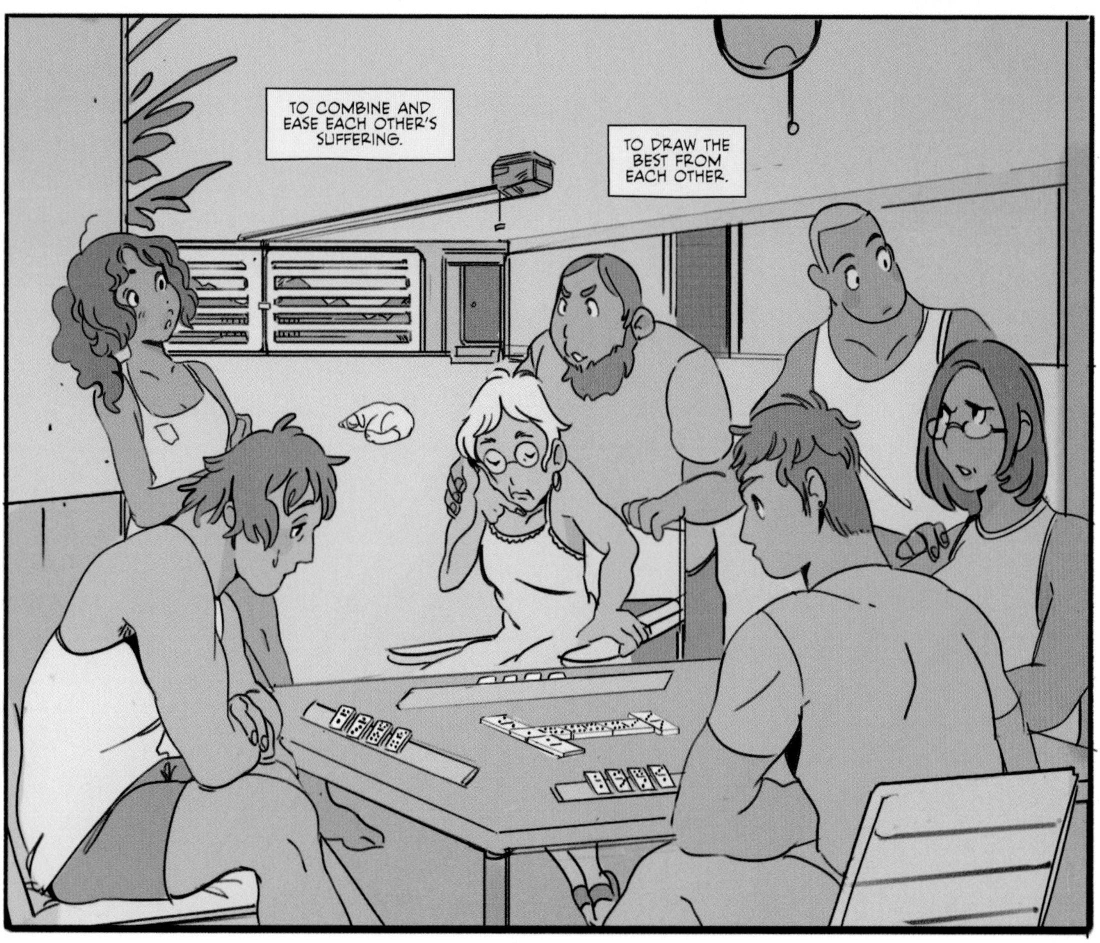
TO COMBINE AND EASE EACH OTHER'S SUFFERING.
TO DRAW THE BEST FROM EACH OTHER.

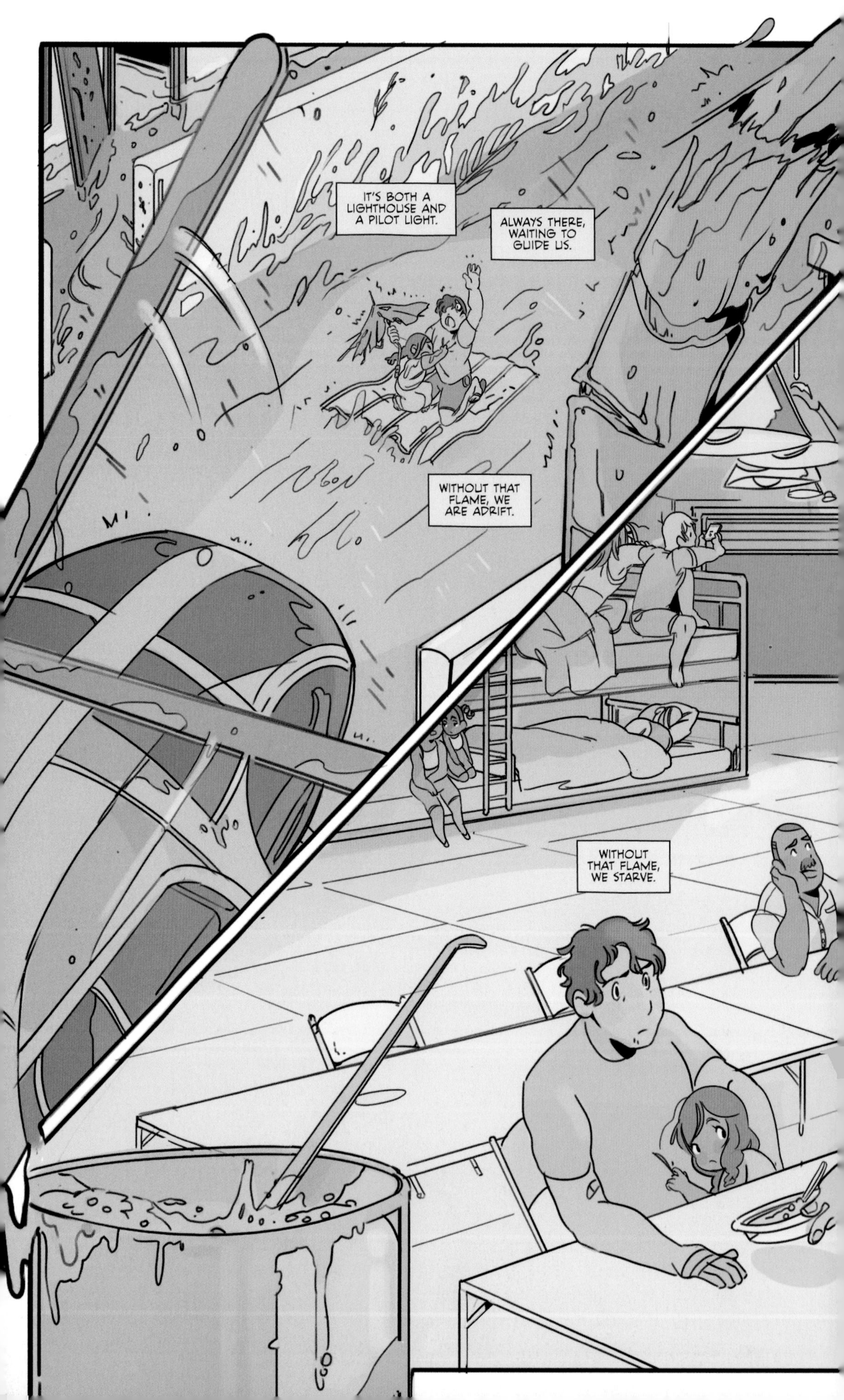
IT'S BOTH A LIGHTHOUSE AND A PILOT LIGHT.
ALWAYS THERE, WAITING TO GUIDE US.
WITHOUT THAT FLAME, WE ARE ADRIFT.
WITHOUT THAT FLAME, WE STARVE.

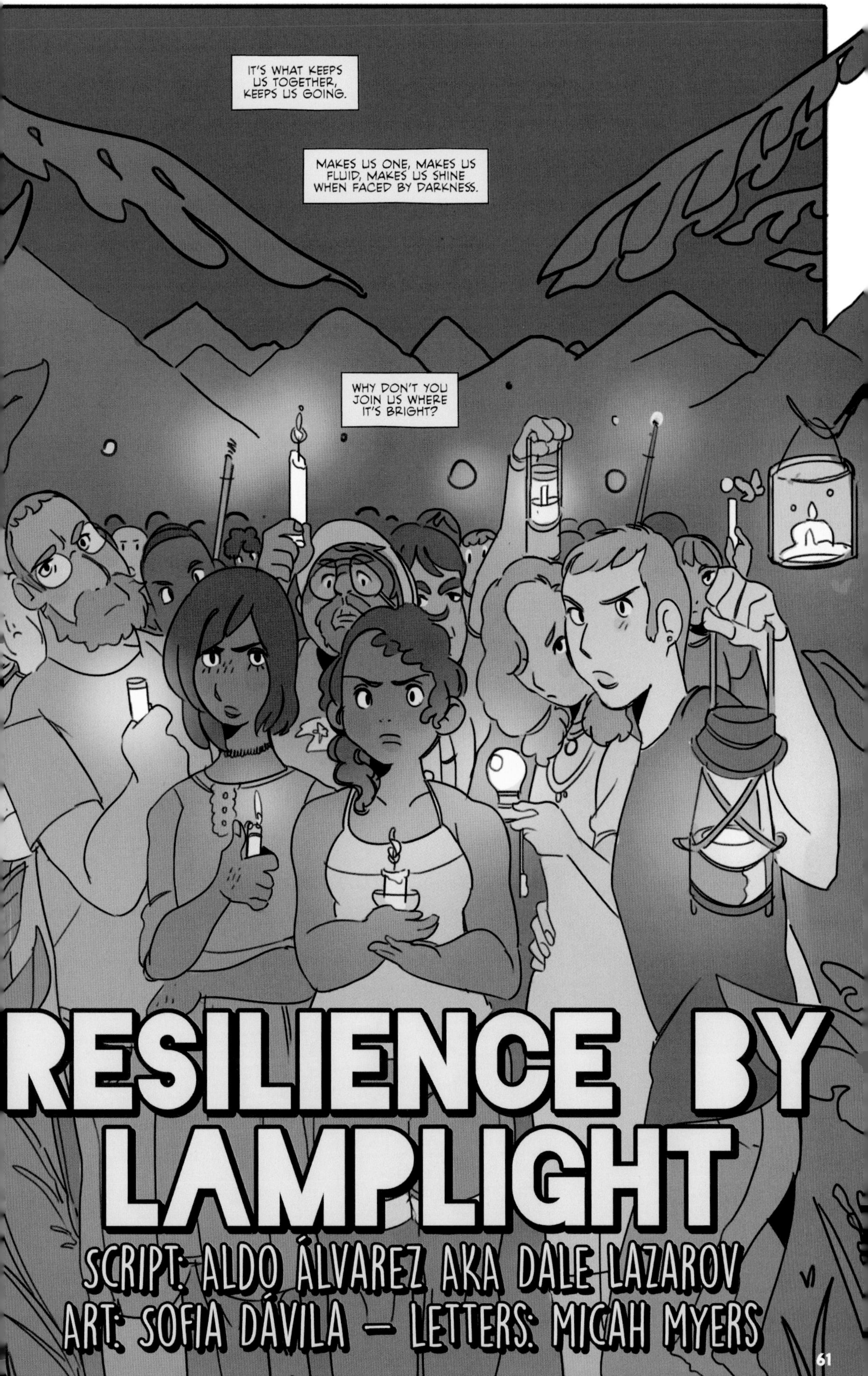
IT'S WHAT KEEPS US TOGETHER, KEEPS US GOING.
MAKES US ONE, MAKES US FLUID, MAKES US SHINE WHEN FACED BY DARKNESS.
WHY DON'T YOU JOIN US WHERE IT'S BRIGHT?
RESILIENCE BY LAMPLIGHT
SCRIPT: ALDO ÁLVAREZ AKA DALE LAZAROV
ART: SOFIA DÁVILA – LETTERS: MICAH MYERS

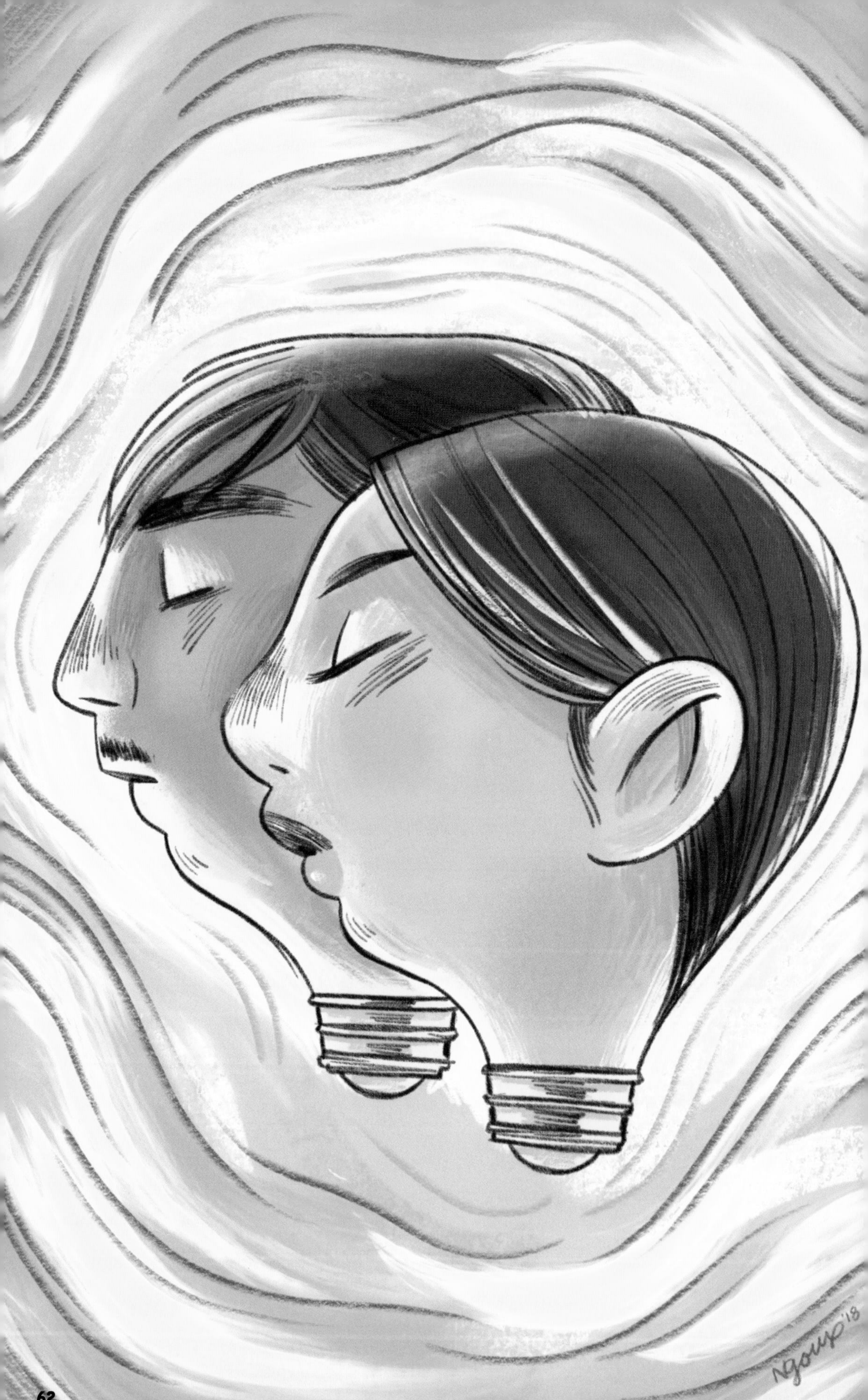

# A BROKEN P.R.O.M.E.S.A. BY ROSA COLÓN

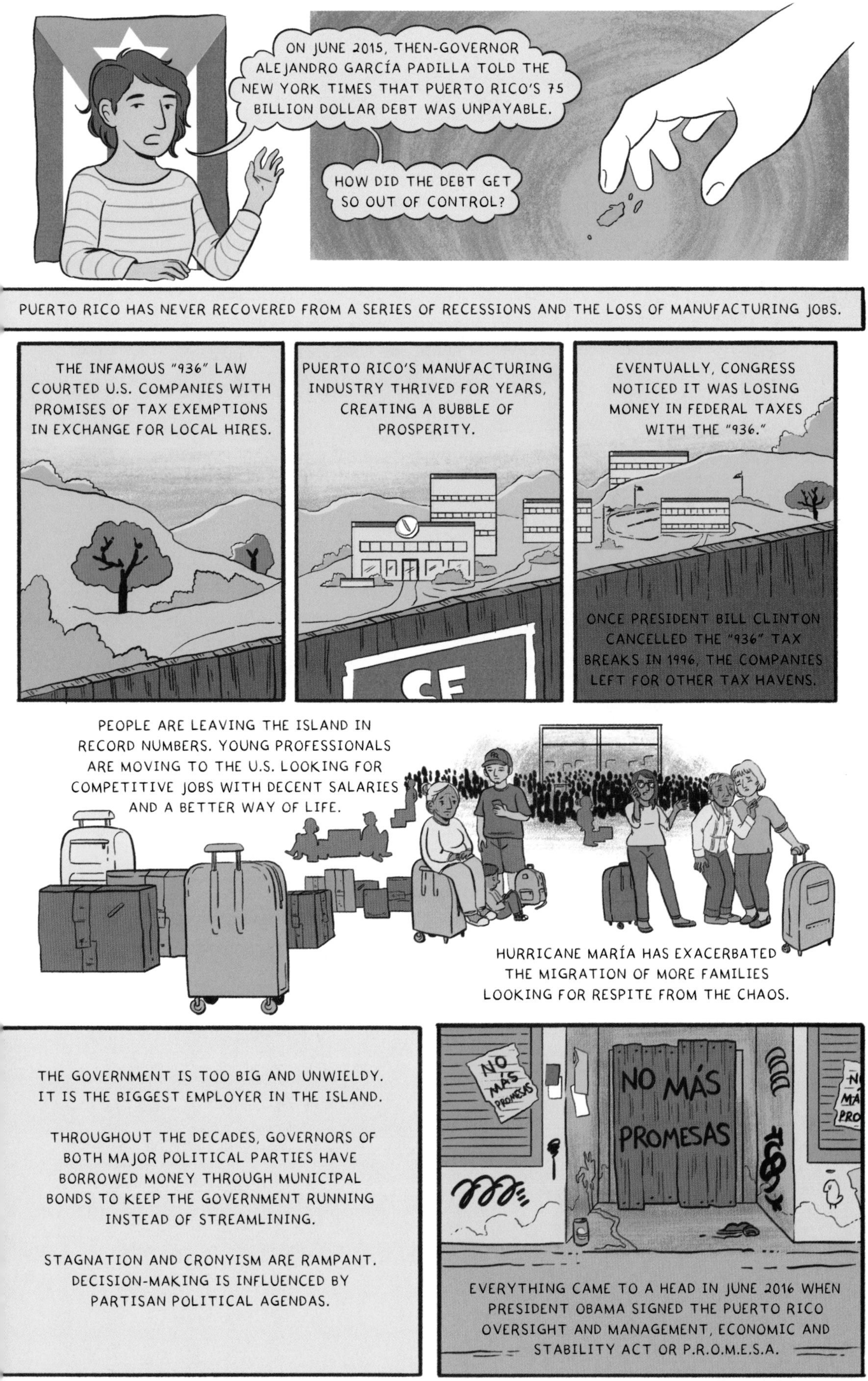

ON JUNE 2015, THEN-GOVERNOR ALEJANDRO GARCÍA PADILLA TOLD THE NEW YORK TIMES THAT PUERTO RICO'S 75 BILLION DOLLAR DEBT WAS UNPAYABLE.
HOW DID THE DEBT GET SO OUT OF CONTROL?
PUERTO RICO HAS NEVER RECOVERED FROM A SERIES OF RECESSIONS AND THE LOSS OF MANUFACTURING JOBS.
THE INFAMOUS "936" LAW COURTED U.S. COMPANIES WITH PROMISES OF TAX EXEMPTIONS IN EXCHANGE FOR LOCAL HIRES.
PUERTO RICO'S MANUFACTURING INDUSTRY THRIVED FOR YEARS, CREATING A BUBBLE OF PROSPERITY.
EVENTUALLY, CONGRESS NOTICED IT WAS LOSING MONEY IN FEDERAL TAXES WITH THE "936."
ONCE PRESIDENT BILL CLINTON CANCELLED THE "936" TAX BREAKS IN 1996, THE COMPANIES LEFT FOR OTHER TAX HAVENS.
PEOPLE ARE LEAVING THE ISLAND IN RECORD NUMBERS. YOUNG PROFESSIONALS ARE MOVING TO THE U.S. LOOKING FOR COMPETITIVE JOBS WITH DECENT SALARIES AND A BETTER WAY OF LIFE.
HURRICANE MARÍA HAS EXACERBATED THE MIGRATION OF MORE FAMILIES LOOKING FOR RESPITE FROM THE CHAOS.
THE GOVERNMENT IS TOO BIG AND UNWIELDY. IT IS THE BIGGEST EMPLOYER IN THE ISLAND.
THROUGHOUT THE DECADES, GOVERNORS OF BOTH MAJOR POLITICAL PARTIES HAVE BORROWED MONEY THROUGH MUNICIPAL BONDS TO KEEP THE GOVERNMENT RUNNING INSTEAD OF STREAMLINING.
STAGNATION AND CRONYISM ARE RAMPANT. DECISION-MAKING IS INFLUENCED BY PARTISAN POLITICAL AGENDAS.
NO MÁS PROMESAS
NO MÁS PROMESAS
EVERYTHING CAME TO A HEAD IN JUNE 2016 WHEN PRESIDENT OBAMA SIGNED THE PUERTO RICO OVERSIGHT AND MANAGEMENT, ECONOMIC AND STABILITY ACT OR P.R.O.M.E.S.A.

PROMESA WAS CREATED BY THE HOUSE COMMITTEE ON NATURAL RESOURCES AND CONGRESS AS A WAY OF HELPING PUERTO RICO THROUGH THE CRISIS AND KEEPING THE BONDHOLDERS FROM SUING THE GOVERNMENT FOR PAYMENTS.

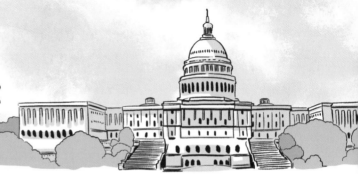

IT HELPS DEFINE ESSENTIAL SERVICES AND PROTECTS THEM FROM BEING PHASED OUT IN FAVOR OF PAYING THE DEBT.

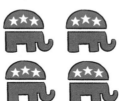

PROMESA IMPLEMENTED THE FINANCIAL OVERSIGHT AND MANAGEMENT BOARD, OR "LA JUNTA" TO MANAGE THE FINANCES PERTAINING TO PUBLIC POLICY. LA JUNTA IS MADE UP OF FOUR REPUBLICANS, TWO DEMOCRATS, AND ONE MEMBER APPOINTED BY THE GOVERNOR OF PUERTO RICO. IT CAN VETO POLICY THAT IS CONSIDERED DETRIMENTAL TO PUERTO RICO'S ECONOMIC GROWTH.

PUBLIC OPINION ON LA JUNTA WAS VARIED AND DIVISIVE.

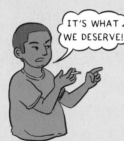

IT'S WHAT WE DESERVE!
WE'RE A COLONY!
THEY'LL CLEAN THIS PLACE UP!

WHILE SOME VIEWED IT AS A MEANS TO REIGN IN A BLOATED GOVERNMENT, OTHERS SAW LA JUNTA AS AN OCCUPATION; A NEW GOVERNMENT IMPOSED BY CONGRESS THREATENING OUR FRAGILE SOVEREIGNTY.

PUERTO RICO HAS ITS CONSTITUTION, EVEN THOUGH IT'S AN UNINCORPORATED TERRITORY. CONGRESS GAVE PUERTO RICO PERMISSION TO WORK ON THE CONSTITUTION AND APPROVED IT. CONGRESS CAN ALSO VOID OUR LAWS IF THEY WISH, ALTHOUGH THEY'VE NEVER DONE SO.

LA JUNTA IS BEHOLDEN TO CONGRESS, AND IT'S HARD NOT TO VIEW IT LIKE ANOTHER WAVE OF CONQUISTADORS, MANAGING THE AFFAIRS OF THE COLONY FROM AFAR.

LA GENTE ANTES DE LA DEUDA

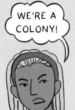

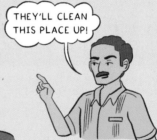

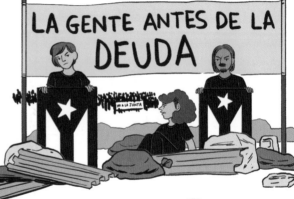

ANY ILLUSION LA JUNTA WOULD PRIORITIZE THE NEEDS OF THE PEOPLE WAS SHATTERED ONCE THE MEMBERS WERE APPOINTED BY CONGRESS.

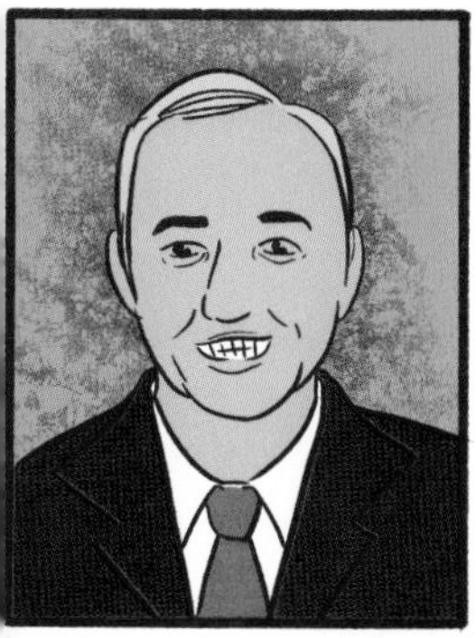

JOSÉ RAMÓN GONZÁLEZ WAS PRESIDENT OF THE GOVERNMENT DEVELOPMENT BANK FOR A SHORT PERIOD DURING THE MID '80s.

THE GOVERNMENT DEVELOPMENT BANK WAS CREATED IN THE '40s AS A FINANCIAL ADVISOR TO THE GOVERNMENT, AND WAS A KEY SELLER OF BONDS, WHICH WOULD DETERIORATE OVER TIME ADDING TO THE DEBT.

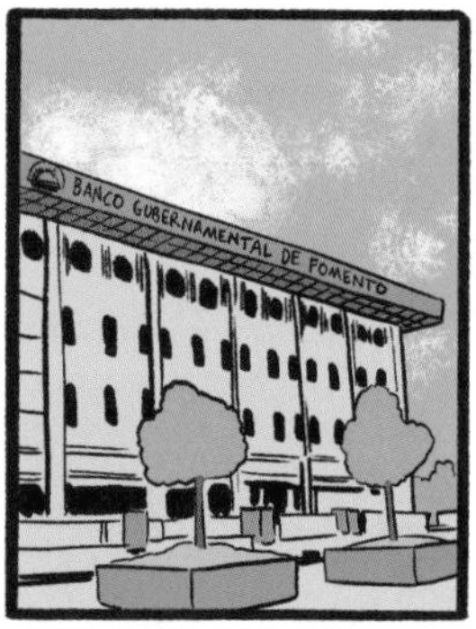
BANCO GUBERNAMENTAL DE FOMENTO

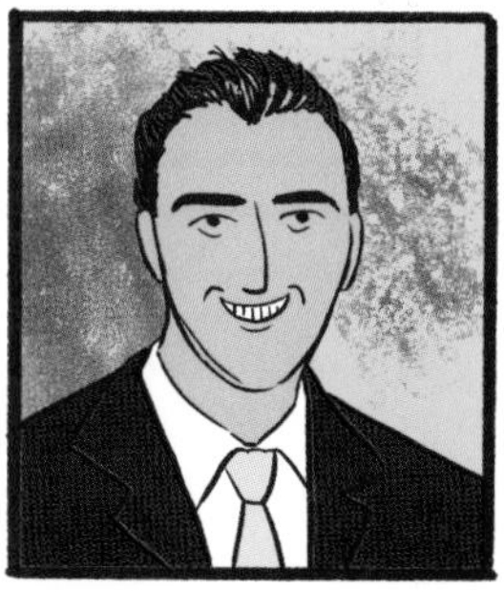

JOSÉ CARRIÓN IS BROTHER-IN-LAW TO PEDRO PIERLUISI, FORMER RESIDENT COMMISSIONER AND RUNNER-UP GOVERNOR CANDIDATE FOR THE PRO-STATEHOOD PARTY, PNP (PARTIDO NUEVO PROGRESISTA).

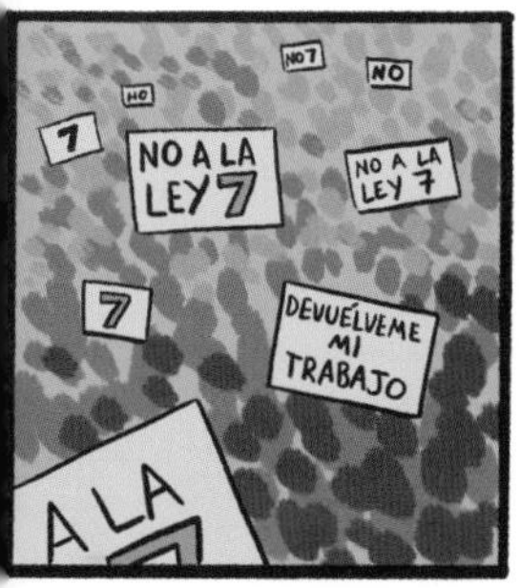
NO 7
NO
NO
7
NO A LA LEY 7
NO A LA LEY 7
7
DEVUÉLVEME MI TRABAJO
A LA

CARLOS GARCÍA WAS THE PRESIDENT OF GOVERNMENT DEVELOPMENT BANK FROM 2009 TO 2011. HE WORKED UNDER GOVERNOR LUIS FORTUÑO ON THE CONTROVERSIAL "LEY 7", WHICH WAS CREATED IN PART TO STABILIZE THE ECONOMY, BUT CAUSED THE FIRING OF THOUSANDS OF GOVERNMENT WORKERS.

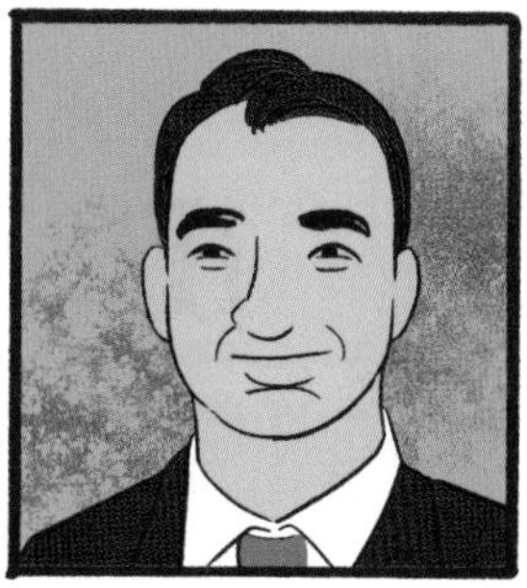

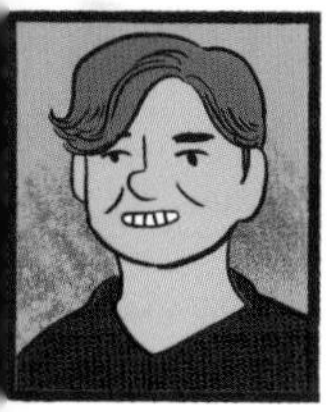

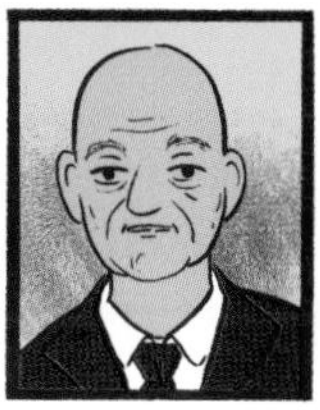

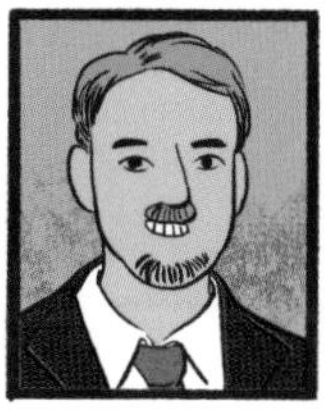

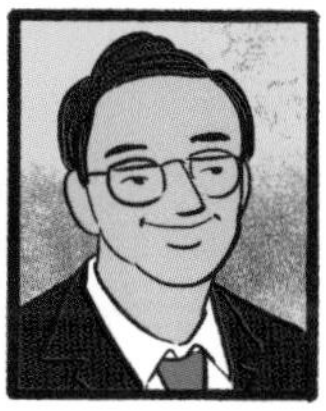

ANA MATOSANTOS, ARTHUR GONZÁLEZ, ANDREW BIGGS, AND DAVID ARTHUR SKEEL ALL HAVE EXPERIENCE WITH BANKRUPTCY IN THE PUBLIC SECTOR IN THE U.S.

LA JUNTA AND GOVERNOR RICARDO ROSELLÓ HAVE CLASHED OVER THE AUSTERITY MEASURES DURING HIS SHORT TIME IN OFFICE, CAUSING LA JUNTA TO ASK CONGRESS FOR EVEN MORE POWER OVER PUERTO RICO.

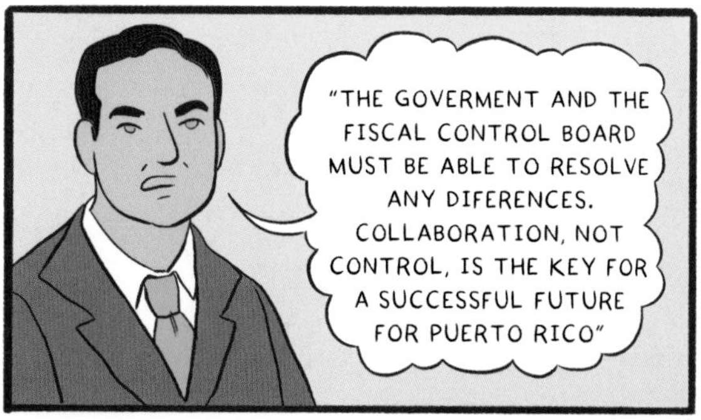
"THE GOVERMENT AND THE FISCAL CONTROL BOARD MUST BE ABLE TO RESOLVE ANY DIFERENCES. COLLABORATION, NOT CONTROL, IS THE KEY FOR A SUCCESSFUL FUTURE FOR PUERTO RICO"

THE GOVERNMENT'S LIQUID ASSETS HAVE BEEN DWINDLING FOR YEARS. THE THREAT OF RUNNING OUT OF MONEY IS ALWAYS PRESENT. IN 2006, THE GOVERNMENT SHUT DOWN FOR TWO WEEKS OVER LACK OF FUNDS.

LONG TERM INVESTMENT PLANS UNDER AN ECONOMIC CRISIS ARE ALMOST IMPOSSIBLE. INFRASTRUCTURE IS NOT UPGRADED, PUTTING ALL PUERTO RICO'S CITIZENS AT RISK DURING NATURAL PHENOMENA.

AFTER HURRICANE MARÍA, LA JUNTA'S PENNY-PINCHING CROSSED THE LINE WHEN GOVERNOR RICARDO ROSELLÓ PARDONED THE IVU TAX ON PREPARED FOODS INDEFINITELY, AND THEY SAW IT AS AN ACT OF DEFIANCE.

IT WAS MORE IMPORTANT TO FILL THE COFFERS THAN FOR FAMILIES TO AFFORD FOOD UNDER A CRISIS.

PUBLIC UTILITIES LIKE WATER AND POWER HAVEN'T BEEN WORKING. THEY HAVEN'T CHARGED FOR SERVICES.

ADD TO THAT THE MASSIVE MIGRATION OF WORKERS AND CONSUMERS WHO ARE NO LONGER CONTRIBUTING TO THE ECONOMY—

AND YOU HAVE A GOVERMENT WEIGHED DOWN WITH MASSIVE DEBT, DESTROYED INFRASTRUCTURES, AND NO WAY OF INVESTING IN ITS FUTURE.

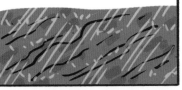

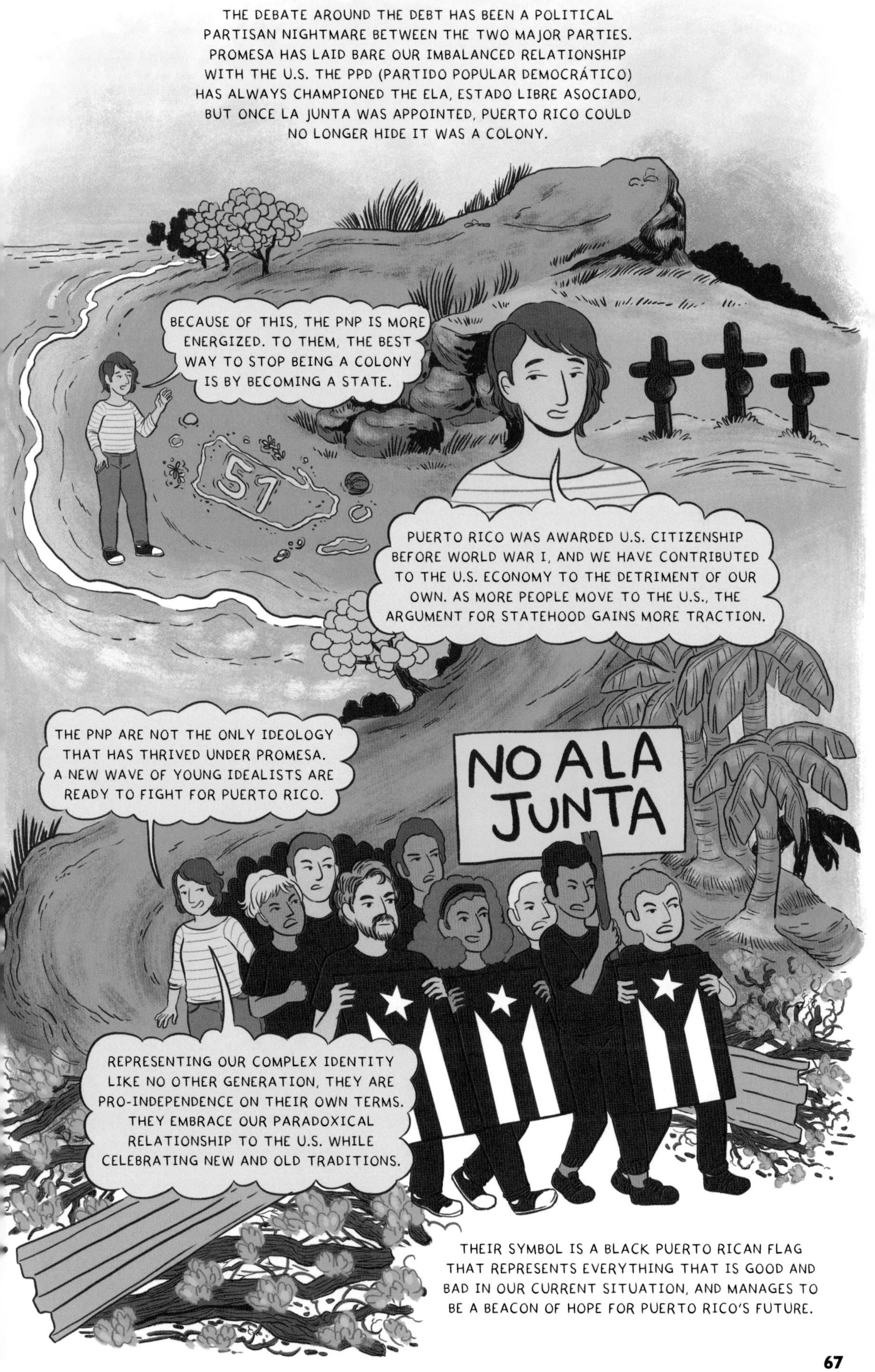
THE DEBATE AROUND THE DEBT HAS BEEN A POLITICAL PARTISAN NIGHTMARE BETWEEN THE TWO MAJOR PARTIES. PROMESA HAS LAID BARE OUR IMBALANCED RELATIONSHIP WITH THE U.S. THE PPD (PARTIDO POPULAR DEMOCRÁTICO) HAS ALWAYS CHAMPIONED THE ELA, ESTADO LIBRE ASOCIADO, BUT ONCE LA JUNTA WAS APPOINTED, PUERTO RICO COULD NO LONGER HIDE IT WAS A COLONY.
BECAUSE OF THIS, THE PNP IS MORE ENERGIZED. TO THEM, THE BEST WAY TO STOP BEING A COLONY IS BY BECOMING A STATE.
51
PUERTO RICO WAS AWARDED U.S. CITIZENSHIP BEFORE WORLD WAR I, AND WE HAVE CONTRIBUTED TO THE U.S. ECONOMY TO THE DETRIMENT OF OUR OWN. AS MORE PEOPLE MOVE TO THE U.S., THE ARGUMENT FOR STATEHOOD GAINS MORE TRACTION.
THE PNP ARE NOT THE ONLY IDEOLOGY THAT HAS THRIVED UNDER PROMESA. A NEW WAVE OF YOUNG IDEALISTS ARE READY TO FIGHT FOR PUERTO RICO.
NO A LA JUNTA
REPRESENTING OUR COMPLEX IDENTITY LIKE NO OTHER GENERATION, THEY ARE PRO-INDEPENDENCE ON THEIR OWN TERMS. THEY EMBRACE OUR PARADOXICAL RELATIONSHIP TO THE U.S. WHILE CELEBRATING NEW AND OLD TRADITIONS.
THEIR SYMBOL IS A BLACK PUERTO RICAN FLAG THAT REPRESENTS EVERYTHING THAT IS GOOD AND BAD IN OUR CURRENT SITUATION, AND MANAGES TO BE A BEACON OF HOPE FOR PUERTO RICO'S FUTURE.

THANKS FOR NOTHING BY TOM BELAND

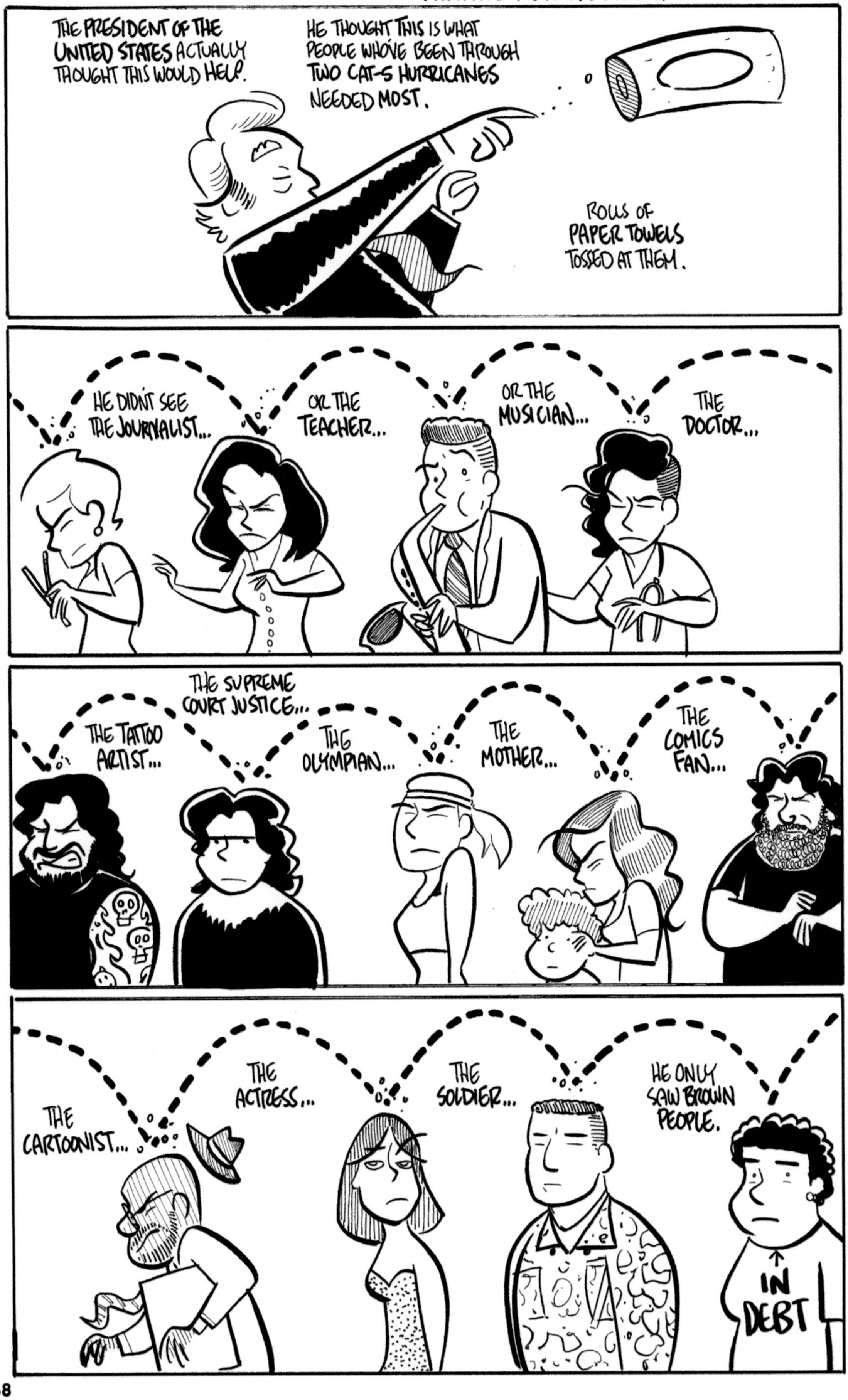

THE PRESIDENT OF THE UNITED STATES ACTUALLY THOUGHT THIS WOULD HELP.
HE THOUGHT THIS IS WHAT PEOPLE WHO'VE BEEN THROUGH TWO CAT-5 HURRICANES NEEDED MOST.
ROLLS OF PAPER TOWELS TOSSED AT THEM.
HE DIDN'T SEE THE JOURNALIST...
OR THE TEACHER...
OR THE MUSICIAN...
THE DOCTOR...
THE TATTOO ARTIST...
THE SUPREME COURT JUSTICE...
THE OLYMPIAN...
THE MOTHER...
THE COMICS FAN...
THE CARTOONIST...
THE ACTRESS...
THE SOLDIER...
HE ONLY SAW BROWN PEOPLE.
IN DEBT

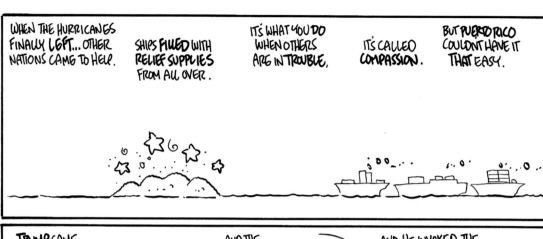

WHEN THE HURRICANES FINALLY LEFT... OTHER NATIONS CAME TO HELP.

SHIPS FILLED WITH RELIEF SUPPLIES FROM ALL OVER.

IT'S WHAT YOU DO WHEN OTHERS ARE IN TROUBLE,

IT'S CALLED COMPASSION.

BUT PUERTO RICO COULDN'T HAVE IT THAT EASY.

TRUMP CAME AND DID WHAT HE DOES BEST.

HE SAID THIS WASN'T A REAL CATASTROPHE LIKE KATRINA.

AND THE ISLAND'S DEBT.

AND HE INVOKED THE JONES ACT AND BLOCKED ALL THOSE SHIPS.

THE WORST THING WAS THE PRIDE HE TOOK IN IT... IN HURTING THE ISLAND.

THAT DAD WHO TAKES PRIDE IN SMACKING HIS KIDS AROUND.

AFTER PUBLIC OUTCRY HE LIFTED THE JONES ACT...

FOR A WEEK.

WHAT'S NEXT..?

*@#@#$$!!

AND WHICH SH**HOLE COUNTRY ARE YOU FROM?

PONCE?

ENGLISH!! YOU'RE IN AMERICA NOW!!

THIS WILL BE NEXT.

HE'S GOT A GUN!!

IT'S A GUILLO!!

TSA

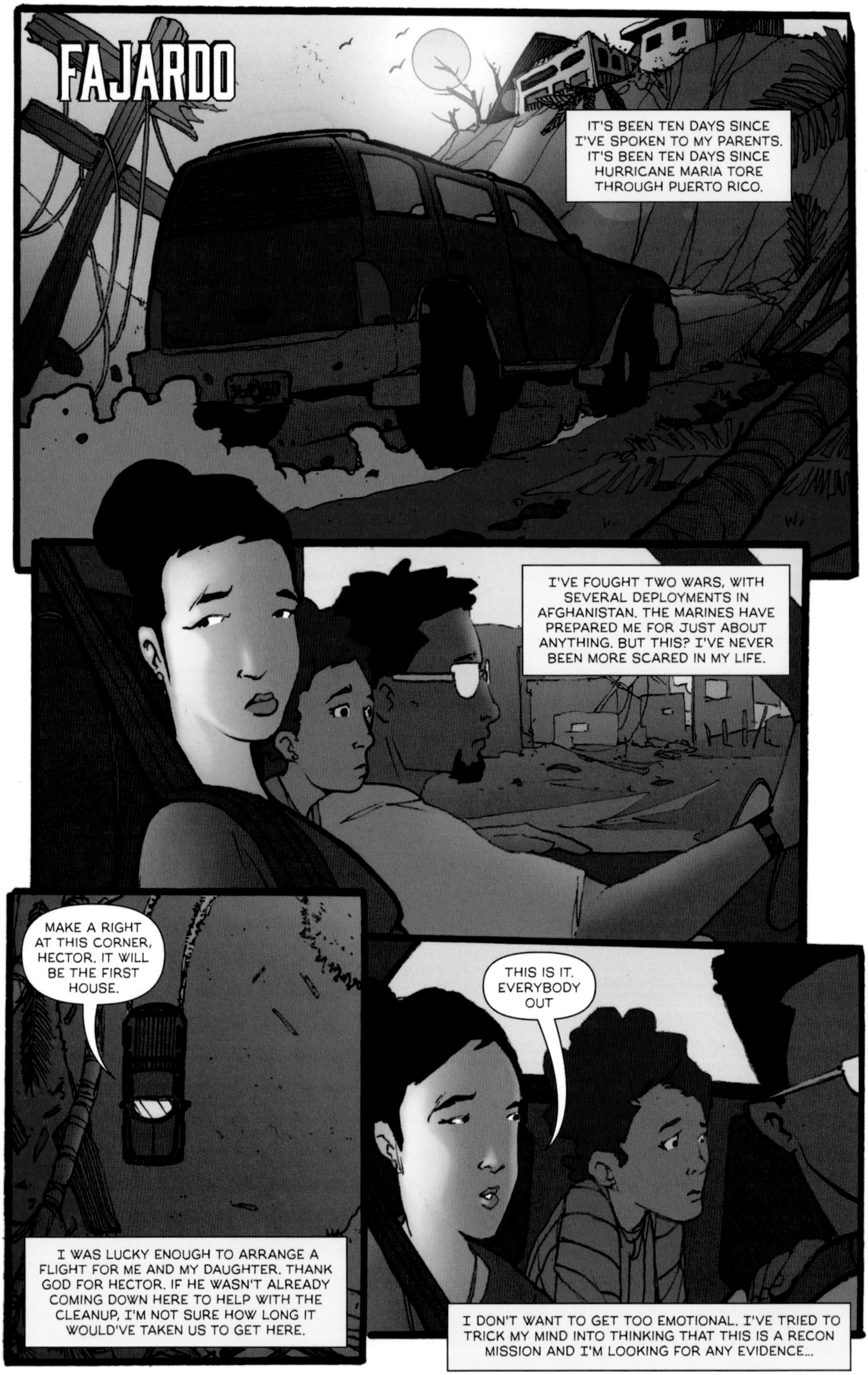
FAJARDO
IT'S BEEN TEN DAYS SINCE I'VE SPOKEN TO MY PARENTS. IT'S BEEN TEN DAYS SINCE HURRICANE MARIA TORE THROUGH PUERTO RICO.
I'VE FOUGHT TWO WARS, WITH SEVERAL DEPLOYMENTS IN AFGHANISTAN. THE MARINES HAVE PREPARED ME FOR JUST ABOUT ANYTHING. BUT THIS? I'VE NEVER BEEN MORE SCARED IN MY LIFE.
MAKE A RIGHT AT THIS CORNER, HECTOR. IT WILL BE THE FIRST HOUSE.
I WAS LUCKY ENOUGH TO ARRANGE A FLIGHT FOR ME AND MY DAUGHTER. THANK GOD FOR HECTOR. IF HE WASN'T ALREADY COMING DOWN HERE TO HELP WITH THE CLEANUP, I'M NOT SURE HOW LONG IT WOULD'VE TAKEN US TO GET HERE.
THIS IS IT. EVERYBODY OUT
I DON'T WANT TO GET TOO EMOTIONAL. I'VE TRIED TO TRICK MY MIND INTO THINKING THAT THIS IS A RECON MISSION AND I'M LOOKING FOR ANY EVIDENCE...

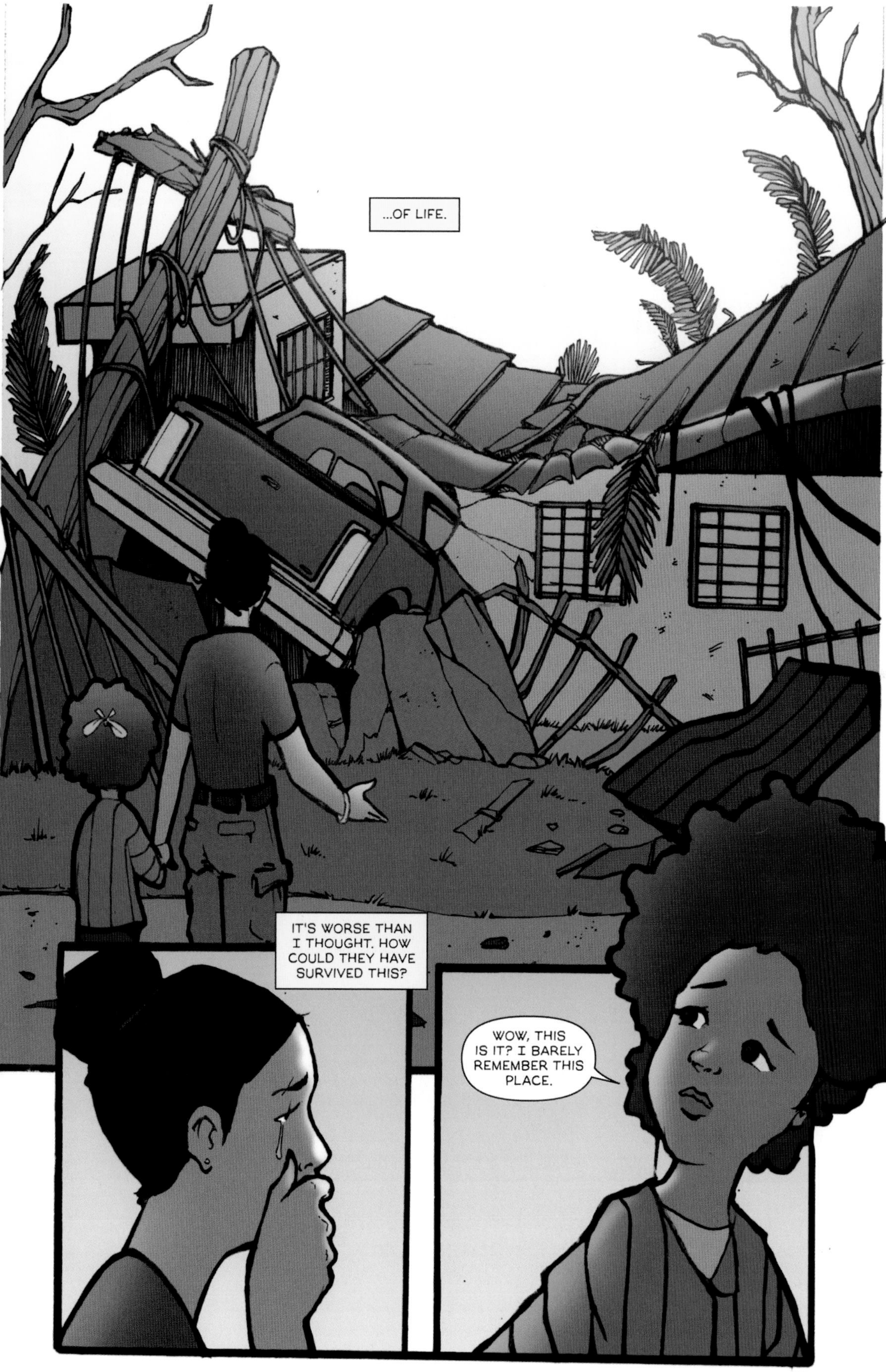
...OF LIFE.
IT'S WORSE THAN I THOUGHT. HOW COULD THEY HAVE SURVIVED THIS?
WOW, THIS IS IT? I BARELY REMEMBER THIS PLACE.

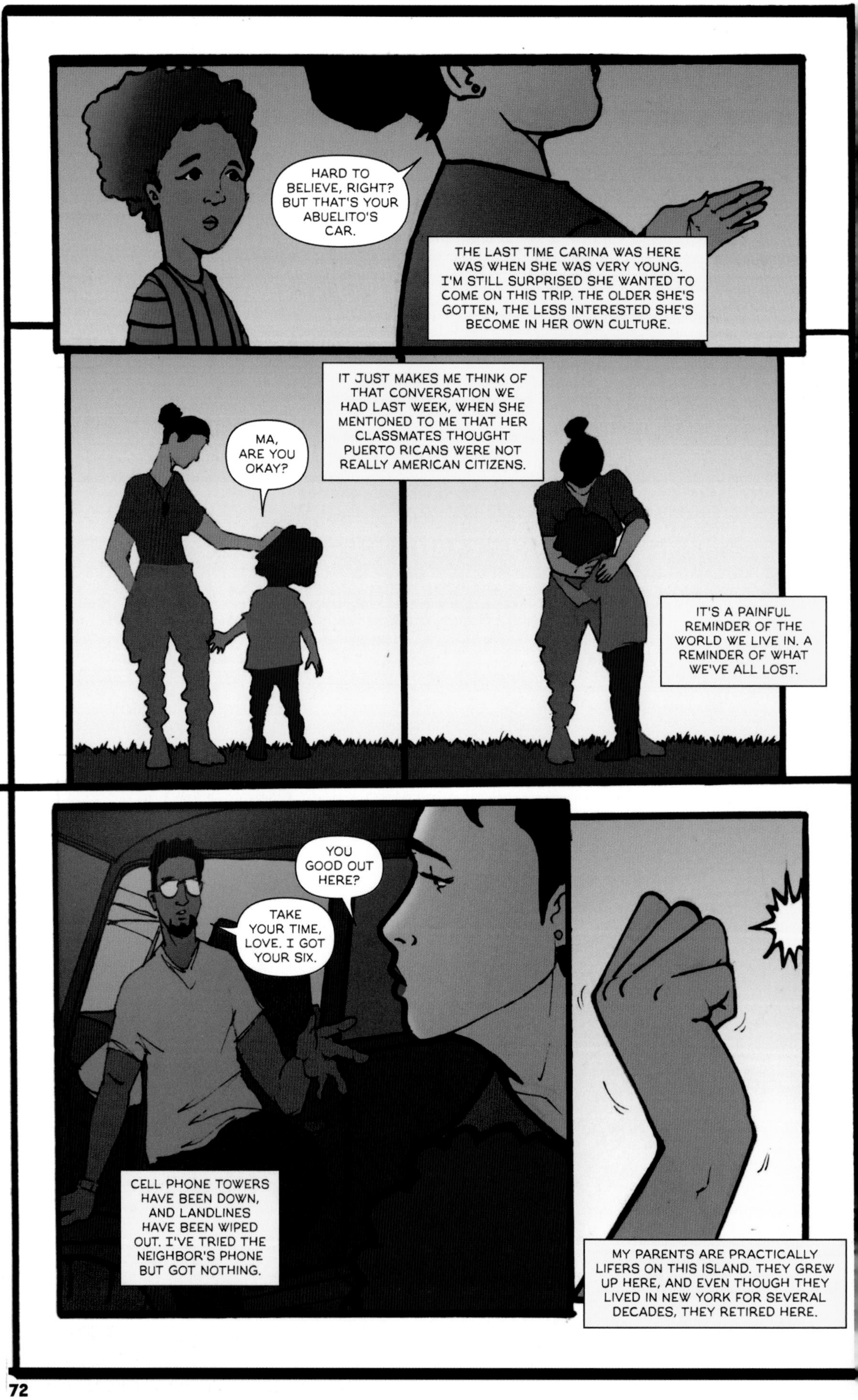
HARD TO BELIEVE, RIGHT? BUT THAT'S YOUR ABUELITO'S CAR.
THE LAST TIME CARINA WAS HERE WAS WHEN SHE WAS VERY YOUNG. I'M STILL SURPRISED SHE WANTED TO COME ON THIS TRIP. THE OLDER SHE'S GOTTEN, THE LESS INTERESTED SHE'S BECOME IN HER OWN CULTURE.
IT JUST MAKES ME THINK OF THAT CONVERSATION WE HAD LAST WEEK, WHEN SHE MENTIONED TO ME THAT HER CLASSMATES THOUGHT PUERTO RICANS WERE NOT REALLY AMERICAN CITIZENS.
MA, ARE YOU OKAY?
IT'S A PAINFUL REMINDER OF THE WORLD WE LIVE IN. A REMINDER OF WHAT WE'VE ALL LOST.
YOU GOOD OUT HERE?
TAKE YOUR TIME, LOVE. I GOT YOUR SIX.
CELL PHONE TOWERS HAVE BEEN DOWN, AND LANDLINES HAVE BEEN WIPED OUT. I'VE TRIED THE NEIGHBOR'S PHONE BUT GOT NOTHING.
MY PARENTS ARE PRACTICALLY LIFERS ON THIS ISLAND. THEY GREW UP HERE, AND EVEN THOUGH THEY LIVED IN NEW YORK FOR SEVERAL DECADES, THEY RETIRED HERE.

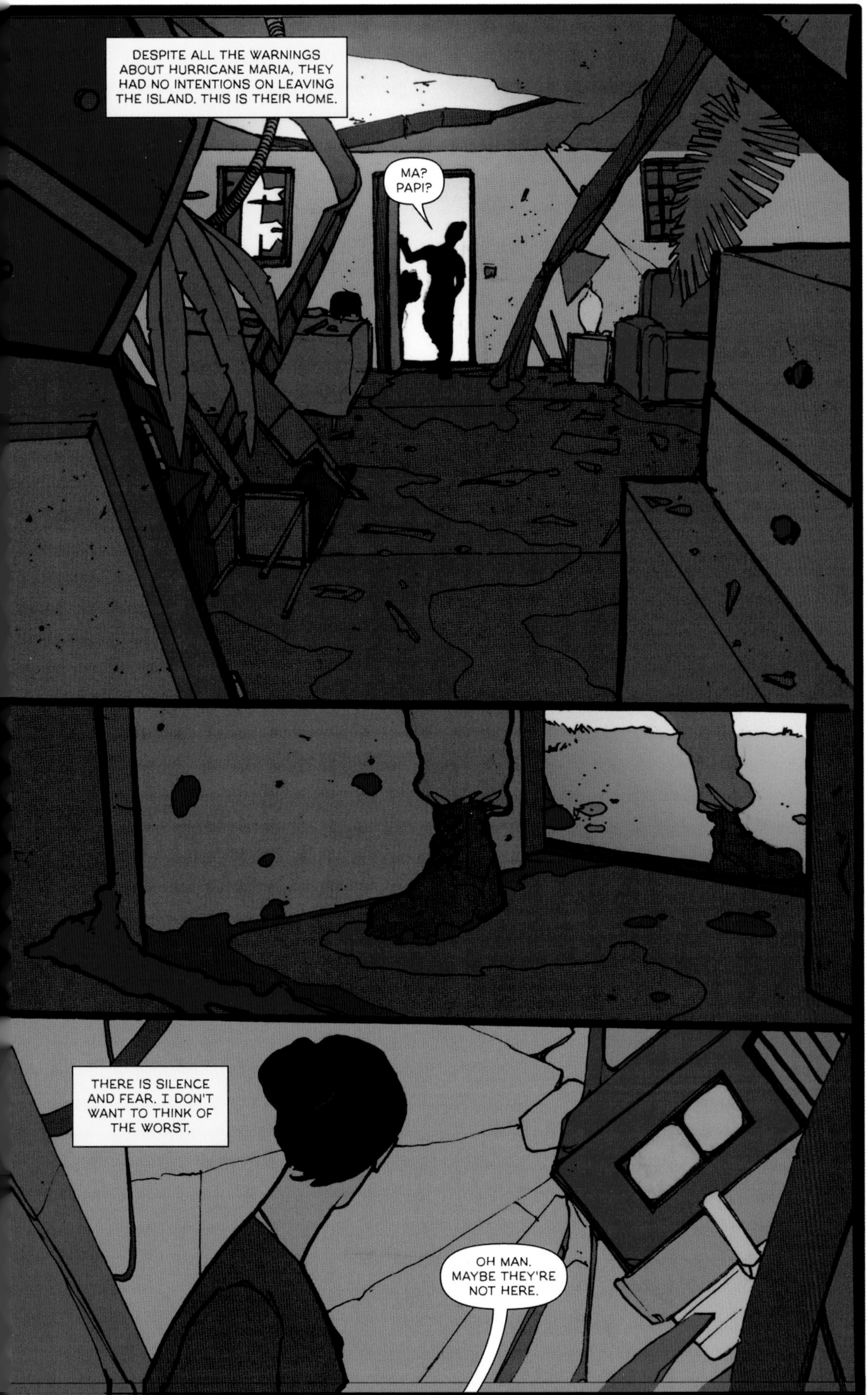
DESPITE ALL THE WARNINGS ABOUT HURRICANE MARIA, THEY HAD NO INTENTIONS ON LEAVING THE ISLAND. THIS IS THEIR HOME.
MA? PAPI?
THERE IS SILENCE AND FEAR. I DON'T WANT TO THINK OF THE WORST.
OH MAN. MAYBE THEY'RE NOT HERE.

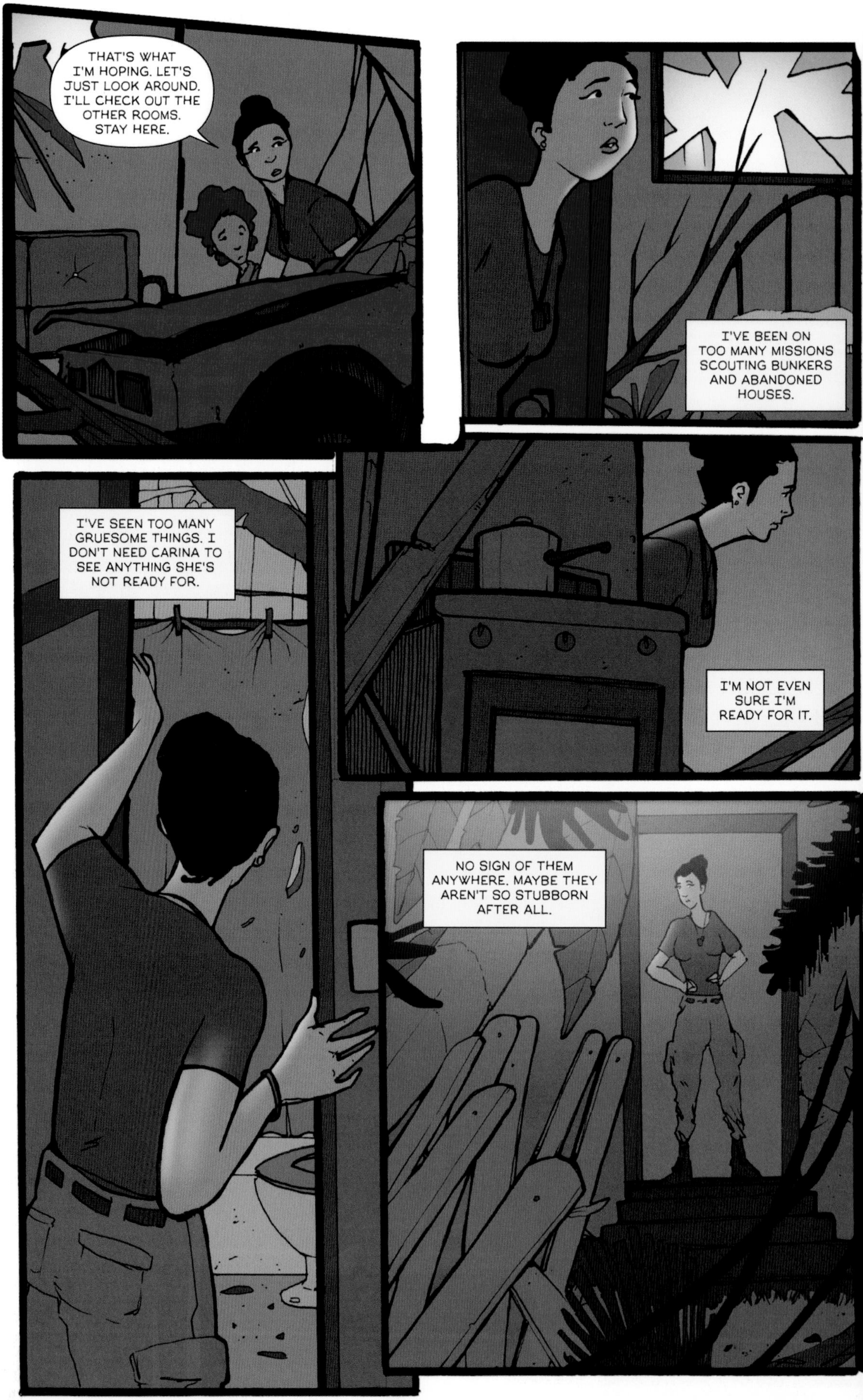
THAT'S WHAT I'M HOPING. LET'S JUST LOOK AROUND. I'LL CHECK OUT THE OTHER ROOMS. STAY HERE.
I'VE BEEN ON TOO MANY MISSIONS SCOUTING BUNKERS AND ABANDONED HOUSES.
I'VE SEEN TOO MANY GRUESOME THINGS. I DON'T NEED CARINA TO SEE ANYTHING SHE'S NOT READY FOR.
I'M NOT EVEN SURE I'M READY FOR IT.
NO SIGN OF THEM ANYWHERE. MAYBE THEY AREN'T SO STUBBORN AFTER ALL.

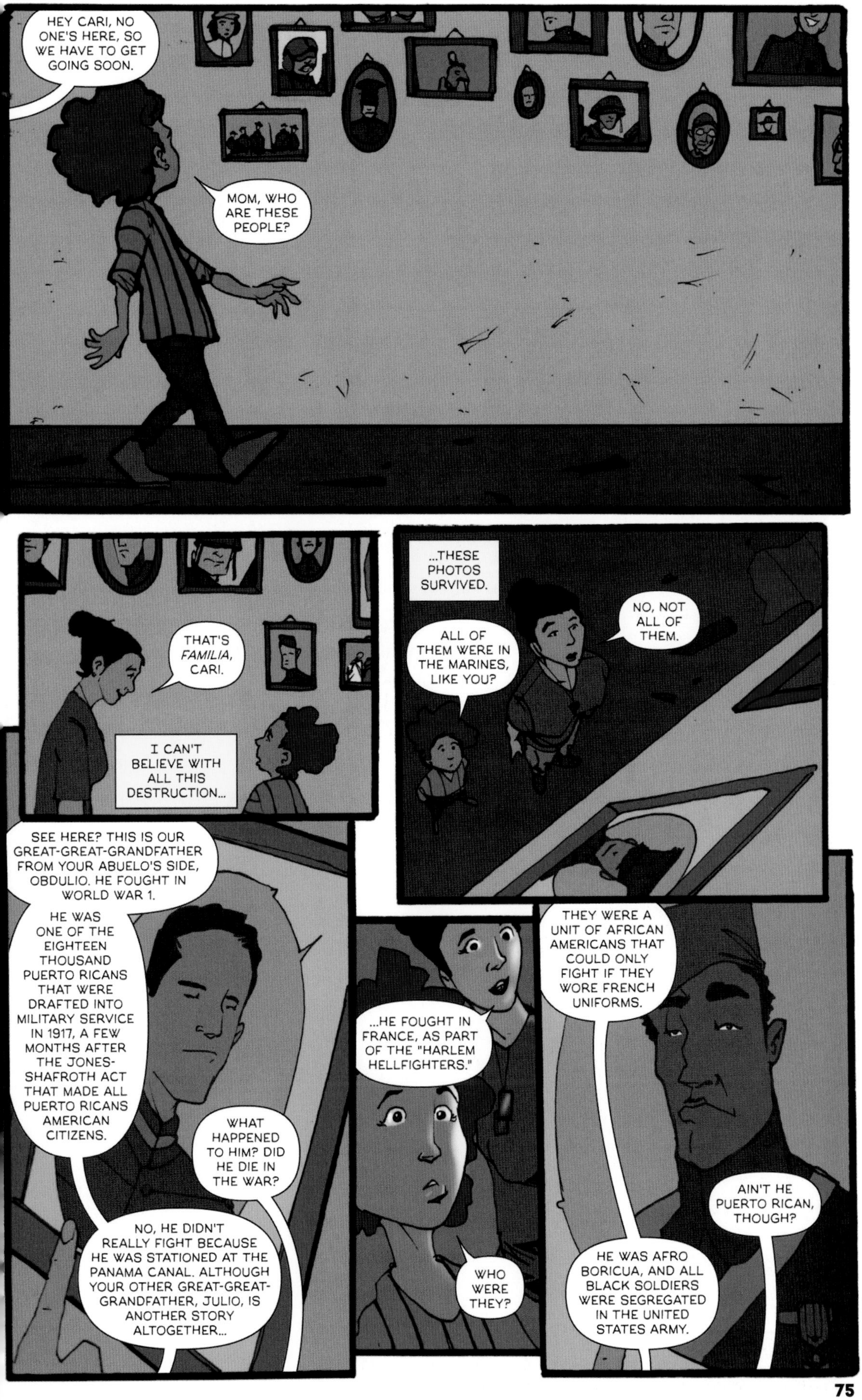

HEY CARI, NO ONE'S HERE, SO WE HAVE TO GET GOING SOON.
MOM, WHO ARE THESE PEOPLE?
THAT'S *FAMILIA*, CARI.
I CAN'T BELIEVE WITH ALL THIS DESTRUCTION...
...THESE PHOTOS SURVIVED.
ALL OF THEM WERE IN THE MARINES, LIKE YOU?
NO, NOT ALL OF THEM.
SEE HERE? THIS IS OUR GREAT-GREAT-GRANDFATHER FROM YOUR ABUELO'S SIDE, OBDULIO. HE FOUGHT IN WORLD WAR 1.
HE WAS ONE OF THE EIGHTEEN THOUSAND PUERTO RICANS THAT WERE DRAFTED INTO MILITARY SERVICE IN 1917, A FEW MONTHS AFTER THE JONES-SHAFROTH ACT THAT MADE ALL PUERTO RICANS AMERICAN CITIZENS.
WHAT HAPPENED TO HIM? DID HE DIE IN THE WAR?
NO, HE DIDN'T REALLY FIGHT BECAUSE HE WAS STATIONED AT THE PANAMA CANAL. ALTHOUGH YOUR OTHER GREAT-GREAT-GRANDFATHER, JULIO, IS ANOTHER STORY ALTOGETHER...
...HE FOUGHT IN FRANCE, AS PART OF THE "HARLEM HELLFIGHTERS."
WHO WERE THEY?
THEY WERE A UNIT OF AFRICAN AMERICANS THAT COULD ONLY FIGHT IF THEY WORE FRENCH UNIFORMS.
AIN'T HE PUERTO RICAN, THOUGH?
HE WAS AFRO BORICUA, AND ALL BLACK SOLDIERS WERE SEGREGATED IN THE UNITED STATES ARMY.

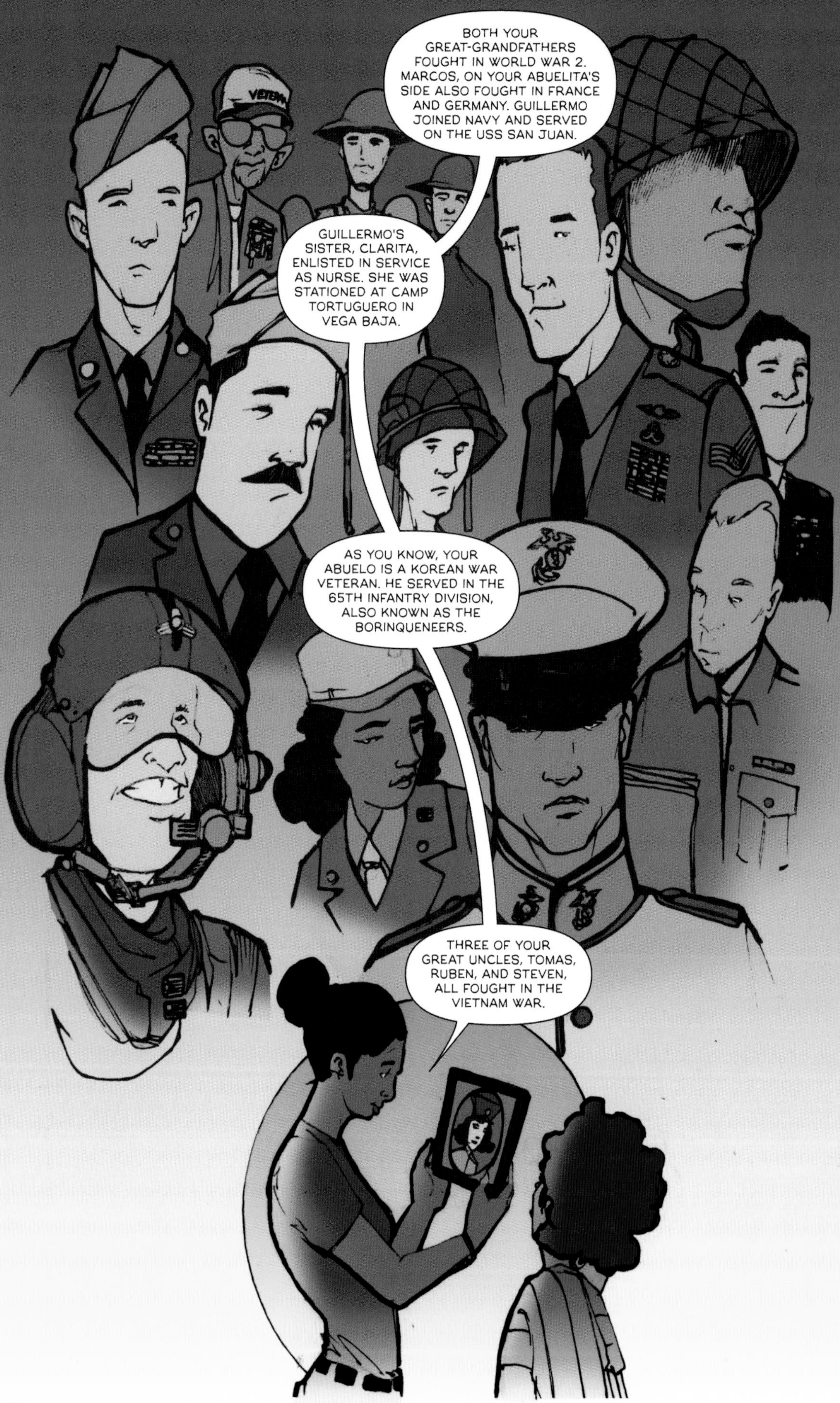
BOTH YOUR GREAT-GRANDFATHERS FOUGHT IN WORLD WAR 2. MARCOS, ON YOUR ABUELITA'S SIDE ALSO FOUGHT IN FRANCE AND GERMANY. GUILLERMO JOINED NAVY AND SERVED ON THE USS SAN JUAN.
GUILLERMO'S SISTER, CLARITA, ENLISTED IN SERVICE AS NURSE. SHE WAS STATIONED AT CAMP TORTUGUERO IN VEGA BAJA.
AS YOU KNOW, YOUR ABUELO IS A KOREAN WAR VETERAN. HE SERVED IN THE 65TH INFANTRY DIVISION, ALSO KNOWN AS THE BORINQUENEERS.
THREE OF YOUR GREAT UNCLES, TOMAS, RUBEN, AND STEVEN, ALL FOUGHT IN THE VIETNAM WAR.

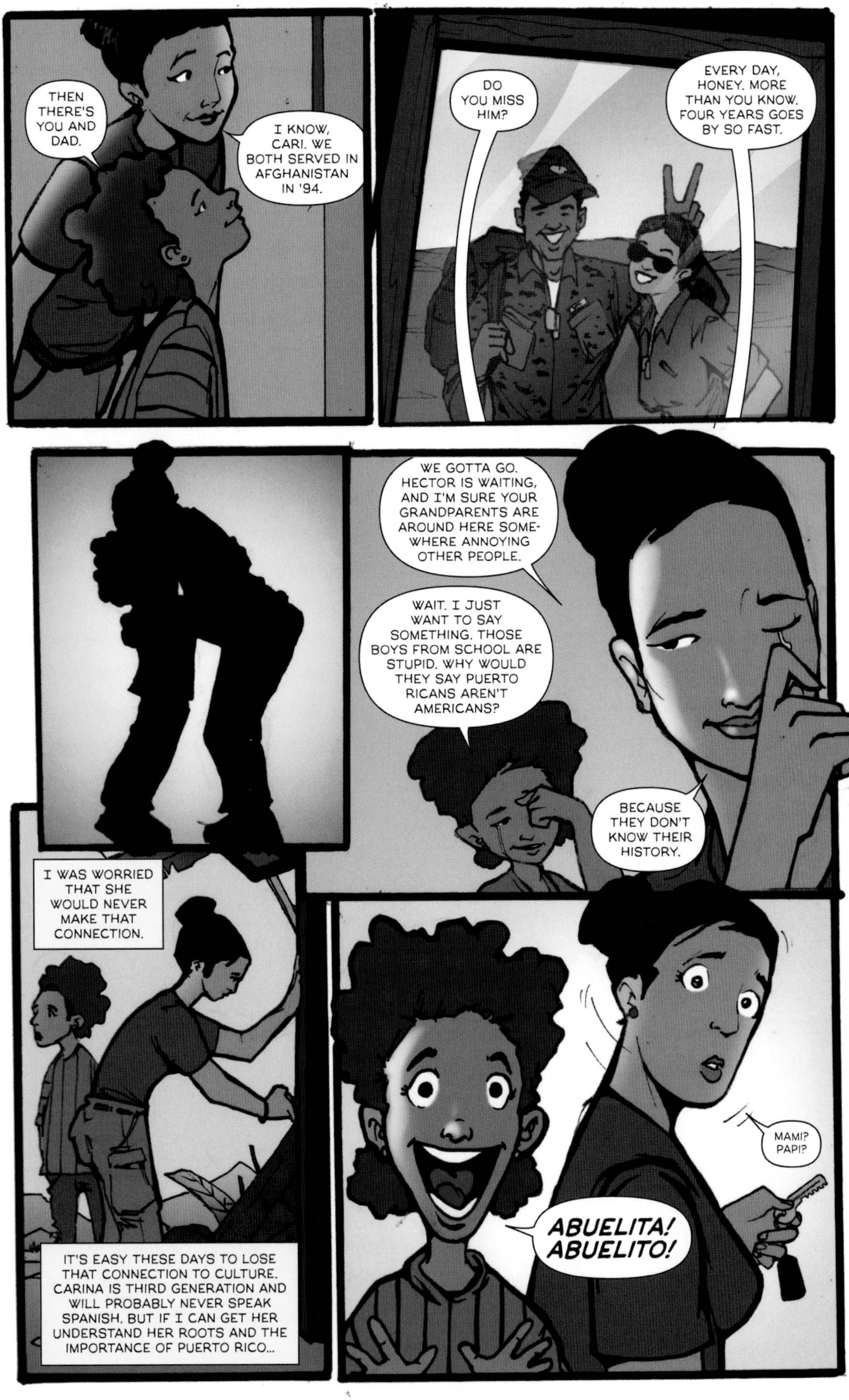

THEN THERE'S YOU AND DAD.
I KNOW, CARI. WE BOTH SERVED IN AFGHANISTAN IN '94.
DO YOU MISS HIM?
EVERY DAY, HONEY. MORE THAN YOU KNOW. FOUR YEARS GOES BY SO FAST.
WE GOTTA GO. HECTOR IS WAITING, AND I'M SURE YOUR GRANDPARENTS ARE AROUND HERE SOME-WHERE ANNOYING OTHER PEOPLE.
WAIT. I JUST WANT TO SAY SOMETHING. THOSE BOYS FROM SCHOOL ARE STUPID. WHY WOULD THEY SAY PUERTO RICANS AREN'T AMERICANS?
BECAUSE THEY DON'T KNOW THEIR HISTORY.
I WAS WORRIED THAT SHE WOULD NEVER MAKE THAT CONNECTION.
IT'S EASY THESE DAYS TO LOSE THAT CONNECTION TO CULTURE. CARINA IS THIRD GENERATION AND WILL PROBABLY NEVER SPEAK SPANISH. BUT IF I CAN GET HER UNDERSTAND HER ROOTS AND THE IMPORTANCE OF PUERTO RICO...
MAMI? PAPI?
ABUELITA! ABUELITO!

# LA CASITA OF AMERICAN HEROES

WRITTEN BY ANTHONY OTERO · ILLUSTRATED BY CHARLES UGAS
COLORED BY DENNIS CALERO · LETTERED BY MICAH MYERS

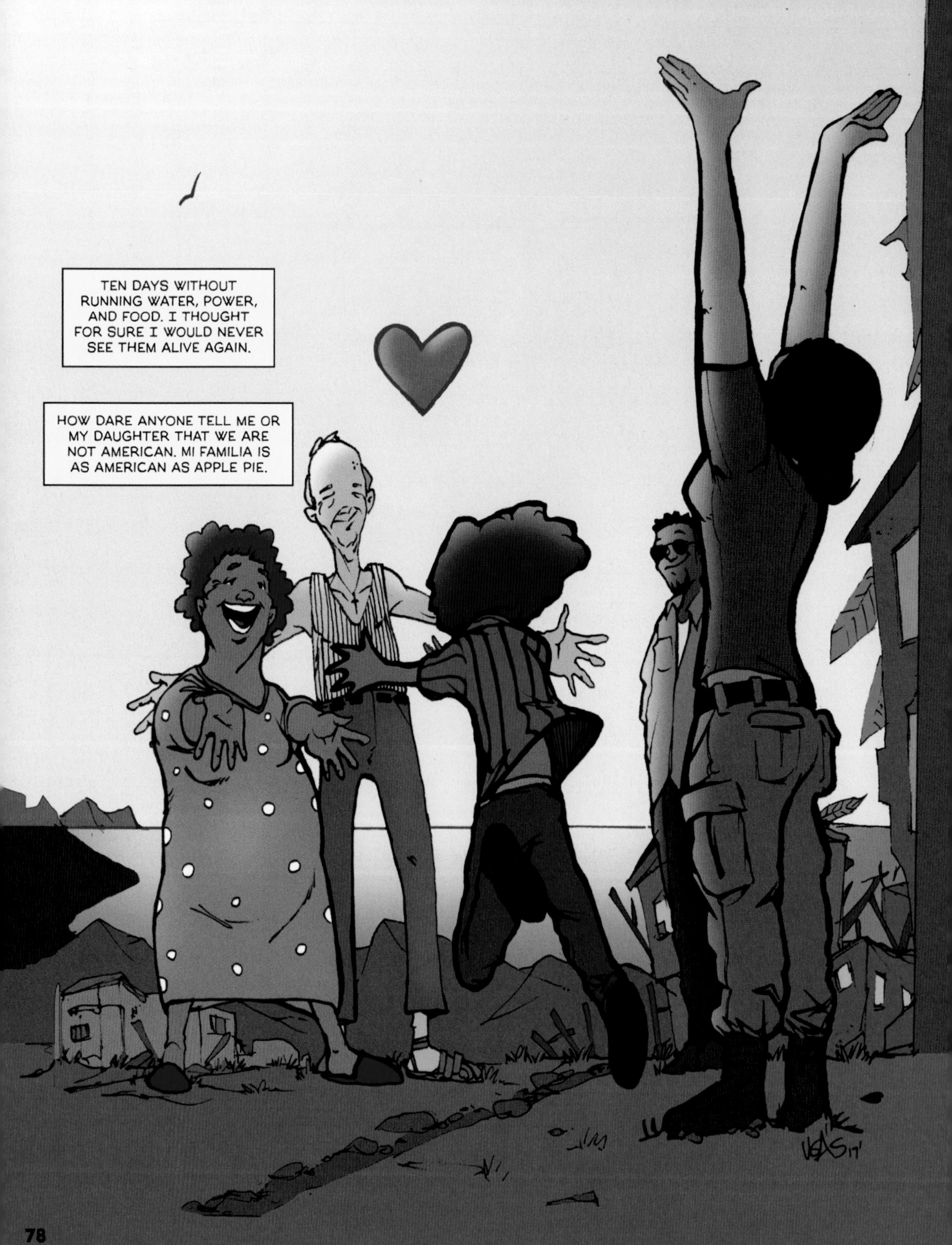
TEN DAYS WITHOUT RUNNING WATER, POWER, AND FOOD. I THOUGHT FOR SURE I WOULD NEVER SEE THEM ALIVE AGAIN.
HOW DARE ANYONE TELL ME OR MY DAUGHTER THAT WE ARE NOT AMERICAN. MI FAMILIA IS AS AMERICAN AS APPLE PIE.

Yúcahu and the creation of the first man

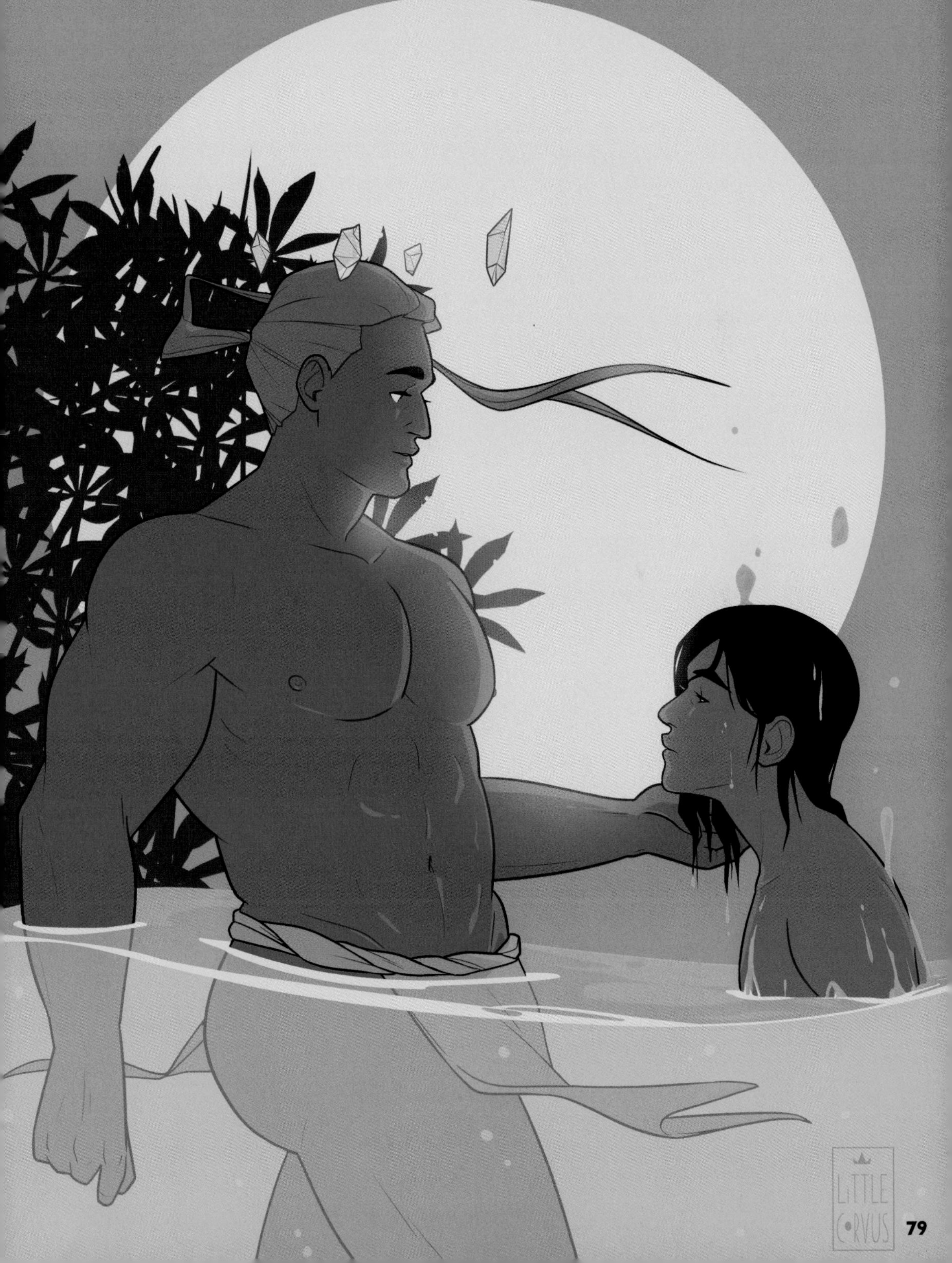
LITTLE
CORVUS

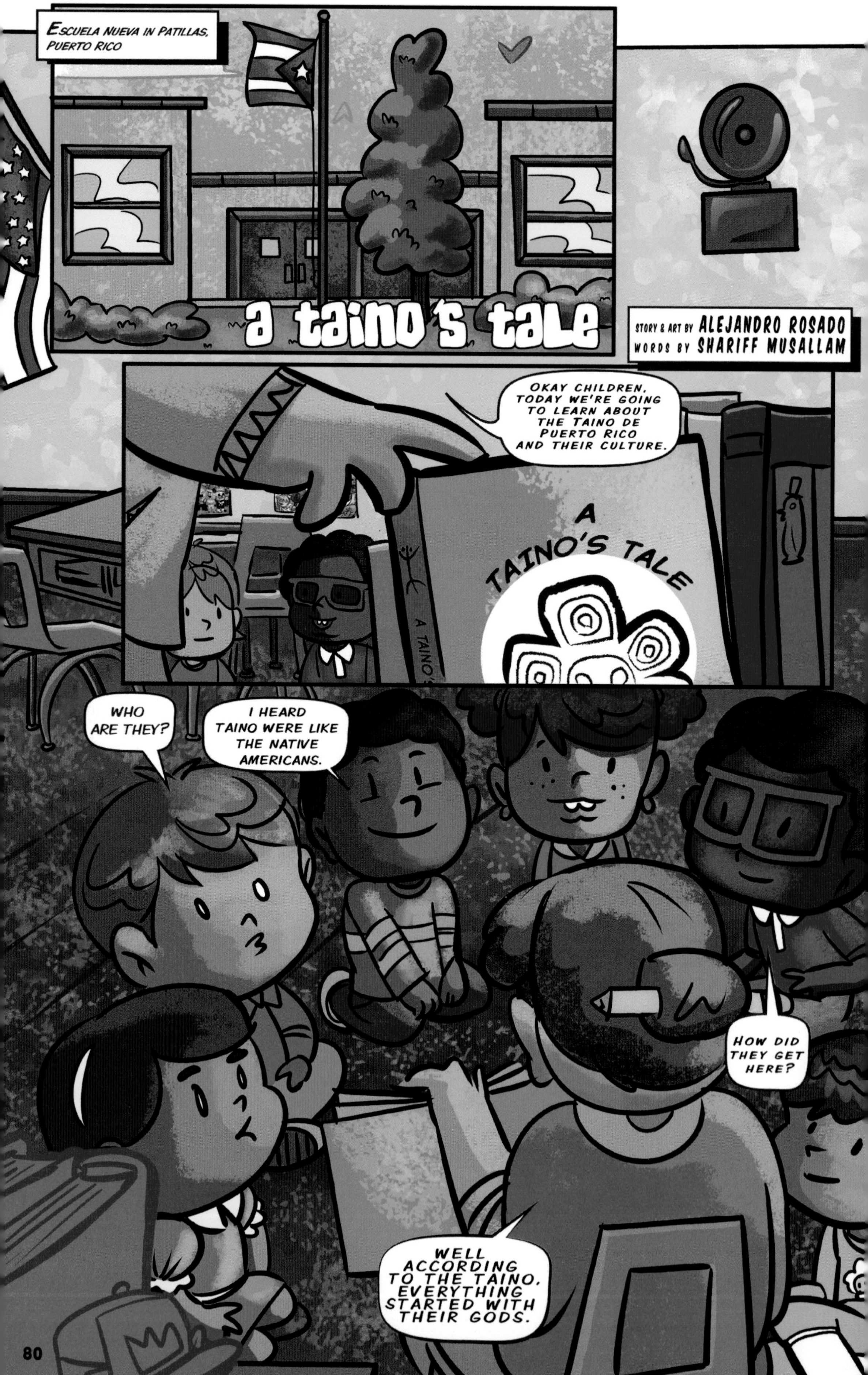
Escuela Nueva in Patillas, Puerto Rico
a taino's tale
STORY & ART BY ALEJANDRO ROSADO
WORDS BY SHARIFF MUSALLAM
OKAY CHILDREN, TODAY WE'RE GOING TO LEARN ABOUT THE TAINO DE PUERTO RICO AND THEIR CULTURE.
A TAINO'S TALE
WHO ARE THEY?
I HEARD TAINO WERE LIKE THE NATIVE AMERICANS.
HOW DID THEY GET HERE?
WELL ACCORDING TO THE TAINO, EVERYTHING STARTED WITH THEIR GODS.

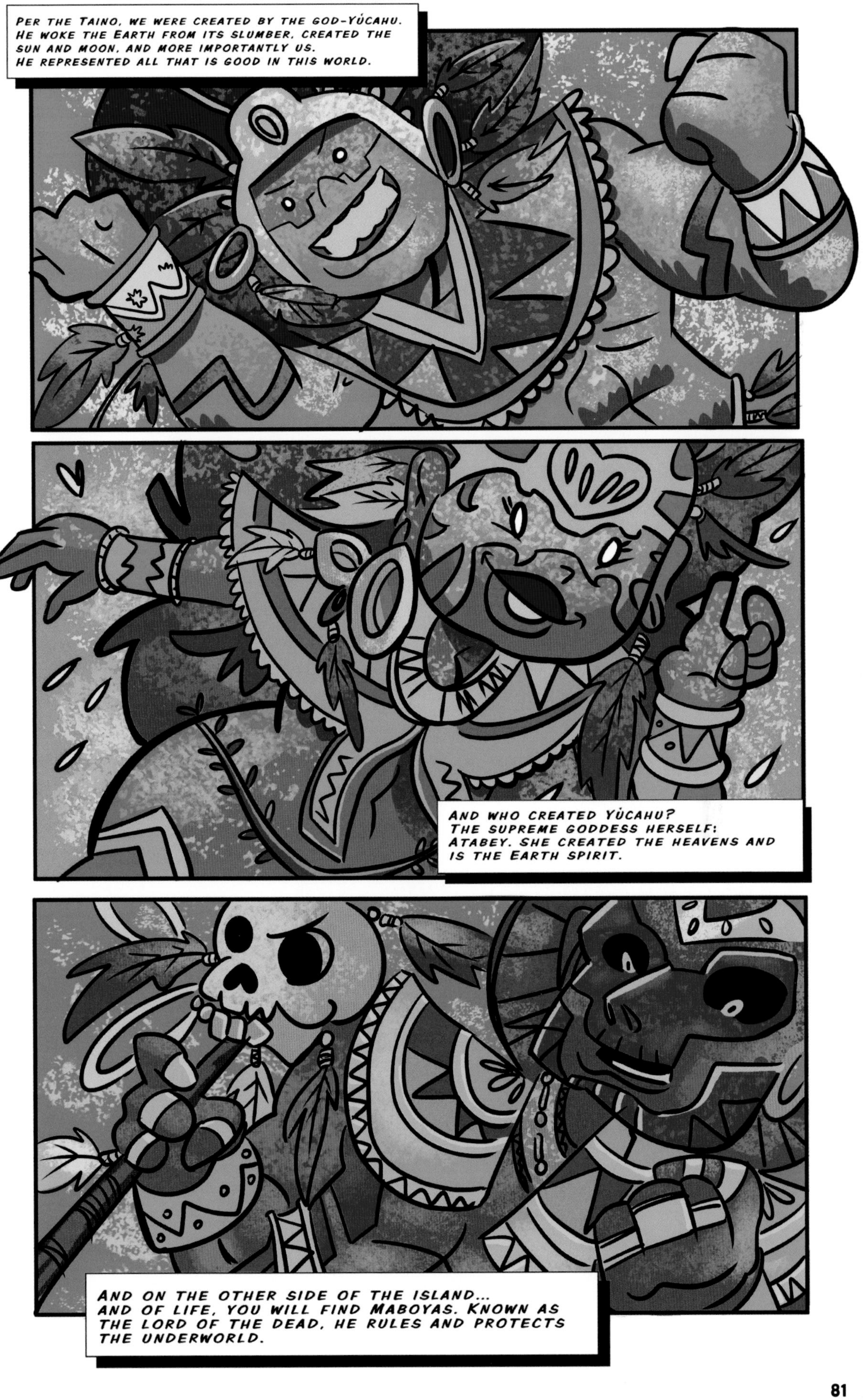
PER THE TAINO, WE WERE CREATED BY THE GOD-YÚCAHU. HE WOKE THE EARTH FROM ITS SLUMBER, CREATED THE SUN AND MOON, AND MORE IMPORTANTLY US. HE REPRESENTED ALL THAT IS GOOD IN THIS WORLD.
AND WHO CREATED YÚCAHU? THE SUPREME GODDESS HERSELF: ATABEY. SHE CREATED THE HEAVENS AND IS THE EARTH SPIRIT.
AND ON THE OTHER SIDE OF THE ISLAND... AND OF LIFE, YOU WILL FIND MABOYAS. KNOWN AS THE LORD OF THE DEAD, HE RULES AND PROTECTS THE UNDERWORLD.

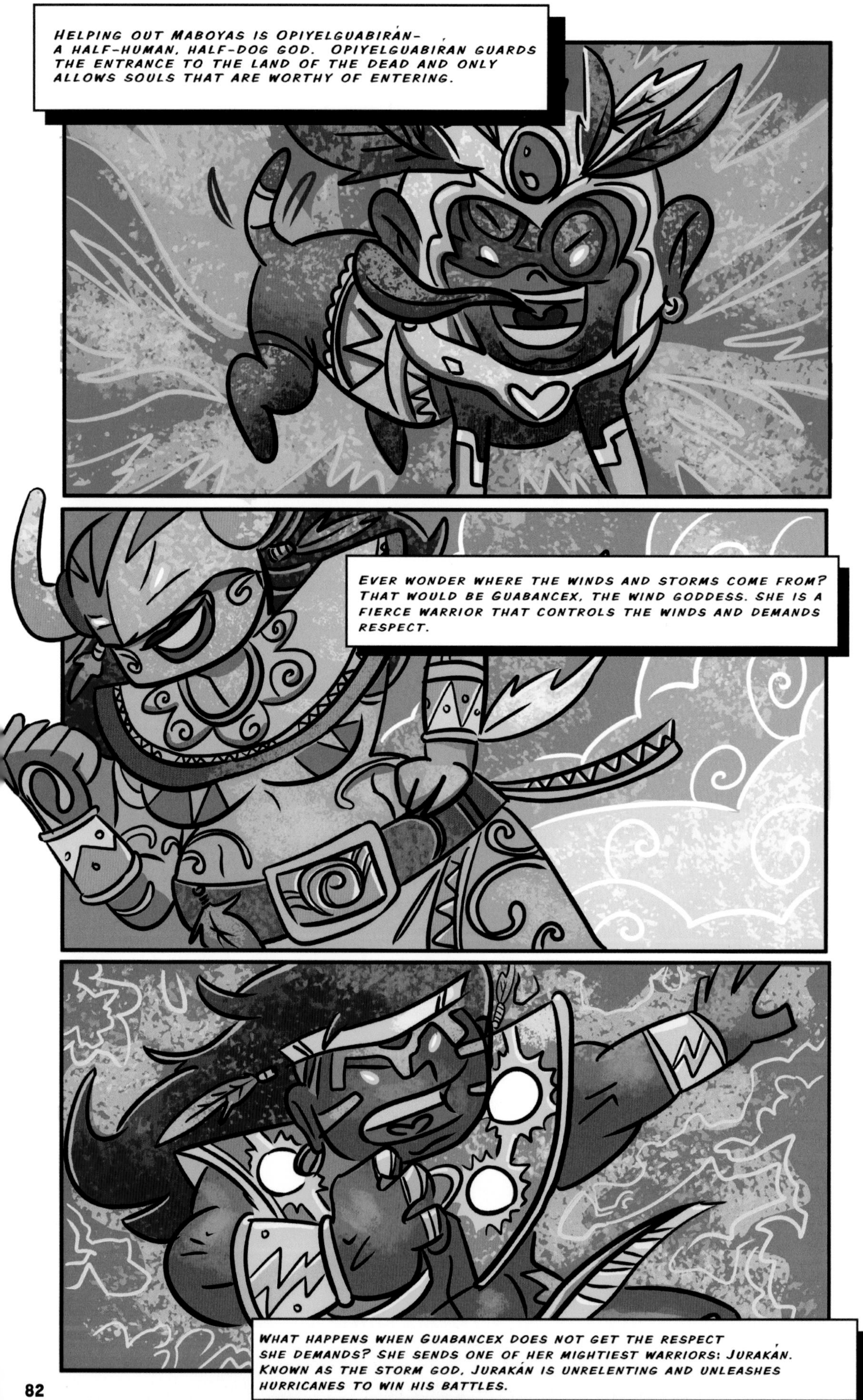
HELPING OUT MABOYAS IS OPIYELGUABIRÁN- A HALF-HUMAN, HALF-DOG GOD. OPIYELGUABIRAN GUARDS THE ENTRANCE TO THE LAND OF THE DEAD AND ONLY ALLOWS SOULS THAT ARE WORTHY OF ENTERING.
EVER WONDER WHERE THE WINDS AND STORMS COME FROM? THAT WOULD BE GUABANCEX, THE WIND GODDESS. SHE IS A FIERCE WARRIOR THAT CONTROLS THE WINDS AND DEMANDS RESPECT.
WHAT HAPPENS WHEN GUABANCEX DOES NOT GET THE RESPECT SHE DEMANDS? SHE SENDS ONE OF HER MIGHTIEST WARRIORS: JURAKÁN. KNOWN AS THE STORM GOD, JURAKÁN IS UNRELENTING AND UNLEASHES HURRICANES TO WIN HIS BATTLES.

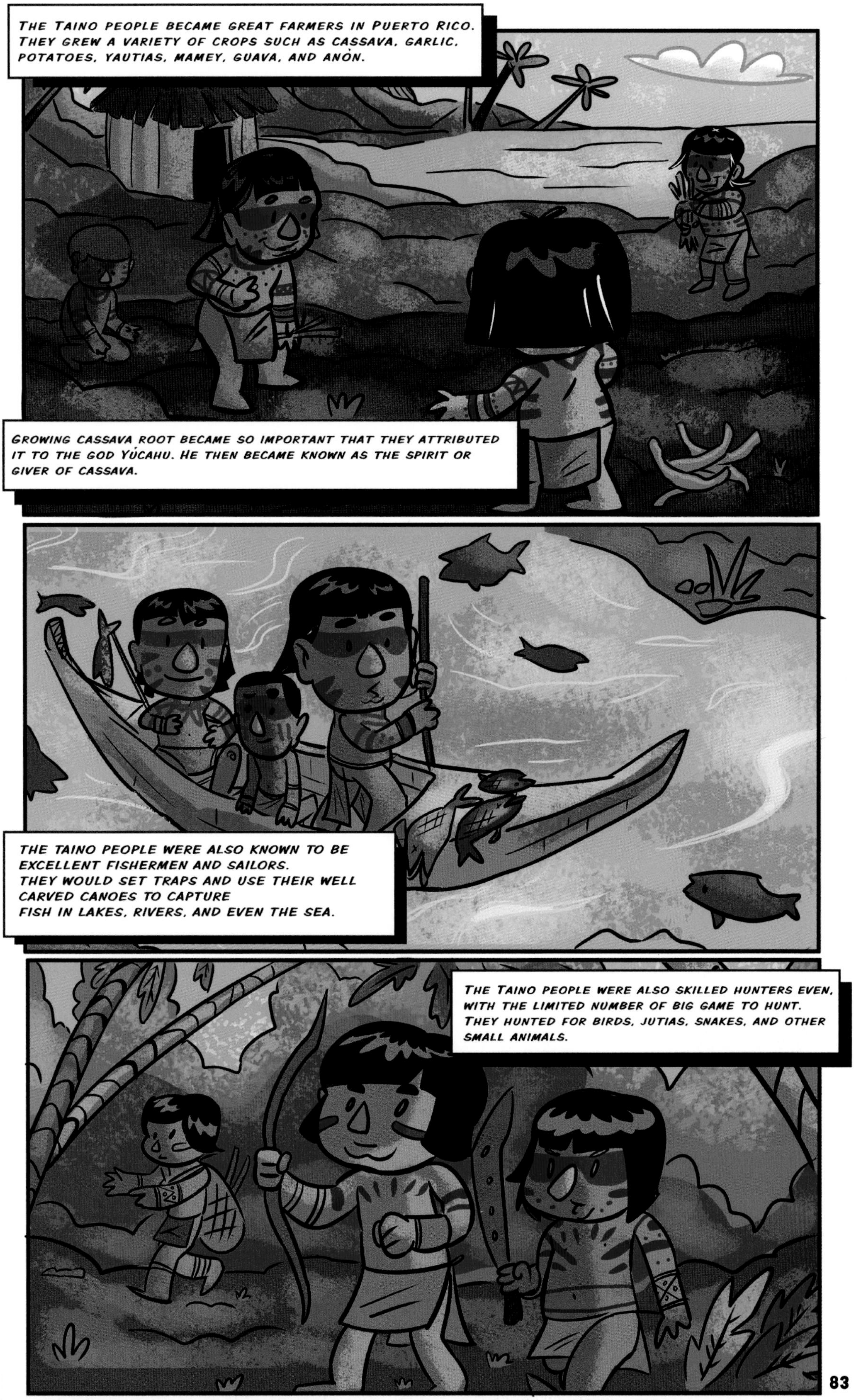
THE TAINO PEOPLE BECAME GREAT FARMERS IN PUERTO RICO. THEY GREW A VARIETY OF CROPS SUCH AS CASSAVA, GARLIC, POTATOES, YAUTIAS, MAMEY, GUAVA, AND ANÓN.
GROWING CASSAVA ROOT BECAME SO IMPORTANT THAT THEY ATTRIBUTED IT TO THE GOD YÚCAHU. HE THEN BECAME KNOWN AS THE SPIRIT OR GIVER OF CASSAVA.
THE TAINO PEOPLE WERE ALSO KNOWN TO BE EXCELLENT FISHERMEN AND SAILORS. THEY WOULD SET TRAPS AND USE THEIR WELL CARVED CANOES TO CAPTURE FISH IN LAKES, RIVERS, AND EVEN THE SEA.
THE TAINO PEOPLE WERE ALSO SKILLED HUNTERS EVEN, WITH THE LIMITED NUMBER OF BIG GAME TO HUNT. THEY HUNTED FOR BIRDS, JUTIAS, SNAKES, AND OTHER SMALL ANIMALS.

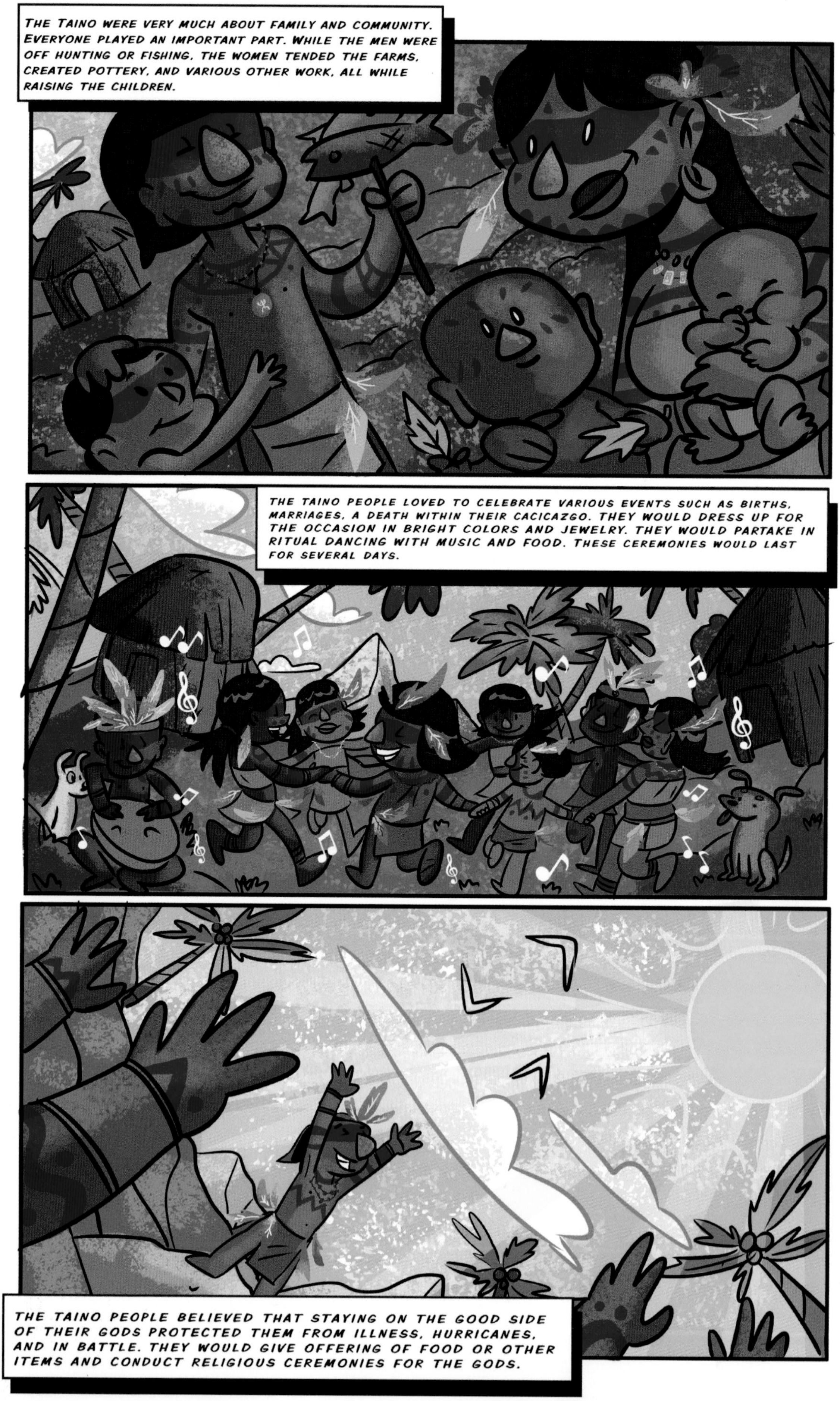
THE TAINO WERE VERY MUCH ABOUT FAMILY AND COMMUNITY. EVERYONE PLAYED AN IMPORTANT PART. WHILE THE MEN WERE OFF HUNTING OR FISHING, THE WOMEN TENDED THE FARMS, CREATED POTTERY, AND VARIOUS OTHER WORK, ALL WHILE RAISING THE CHILDREN.
THE TAINO PEOPLE LOVED TO CELEBRATE VARIOUS EVENTS SUCH AS BIRTHS, MARRIAGES, A DEATH WITHIN THEIR CACICAZGO. THEY WOULD DRESS UP FOR THE OCCASION IN BRIGHT COLORS AND JEWELRY. THEY WOULD PARTAKE IN RITUAL DANCING WITH MUSIC AND FOOD. THESE CEREMONIES WOULD LAST FOR SEVERAL DAYS.
THE TAINO PEOPLE BELIEVED THAT STAYING ON THE GOOD SIDE OF THEIR GODS PROTECTED THEM FROM ILLNESS, HURRICANES, AND IN BATTLE. THEY WOULD GIVE OFFERING OF FOOD OR OTHER ITEMS AND CONDUCT RELIGIOUS CEREMONIES FOR THE GODS.

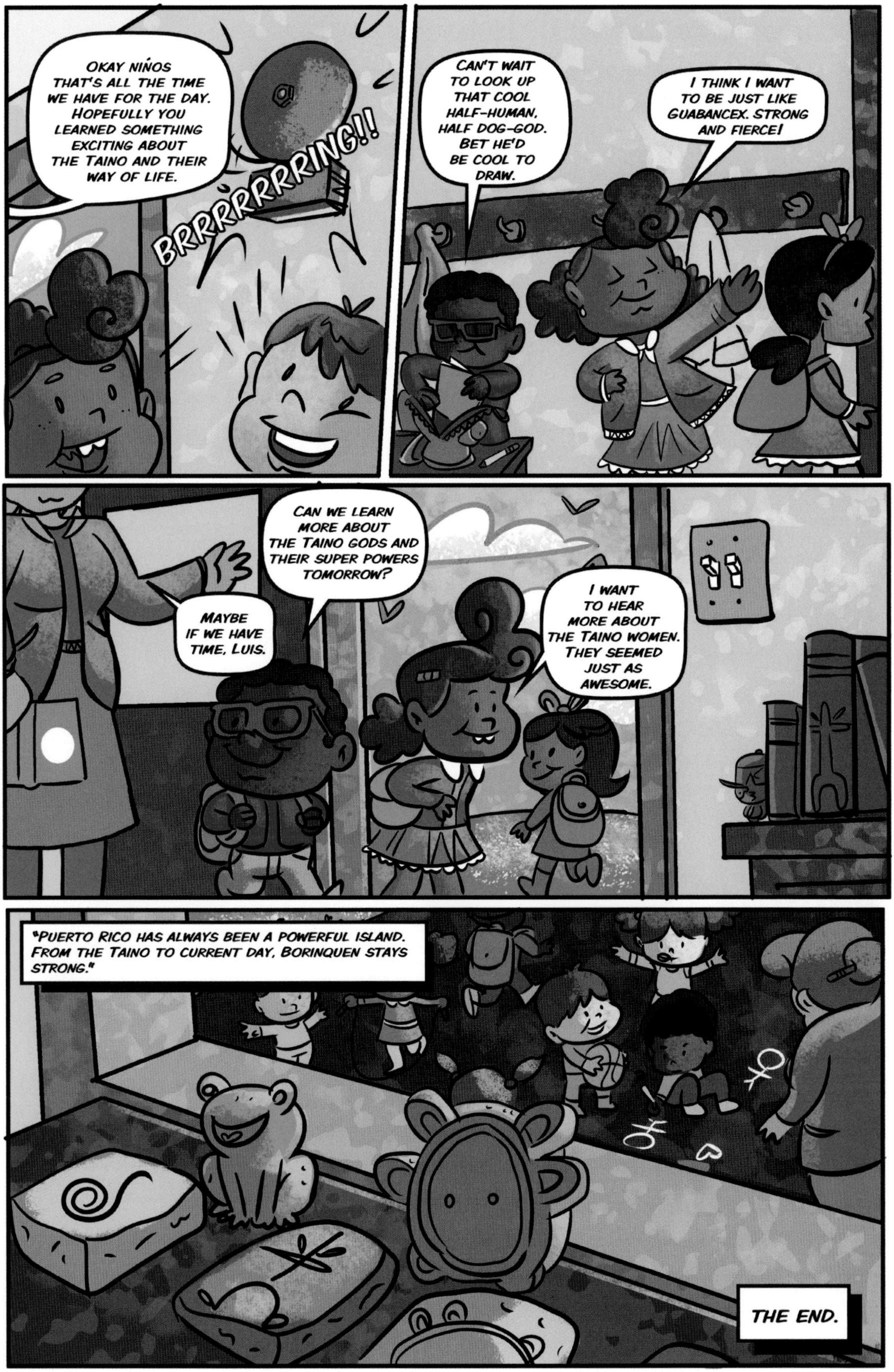
OKAY NIÑOS THAT'S ALL THE TIME WE HAVE FOR THE DAY. HOPEFULLY YOU LEARNED SOMETHING EXCITING ABOUT THE TAINO AND THEIR WAY OF LIFE.
BRRRRRRRRING!!
CAN'T WAIT TO LOOK UP THAT COOL HALF-HUMAN, HALF DOG-GOD. BET HE'D BE COOL TO DRAW.
I THINK I WANT TO BE JUST LIKE GUABANCEX. STRONG AND FIERCE!
CAN WE LEARN MORE ABOUT THE TAINO GODS AND THEIR SUPER POWERS TOMORROW?
MAYBE IF WE HAVE TIME, LUIS.
I WANT TO HEAR MORE ABOUT THE TAINO WOMEN. THEY SEEMED JUST AS AWESOME.
"PUERTO RICO HAS ALWAYS BEEN A POWERFUL ISLAND. FROM THE TAINO TO CURRENT DAY, BORINQUEN STAYS STRONG."
THE END.

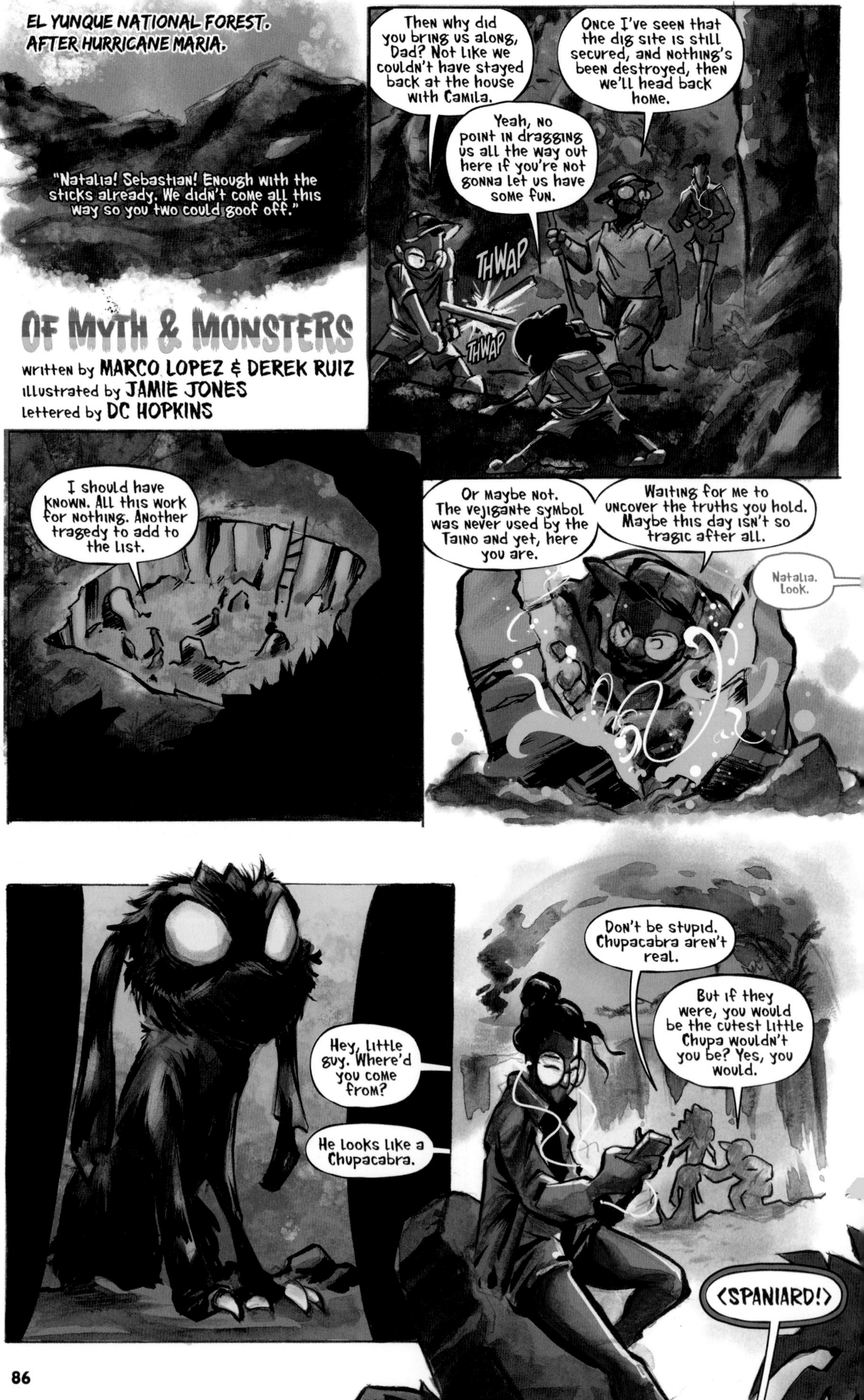
EL YUNQUE NATIONAL FOREST. AFTER HURRICANE MARIA.
"Natalia! Sebastian! Enough with the sticks already. We didn't come all this way so you two could goof off."
OF MYTH & MONSTERS
written by MARCO LOPEZ & DEREK RUIZ
illustrated by JAMIE JONES
lettered by DC HOPKINS
Then why did you bring us along, Dad? Not like we couldn't have stayed back at the house with Camila.
Once I've seen that the dig site is still secured, and nothing's been destroyed, then we'll head back home.
Yeah, no point in dragging us all the way out here if you're not gonna let us have some fun.
THWAP
THWAP
I should have known. All this work for nothing. Another tragedy to add to the list.
Or maybe not. The vejigante symbol was never used by the Taino and yet, here you are.
Waiting for me to uncover the truths you hold. Maybe this day isn't so tragic after all.
Natalia. Look.
Hey, little guy. Where'd you come from?
He looks like a Chupacabra.
Don't be stupid. Chupacabra aren't real.
But if they were, you would be the cutest little Chupa wouldn't you be? Yes, you would.
<SPANIARD!>

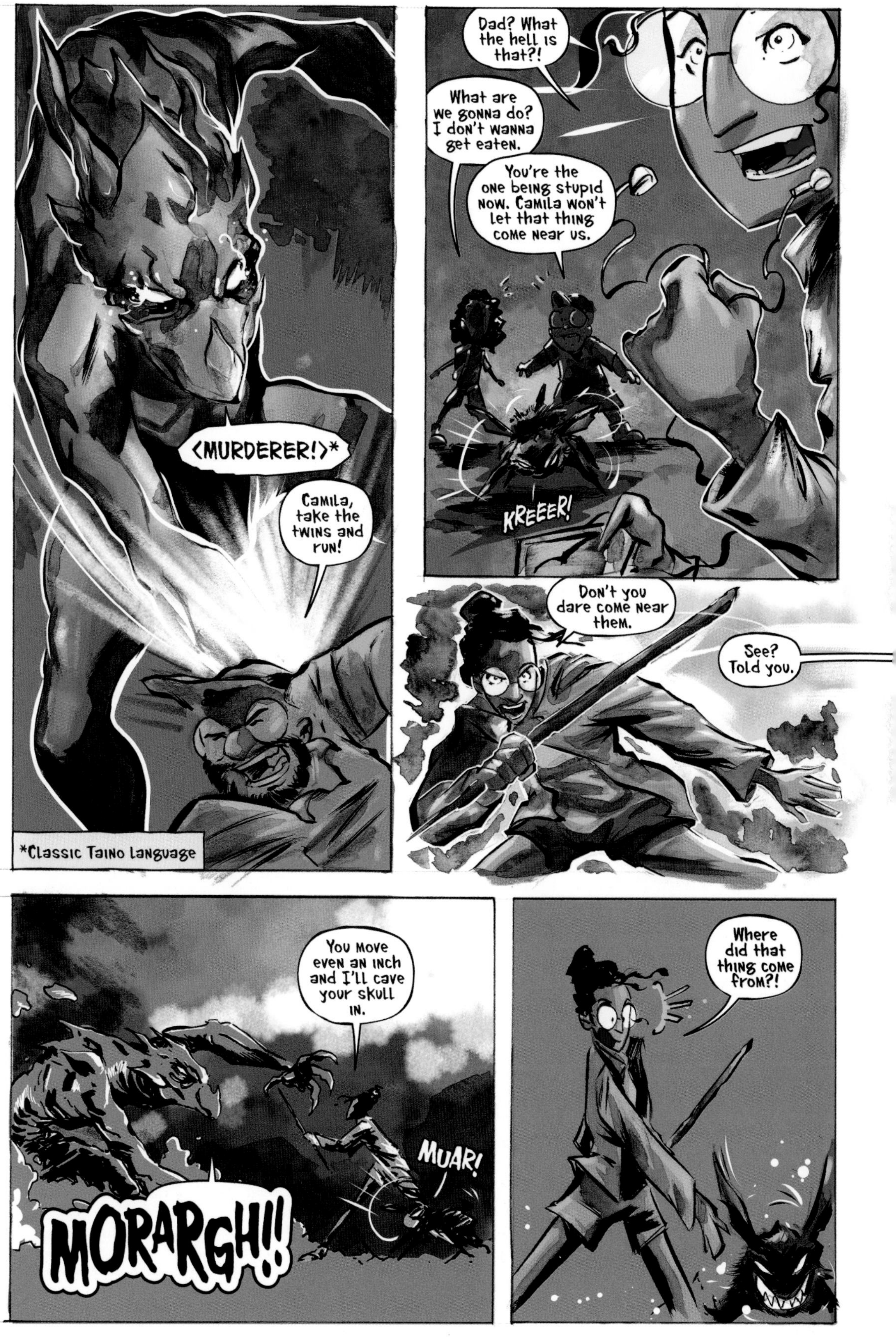

<MURDERER!>*
Camila, take the twins and run!
*Classic Taino Language
Dad? What the hell is that?!
What are we gonna do? I don't wanna get eaten.
You're the one being stupid now. Camila won't let that thing come near us.
KREEER!
Don't you dare come near them.
See? Told you.
You move even an inch and I'll cave your skull in.
MUAR!
MORARGH!!
Where did that thing come from?!

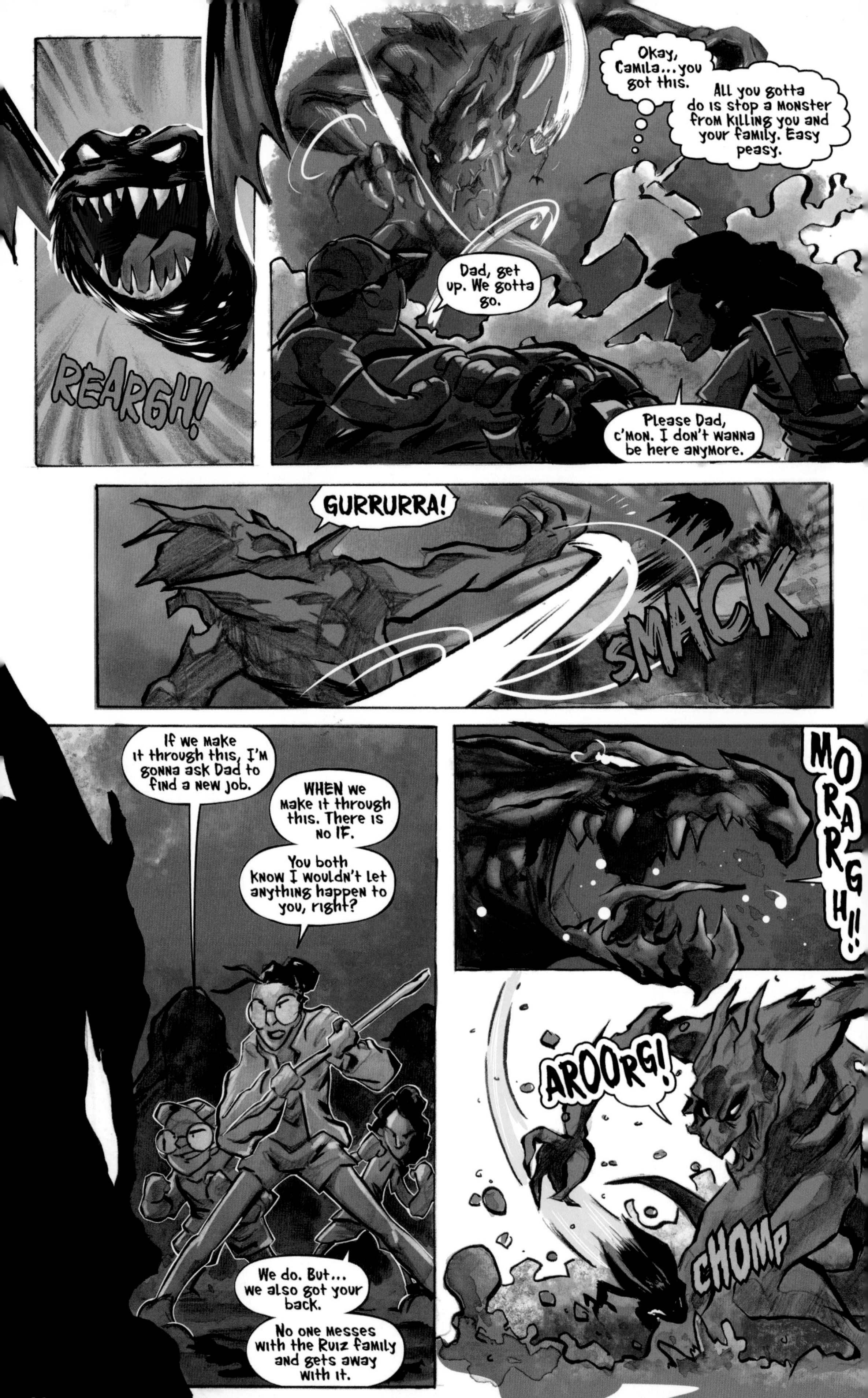
REARGH!
Okay, Camila... you got this.
All you gotta do is stop a monster from killing you and your family. Easy peasy.
Dad, get up. We gotta go.
Please Dad, c'mon. I don't wanna be here anymore.
GURRURRA!
SMACK
If we make it through this, I'm gonna ask Dad to find a new job.
WHEN we make it through this. There is no IF.
You both know I wouldn't let anything happen to you, right?
We do. But... we also got your back.
No one messes with the Ruiz family and gets away with it.
MORARGH!!
AROORG!
CHOMP

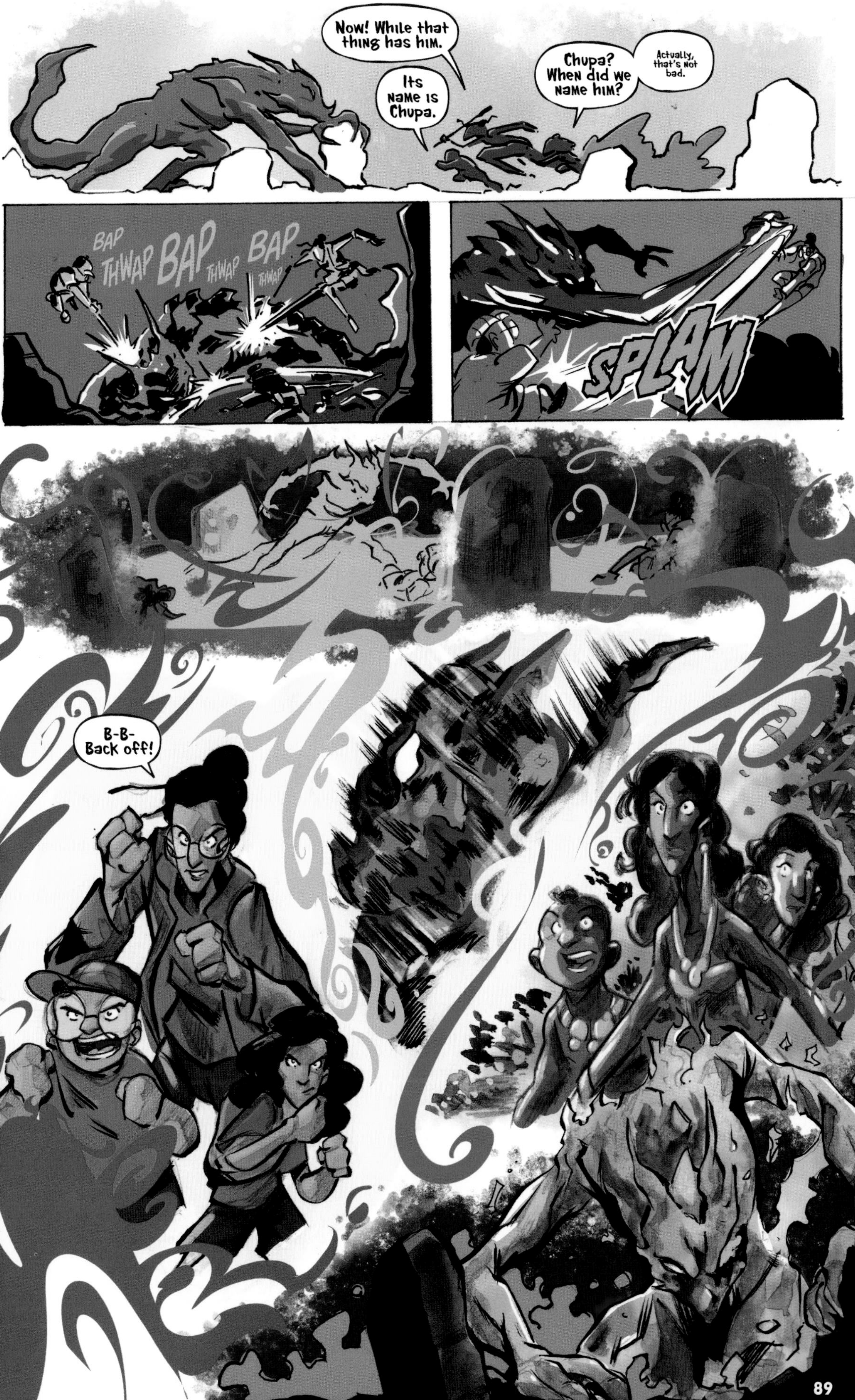
Now! While that thing has him.
Its name is Chupa.
Chupa? When did we name him?
Actually, that's not bad.
BAP THWAP BAP THWAP BAP THWAP
SPLAM
B-B- Back off!

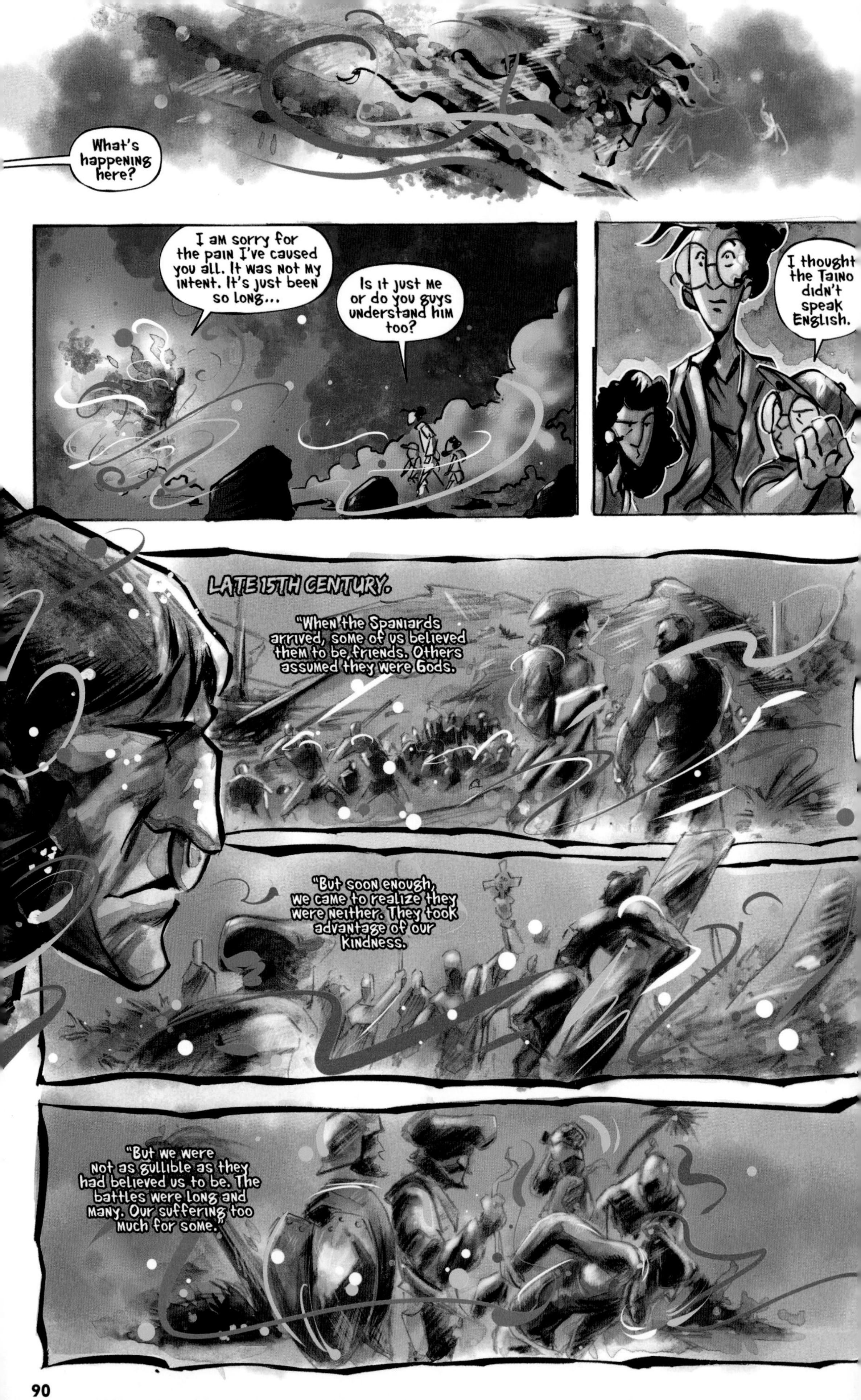
What's happening here?
I am sorry for the pain I've caused you all. It was not my intent. It's just been so long...
Is it just me or do you guys understand him too?
I thought the Taino didn't speak English.
LATE 15TH CENTURY.
"When the Spaniards arrived, some of us believed them to be friends. Others assumed they were Gods.
"But soon enough, we came to realize they were neither. They took advantage of our kindness.
"But we were not as gullible as they had believed us to be. The battles were long and many. Our suffering too much for some."

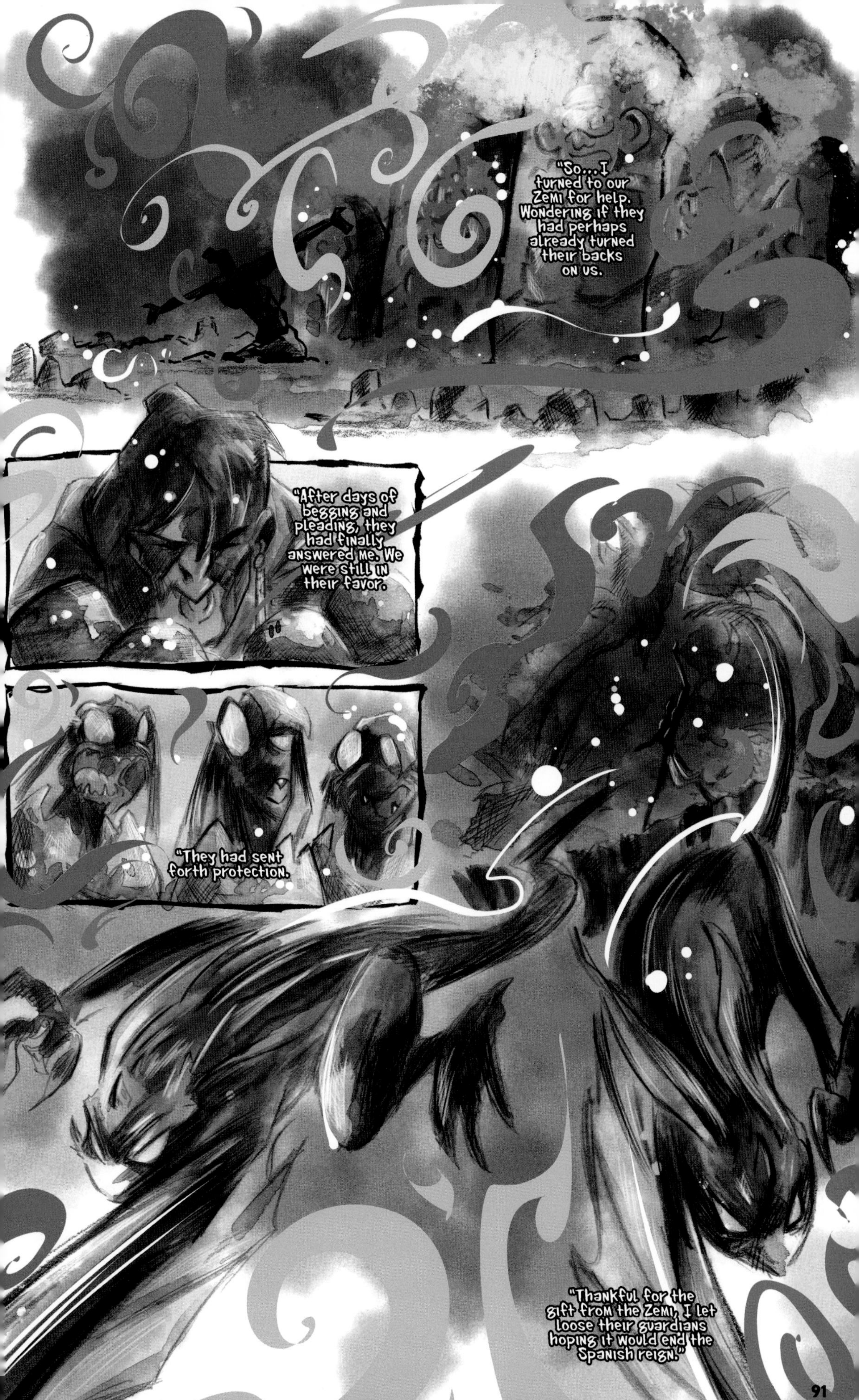
"So... I turned to our Zemi for help. Wondering if they had perhaps already turned their backs on us.
"After days of begging and pleading, they had finally answered me. We were still in their favor.
"They had sent forth protection.
"Thankful for the gift from the Zemi, I let loose their guardians hoping it would end the Spanish reign."

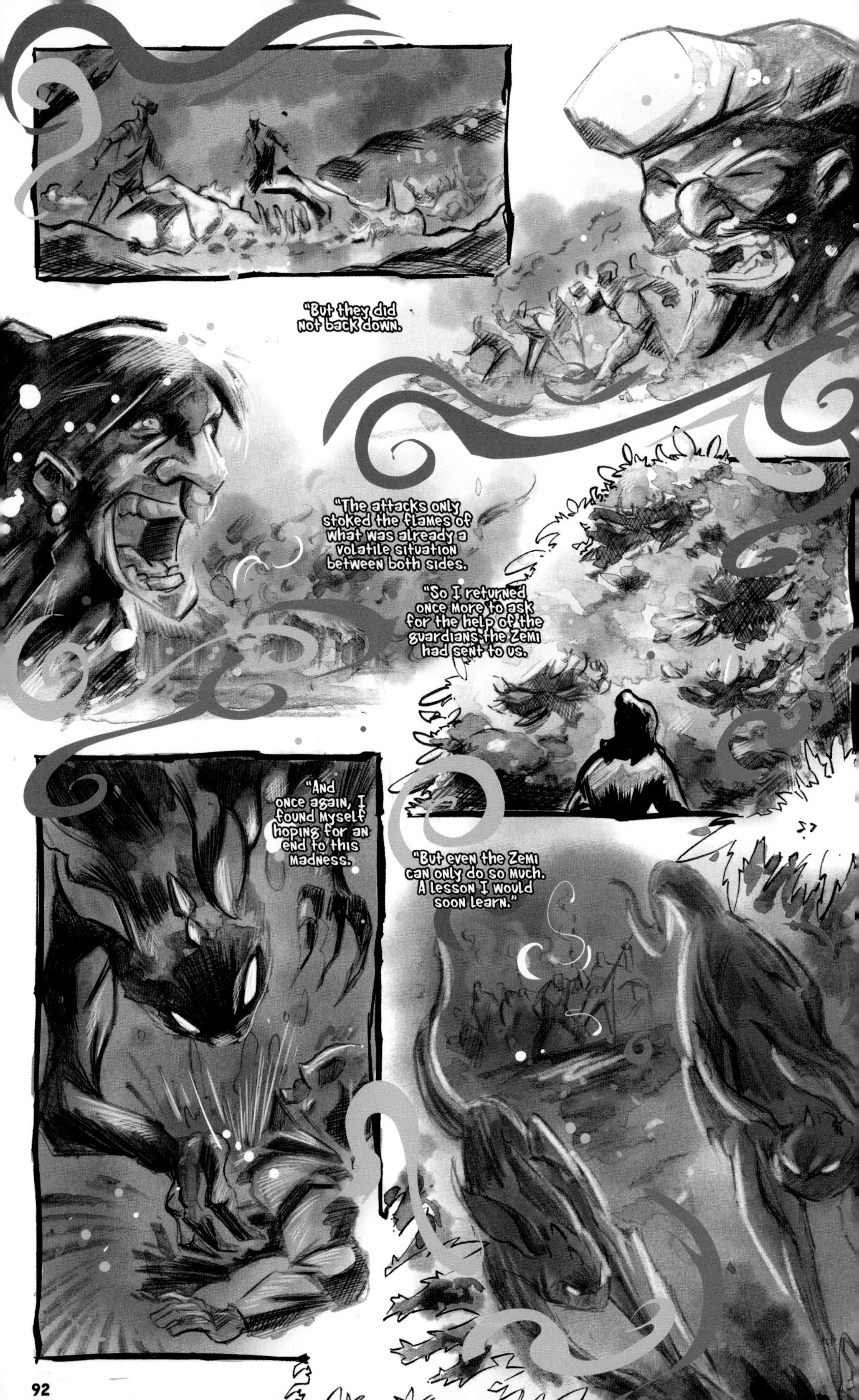
"But they did not back down.
"The attacks only stoked the flames of what was already a volatile situation between both sides.
"So I returned once more to ask for the help of the guardians the Zemi had sent to us.
"And once again, I found myself hoping for an end to this madness.
"But even the Zemi can only do so much. A lesson I would soon learn."

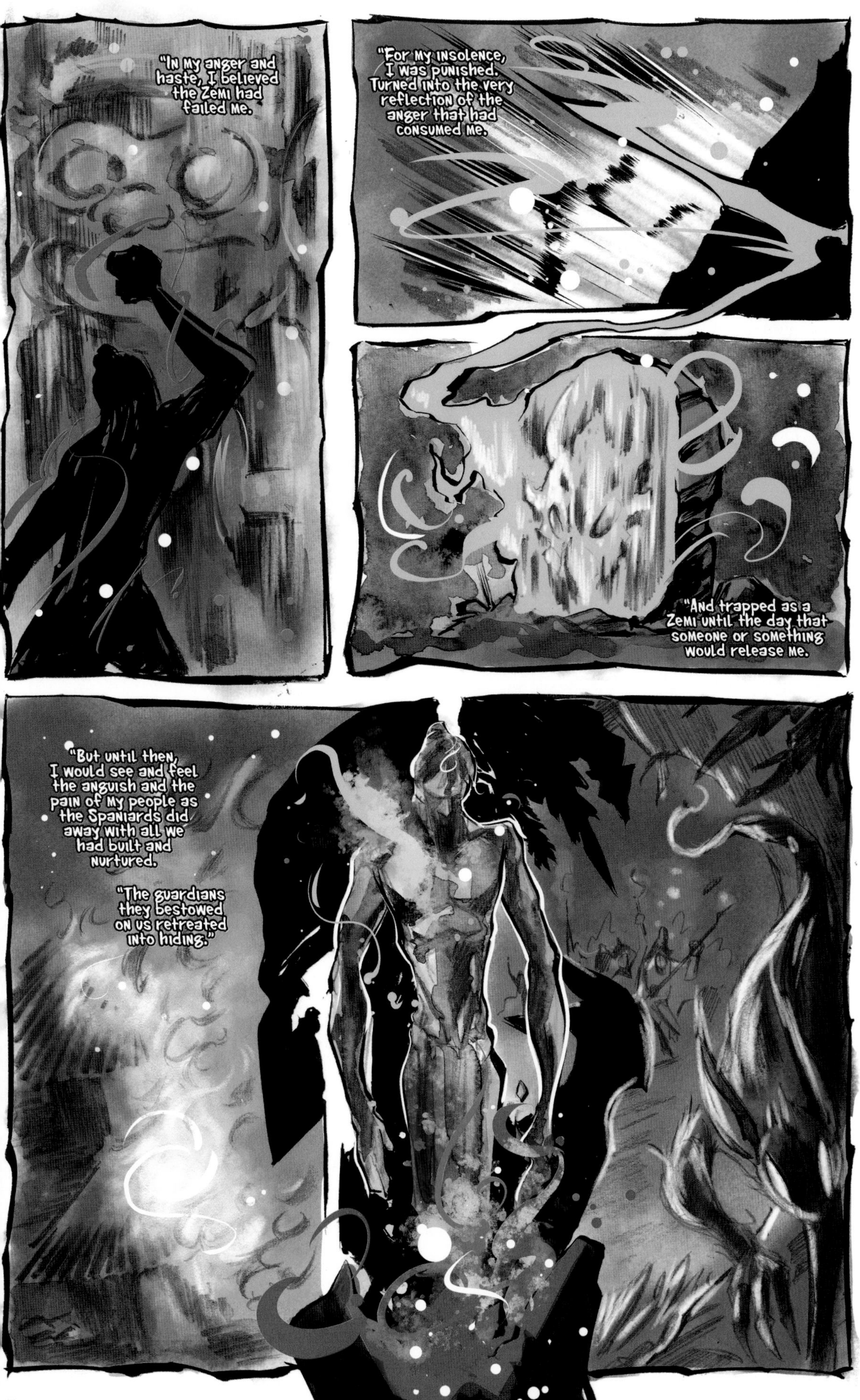
"In my anger and haste, I believed the Zemi had failed me.
"For my insolence, I was punished. Turned into the very reflection of the anger that had consumed me.
"And trapped as a Zemi until the day that someone or something would release me.
"But until then, I would see and feel the anguish and the pain of my people as the Spaniards did away with all we had built and nurtured.
"The guardians they bestowed on us retreated into hiding."

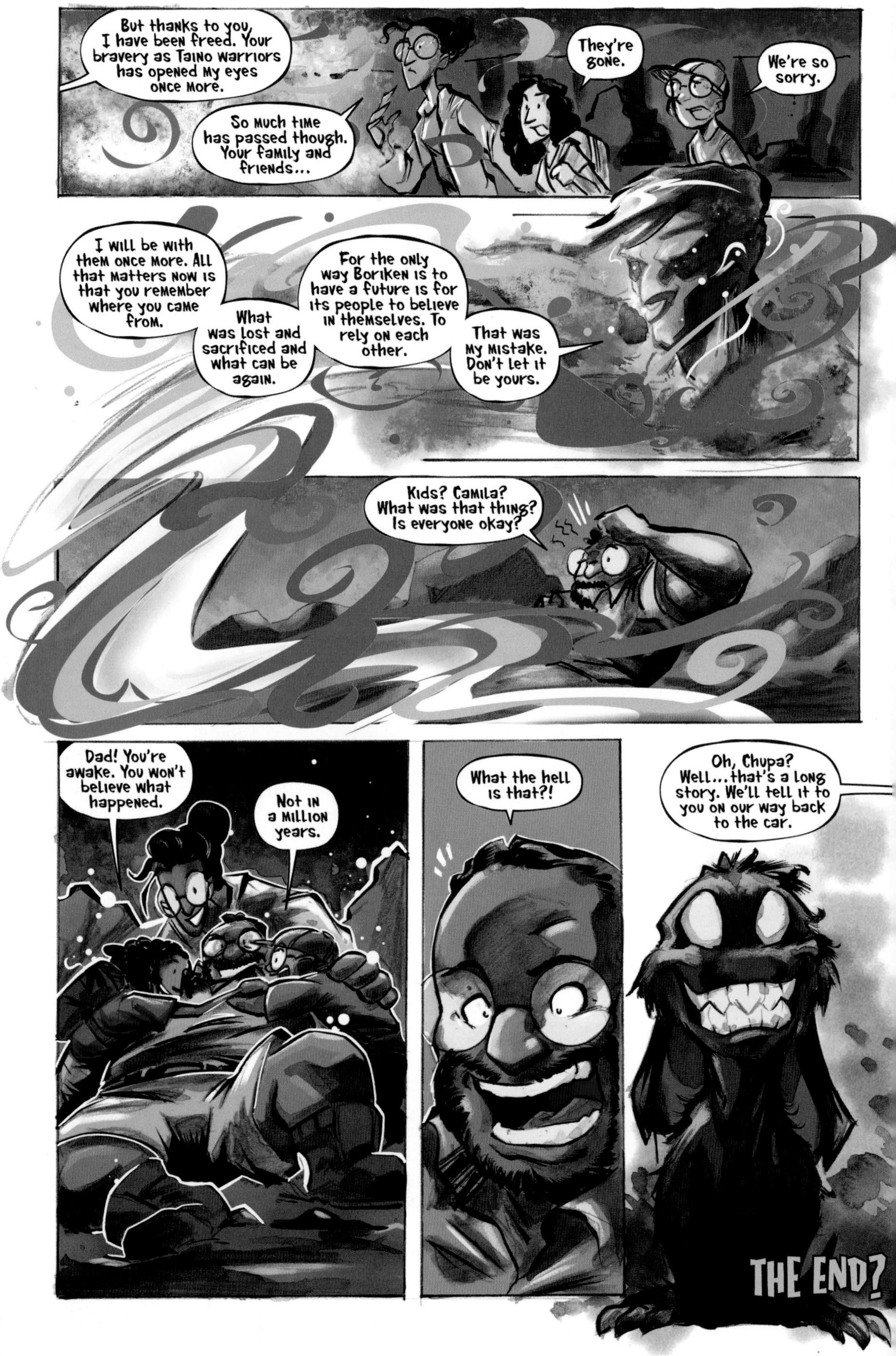

But thanks to you, I have been freed. Your bravery as Taino warriors has opened my eyes once more.
So much time has passed though. Your family and friends...
They're gone.
We're so sorry.
I will be with them once more. All that matters now is that you remember where you came from.
What was lost and sacrificed and what can be again.
For the only way Boriken is to have a future is for its people to believe in themselves. To rely on each other.
That was my mistake. Don't let it be yours.
Kids? Camila? What was that thing? Is everyone okay?
Dad! You're awake. You won't believe what happened.
Not in a million years.
What the hell is that?!
Oh, Chupa? Well...that's a long story. We'll tell it to you on our way back to the car.
THE END?

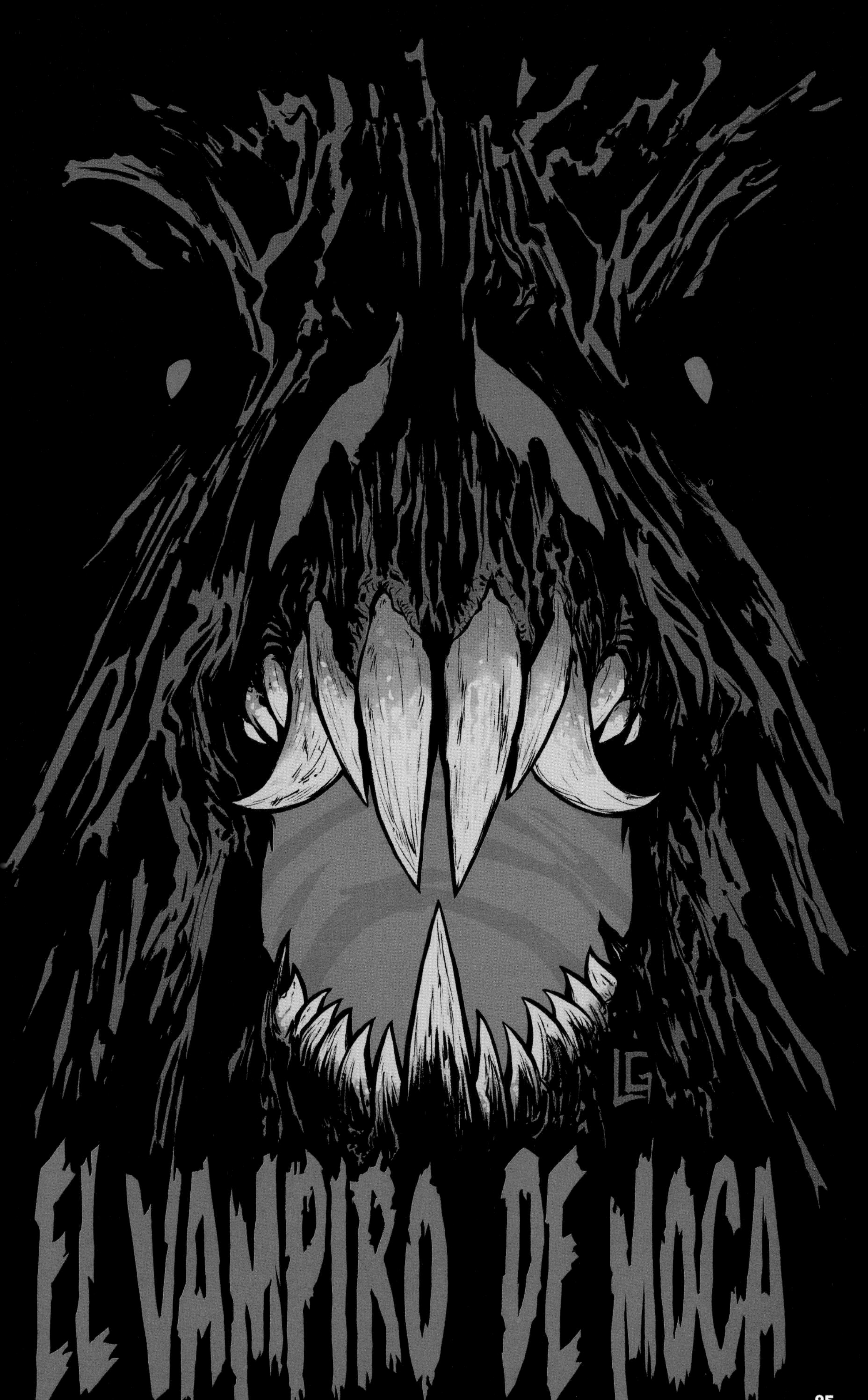
EL VAMPIRO DE MOCA

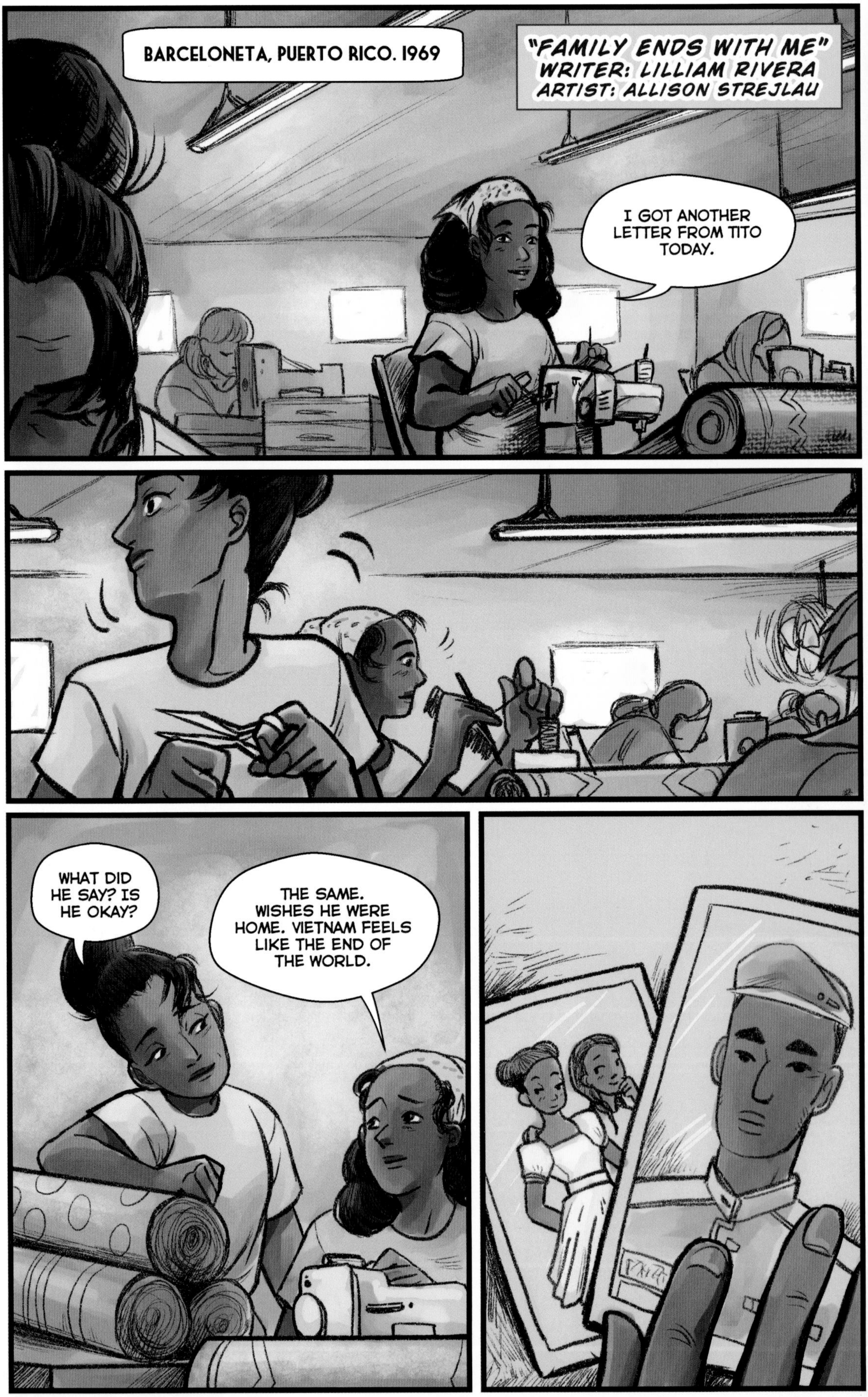
BARCELONETA, PUERTO RICO. 1969
"FAMILY ENDS WITH ME"
WRITER: LILLIAM RIVERA
ARTIST: ALLISON STREJLAU
I GOT ANOTHER LETTER FROM TITO TODAY.
WHAT DID HE SAY? IS HE OKAY?
THE SAME. WISHES HE WERE HOME. VIETNAM FEELS LIKE THE END OF THE WORLD.

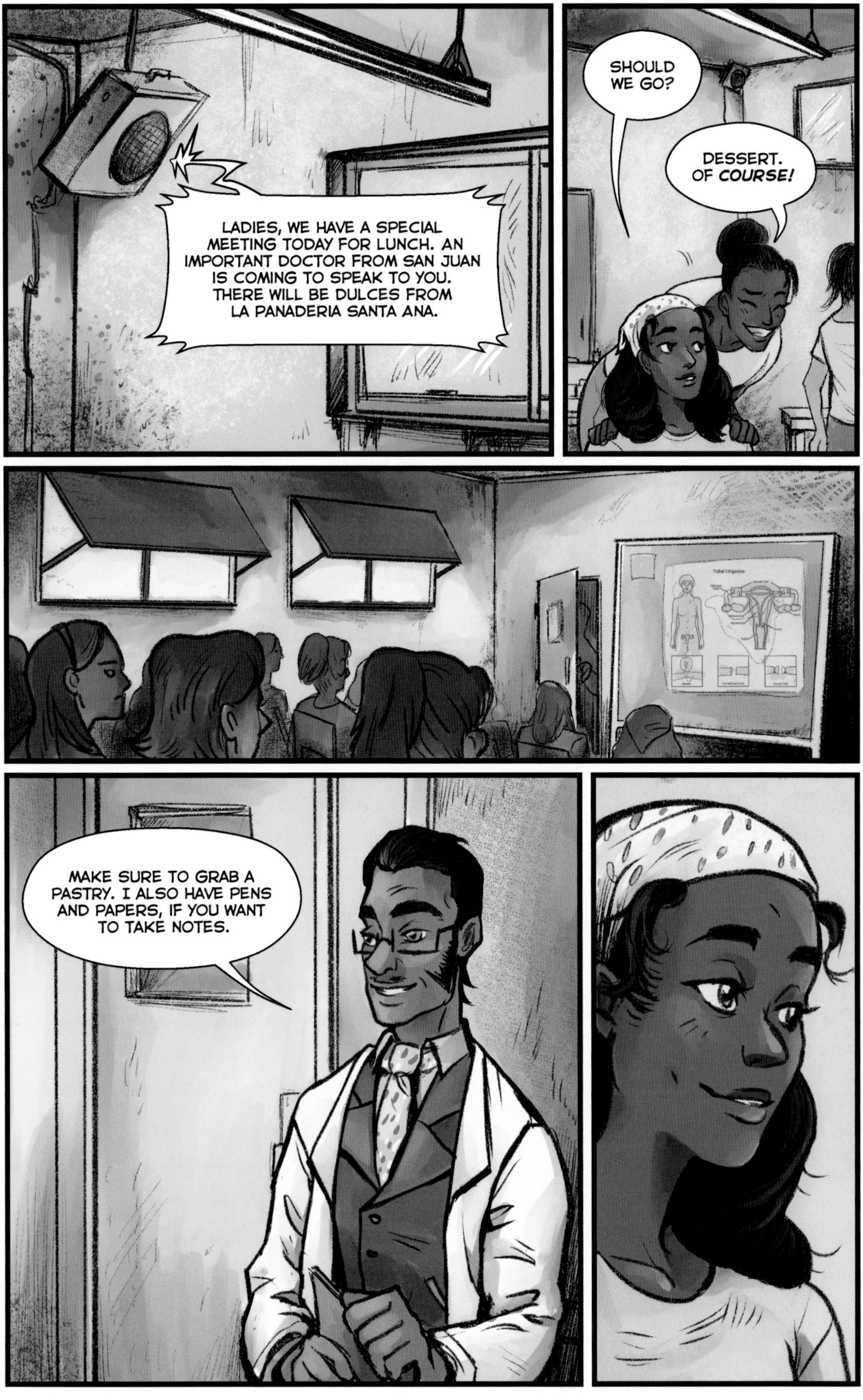
LADIES, WE HAVE A SPECIAL MEETING TODAY FOR LUNCH. AN IMPORTANT DOCTOR FROM SAN JUAN IS COMING TO SPEAK TO YOU. THERE WILL BE DULCES FROM LA PANADERIA SANTA ANA.
SHOULD WE GO?
DESSERT. OF *COURSE!*
MAKE SURE TO GRAB A PASTRY. I ALSO HAVE PENS AND PAPERS, IF YOU WANT TO TAKE NOTES.

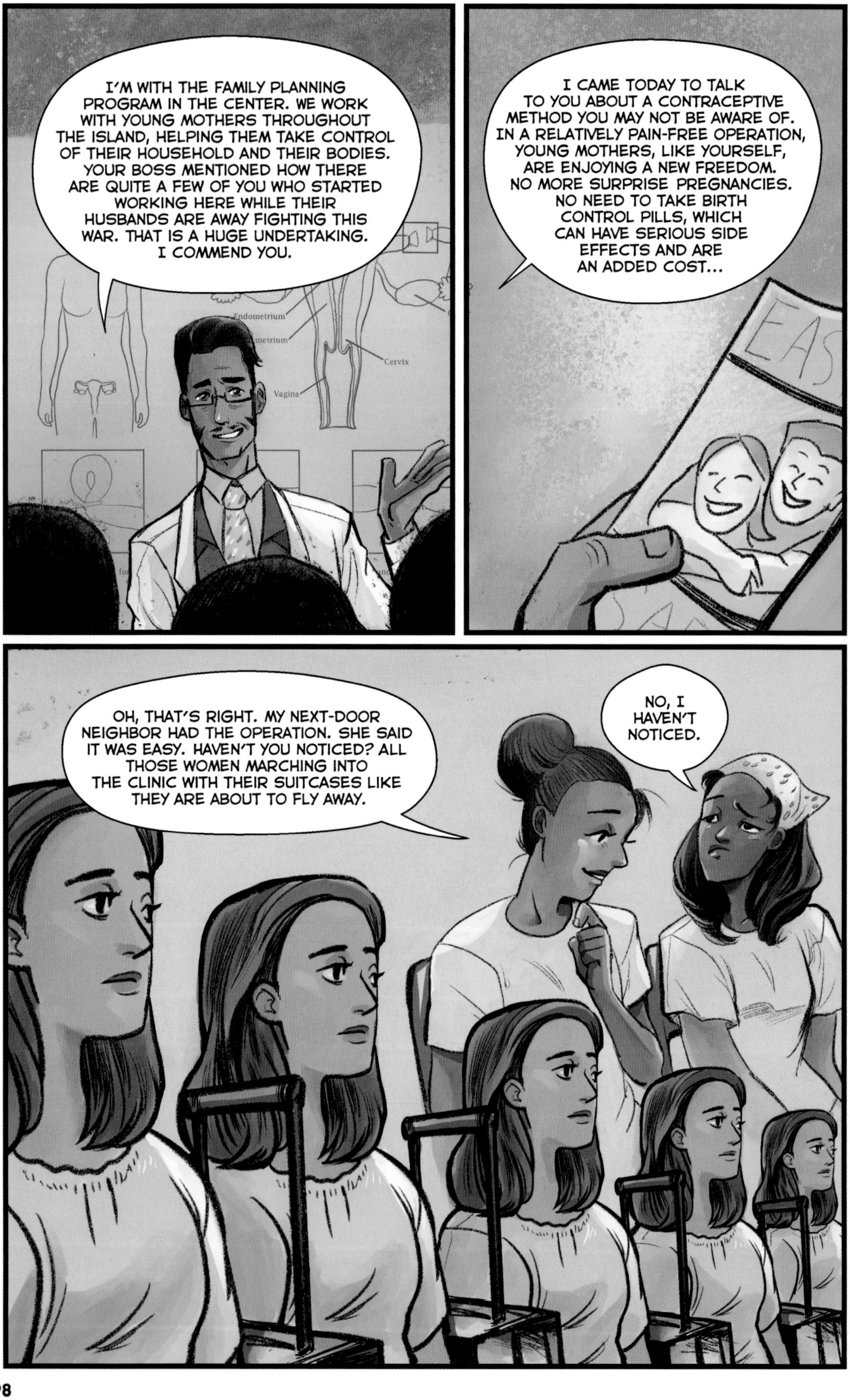
I'M WITH THE FAMILY PLANNING PROGRAM IN THE CENTER. WE WORK WITH YOUNG MOTHERS THROUGHOUT THE ISLAND, HELPING THEM TAKE CONTROL OF THEIR HOUSEHOLD AND THEIR BODIES. YOUR BOSS MENTIONED HOW THERE ARE QUITE A FEW OF YOU WHO STARTED WORKING HERE WHILE THEIR HUSBANDS ARE AWAY FIGHTING THIS WAR. THAT IS A HUGE UNDERTAKING. I COMMEND YOU.
Endometrium
Cervix
Vagina
I CAME TODAY TO TALK TO YOU ABOUT A CONTRACEPTIVE METHOD YOU MAY NOT BE AWARE OF. IN A RELATIVELY PAIN-FREE OPERATION, YOUNG MOTHERS, LIKE YOURSELF, ARE ENJOYING A NEW FREEDOM. NO MORE SURPRISE PREGNANCIES. NO NEED TO TAKE BIRTH CONTROL PILLS, WHICH CAN HAVE SERIOUS SIDE EFFECTS AND ARE AN ADDED COST...
OH, THAT'S RIGHT. MY NEXT-DOOR NEIGHBOR HAD THE OPERATION. SHE SAID IT WAS EASY. HAVEN'T YOU NOTICED? ALL THOSE WOMEN MARCHING INTO THE CLINIC WITH THEIR SUITCASES LIKE THEY ARE ABOUT TO FLY AWAY.
NO, I HAVEN'T NOTICED.

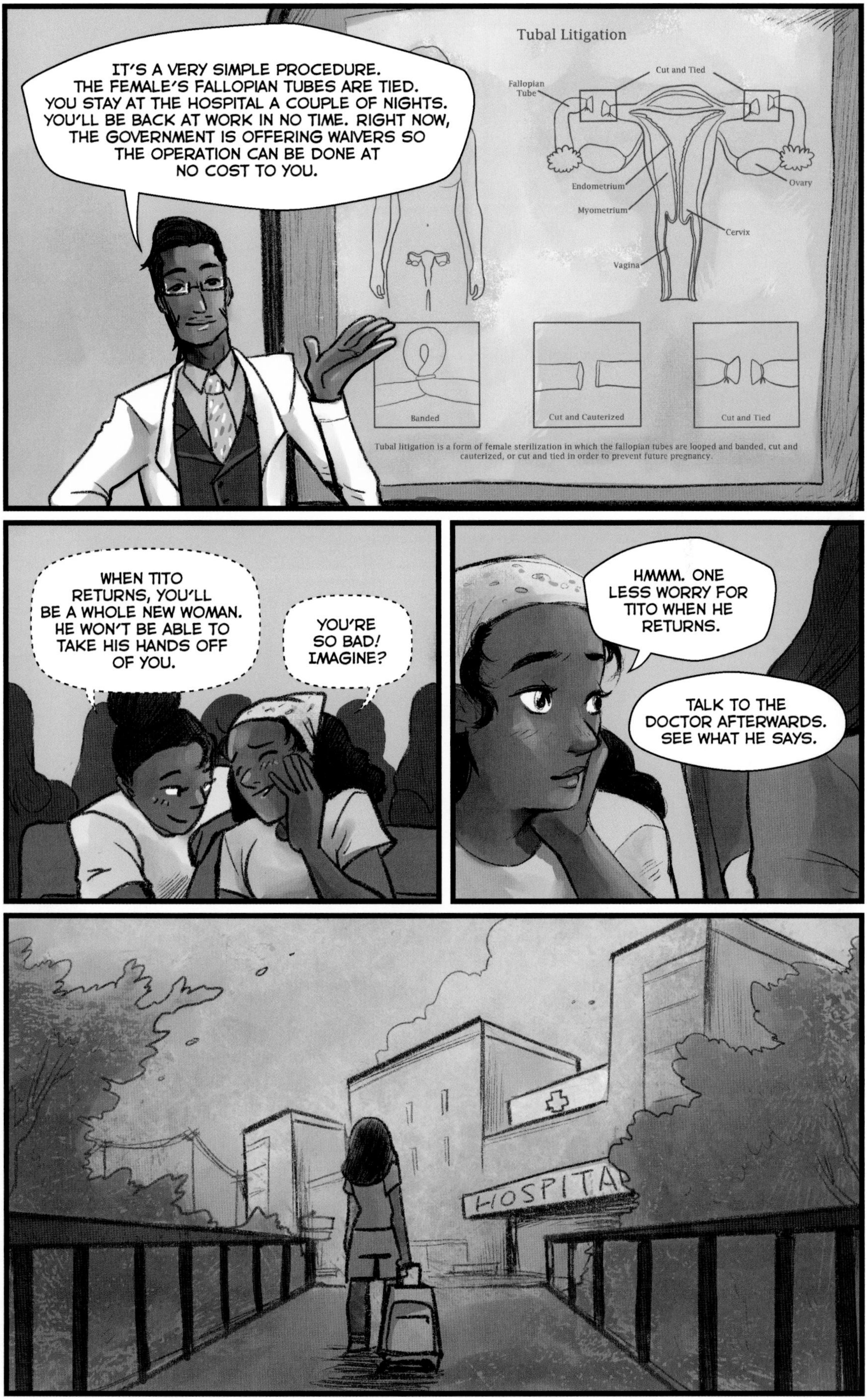
IT'S A VERY SIMPLE PROCEDURE. THE FEMALE'S FALLOPIAN TUBES ARE TIED. YOU STAY AT THE HOSPITAL A COUPLE OF NIGHTS. YOU'LL BE BACK AT WORK IN NO TIME. RIGHT NOW, THE GOVERNMENT IS OFFERING WAIVERS SO THE OPERATION CAN BE DONE AT NO COST TO YOU.
Tubal Litigation
Cut and Tied
Fallopian Tube
Endometrium
Myometrium
Ovary
Cervix
Vagina
Banded
Cut and Cauterized
Cut and Tied
Tubal litigation is a form of female sterilization in which the fallopian tubes are looped and banded, cut and cauterized, or cut and tied in order to prevent future pregnancy.
WHEN TITO RETURNS, YOU'LL BE A WHOLE NEW WOMAN. HE WON'T BE ABLE TO TAKE HIS HANDS OFF OF YOU.
YOU'RE SO BAD! IMAGINE?
HMMM. ONE LESS WORRY FOR TITO WHEN HE RETURNS.
TALK TO THE DOCTOR AFTERWARDS. SEE WHAT HE SAYS.
HOSPITA

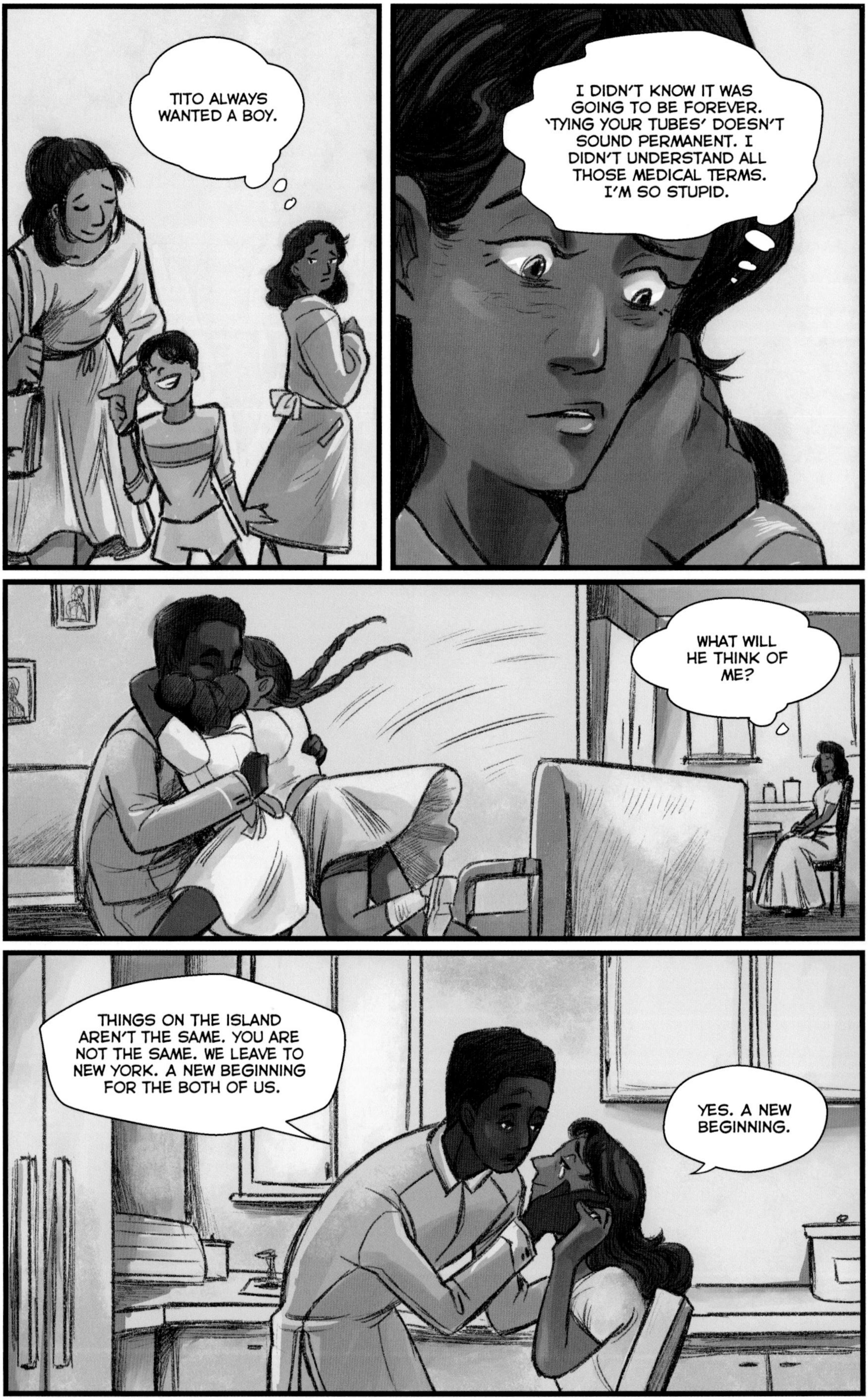
TITO ALWAYS WANTED A BOY.
I DIDN'T KNOW IT WAS GOING TO BE FOREVER. 'TYING YOUR TUBES' DOESN'T SOUND PERMANENT. I DIDN'T UNDERSTAND ALL THOSE MEDICAL TERMS. I'M SO STUPID.
WHAT WILL HE THINK OF ME?
THINGS ON THE ISLAND AREN'T THE SAME. YOU ARE NOT THE SAME. WE LEAVE TO NEW YORK. A NEW BEGINNING FOR THE BOTH OF US.
YES. A NEW BEGINNING.

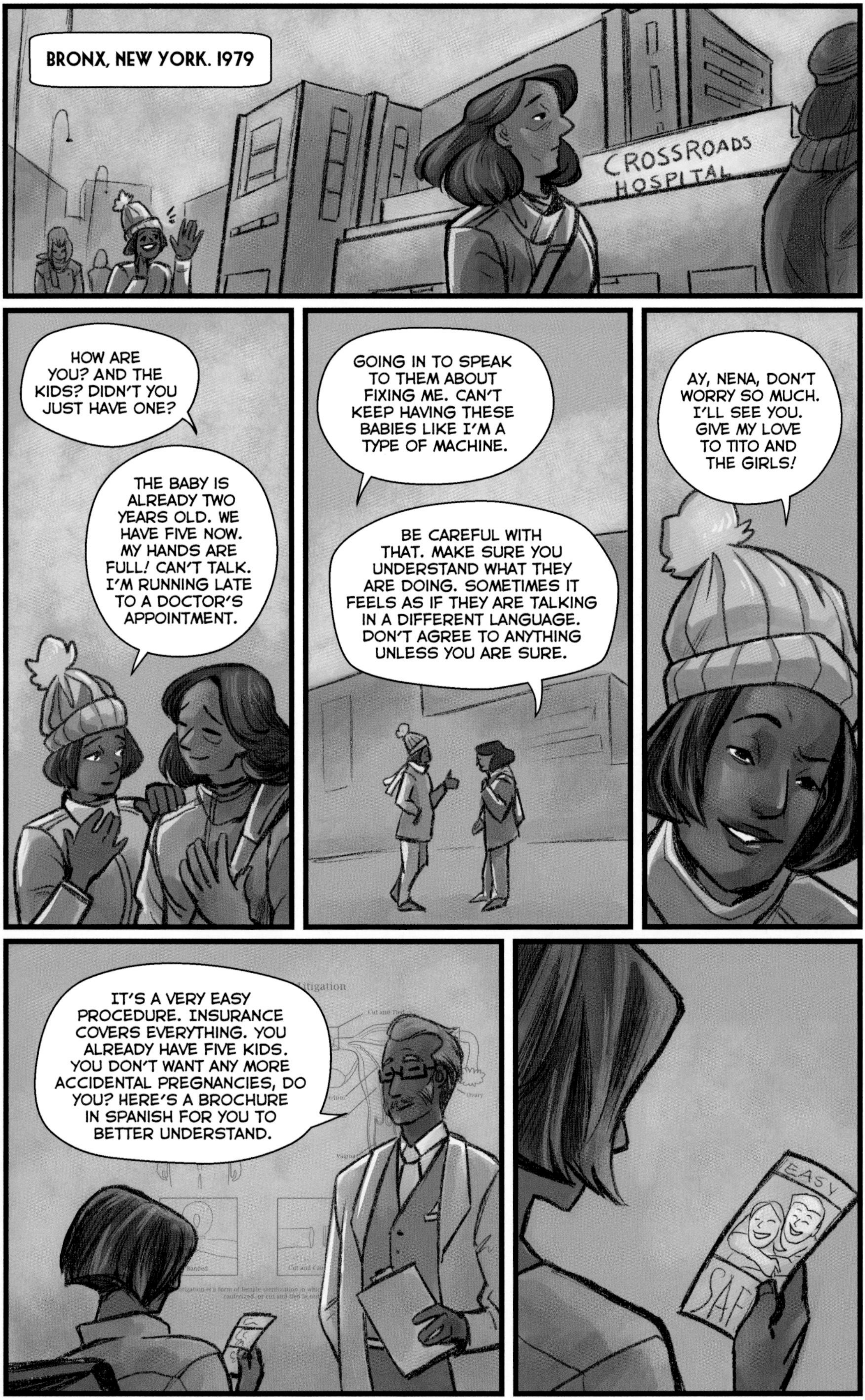
BRONX, NEW YORK. 1979
CROSSROADS HOSPITAL
HOW ARE YOU? AND THE KIDS? DIDN'T YOU JUST HAVE ONE?
THE BABY IS ALREADY TWO YEARS OLD. WE HAVE FIVE NOW. MY HANDS ARE FULL! CAN'T TALK. I'M RUNNING LATE TO A DOCTOR'S APPOINTMENT.
GOING IN TO SPEAK TO THEM ABOUT FIXING ME. CAN'T KEEP HAVING THESE BABIES LIKE I'M A TYPE OF MACHINE.
BE CAREFUL WITH THAT. MAKE SURE YOU UNDERSTAND WHAT THEY ARE DOING. SOMETIMES IT FEELS AS IF THEY ARE TALKING IN A DIFFERENT LANGUAGE. DON'T AGREE TO ANYTHING UNLESS YOU ARE SURE.
AY, NENA, DON'T WORRY SO MUCH. I'LL SEE YOU. GIVE MY LOVE TO TITO AND THE GIRLS!
IT'S A VERY EASY PROCEDURE. INSURANCE COVERS EVERYTHING. YOU ALREADY HAVE FIVE KIDS. YOU DON'T WANT ANY MORE ACCIDENTAL PREGNANCIES, DO YOU? HERE'S A BROCHURE IN SPANISH FOR YOU TO BETTER UNDERSTAND.
Cut and Tied
Ovary
Vagina
Banded
EASY

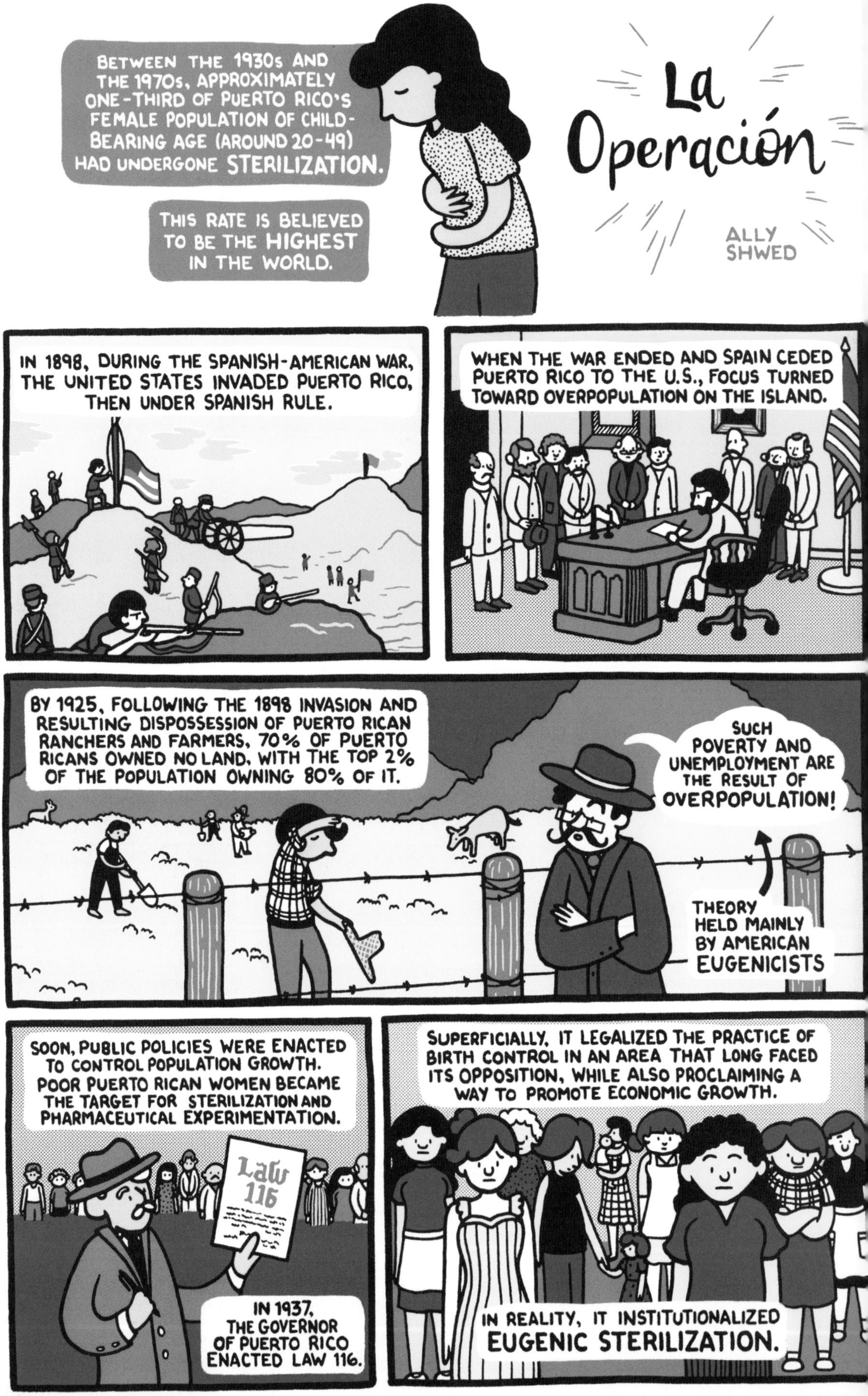
BETWEEN THE 1930s AND THE 1970s, APPROXIMATELY ONE-THIRD OF PUERTO RICO'S FEMALE POPULATION OF CHILD-BEARING AGE (AROUND 20-49) HAD UNDERGONE STERILIZATION.
THIS RATE IS BELIEVED TO BE THE HIGHEST IN THE WORLD.
La Operación
ALLY SHWED
IN 1898, DURING THE SPANISH-AMERICAN WAR, THE UNITED STATES INVADED PUERTO RICO, THEN UNDER SPANISH RULE.
WHEN THE WAR ENDED AND SPAIN CEDED PUERTO RICO TO THE U.S., FOCUS TURNED TOWARD OVERPOPULATION ON THE ISLAND.
BY 1925, FOLLOWING THE 1898 INVASION AND RESULTING DISPOSSESSION OF PUERTO RICAN RANCHERS AND FARMERS, 70% OF PUERTO RICANS OWNED NO LAND, WITH THE TOP 2% OF THE POPULATION OWNING 80% OF IT.
SUCH POVERTY AND UNEMPLOYMENT ARE THE RESULT OF OVERPOPULATION!
THEORY HELD MAINLY BY AMERICAN EUGENICISTS
SOON, PUBLIC POLICIES WERE ENACTED TO CONTROL POPULATION GROWTH. POOR PUERTO RICAN WOMEN BECAME THE TARGET FOR STERILIZATION AND PHARMACEUTICAL EXPERIMENTATION.
LAW 116
IN 1937, THE GOVERNOR OF PUERTO RICO ENACTED LAW 116.
SUPERFICIALLY, IT LEGALIZED THE PRACTICE OF BIRTH CONTROL IN AN AREA THAT LONG FACED ITS OPPOSITION, WHILE ALSO PROCLAIMING A WAY TO PROMOTE ECONOMIC GROWTH.
IN REALITY, IT INSTITUTIONALIZED EUGENIC STERILIZATION.

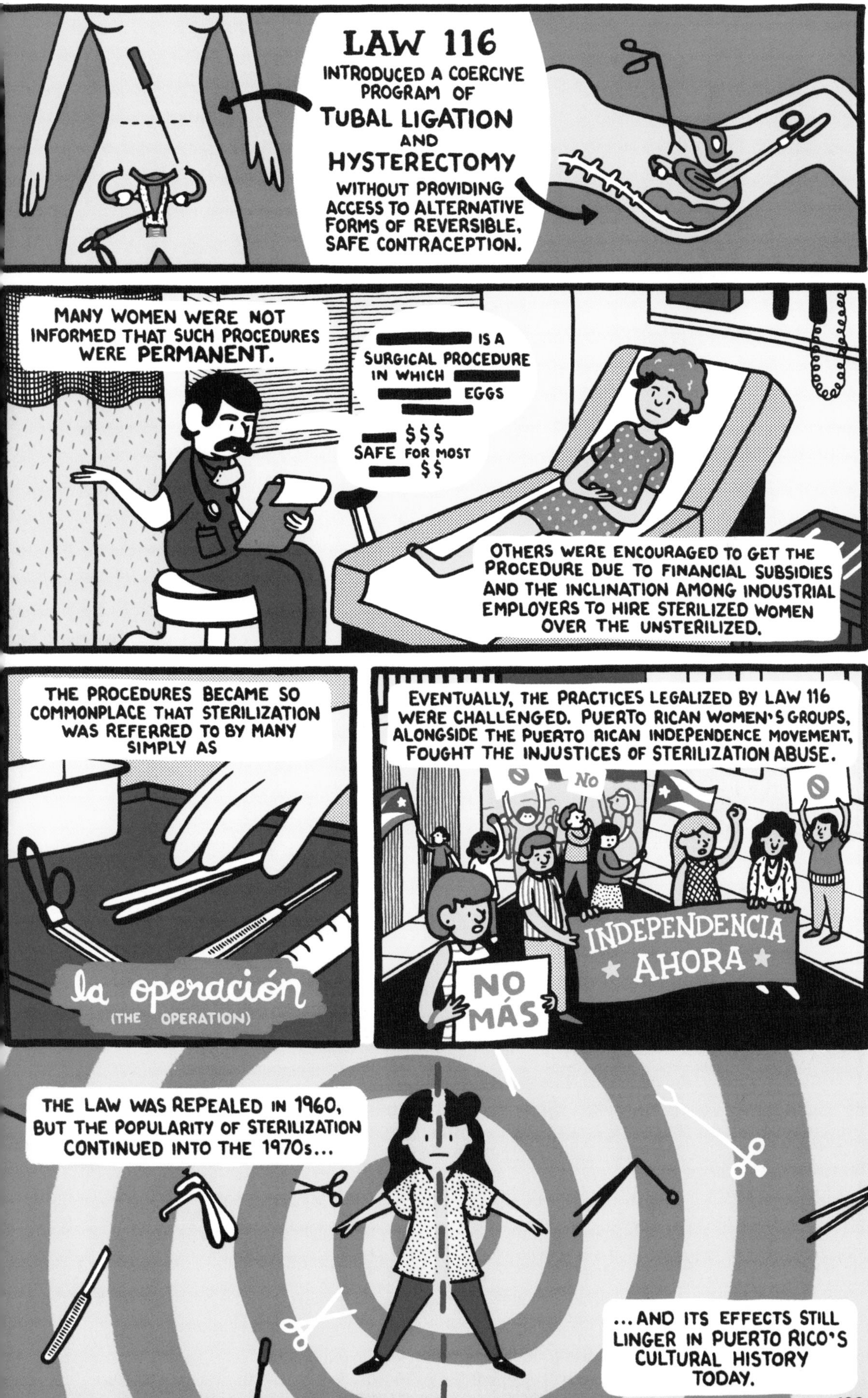
LAW 116 INTRODUCED A COERCIVE PROGRAM OF TUBAL LIGATION AND HYSTERECTOMY WITHOUT PROVIDING ACCESS TO ALTERNATIVE FORMS OF REVERSIBLE, SAFE CONTRACEPTION.
MANY WOMEN WERE NOT INFORMED THAT SUCH PROCEDURES WERE PERMANENT.
[redacted] IS A SURGICAL PROCEDURE IN WHICH [redacted] EGGS [redacted] $$$ SAFE FOR MOST [redacted] $$
OTHERS WERE ENCOURAGED TO GET THE PROCEDURE DUE TO FINANCIAL SUBSIDIES AND THE INCLINATION AMONG INDUSTRIAL EMPLOYERS TO HIRE STERILIZED WOMEN OVER THE UNSTERILIZED.
THE PROCEDURES BECAME SO COMMONPLACE THAT STERILIZATION WAS REFERRED TO BY MANY SIMPLY AS
la operación
(THE OPERATION)
EVENTUALLY, THE PRACTICES LEGALIZED BY LAW 116 WERE CHALLENGED. PUERTO RICAN WOMEN'S GROUPS, ALONGSIDE THE PUERTO RICAN INDEPENDENCE MOVEMENT, FOUGHT THE INJUSTICES OF STERILIZATION ABUSE.
No
INDEPENDENCIA ★ AHORA ★
NO MÁS
THE LAW WAS REPEALED IN 1960, BUT THE POPULARITY OF STERILIZATION CONTINUED INTO THE 1970s...
...AND ITS EFFECTS STILL LINGER IN PUERTO RICO'S CULTURAL HISTORY TODAY.

# The Puerto Rican BIRTH CONTROL Trials

ALLY SHWED

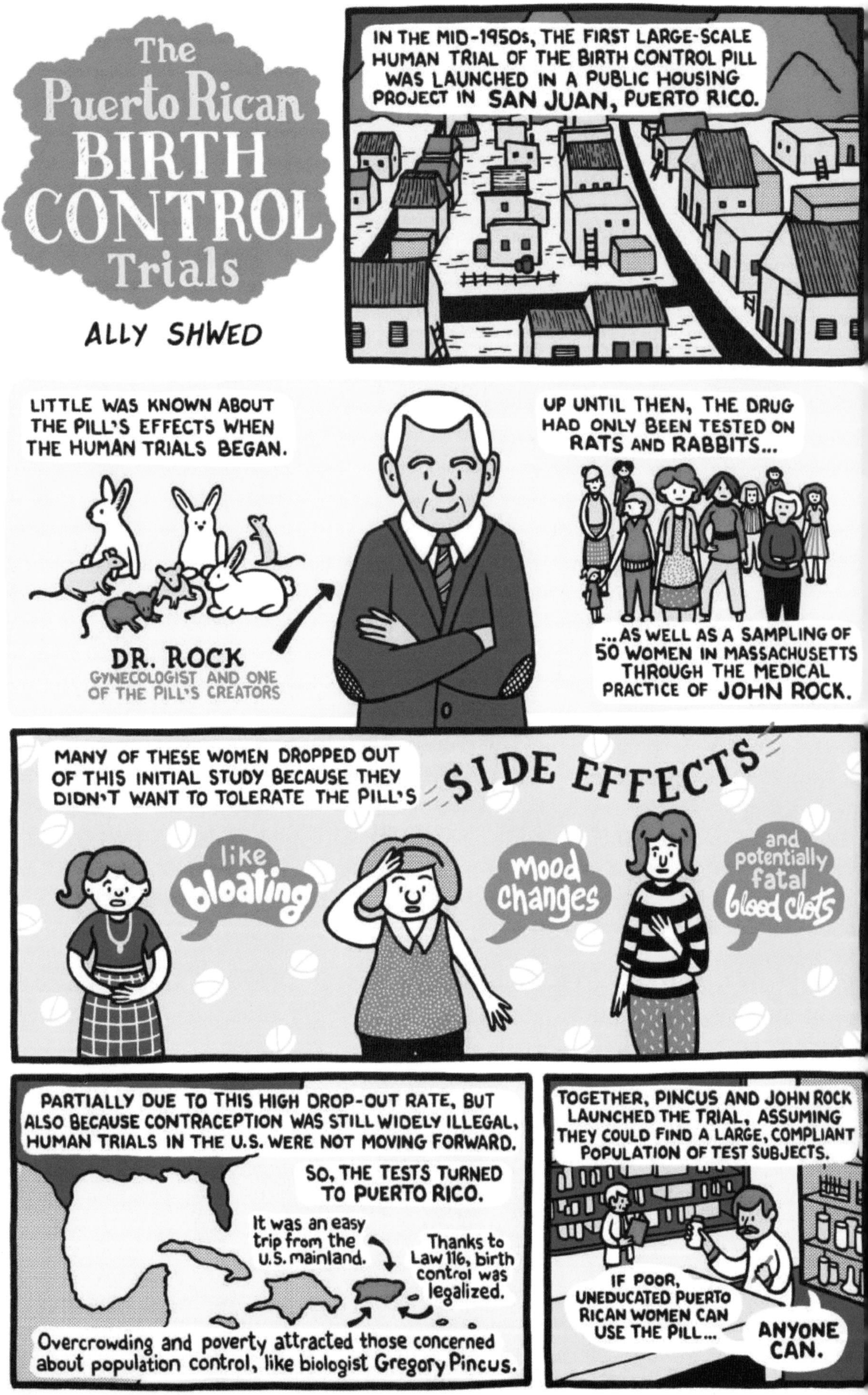
IN THE MID-1950s, THE FIRST LARGE-SCALE HUMAN TRIAL OF THE BIRTH CONTROL PILL WAS LAUNCHED IN A PUBLIC HOUSING PROJECT IN SAN JUAN, PUERTO RICO.
LITTLE WAS KNOWN ABOUT THE PILL'S EFFECTS WHEN THE HUMAN TRIALS BEGAN.
DR. ROCK
GYNECOLOGIST AND ONE OF THE PILL'S CREATORS
UP UNTIL THEN, THE DRUG HAD ONLY BEEN TESTED ON RATS AND RABBITS...
...AS WELL AS A SAMPLING OF 50 WOMEN IN MASSACHUSETTS THROUGH THE MEDICAL PRACTICE OF JOHN ROCK.
MANY OF THESE WOMEN DROPPED OUT OF THIS INITIAL STUDY BECAUSE THEY DIDN'T WANT TO TOLERATE THE PILL'S
SIDE EFFECTS
like bloating
mood changes
and potentially fatal blood clots
PARTIALLY DUE TO THIS HIGH DROP-OUT RATE, BUT ALSO BECAUSE CONTRACEPTION WAS STILL WIDELY ILLEGAL, HUMAN TRIALS IN THE U.S. WERE NOT MOVING FORWARD.
SO, THE TESTS TURNED TO PUERTO RICO.
It was an easy trip from the U.S. mainland.
Thanks to Law 116, birth control was legalized.
Overcrowding and poverty attracted those concerned about population control, like biologist Gregory Pincus.
TOGETHER, PINCUS AND JOHN ROCK LAUNCHED THE TRIAL, ASSUMING THEY COULD FIND A LARGE, COMPLIANT POPULATION OF TEST SUBJECTS.
IF POOR, UNEDUCATED PUERTO RICAN WOMEN CAN USE THE PILL...
ANYONE CAN.

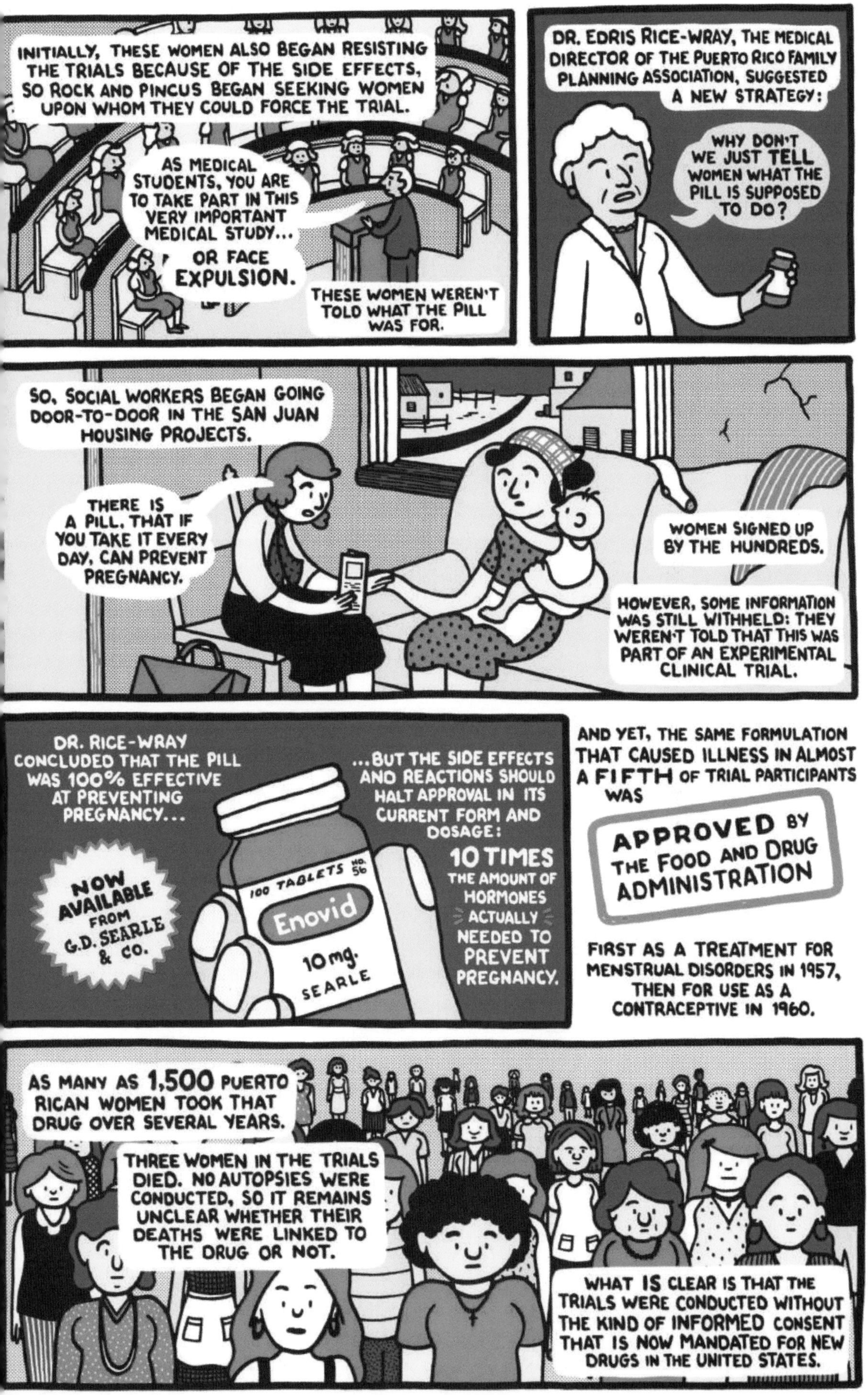

INITIALLY, THESE WOMEN ALSO BEGAN RESISTING THE TRIALS BECAUSE OF THE SIDE EFFECTS, SO ROCK AND PINCUS BEGAN SEEKING WOMEN UPON WHOM THEY COULD FORCE THE TRIAL.
AS MEDICAL STUDENTS, YOU ARE TO TAKE PART IN THIS VERY IMPORTANT MEDICAL STUDY... OR FACE EXPULSION.
THESE WOMEN WEREN'T TOLD WHAT THE PILL WAS FOR.
DR. EDRIS RICE-WRAY, THE MEDICAL DIRECTOR OF THE PUERTO RICO FAMILY PLANNING ASSOCIATION, SUGGESTED A NEW STRATEGY:
WHY DON'T WE JUST TELL WOMEN WHAT THE PILL IS SUPPOSED TO DO?
SO, SOCIAL WORKERS BEGAN GOING DOOR-TO-DOOR IN THE SAN JUAN HOUSING PROJECTS.
THERE IS A PILL, THAT IF YOU TAKE IT EVERY DAY, CAN PREVENT PREGNANCY.
WOMEN SIGNED UP BY THE HUNDREDS.
HOWEVER, SOME INFORMATION WAS STILL WITHHELD: THEY WEREN'T TOLD THAT THIS WAS PART OF AN EXPERIMENTAL CLINICAL TRIAL.
DR. RICE-WRAY CONCLUDED THAT THE PILL WAS 100% EFFECTIVE AT PREVENTING PREGNANCY...
...BUT THE SIDE EFFECTS AND REACTIONS SHOULD HALT APPROVAL IN ITS CURRENT FORM AND DOSAGE:
10 TIMES THE AMOUNT OF HORMONES ACTUALLY NEEDED TO PREVENT PREGNANCY.
NOW AVAILABLE FROM G.D. SEARLE & CO.
100 TABLETS NO. 56
Enovid
10 mg.
SEARLE
AND YET, THE SAME FORMULATION THAT CAUSED ILLNESS IN ALMOST A FIFTH OF TRIAL PARTICIPANTS WAS
APPROVED BY THE FOOD AND DRUG ADMINISTRATION
FIRST AS A TREATMENT FOR MENSTRUAL DISORDERS IN 1957, THEN FOR USE AS A CONTRACEPTIVE IN 1960.
AS MANY AS 1,500 PUERTO RICAN WOMEN TOOK THAT DRUG OVER SEVERAL YEARS.
THREE WOMEN IN THE TRIALS DIED. NO AUTOPSIES WERE CONDUCTED, SO IT REMAINS UNCLEAR WHETHER THEIR DEATHS WERE LINKED TO THE DRUG OR NOT.
WHAT IS CLEAR IS THAT THE TRIALS WERE CONDUCTED WITHOUT THE KIND OF INFORMED CONSENT THAT IS NOW MANDATED FOR NEW DRUGS IN THE UNITED STATES.

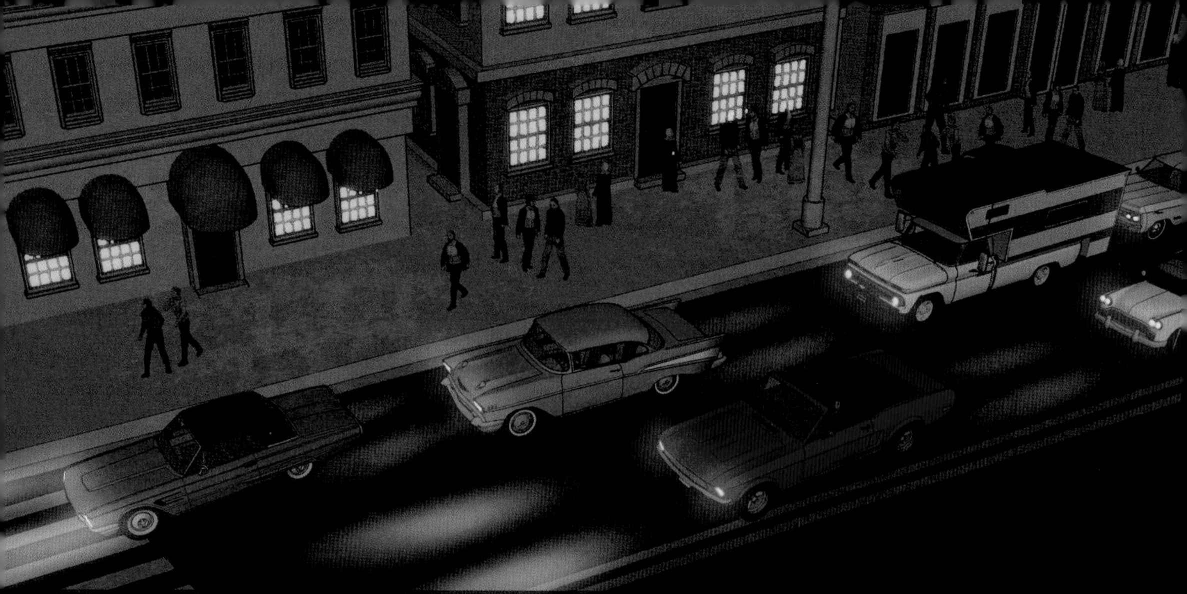

# "Breaking Bread"

Story By Tara Martinez · Artwork by Rod Espinosa

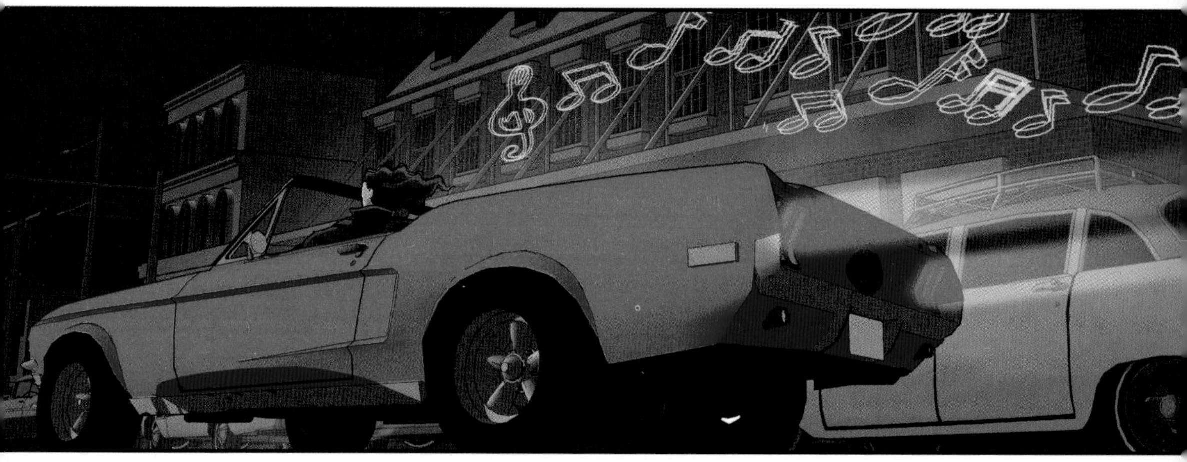

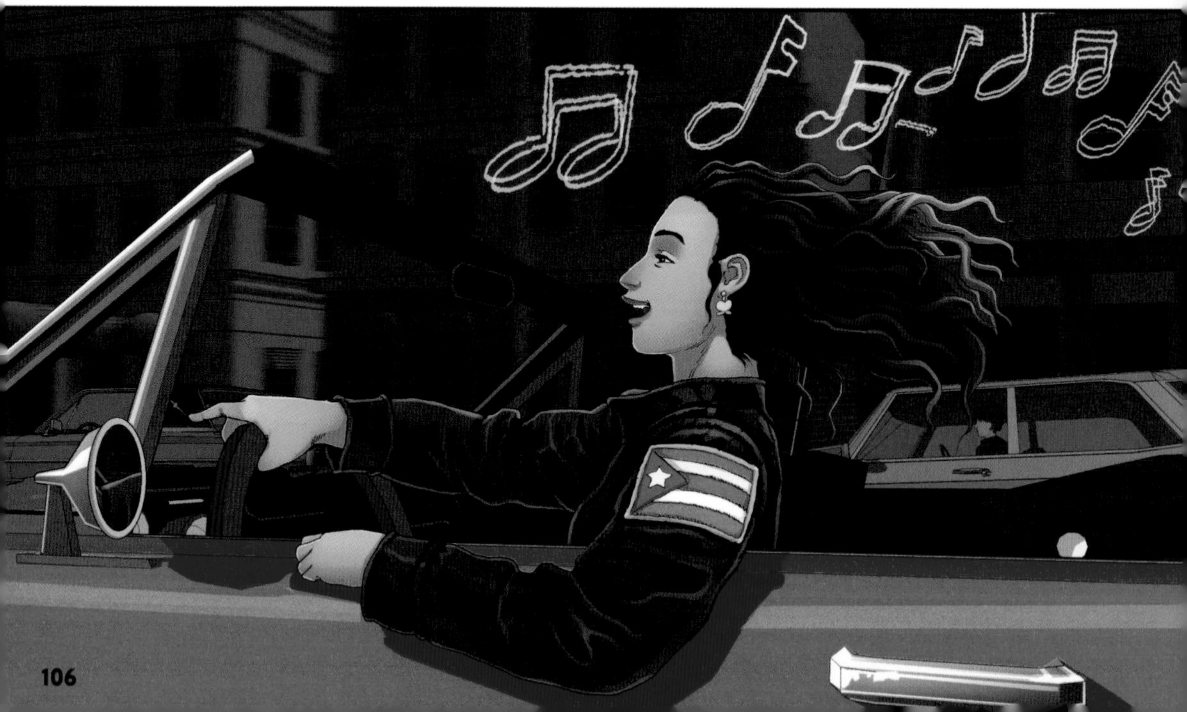

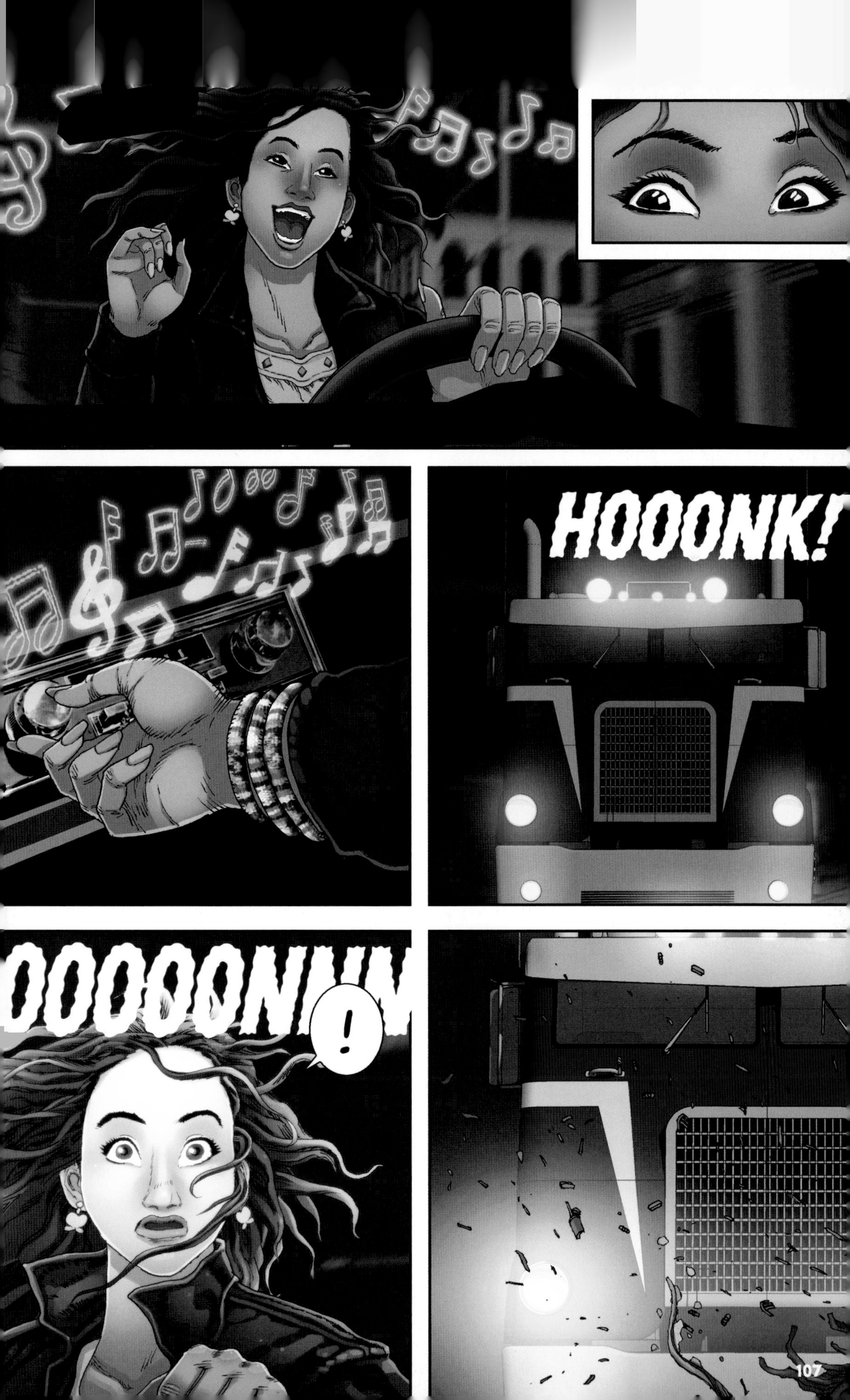
HOOONK!
OOOOONNN
!

LATER...

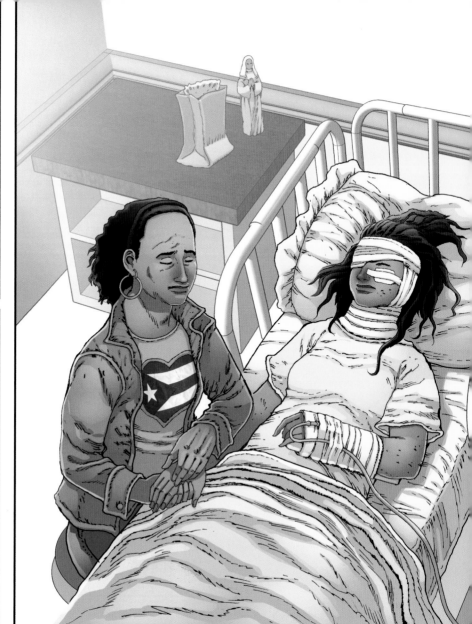

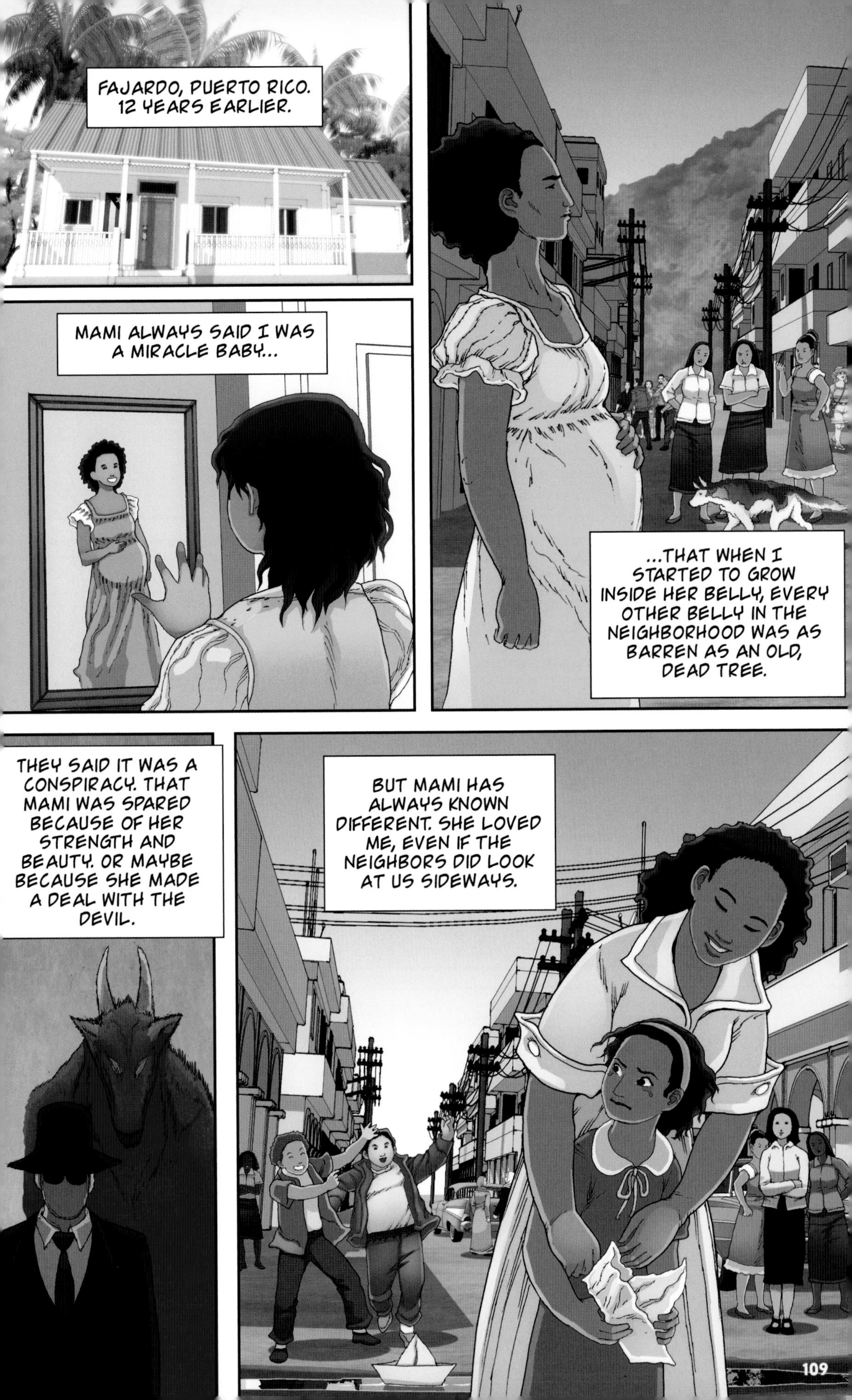
FAJARDO, PUERTO RICO. 12 YEARS EARLIER.
MAMI ALWAYS SAID I WAS A MIRACLE BABY...
...THAT WHEN I STARTED TO GROW INSIDE HER BELLY, EVERY OTHER BELLY IN THE NEIGHBORHOOD WAS AS BARREN AS AN OLD, DEAD TREE.
THEY SAID IT WAS A CONSPIRACY. THAT MAMI WAS SPARED BECAUSE OF HER STRENGTH AND BEAUTY. OR MAYBE BECAUSE SHE MADE A DEAL WITH THE DEVIL.
BUT MAMI HAS ALWAYS KNOWN DIFFERENT. SHE LOVED ME, EVEN IF THE NEIGHBORS DID LOOK AT US SIDEWAYS.

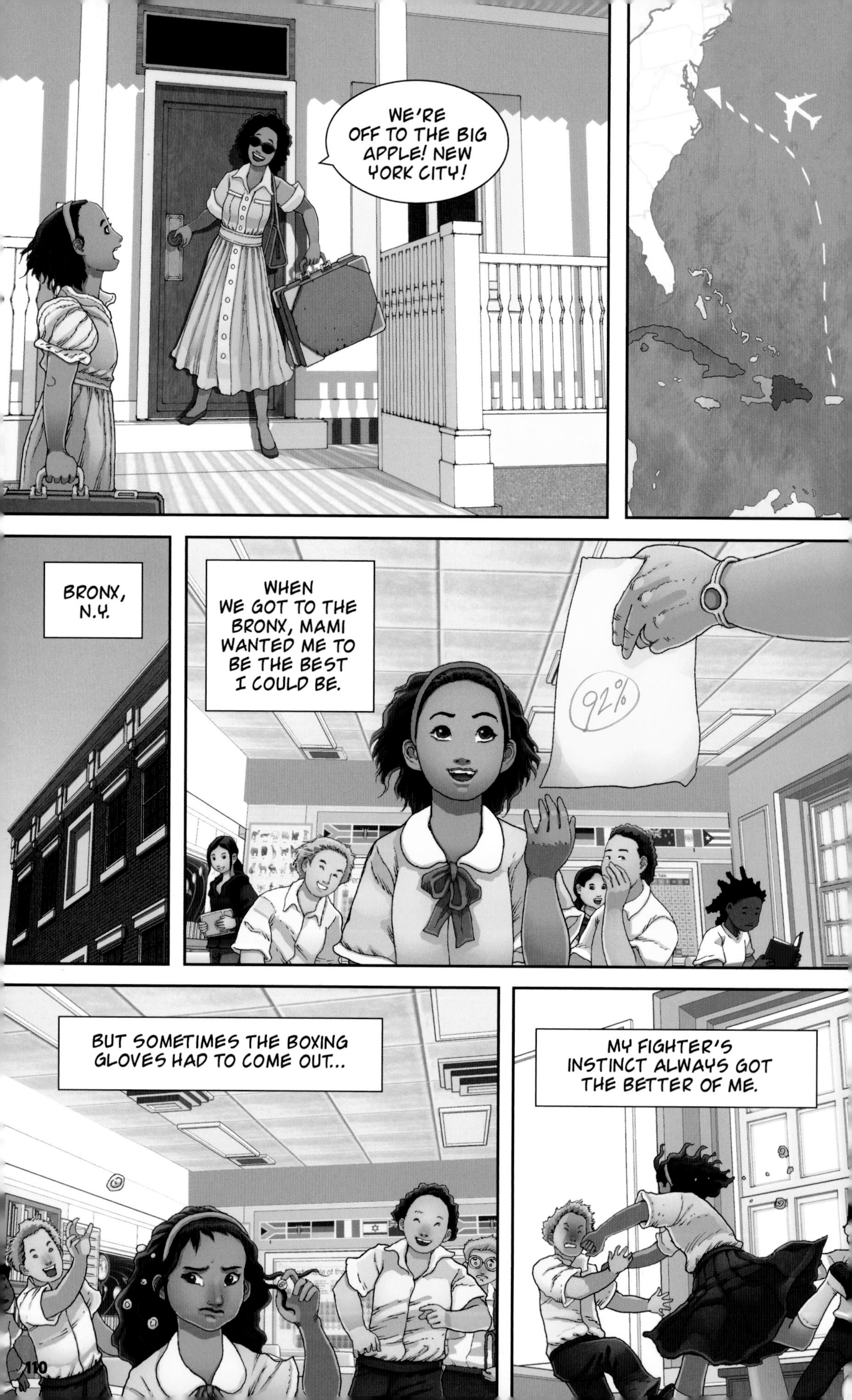
WE'RE OFF TO THE BIG APPLE! NEW YORK CITY!
BRONX, N.Y.
WHEN WE GOT TO THE BRONX, MAMI WANTED ME TO BE THE BEST I COULD BE.
92%
BUT SOMETIMES THE BOXING GLOVES HAD TO COME OUT...
MY FIGHTER'S INSTINCT ALWAYS GOT THE BETTER OF ME.

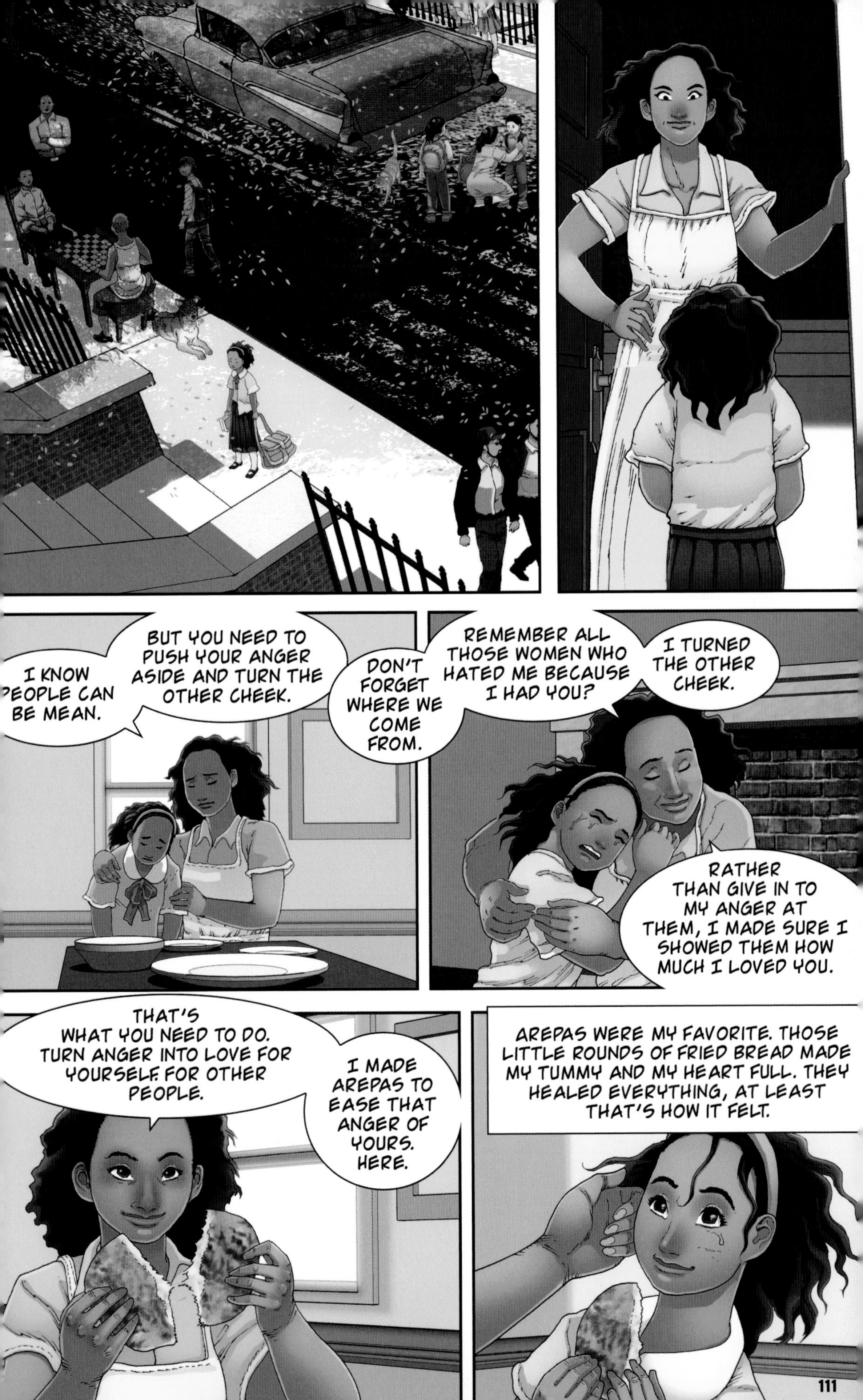
I KNOW PEOPLE CAN BE MEAN.
BUT YOU NEED TO PUSH YOUR ANGER ASIDE AND TURN THE OTHER CHEEK.
DON'T FORGET WHERE WE COME FROM.
REMEMBER ALL THOSE WOMEN WHO HATED ME BECAUSE I HAD YOU?
I TURNED THE OTHER CHEEK.
RATHER THAN GIVE IN TO MY ANGER AT THEM, I MADE SURE I SHOWED THEM HOW MUCH I LOVED YOU.
THAT'S WHAT YOU NEED TO DO. TURN ANGER INTO LOVE FOR YOURSELF. FOR OTHER PEOPLE.
I MADE AREPAS TO EASE THAT ANGER OF YOURS. HERE.
AREPAS WERE MY FAVORITE. THOSE LITTLE ROUNDS OF FRIED BREAD MADE MY TUMMY AND MY HEART FULL. THEY HEALED EVERYTHING, AT LEAST THAT'S HOW IT FELT.

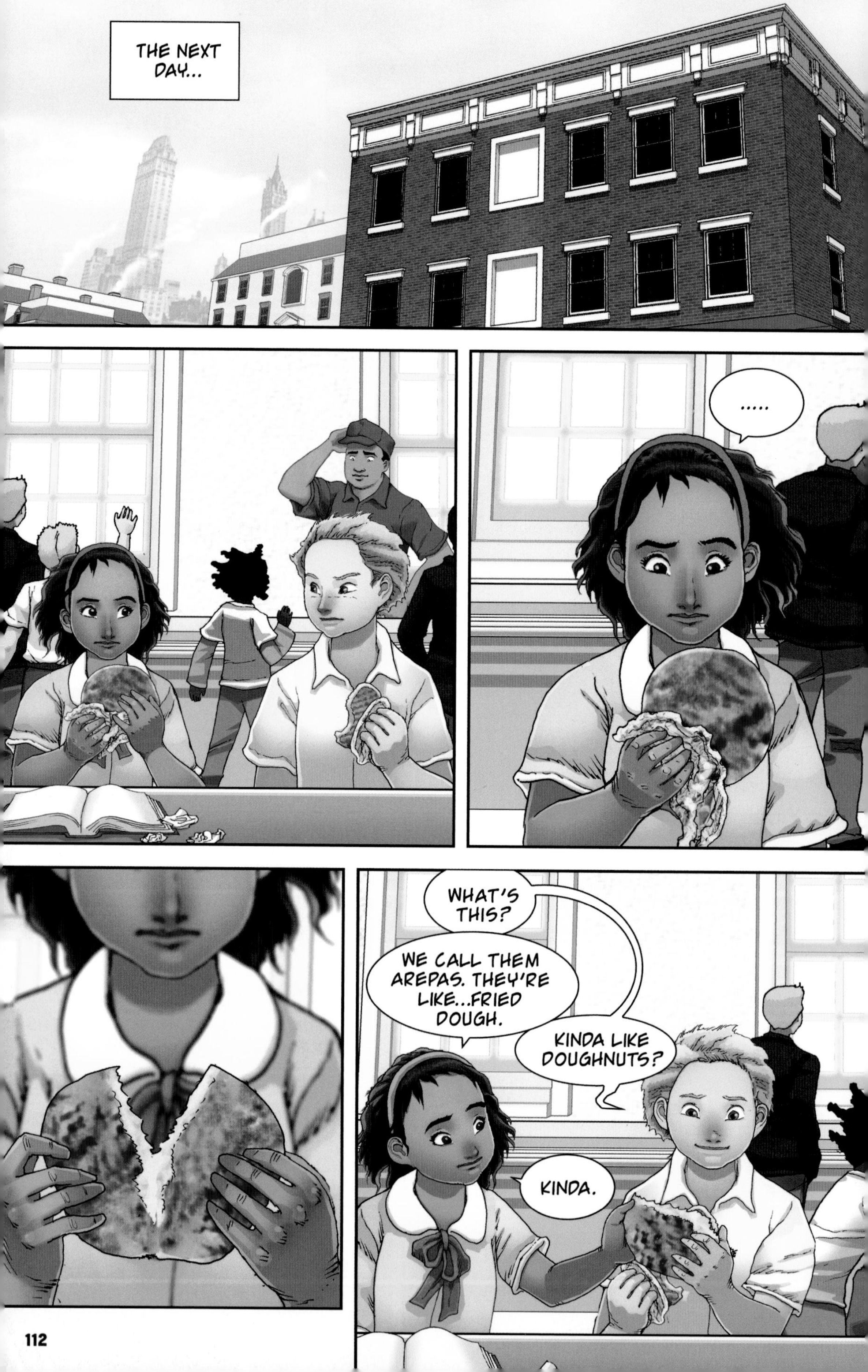
THE NEXT DAY...
.....
WHAT'S THIS?
WE CALL THEM AREPAS. THEY'RE LIKE...FRIED DOUGH.
KINDA LIKE DOUGHNUTS?
KINDA.

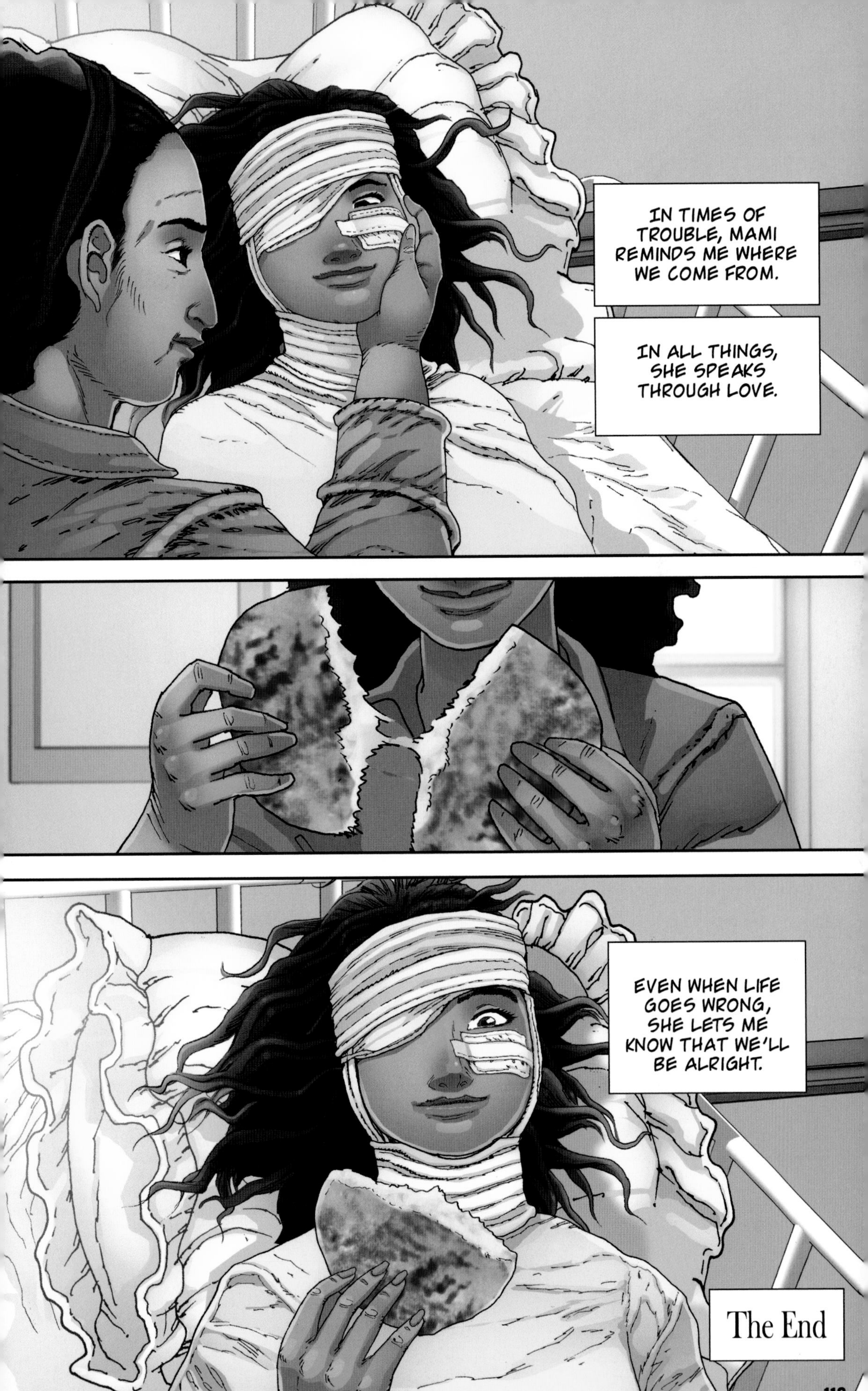
IN TIMES OF TROUBLE, MAMI REMINDS ME WHERE WE COME FROM.
IN ALL THINGS, SHE SPEAKS THROUGH LOVE.
EVEN WHEN LIFE GOES WRONG, SHE LETS ME KNOW THAT WE'LL BE ALRIGHT.
The End

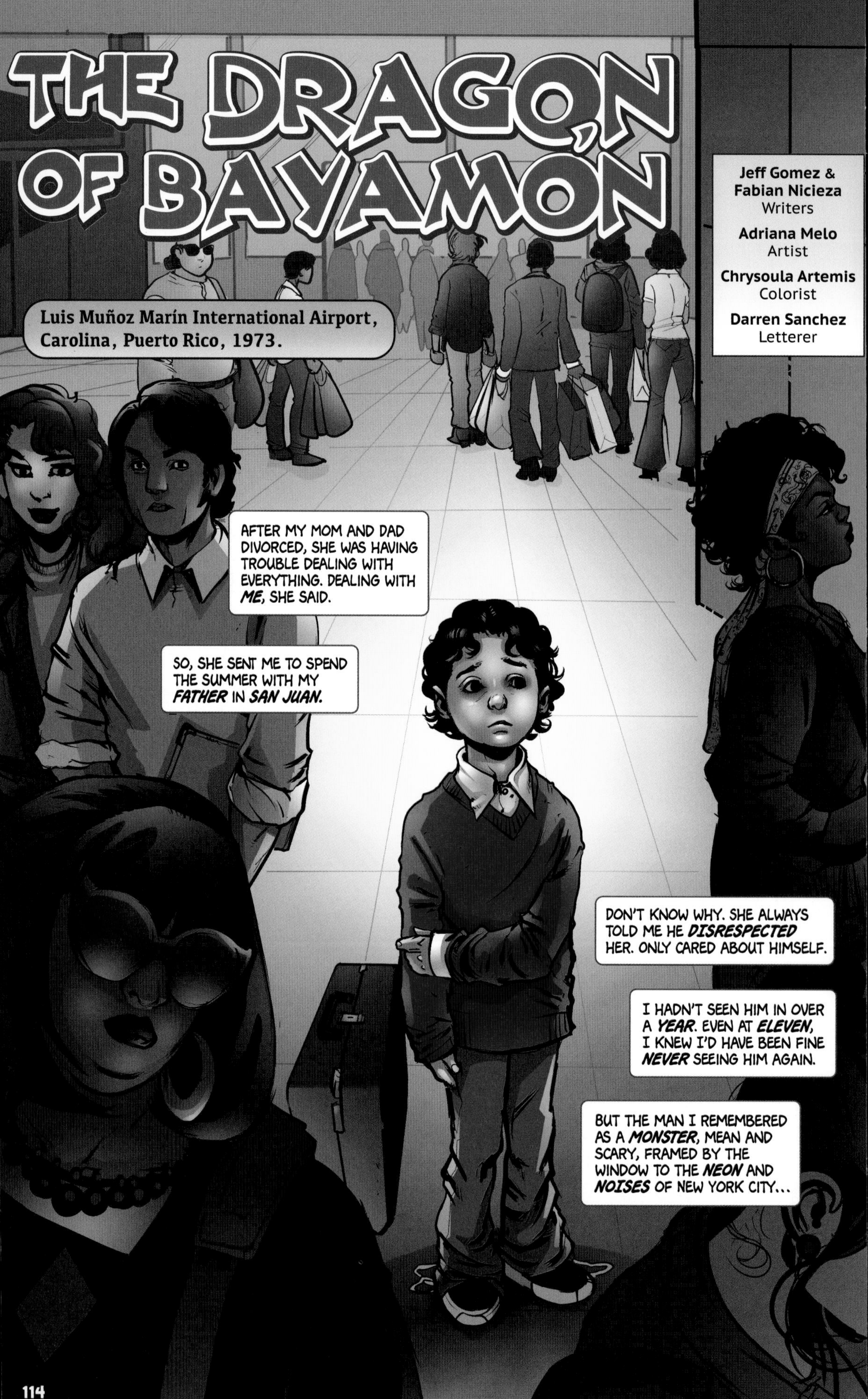
THE DRAGON OF BAYAMÓN
Jeff Gomez & Fabian Nicieza Writers
Adriana Melo Artist
Chrysoula Artemis Colorist
Darren Sanchez Letterer
Luis Muñoz Marín International Airport, Carolina, Puerto Rico, 1973.
AFTER MY MOM AND DAD DIVORCED, SHE WAS HAVING TROUBLE DEALING WITH EVERYTHING. DEALING WITH *ME*, SHE SAID.
SO, SHE SENT ME TO SPEND THE SUMMER WITH MY *FATHER* IN *SAN JUAN.*
DON'T KNOW WHY. SHE ALWAYS TOLD ME HE *DISRESPECTED* HER. ONLY CARED ABOUT HIMSELF.
I HADN'T SEEN HIM IN OVER A *YEAR*. EVEN AT *ELEVEN*, I KNEW I'D HAVE BEEN FINE *NEVER* SEEING HIM AGAIN.
BUT THE MAN I REMEMBERED AS A *MONSTER*, MEAN AND SCARY, FRAMED BY THE WINDOW TO THE *NEON* AND *NOISES* OF NEW YORK CITY...

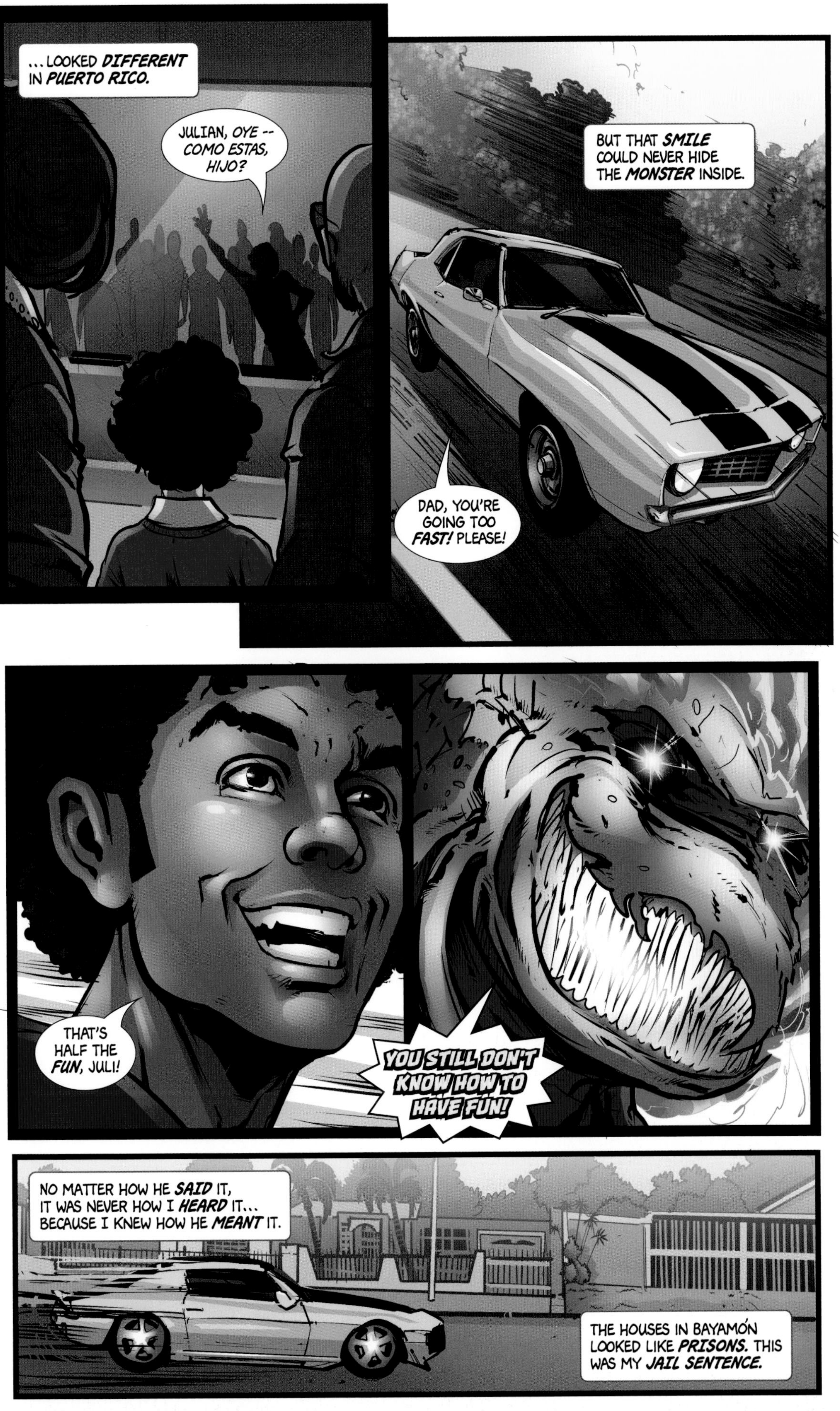

...LOOKED DIFFERENT IN PUERTO RICO.
JULIAN, OYE -- COMO ESTAS, HIJO?
BUT THAT SMILE COULD NEVER HIDE THE MONSTER INSIDE.
DAD, YOU'RE GOING TOO FAST! PLEASE!
THAT'S HALF THE FUN, JULI!
YOU STILL DON'T KNOW HOW TO HAVE FUN!
NO MATTER HOW HE SAID IT, IT WAS NEVER HOW I HEARD IT... BECAUSE I KNEW HOW HE MEANT IT.
THE HOUSES IN BAYAMÓN LOOKED LIKE PRISONS. THIS WAS MY JAIL SENTENCE.

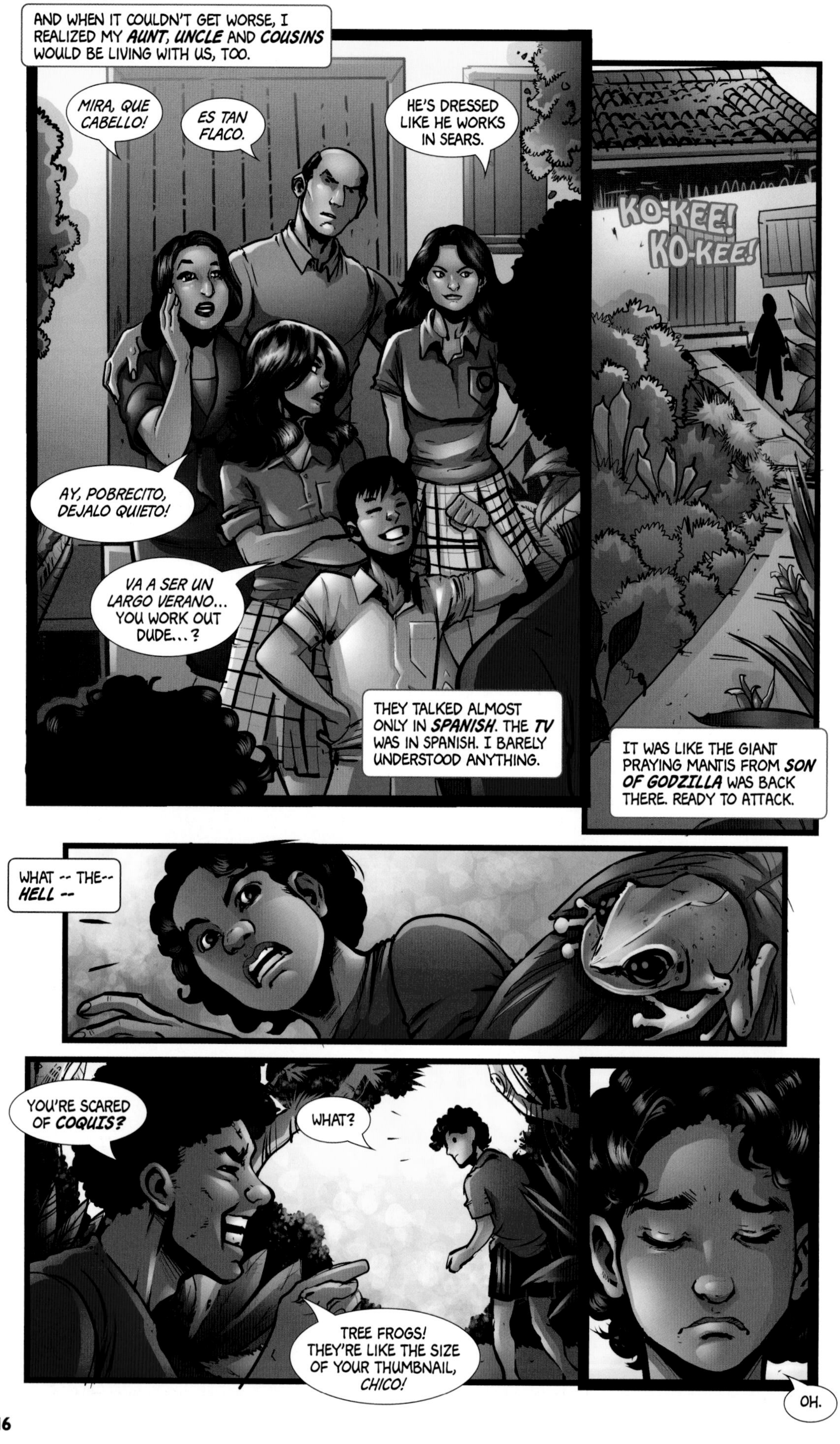
AND WHEN IT COULDN'T GET WORSE, I REALIZED MY AUNT, UNCLE AND COUSINS WOULD BE LIVING WITH US, TOO.
MIRA, QUE CABELLO!
ES TAN FLACO.
HE'S DRESSED LIKE HE WORKS IN SEARS.
AY, POBRECITO, DEJALO QUIETO!
VA A SER UN LARGO VERANO... YOU WORK OUT DUDE...?
THEY TALKED ALMOST ONLY IN SPANISH. THE TV WAS IN SPANISH. I BARELY UNDERSTOOD ANYTHING.
KO-KEE! KO-KEE!
IT WAS LIKE THE GIANT PRAYING MANTIS FROM SON OF GODZILLA WAS BACK THERE. READY TO ATTACK.
WHAT -- THE-- HELL --
YOU'RE SCARED OF COQUIS?
WHAT?
TREE FROGS! THEY'RE LIKE THE SIZE OF YOUR THUMBNAIL, CHICO!
OH.

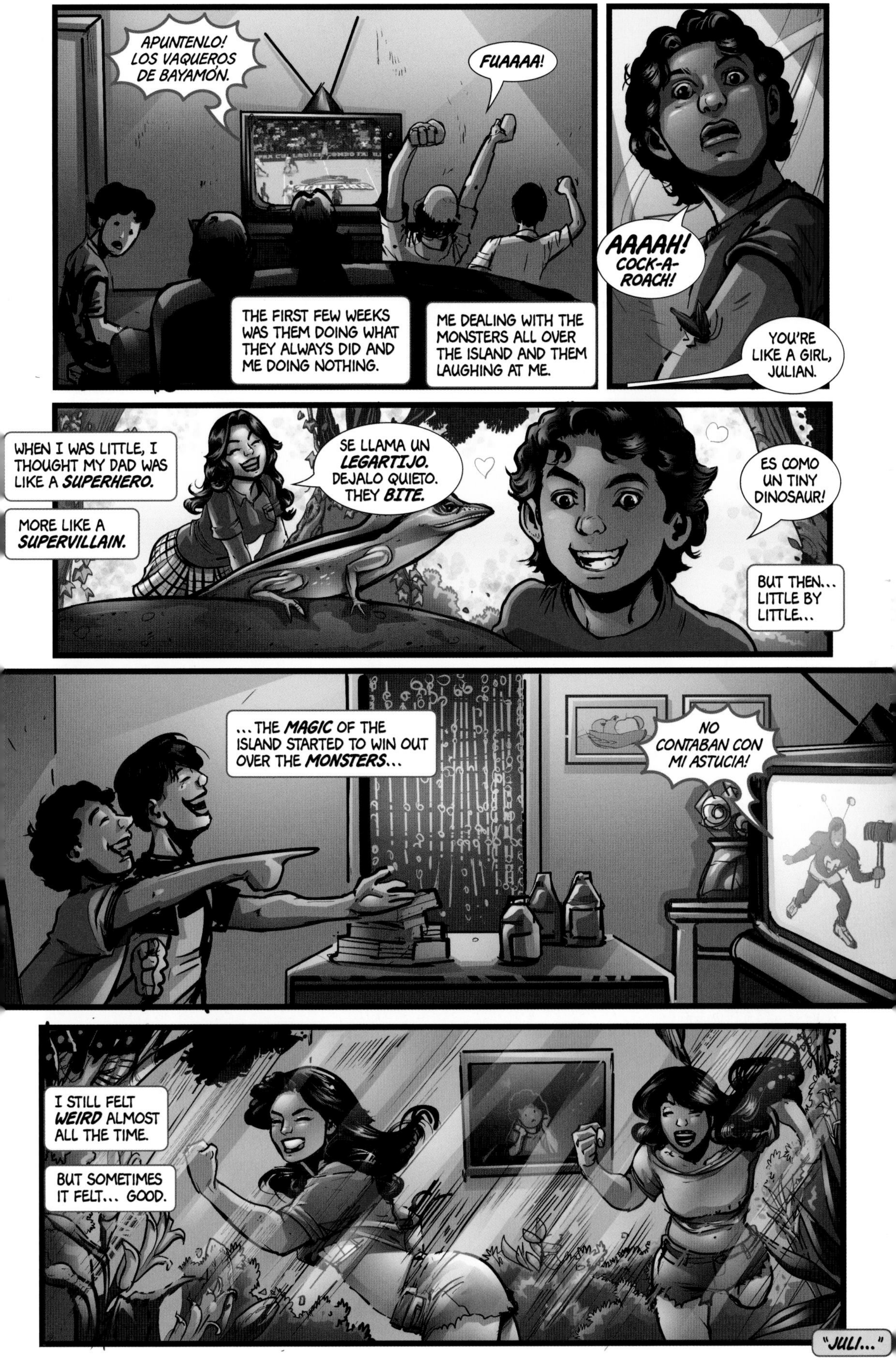

APUNTENLO! LOS VAQUEROS DE BAYAMÓN.
FUAAAA!
THE FIRST FEW WEEKS WAS THEM DOING WHAT THEY ALWAYS DID AND ME DOING NOTHING.
ME DEALING WITH THE MONSTERS ALL OVER THE ISLAND AND THEM LAUGHING AT ME.
AAAAH! COCK-A-ROACH!
YOU'RE LIKE A GIRL, JULIAN.
WHEN I WAS LITTLE, I THOUGHT MY DAD WAS LIKE A SUPERHERO.
MORE LIKE A SUPERVILLAIN.
SE LLAMA UN LEGARTIJO. DEJALO QUIETO. THEY BITE.
ES COMO UN TINY DINOSAUR!
BUT THEN... LITTLE BY LITTLE...
...THE MAGIC OF THE ISLAND STARTED TO WIN OUT OVER THE MONSTERS...
NO CONTABAN CON MI ASTUCIA!
I STILL FELT WEIRD ALMOST ALL THE TIME.
BUT SOMETIMES IT FELT... GOOD.
"JULI..."

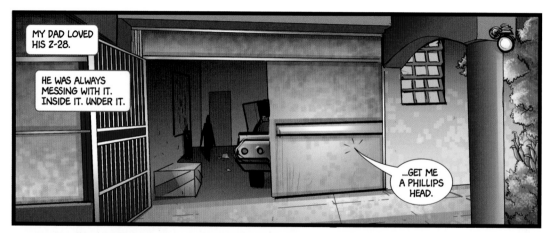

MY DAD LOVED HIS Z-28.

HE WAS ALWAYS MESSING WITH IT. INSIDE IT. UNDER IT.

...GET ME A PHILLIPS HEAD.

TO ME, IT MIGHT AS WELL HAVE BEEN *ALGEBRA.*

JULI, C'MON!

YOU GOT NO IDEA WHICH IS THE PHILLIPS. ISN'T ANYONE TEACHING YOU ANYTHING...?

WELL, HOW AM I SUPPOSED TO KNOW?

I SHOULDN'T HAVE TALKED BACK. HE HAD HIT ME BEFORE FOR LESS.

SEE THIS? THERE'S LIKE AN *X* ON THE END. FITS INTO THOSE SCREWS WITH X-HEADS. PHILLIPS. SABE?

SI.

COME WITH ME TO THE PHARMACY.

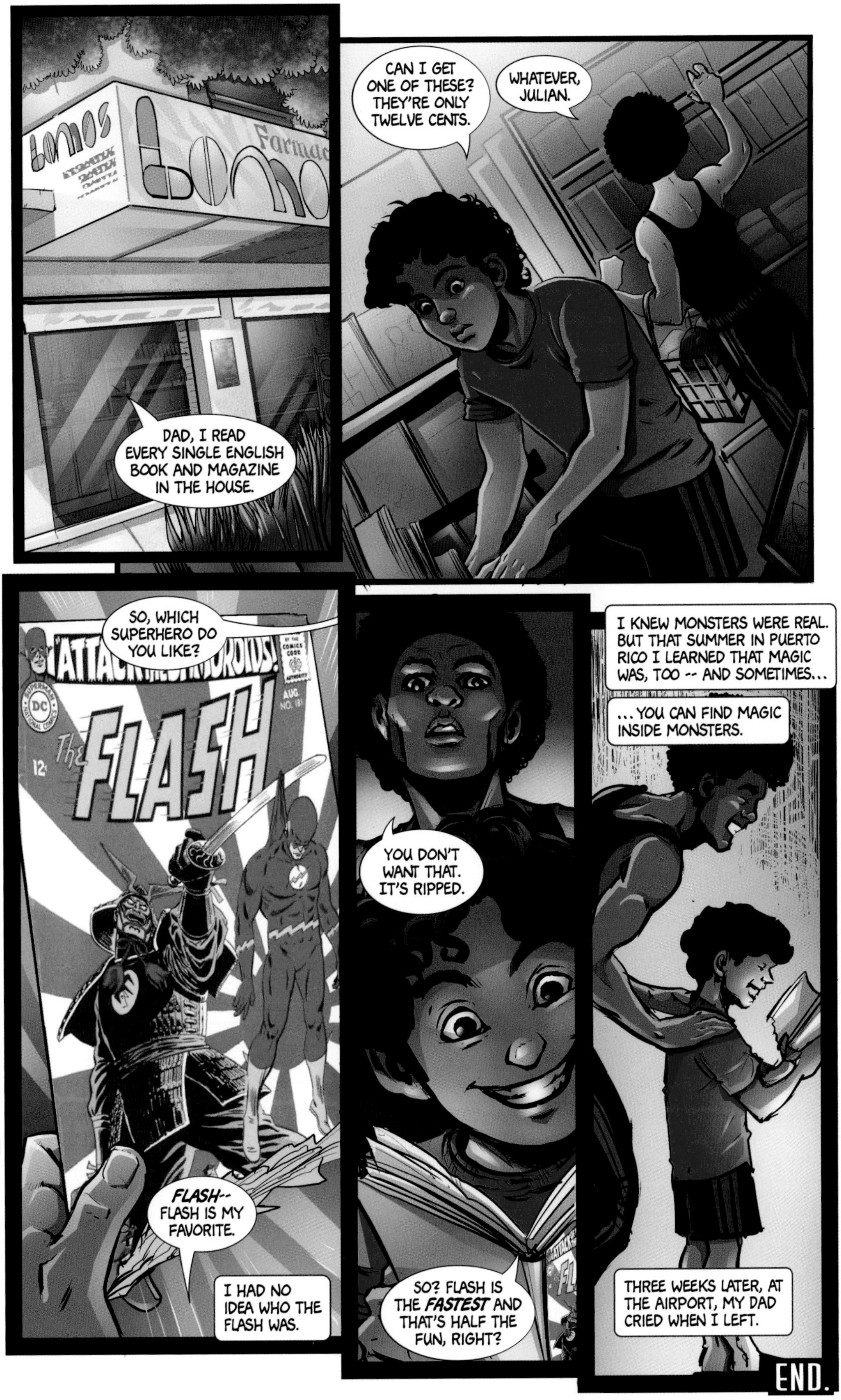
DAD, I READ EVERY SINGLE ENGLISH BOOK AND MAGAZINE IN THE HOUSE.
CAN I GET ONE OF THESE? THEY'RE ONLY TWELVE CENTS.
WHATEVER, JULIAN.
SO, WHICH SUPERHERO DO YOU LIKE?
The FLASH
FLASH-- FLASH IS MY FAVORITE.
I HAD NO IDEA WHO THE FLASH WAS.
YOU DON'T WANT THAT. IT'S RIPPED.
SO? FLASH IS THE FASTEST AND THAT'S HALF THE FUN, RIGHT?
I KNEW MONSTERS WERE REAL. BUT THAT SUMMER IN PUERTO RICO I LEARNED THAT MAGIC WAS, TOO -- AND SOMETIMES...
...YOU CAN FIND MAGIC INSIDE MONSTERS.
THREE WEEKS LATER, AT THE AIRPORT, MY DAD CRIED WHEN I LEFT.
END.

# On Traditions & Being Homesick

BY- JESENIA SANTANA

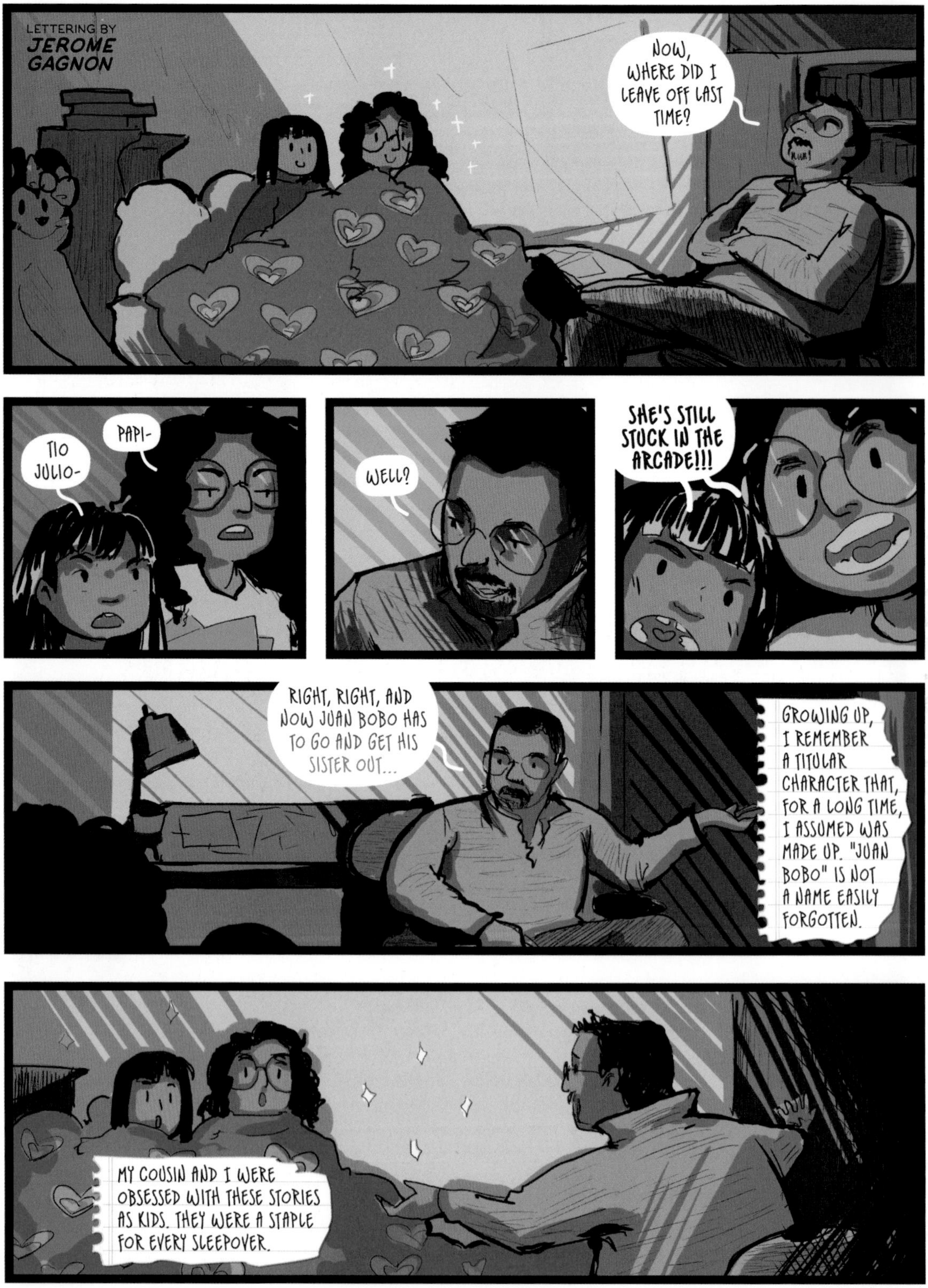
LETTERING BY JEROME GAGNON
NOW, WHERE DID I LEAVE OFF LAST TIME?
TIO JULIO-
PAPI-
WELL?
SHE'S STILL STUCK IN THE ARCADE!!!
RIGHT, RIGHT, AND NOW JUAN BOBO HAS TO GO AND GET HIS SISTER OUT...
GROWING UP, I REMEMBER A TITULAR CHARACTER THAT, FOR A LONG TIME, I ASSUMED WAS MADE UP. "JUAN BOBO" IS NOT A NAME EASILY FORGOTTEN.
MY COUSIN AND I WERE OBSESSED WITH THESE STORIES AS KIDS. THEY WERE A STAPLE FOR EVERY SLEEPOVER.

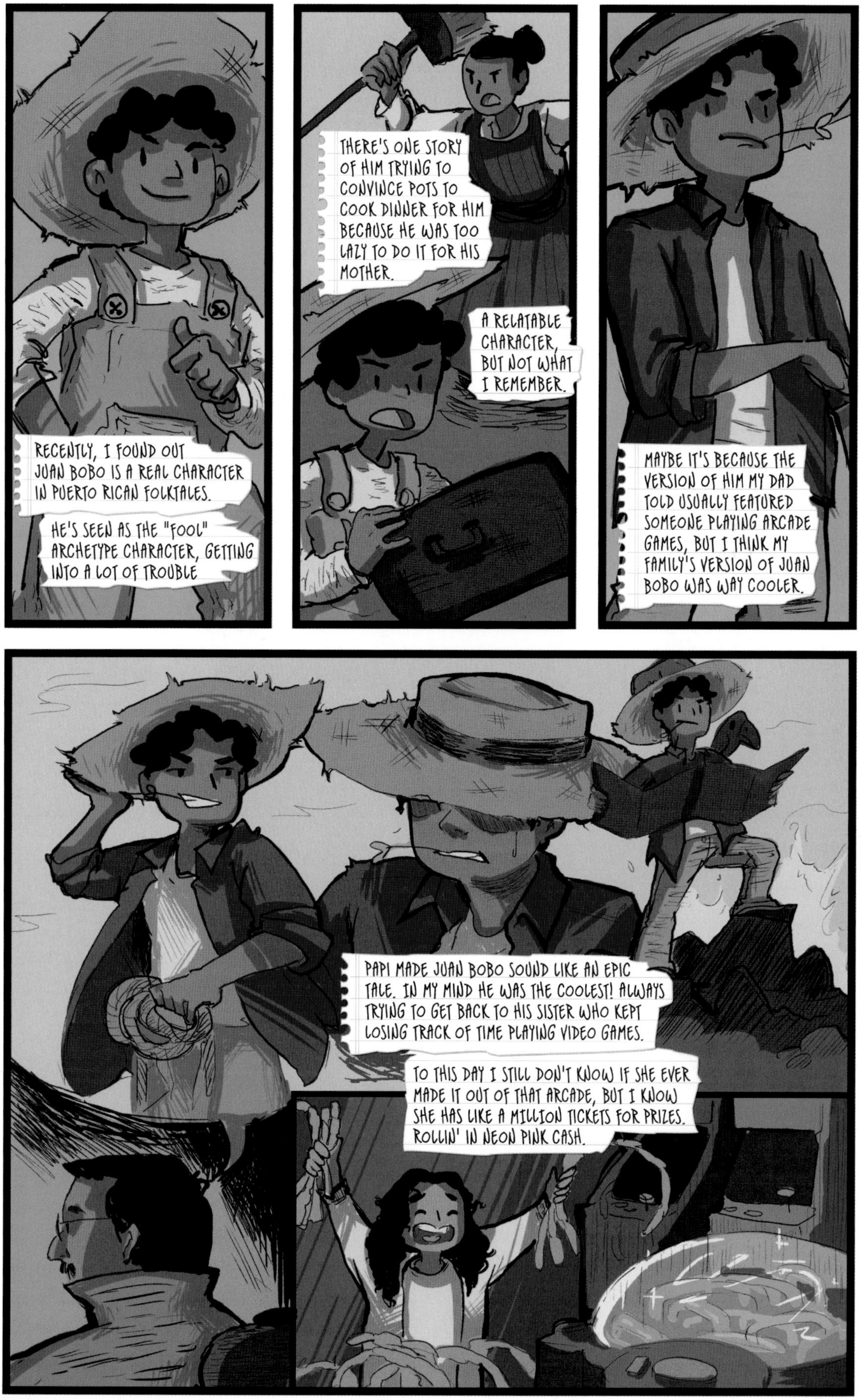
RECENTLY, I FOUND OUT JUAN BOBO IS A REAL CHARACTER IN PUERTO RICAN FOLKTALES.
HE'S SEEN AS THE "FOOL" ARCHETYPE CHARACTER, GETTING INTO A LOT OF TROUBLE
THERE'S ONE STORY OF HIM TRYING TO CONVINCE POTS TO COOK DINNER FOR HIM BECAUSE HE WAS TOO LAZY TO DO IT FOR HIS MOTHER.
A RELATABLE CHARACTER, BUT NOT WHAT I REMEMBER.
MAYBE IT'S BECAUSE THE VERSION OF HIM MY DAD TOLD USUALLY FEATURED SOMEONE PLAYING ARCADE GAMES, BUT I THINK MY FAMILY'S VERSION OF JUAN BOBO WAS WAY COOLER.
PAPI MADE JUAN BOBO SOUND LIKE AN EPIC TALE. IN MY MIND HE WAS THE COOLEST! ALWAYS TRYING TO GET BACK TO HIS SISTER WHO KEPT LOSING TRACK OF TIME PLAYING VIDEO GAMES.
TO THIS DAY I STILL DON'T KNOW IF SHE EVER MADE IT OUT OF THAT ARCADE, BUT I KNOW SHE HAS LIKE A MILLION TICKETS FOR PRIZES. ROLLIN' IN NEON PINK CASH.

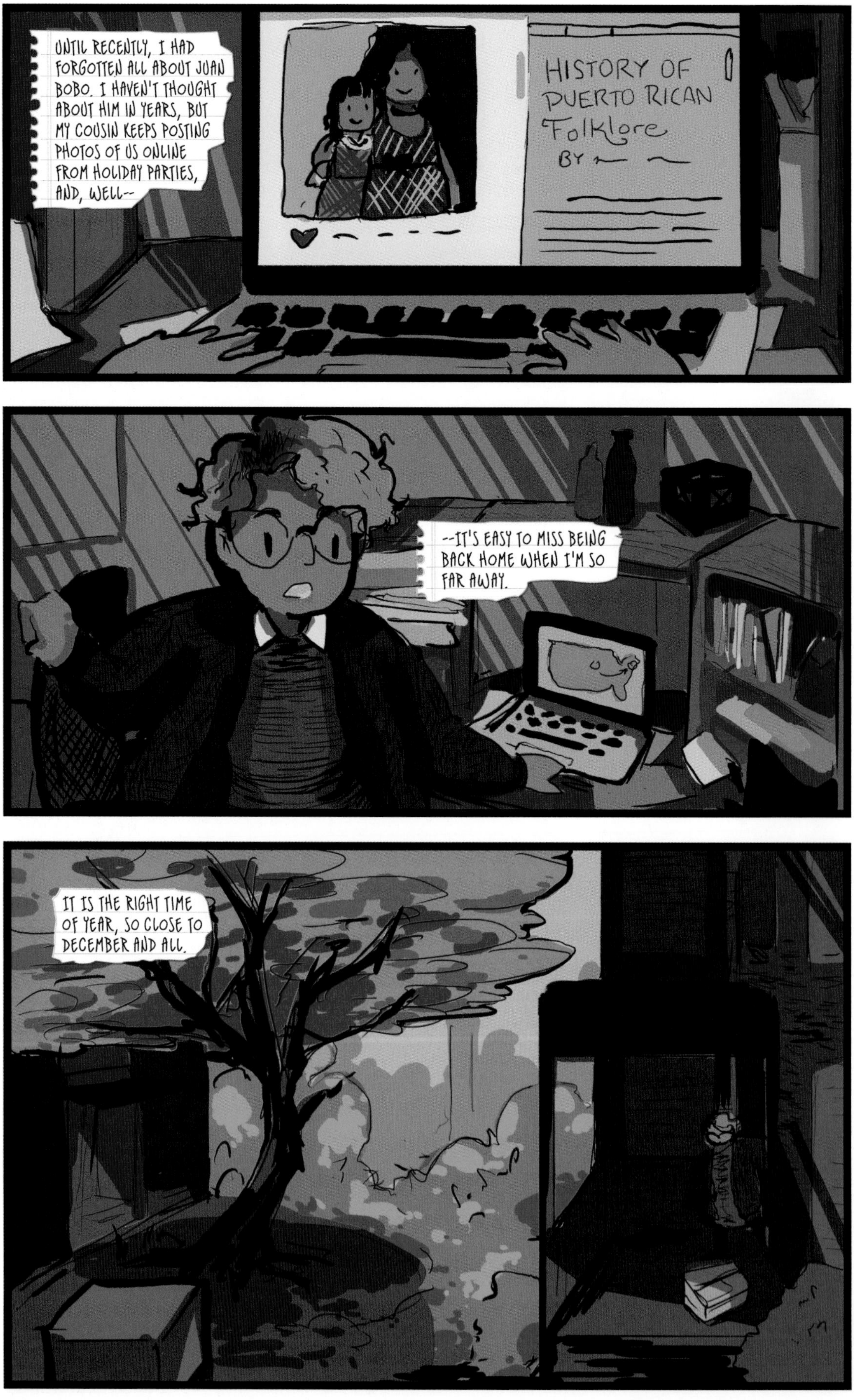
UNTIL RECENTLY, I HAD FORGOTTEN ALL ABOUT JUAN BOBO. I HAVEN'T THOUGHT ABOUT HIM IN YEARS, BUT MY COUSIN KEEPS POSTING PHOTOS OF US ONLINE FROM HOLIDAY PARTIES, AND, WELL--
HISTORY OF PUERTO RICAN Folklore
BY
--IT'S EASY TO MISS BEING BACK HOME WHEN I'M SO FAR AWAY.
IT IS THE RIGHT TIME OF YEAR, SO CLOSE TO DECEMBER AND ALL.

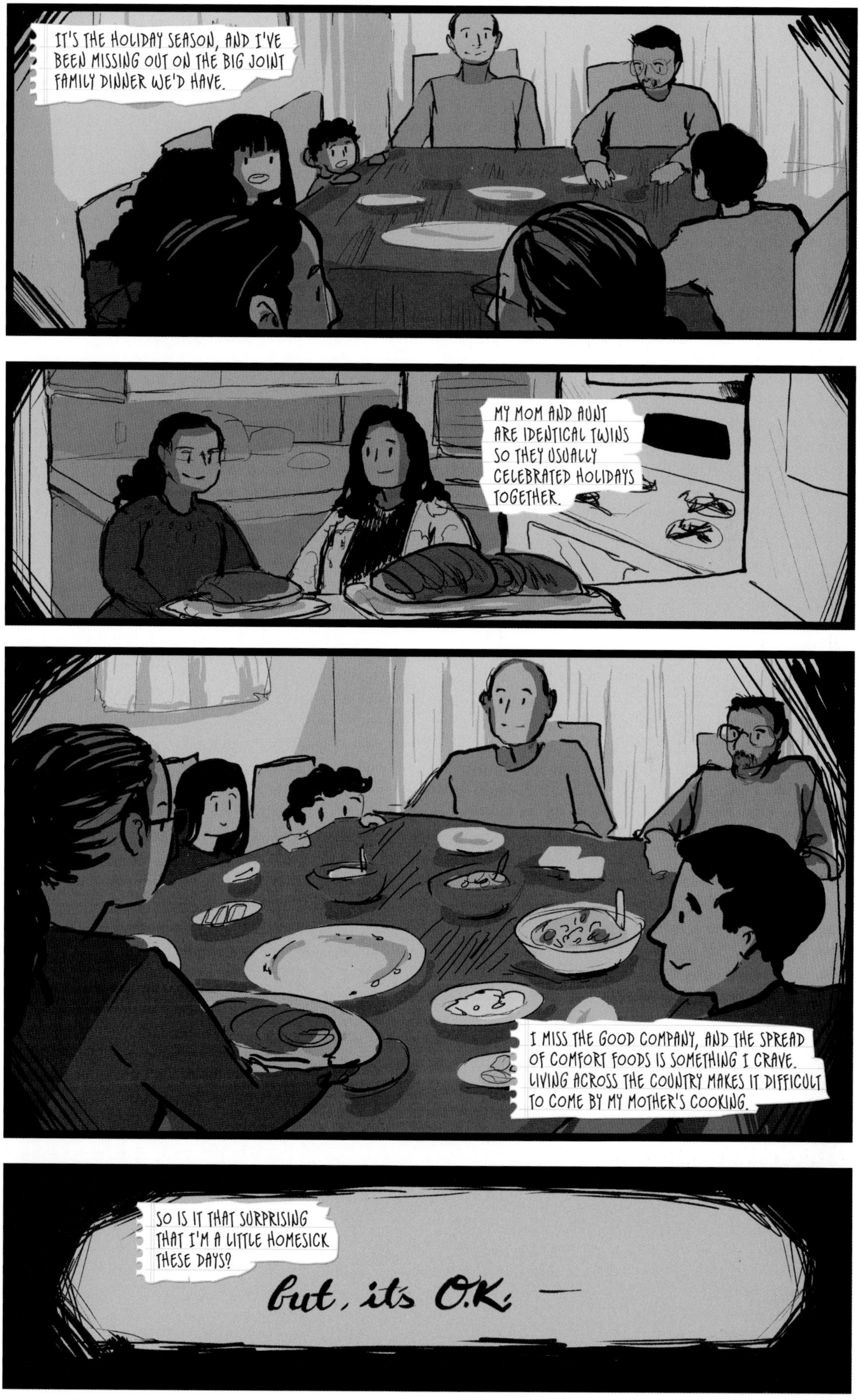
IT'S THE HOLIDAY SEASON, AND I'VE BEEN MISSING OUT ON THE BIG JOINT FAMILY DINNER WE'D HAVE.
MY MOM AND AUNT ARE IDENTICAL TWINS SO THEY USUALLY CELEBRATED HOLIDAYS TOGETHER.
I MISS THE GOOD COMPANY, AND THE SPREAD OF COMFORT FOODS IS SOMETHING I CRAVE. LIVING ACROSS THE COUNTRY MAKES IT DIFFICULT TO COME BY MY MOTHER'S COOKING.
SO IS IT THAT SURPRISING THAT I'M A LITTLE HOMESICK THESE DAYS?
but, it's O.K. —

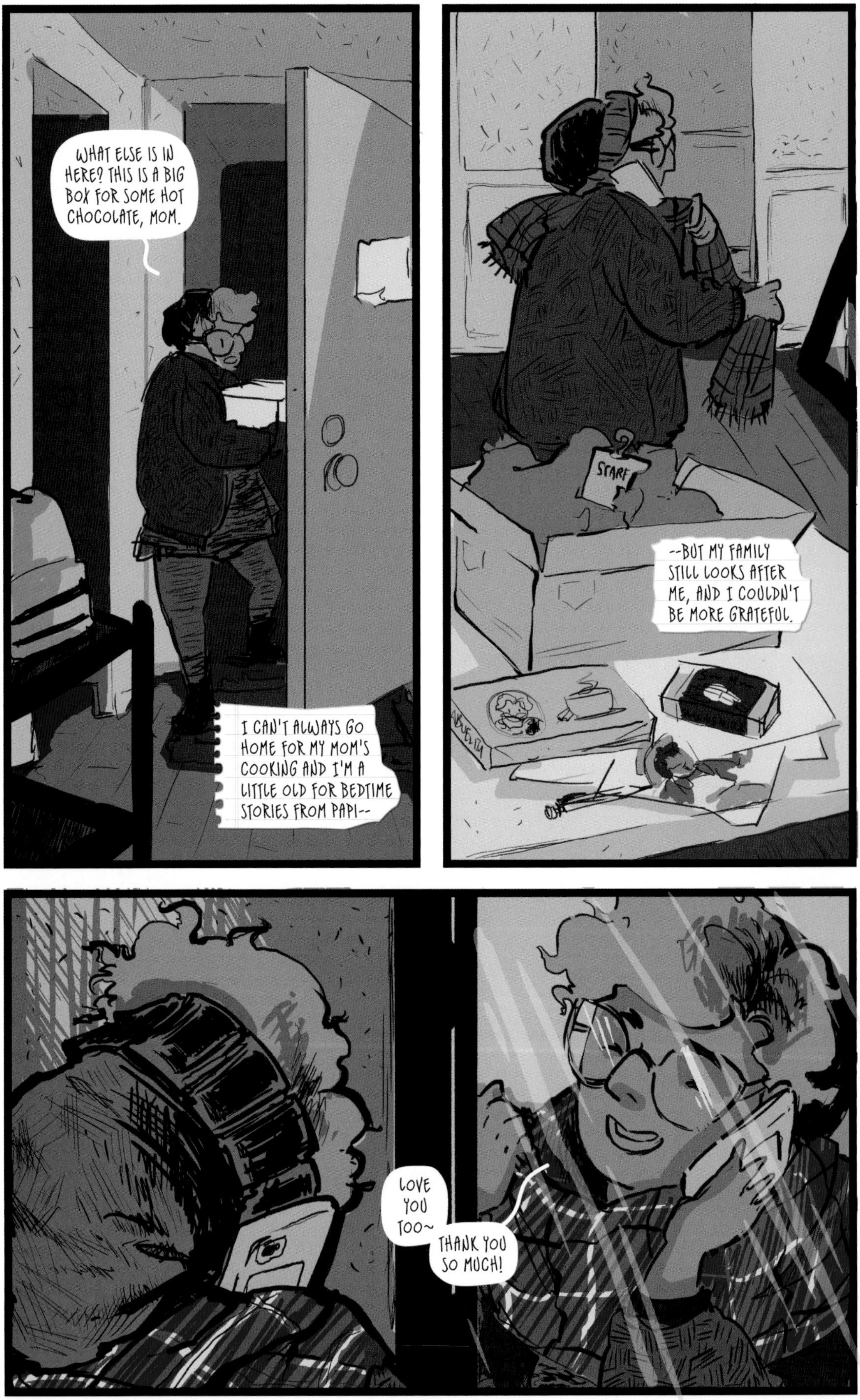
WHAT ELSE IS IN HERE? THIS IS A BIG BOX FOR SOME HOT CHOCOLATE, MOM.
I CAN'T ALWAYS GO HOME FOR MY MOM'S COOKING AND I'M A LITTLE OLD FOR BEDTIME STORIES FROM PAPI--
SCARF
--BUT MY FAMILY STILL LOOKS AFTER ME, AND I COULDN'T BE MORE GRATEFUL.
LOVE YOU TOO~
THANK YOU SO MUCH!

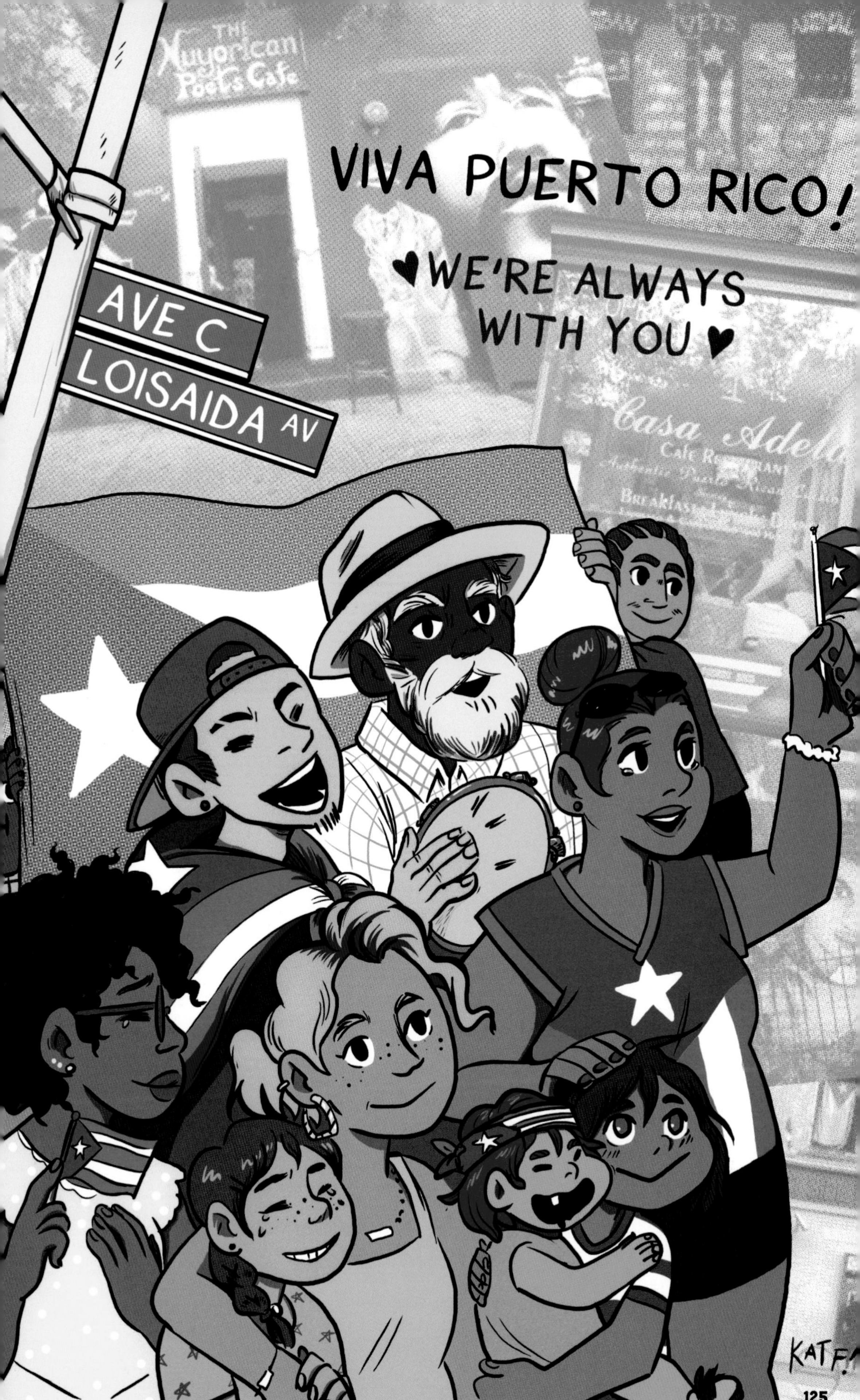
THE Nuyorican Poets Cafe
VIVA PUERTO RICO!
♥WE'RE ALWAYS WITH YOU♥
AVE C
LOISAIDA AV
Casa Adel
Cafe Restaurant
Breakfast
KAT F.

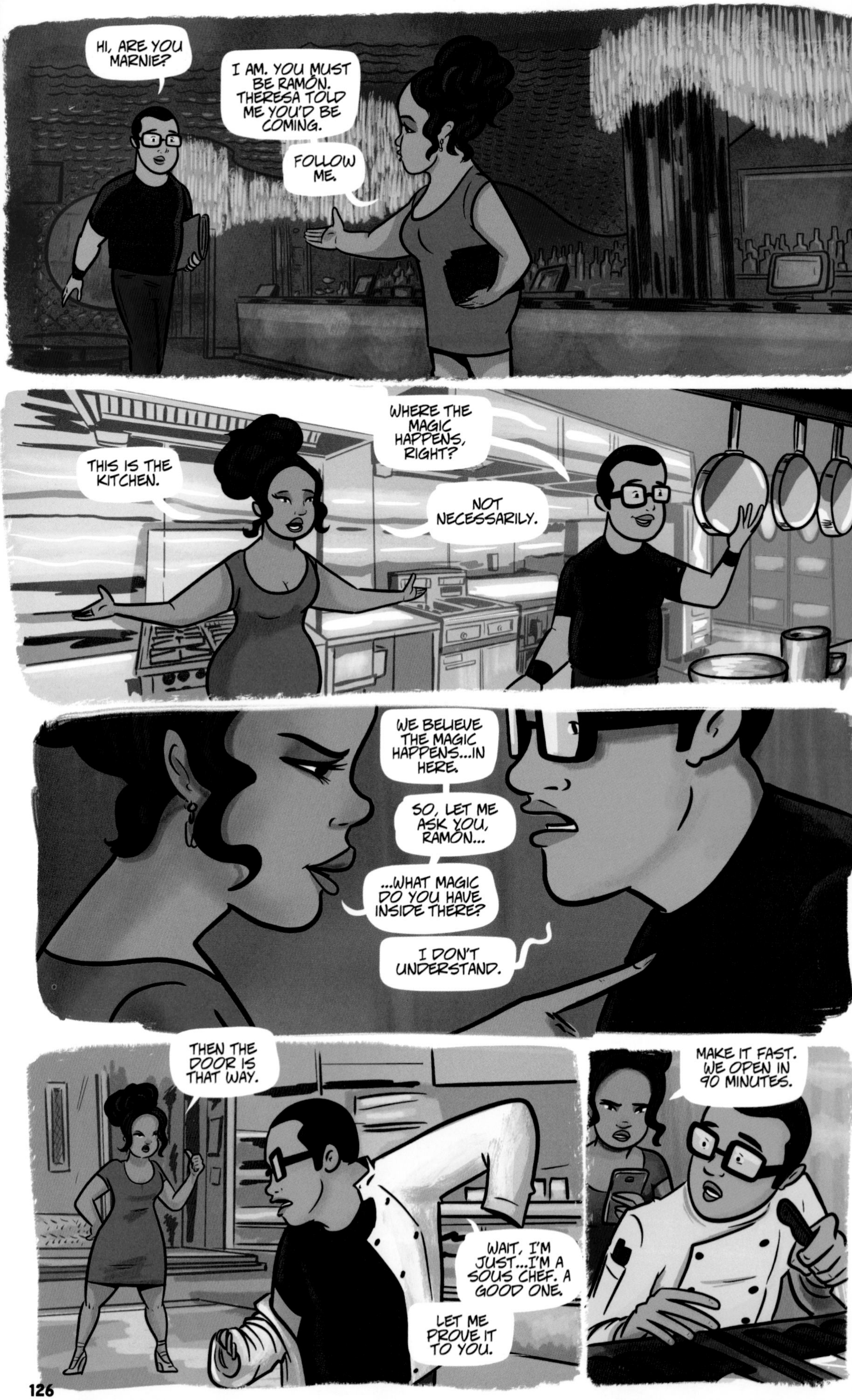
HI, ARE YOU MARNIE?
I AM. YOU MUST BE RAMÓN. THERESA TOLD ME YOU'D BE COMING.
FOLLOW ME.
THIS IS THE KITCHEN.
WHERE THE MAGIC HAPPENS, RIGHT?
NOT NECESSARILY.
WE BELIEVE THE MAGIC HAPPENS...IN HERE.
SO, LET ME ASK YOU, RAMÓN...
...WHAT MAGIC DO YOU HAVE INSIDE THERE?
I DON'T UNDERSTAND.
THEN THE DOOR IS THAT WAY.
WAIT, I'M JUST...I'M A SOUS CHEF. A GOOD ONE.
LET ME PROVE IT TO YOU.
MAKE IT FAST. WE OPEN IN 90 MINUTES.

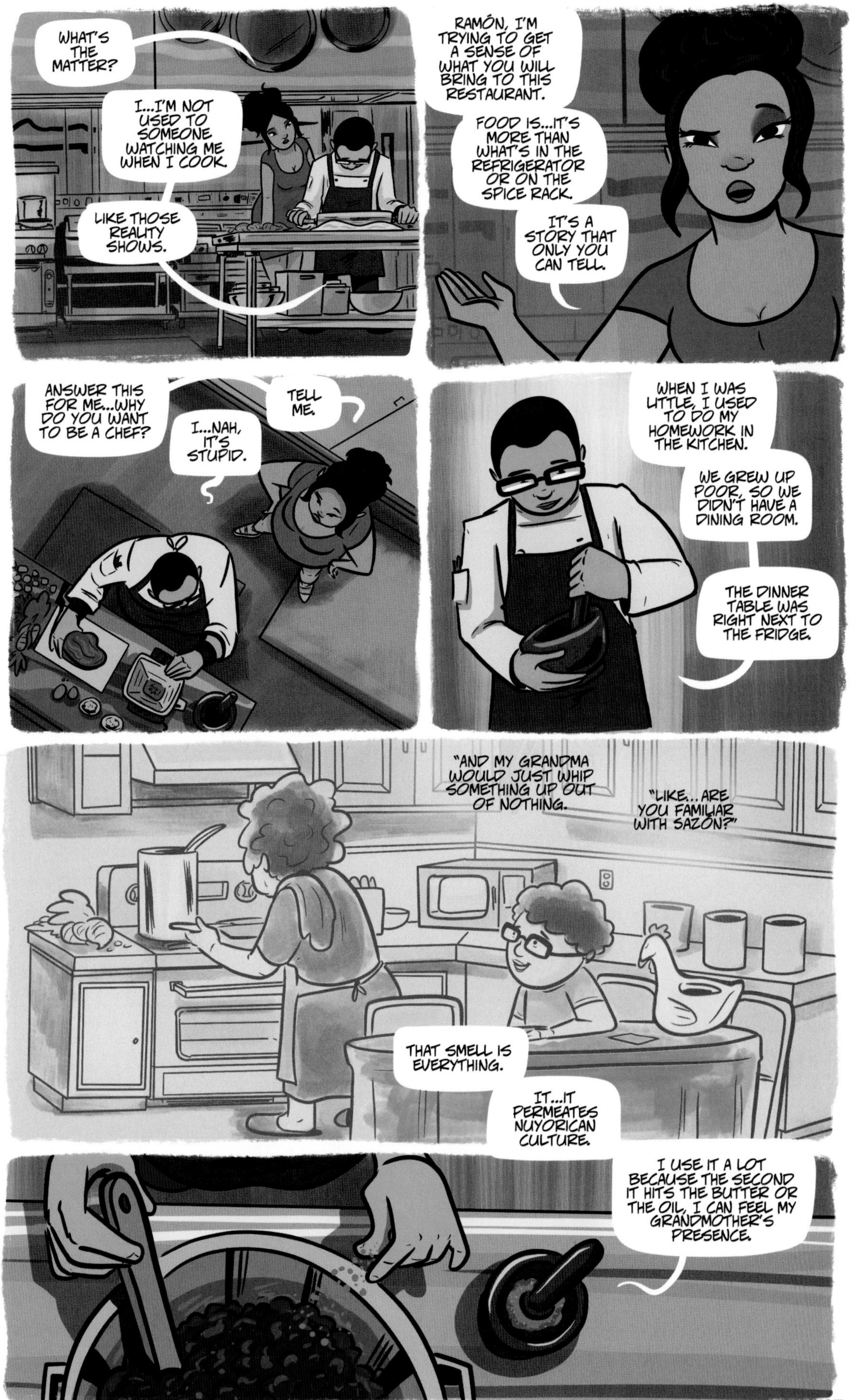
WHAT'S THE MATTER?
I...I'M NOT USED TO SOMEONE WATCHING ME WHEN I COOK.
LIKE THOSE REALITY SHOWS.
RAMÓN, I'M TRYING TO GET A SENSE OF WHAT YOU WILL BRING TO THIS RESTAURANT.
FOOD IS...IT'S MORE THAN WHAT'S IN THE REFRIGERATOR OR ON THE SPICE RACK.
IT'S A STORY THAT ONLY YOU CAN TELL.
ANSWER THIS FOR ME...WHY DO YOU WANT TO BE A CHEF?
I...NAH, IT'S STUPID.
TELL ME.
WHEN I WAS LITTLE, I USED TO DO MY HOMEWORK IN THE KITCHEN.
WE GREW UP POOR, SO WE DIDN'T HAVE A DINING ROOM.
THE DINNER TABLE WAS RIGHT NEXT TO THE FRIDGE.
"AND MY GRANDMA WOULD JUST WHIP SOMETHING UP OUT OF NOTHING.
"LIKE... ARE YOU FAMILIAR WITH SAZÓN?"
THAT SMELL IS EVERYTHING.
IT...IT PERMEATES NUYORICAN CULTURE.
I USE IT A LOT BECAUSE THE SECOND IT HITS THE BUTTER OR THE OIL, I CAN FEEL MY GRANDMOTHER'S PRESENCE.

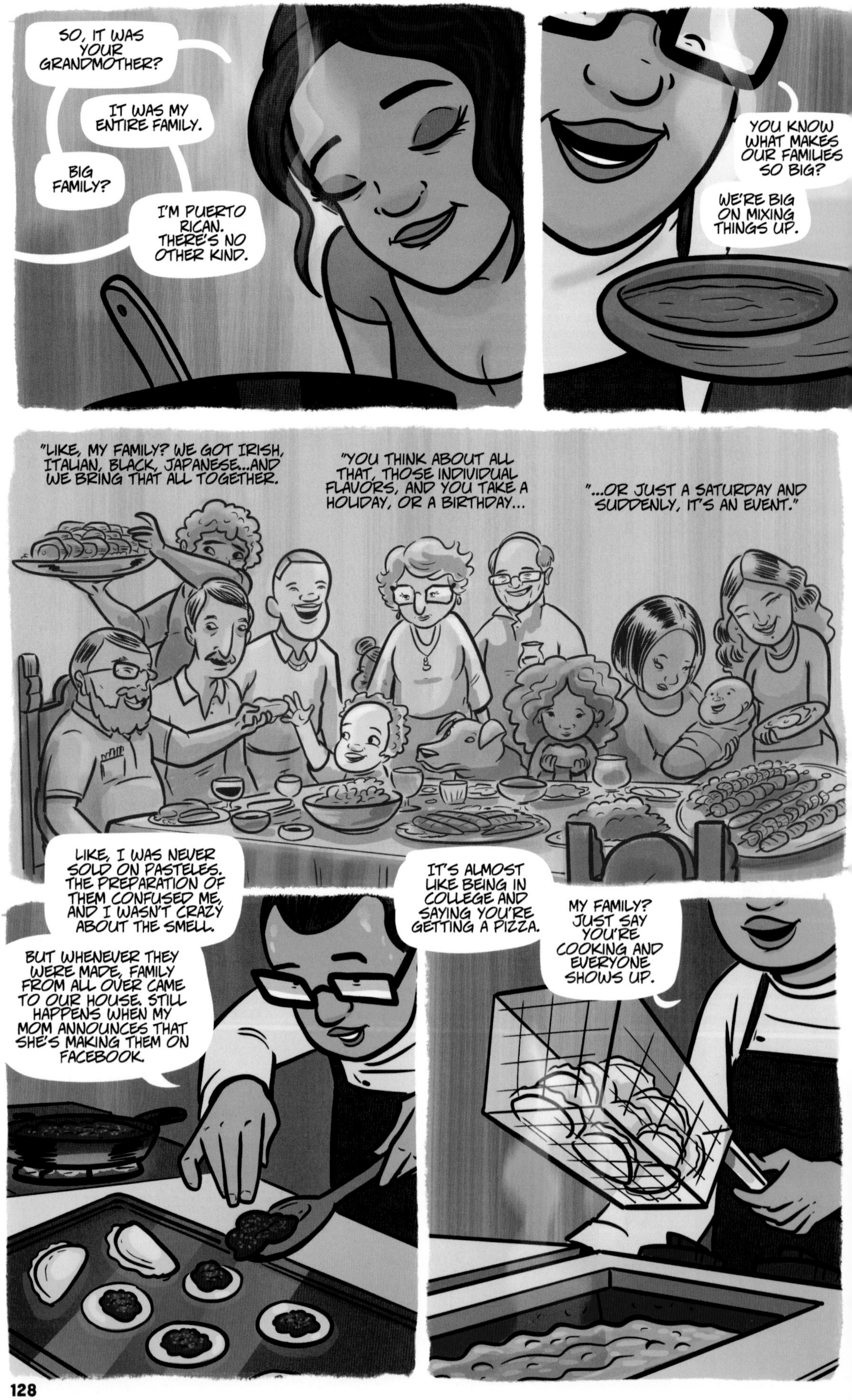
SO, IT WAS YOUR GRANDMOTHER?
IT WAS MY ENTIRE FAMILY.
BIG FAMILY?
I'M PUERTO RICAN. THERE'S NO OTHER KIND.
YOU KNOW WHAT MAKES OUR FAMILIES SO BIG?
WE'RE BIG ON MIXING THINGS UP.
"LIKE, MY FAMILY? WE GOT IRISH, ITALIAN, BLACK, JAPANESE...AND WE BRING THAT ALL TOGETHER.
"YOU THINK ABOUT ALL THAT, THOSE INDIVIDUAL FLAVORS, AND YOU TAKE A HOLIDAY, OR A BIRTHDAY...
"...OR JUST A SATURDAY AND SUDDENLY, IT'S AN EVENT."
LIKE, I WAS NEVER SOLD ON PASTELES. THE PREPARATION OF THEM CONFUSED ME, AND I WASN'T CRAZY ABOUT THE SMELL.
BUT WHENEVER THEY WERE MADE, FAMILY FROM ALL OVER CAME TO OUR HOUSE. STILL HAPPENS WHEN MY MOM ANNOUNCES THAT SHE'S MAKING THEM ON FACEBOOK.
IT'S ALMOST LIKE BEING IN COLLEGE AND SAYING YOU'RE GETTING A PIZZA.
MY FAMILY? JUST SAY YOU'RE COOKING AND EVERYONE SHOWS UP.

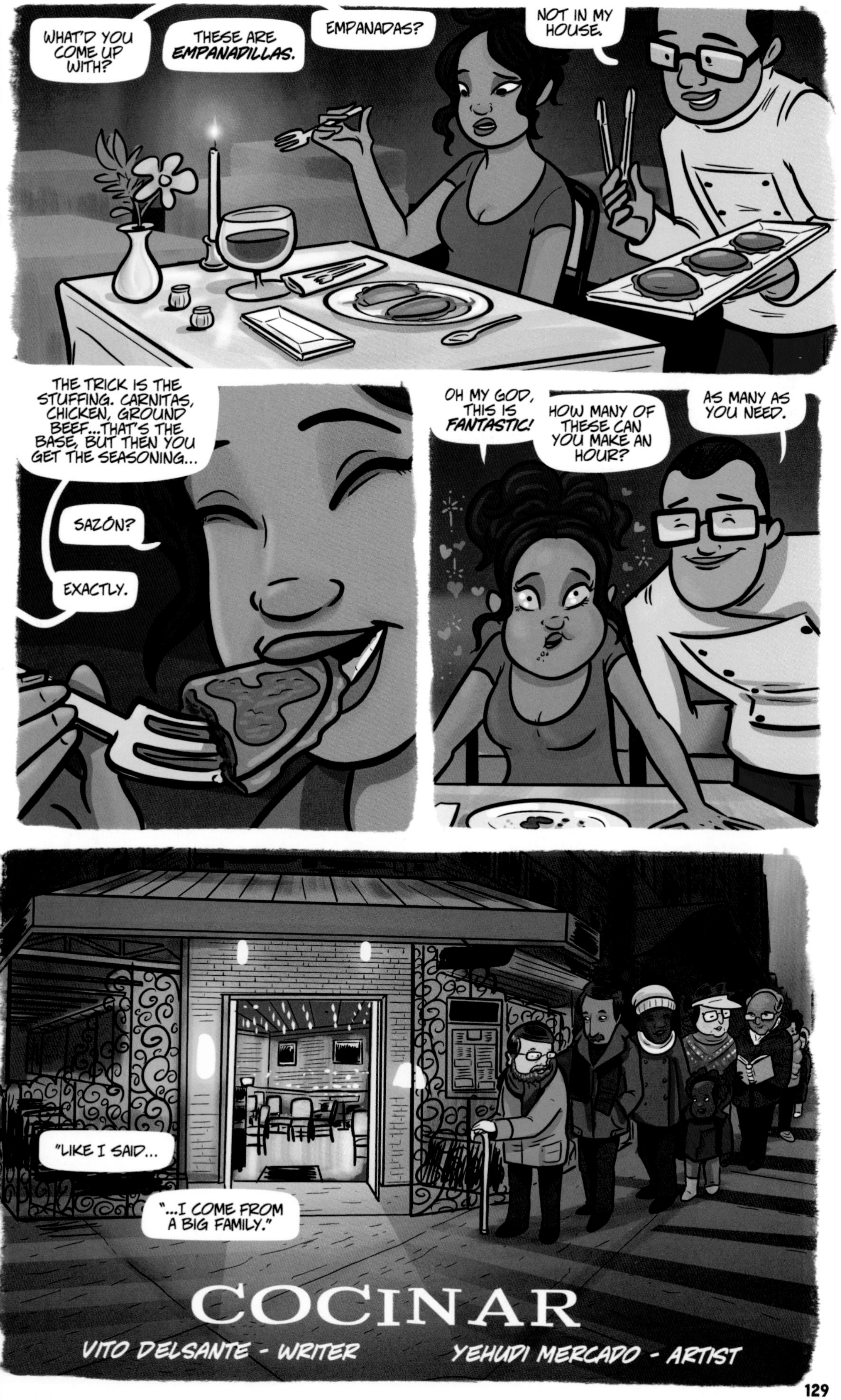
WHAT'D YOU COME UP WITH?
THESE ARE EMPANADILLAS.
EMPANADAS?
NOT IN MY HOUSE.
THE TRICK IS THE STUFFING. CARNITAS, CHICKEN, GROUND BEEF...THAT'S THE BASE, BUT THEN YOU GET THE SEASONING...
SAZÓN?
EXACTLY.
OH MY GOD, THIS IS FANTASTIC!
HOW MANY OF THESE CAN YOU MAKE AN HOUR?
AS MANY AS YOU NEED.
"LIKE I SAID...
"...I COME FROM A BIG FAMILY."
COCINAR
VITO DELSANTE - WRITER
YEHUDI MERCADO - ARTIST

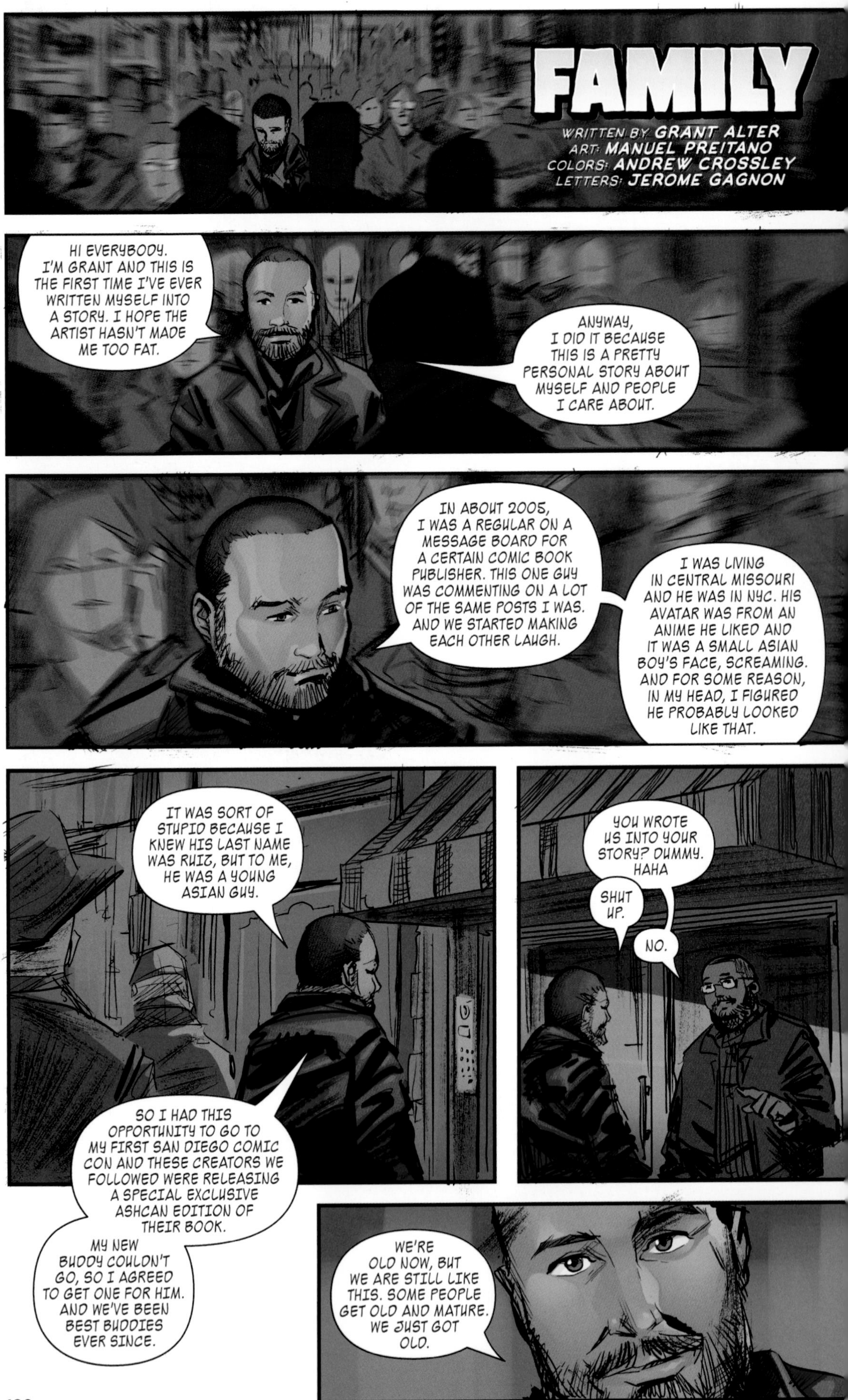

FAMILY
WRITTEN BY: GRANT ALTER
ART: MANUEL PREITANO
COLORS: ANDREW CROSSLEY
LETTERS: JEROME GAGNON
HI EVERYBODY. I'M GRANT AND THIS IS THE FIRST TIME I'VE EVER WRITTEN MYSELF INTO A STORY. I HOPE THE ARTIST HASN'T MADE ME TOO FAT.
ANYWAY, I DID IT BECAUSE THIS IS A PRETTY PERSONAL STORY ABOUT MYSELF AND PEOPLE I CARE ABOUT.
IN ABOUT 2005, I WAS A REGULAR ON A MESSAGE BOARD FOR A CERTAIN COMIC BOOK PUBLISHER. THIS ONE GUY WAS COMMENTING ON A LOT OF THE SAME POSTS I WAS. AND WE STARTED MAKING EACH OTHER LAUGH.
I WAS LIVING IN CENTRAL MISSOURI AND HE WAS IN NYC. HIS AVATAR WAS FROM AN ANIME HE LIKED AND IT WAS A SMALL ASIAN BOY'S FACE, SCREAMING. AND FOR SOME REASON, IN MY HEAD, I FIGURED HE PROBABLY LOOKED LIKE THAT.
IT WAS SORT OF STUPID BECAUSE I KNEW HIS LAST NAME WAS RUIZ, BUT TO ME, HE WAS A YOUNG ASIAN GUY.
SO I HAD THIS OPPORTUNITY TO GO TO MY FIRST SAN DIEGO COMIC CON AND THESE CREATORS WE FOLLOWED WERE RELEASING A SPECIAL EXCLUSIVE ASHCAN EDITION OF THEIR BOOK.
MY NEW BUDDY COULDN'T GO, SO I AGREED TO GET ONE FOR HIM. AND WE'VE BEEN BEST BUDDIES EVER SINCE.
YOU WROTE US INTO YOUR STORY? DUMMY. HAHA
SHUT UP.
NO.
WE'RE OLD NOW, BUT WE ARE STILL LIKE THIS. SOME PEOPLE GET OLD AND MATURE. WE JUST GOT OLD.

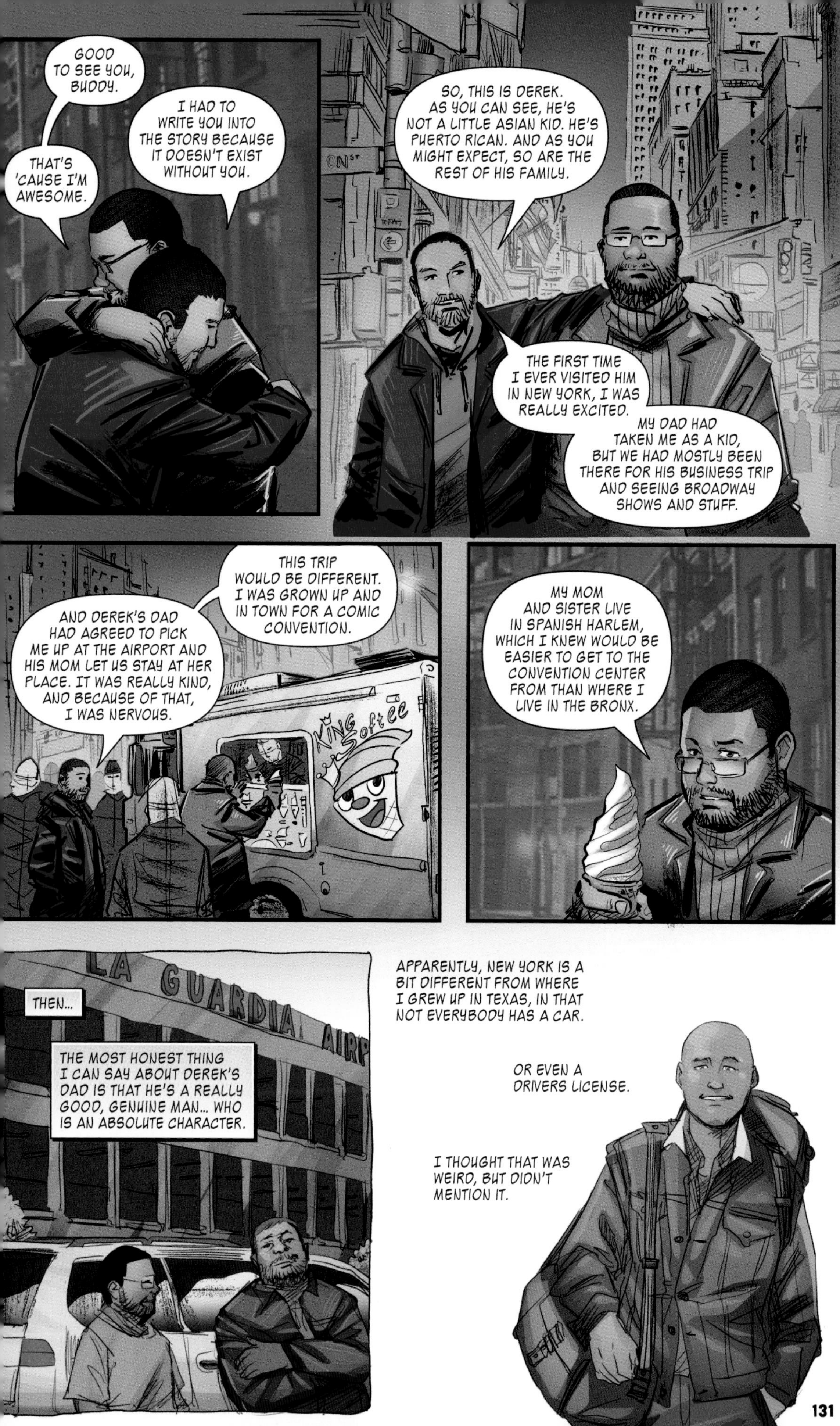
GOOD TO SEE YOU, BUDDY.
I HAD TO WRITE YOU INTO THE STORY BECAUSE IT DOESN'T EXIST WITHOUT YOU.
THAT'S 'CAUSE I'M AWESOME.
SO, THIS IS DEREK. AS YOU CAN SEE, HE'S NOT A LITTLE ASIAN KID. HE'S PUERTO RICAN. AND AS YOU MIGHT EXPECT, SO ARE THE REST OF HIS FAMILY.
THE FIRST TIME I EVER VISITED HIM IN NEW YORK, I WAS REALLY EXCITED.
MY DAD HAD TAKEN ME AS A KID, BUT WE HAD MOSTLY BEEN THERE FOR HIS BUSINESS TRIP AND SEEING BROADWAY SHOWS AND STUFF.
THIS TRIP WOULD BE DIFFERENT. I WAS GROWN UP AND IN TOWN FOR A COMIC CONVENTION.
AND DEREK'S DAD HAD AGREED TO PICK ME UP AT THE AIRPORT AND HIS MOM LET US STAY AT HER PLACE. IT WAS REALLY KIND, AND BECAUSE OF THAT, I WAS NERVOUS.
KING Softee
MY MOM AND SISTER LIVE IN SPANISH HARLEM, WHICH I KNEW WOULD BE EASIER TO GET TO THE CONVENTION CENTER FROM THAN WHERE I LIVE IN THE BRONX.
LA GUARDIA AIRP
THEN...
THE MOST HONEST THING I CAN SAY ABOUT DEREK'S DAD IS THAT HE'S A REALLY GOOD, GENUINE MAN... WHO IS AN ABSOLUTE CHARACTER.
APPARENTLY, NEW YORK IS A BIT DIFFERENT FROM WHERE I GREW UP IN TEXAS, IN THAT NOT EVERYBODY HAS A CAR.
OR EVEN A DRIVERS LICENSE.
I THOUGHT THAT WAS WEIRD, BUT DIDN'T MENTION IT.

HI. I'M DEREK'S DAD. I'VE HEARD A LOT ABOUT YOU, AND I'M GLAD I FINALLY GET TO MEET YOU. YOU'RE FAMILY NOW.

MAKE SURE YOU'RE BUCKLED REALLY GOOD. THIS ISN'T... WHERE DO YOU LIVE? MISSOURI? YEAH, THIS ISN'T MISSOURI.

I HAD BEEN TO NEW YORK, AND THOUGHT I KNEW WHAT TO EXPECT.

HE TOLD ME IN PRETTY COLORFUL LANGUAGE WHAT HE THOUGHT ABOUT TAXI DRIVERS.

APPARENTLY, HE DOESN'T LIKE THEM MUCH.

BEEEEEEEEEEEEEEEEEEEEEEEEPP

WHO DID YOU BRIBE TO GET THAT LICENSE, YOU CENSORED ?!

THAT PIECE OF CENSORED. DID YOU SEE WHAT HE DID?

SO, HOW'S YOUR FAMILY DOING? EVERYBODY HEALTHY?

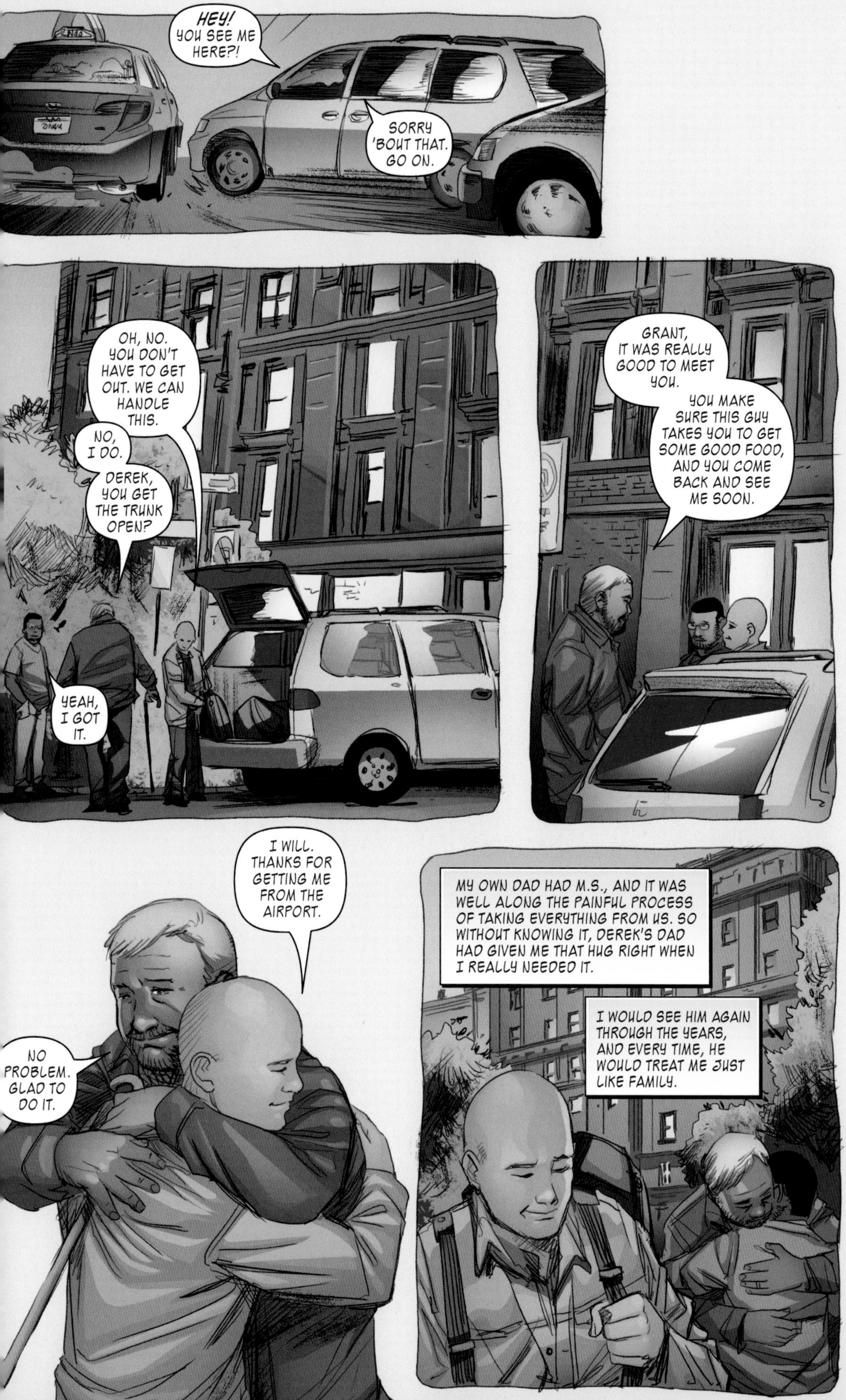
HEY! YOU SEE ME HERE?!
SORRY 'BOUT THAT. GO ON.
OH, NO. YOU DON'T HAVE TO GET OUT. WE CAN HANDLE THIS.
NO, I DO.
DEREK, YOU GET THE TRUNK OPEN?
YEAH, I GOT IT.
GRANT, IT WAS REALLY GOOD TO MEET YOU.
YOU MAKE SURE THIS GUY TAKES YOU TO GET SOME GOOD FOOD, AND YOU COME BACK AND SEE ME SOON.
I WILL. THANKS FOR GETTING ME FROM THE AIRPORT.
NO PROBLEM. GLAD TO DO IT.
MY OWN DAD HAD M.S., AND IT WAS WELL ALONG THE PAINFUL PROCESS OF TAKING EVERYTHING FROM US. SO WITHOUT KNOWING IT, DEREK'S DAD HAD GIVEN ME THAT HUG RIGHT WHEN I REALLY NEEDED IT.
I WOULD SEE HIM AGAIN THROUGH THE YEARS, AND EVERY TIME, HE WOULD TREAT ME JUST LIKE FAMILY.

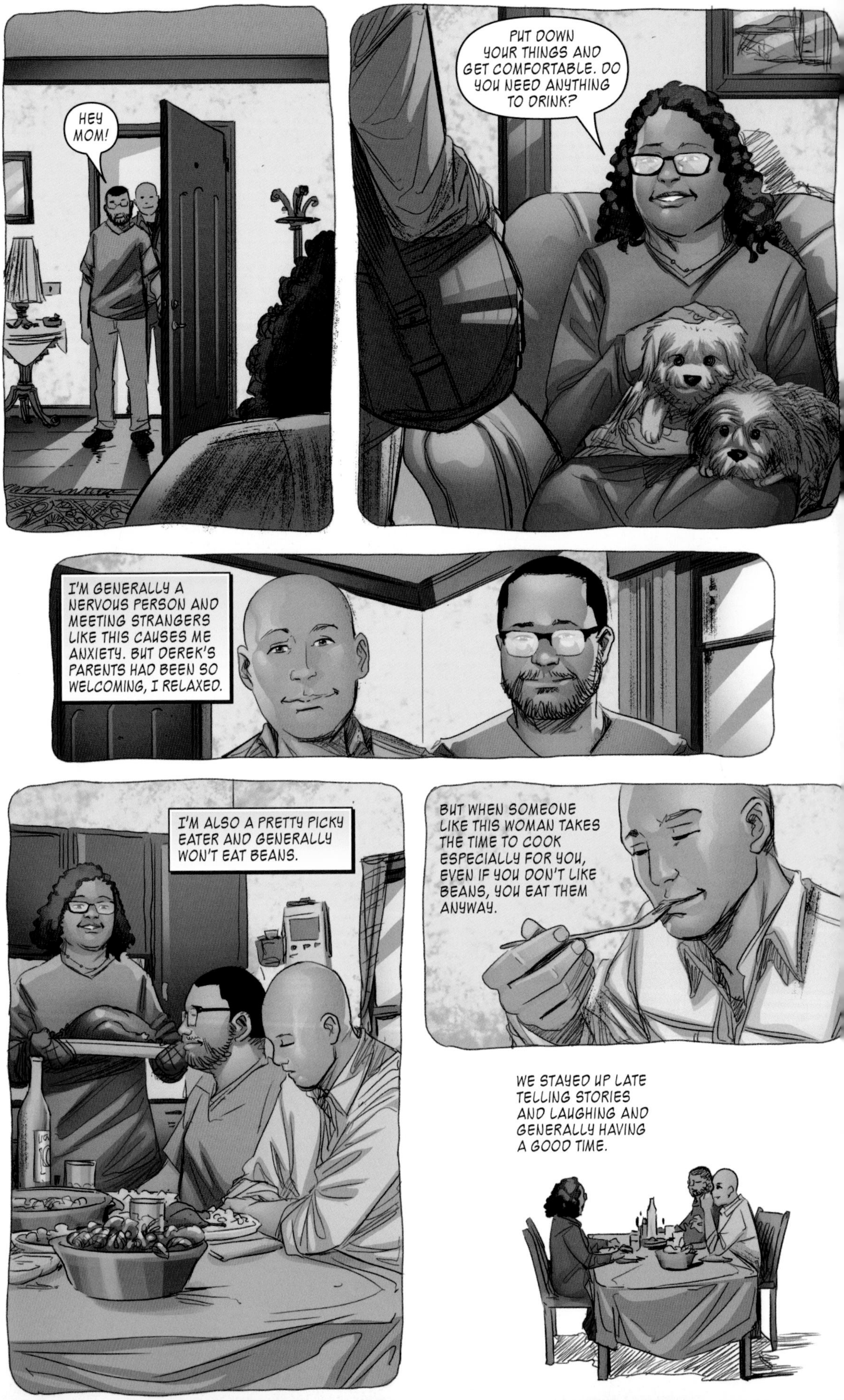
HEY MOM!
PUT DOWN YOUR THINGS AND GET COMFORTABLE. DO YOU NEED ANYTHING TO DRINK?
I'M GENERALLY A NERVOUS PERSON AND MEETING STRANGERS LIKE THIS CAUSES ME ANXIETY. BUT DEREK'S PARENTS HAD BEEN SO WELCOMING, I RELAXED.
I'M ALSO A PRETTY PICKY EATER AND GENERALLY WON'T EAT BEANS.
BUT WHEN SOMEONE LIKE THIS WOMAN TAKES THE TIME TO COOK ESPECIALLY FOR YOU, EVEN IF YOU DON'T LIKE BEANS, YOU EAT THEM ANYWAY.
WE STAYED UP LATE TELLING STORIES AND LAUGHING AND GENERALLY HAVING A GOOD TIME.

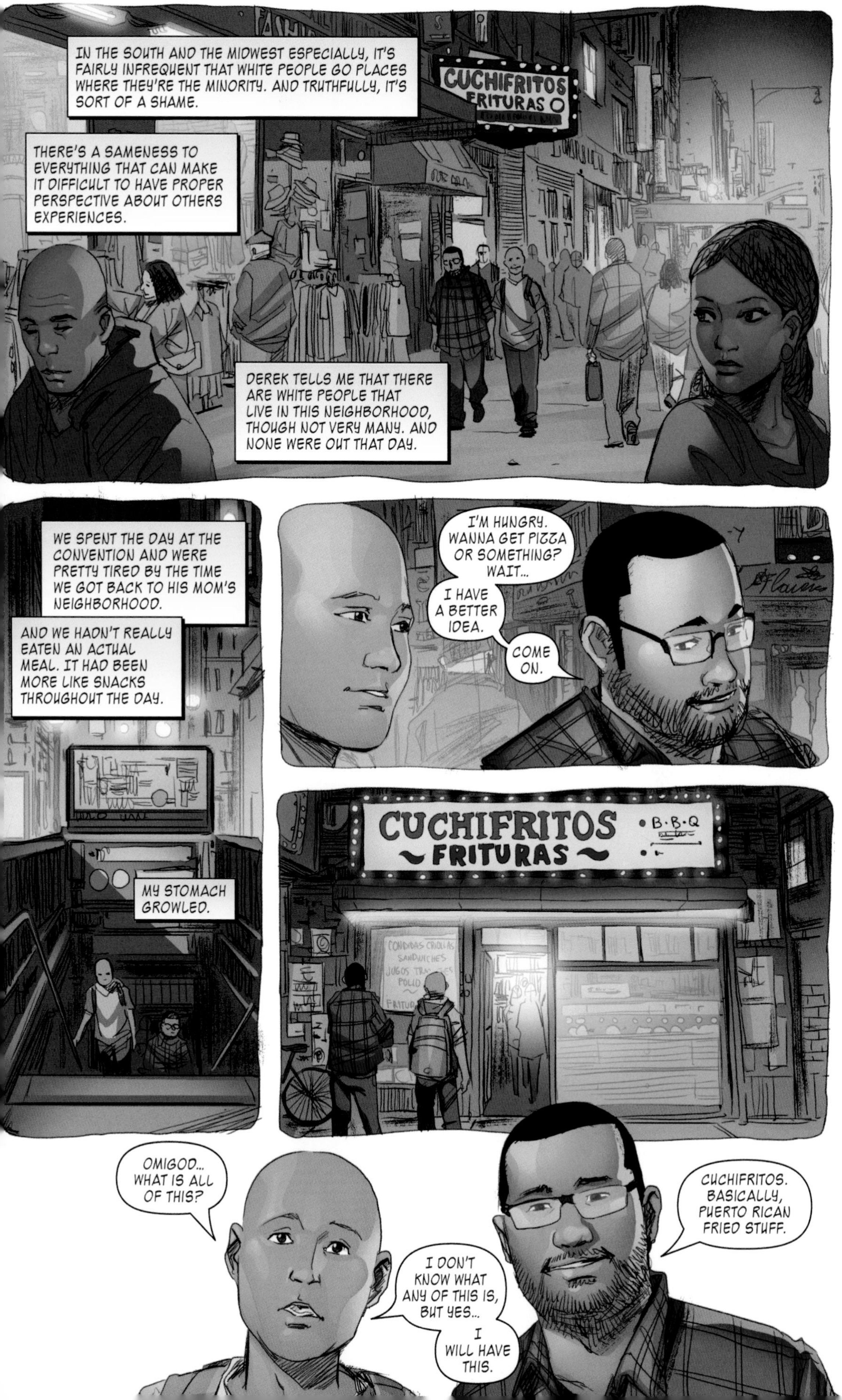
IN THE SOUTH AND THE MIDWEST ESPECIALLY, IT'S FAIRLY INFREQUENT THAT WHITE PEOPLE GO PLACES WHERE THEY'RE THE MINORITY. AND TRUTHFULLY, IT'S SORT OF A SHAME.
CUCHIFRITOS
FRITURAS
THERE'S A SAMENESS TO EVERYTHING THAT CAN MAKE IT DIFFICULT TO HAVE PROPER PERSPECTIVE ABOUT OTHERS EXPERIENCES.
DEREK TELLS ME THAT THERE ARE WHITE PEOPLE THAT LIVE IN THIS NEIGHBORHOOD, THOUGH NOT VERY MANY. AND NONE WERE OUT THAT DAY.
WE SPENT THE DAY AT THE CONVENTION AND WERE PRETTY TIRED BY THE TIME WE GOT BACK TO HIS MOM'S NEIGHBORHOOD.
AND WE HADN'T REALLY EATEN AN ACTUAL MEAL. IT HAD BEEN MORE LIKE SNACKS THROUGHOUT THE DAY.
MY STOMACH GROWLED.
I'M HUNGRY. WANNA GET PIZZA OR SOMETHING? WAIT...
I HAVE A BETTER IDEA.
COME ON.
CUCHIFRITOS
B·B·Q
~FRITURAS~
OMIGOD... WHAT IS ALL OF THIS?
CUCHIFRITOS. BASICALLY, PUERTO RICAN FRIED STUFF.
I DON'T KNOW WHAT ANY OF THIS IS, BUT YES...
I WILL HAVE THIS.

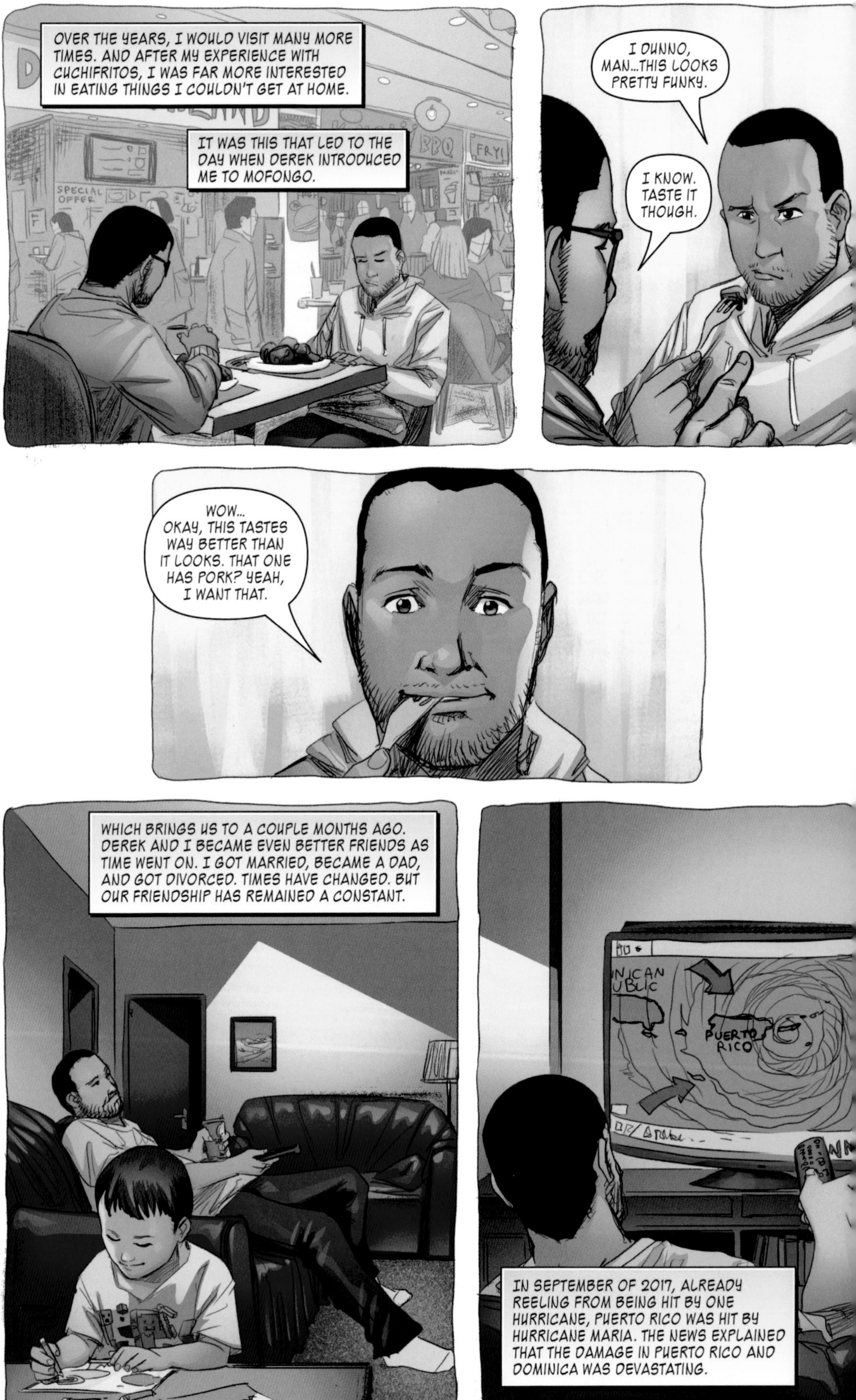
OVER THE YEARS, I WOULD VISIT MANY MORE TIMES. AND AFTER MY EXPERIENCE WITH CUCHIFRITOS, I WAS FAR MORE INTERESTED IN EATING THINGS I COULDN'T GET AT HOME.
IT WAS THIS THAT LED TO THE DAY WHEN DEREK INTRODUCED ME TO MOFONGO.
SPECIAL OFFER
BBQ
FRY!
I DUNNO, MAN...THIS LOOKS PRETTY FUNKY.
I KNOW. TASTE IT THOUGH.
WOW... OKAY, THIS TASTES WAY BETTER THAN IT LOOKS. THAT ONE HAS PORK? YEAH, I WANT THAT.
WHICH BRINGS US TO A COUPLE MONTHS AGO. DEREK AND I BECAME EVEN BETTER FRIENDS AS TIME WENT ON. I GOT MARRIED, BECAME A DAD, AND GOT DIVORCED. TIMES HAVE CHANGED. BUT OUR FRIENDSHIP HAS REMAINED A CONSTANT.
PUERTO RICO
IN SEPTEMBER OF 2017, ALREADY REELING FROM BEING HIT BY ONE HURRICANE, PUERTO RICO WAS HIT BY HURRICANE MARIA. THE NEWS EXPLAINED THAT THE DAMAGE IN PUERTO RICO AND DOMINICA WAS DEVASTATING.

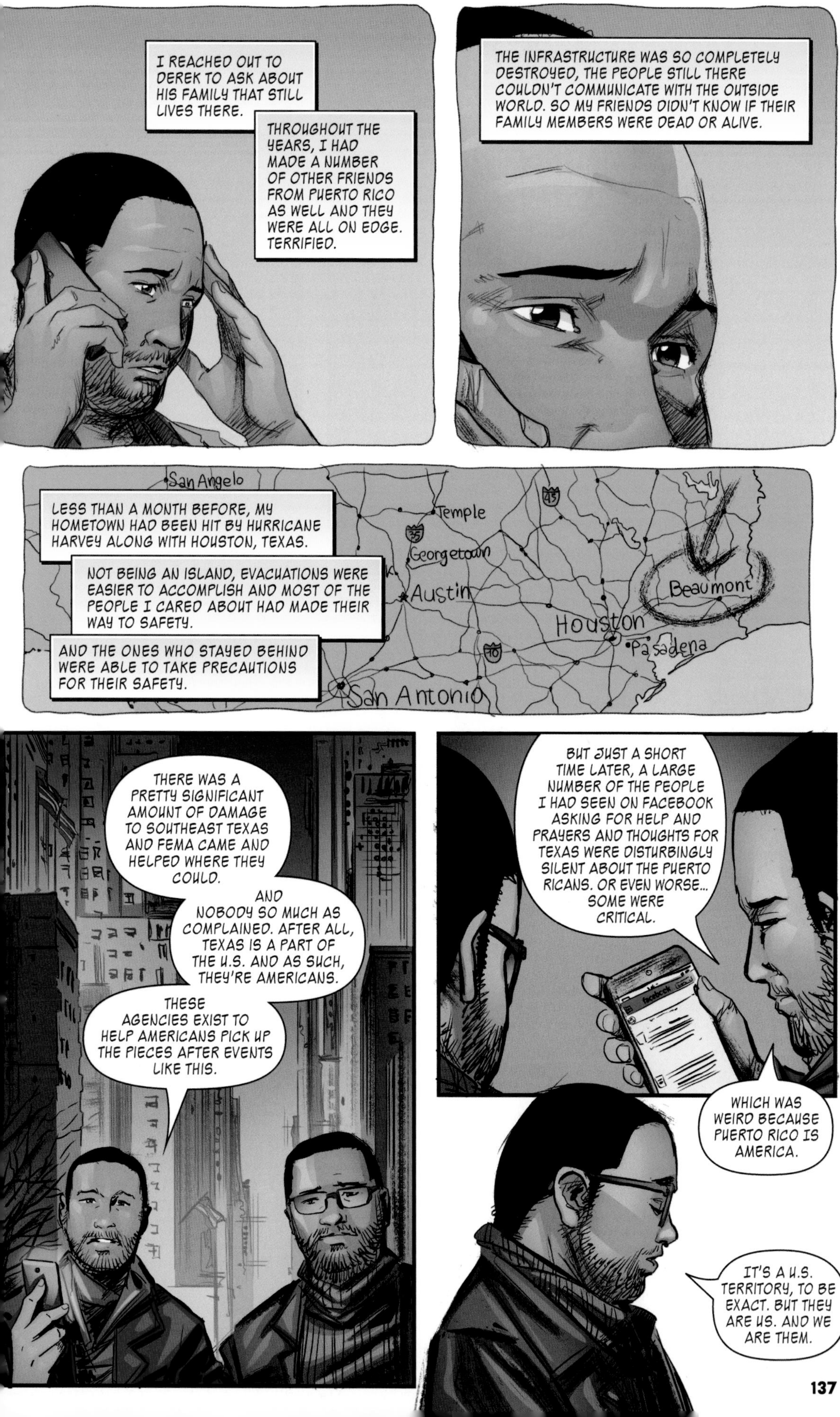
I REACHED OUT TO DEREK TO ASK ABOUT HIS FAMILY THAT STILL LIVES THERE.
THROUGHOUT THE YEARS, I HAD MADE A NUMBER OF OTHER FRIENDS FROM PUERTO RICO AS WELL AND THEY WERE ALL ON EDGE. TERRIFIED.
THE INFRASTRUCTURE WAS SO COMPLETELY DESTROYED, THE PEOPLE STILL THERE COULDN'T COMMUNICATE WITH THE OUTSIDE WORLD. SO MY FRIENDS DIDN'T KNOW IF THEIR FAMILY MEMBERS WERE DEAD OR ALIVE.
LESS THAN A MONTH BEFORE, MY HOMETOWN HAD BEEN HIT BY HURRICANE HARVEY ALONG WITH HOUSTON, TEXAS.
NOT BEING AN ISLAND, EVACUATIONS WERE EASIER TO ACCOMPLISH AND MOST OF THE PEOPLE I CARED ABOUT HAD MADE THEIR WAY TO SAFETY.
AND THE ONES WHO STAYED BEHIND WERE ABLE TO TAKE PRECAUTIONS FOR THEIR SAFETY.
San Angelo
Temple
35
Georgetown
45
Austin
Beaumont
Houston
Pasadena
10
San Antonio
THERE WAS A PRETTY SIGNIFICANT AMOUNT OF DAMAGE TO SOUTHEAST TEXAS AND FEMA CAME AND HELPED WHERE THEY COULD.
AND NOBODY SO MUCH AS COMPLAINED. AFTER ALL, TEXAS IS A PART OF THE U.S. AND AS SUCH, THEY'RE AMERICANS.
THESE AGENCIES EXIST TO HELP AMERICANS PICK UP THE PIECES AFTER EVENTS LIKE THIS.
BUT JUST A SHORT TIME LATER, A LARGE NUMBER OF THE PEOPLE I HAD SEEN ON FACEBOOK ASKING FOR HELP AND PRAYERS AND THOUGHTS FOR TEXAS WERE DISTURBINGLY SILENT ABOUT THE PUERTO RICANS. OR EVEN WORSE... SOME WERE CRITICAL.
WHICH WAS WEIRD BECAUSE PUERTO RICO IS AMERICA.
IT'S A U.S. TERRITORY, TO BE EXACT. BUT THEY ARE US. AND WE ARE THEM.

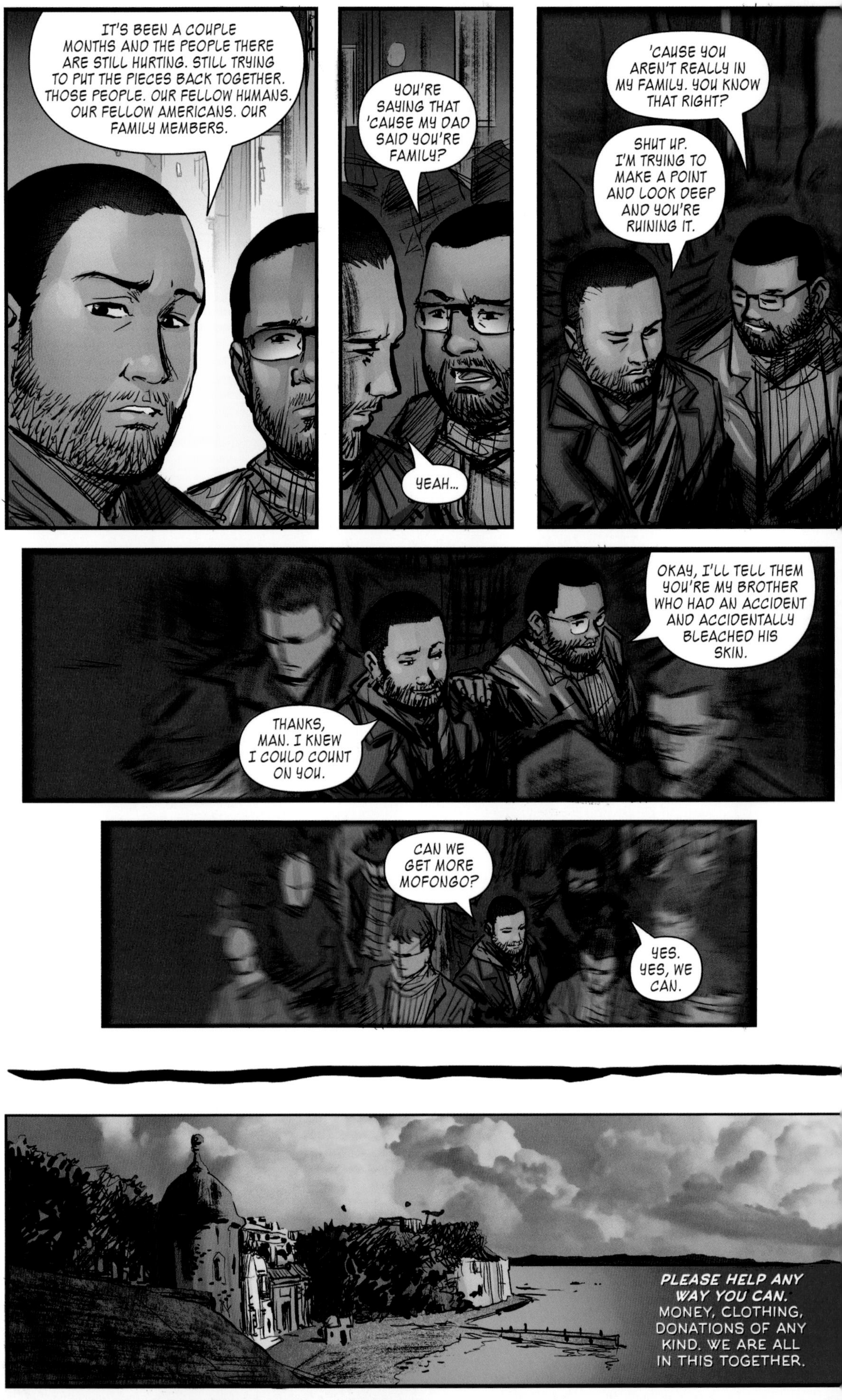
IT'S BEEN A COUPLE MONTHS AND THE PEOPLE THERE ARE STILL HURTING. STILL TRYING TO PUT THE PIECES BACK TOGETHER. THOSE PEOPLE. OUR FELLOW HUMANS. OUR FELLOW AMERICANS. OUR FAMILY MEMBERS.
YOU'RE SAYING THAT 'CAUSE MY DAD SAID YOU'RE FAMILY?
YEAH...
'CAUSE YOU AREN'T REALLY IN MY FAMILY. YOU KNOW THAT RIGHT?
SHUT UP. I'M TRYING TO MAKE A POINT AND LOOK DEEP AND YOU'RE RUINING IT.
OKAY, I'LL TELL THEM YOU'RE MY BROTHER WHO HAD AN ACCIDENT AND ACCIDENTALLY BLEACHED HIS SKIN.
THANKS, MAN. I KNEW I COULD COUNT ON YOU.
CAN WE GET MORE MOFONGO?
YES. YES, WE CAN.
PLEASE HELP ANY WAY YOU CAN. MONEY, CLOTHING, DONATIONS OF ANY KIND. WE ARE ALL IN THIS TOGETHER.

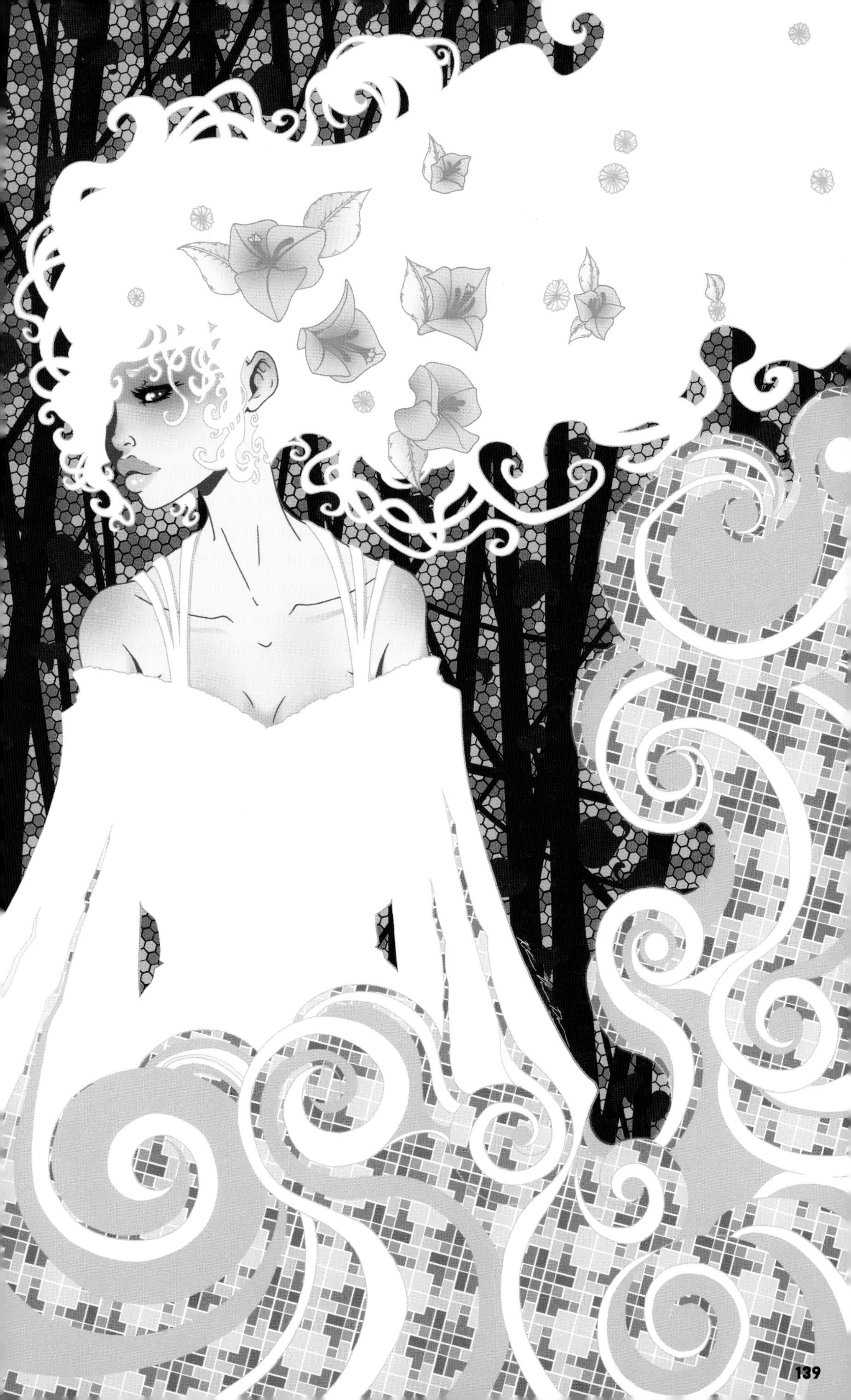

# TAINO ONLINE

Comic by Joamette Gil

Colors by Christopher Sotomayor

This was my reaction when my tía told me about my maternal great-grandmother's Taino roots.

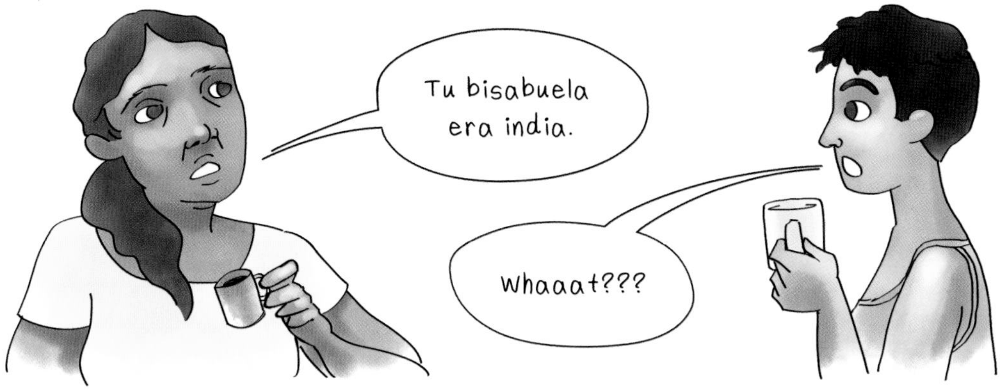

Tu bisabuela era india.
Whaaat???


For those of you who aren't in the know: the Taino were an Arawak-speaking people who settled throughout the Caribbean thousands of years ago.

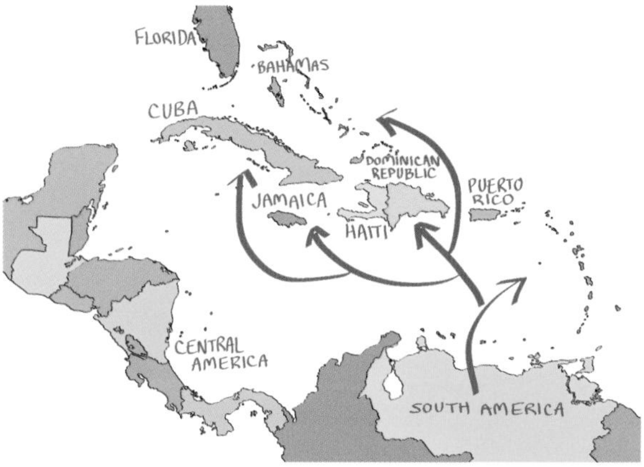

FLORIDA
BAHAMAS
CUBA
DOMINICAN REPUBLIC
PUERTO RICO
JAMAICA
HAITI
CENTRAL AMERICA
SOUTH AMERICA


They were the "Indians" Christopher Columbus claimed to have "discovered."

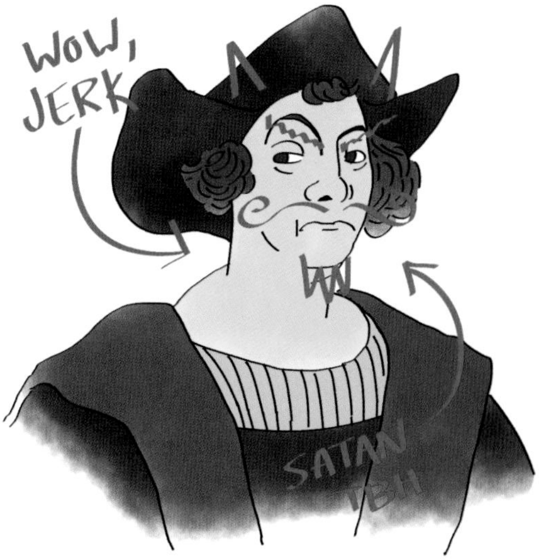

WOW, JERK
SATAN TBH


I decided to make up for my family's total silence on the matter by doing my own research on Taino history and culture.

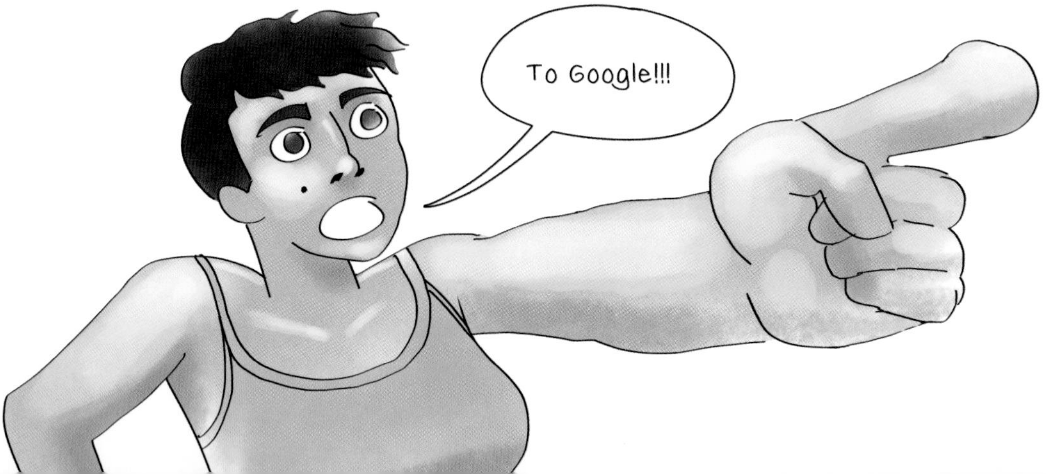

To Google!!!

I inhaled every Taino fact I could find: the food they ate, the games they played, their genders, their gods, their monsters...

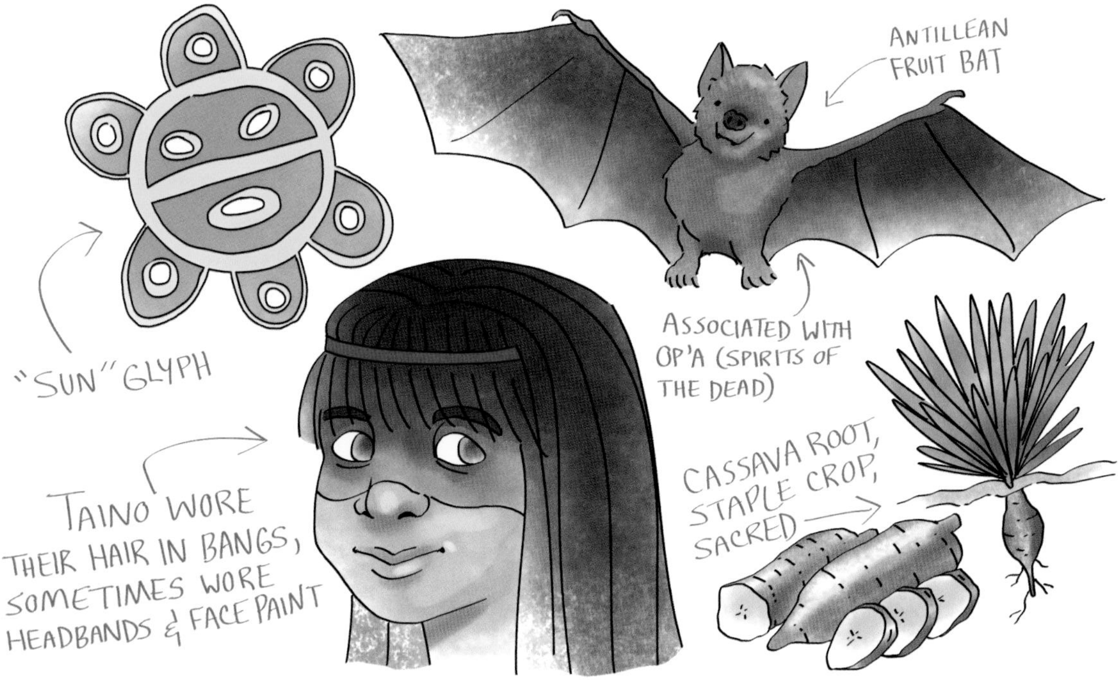
ANTILLEAN FRUIT BAT
"SUN" GLYPH
ASSOCIATED WITH OP'A (SPIRITS OF THE DEAD)
TAINO WORE THEIR HAIR IN BANGS, SOMETIMES WORE HEADBANDS & FACE PAINT
CASSAVA ROOT, STAPLE CROP, SACRED

...And I was surprised by how many common English words were Arawak in origin: hammock, barbecue, canoe, hurricane, guava, and even tobacco.

One Taino word stood out the most:

# BORICUA

I'd heard Puerto Ricans call themselves Boricuas (instead of "Puerto Ricans") my whole life, but I never knew why.

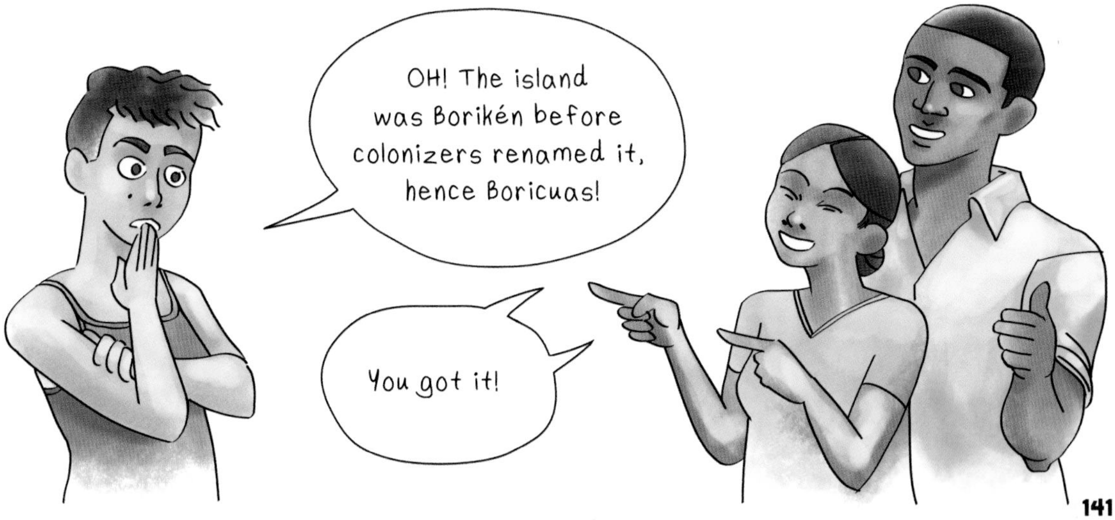
OH! The island was Borikén before colonizers renamed it, hence Boricuas!
You got it!

The Spanish completely destroyed the Taino civilization, but in addition to words and foods and legends, Taino *genes* lived on, *especially* in Borikén.

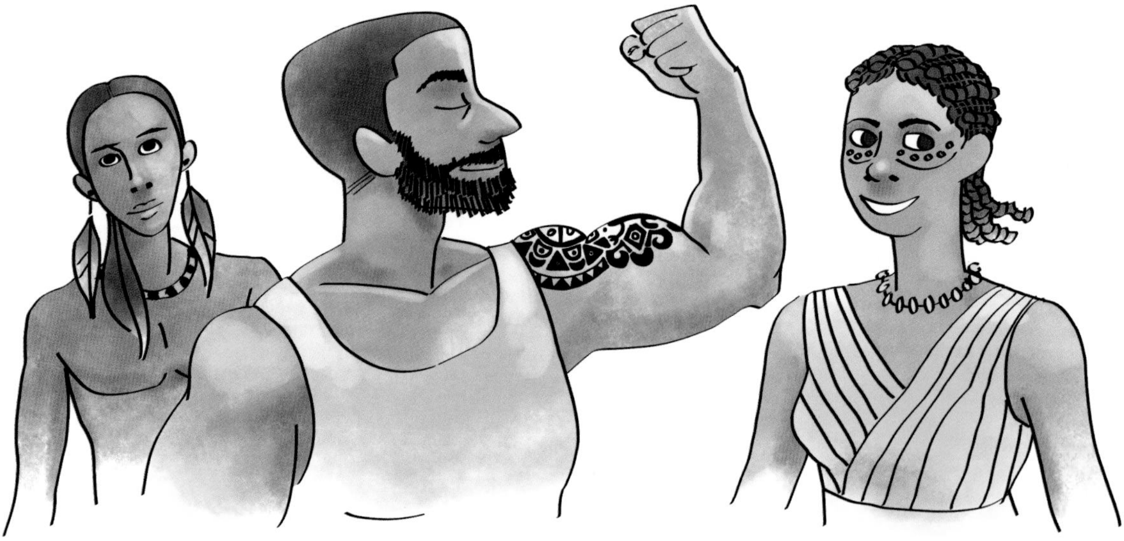

According to mtDNA studies, roughly 60% of all mothers from the inception of Puerto Rico were of Taino descent.

In Cuba, that number is only around 34%, but hey - that's not nothing!

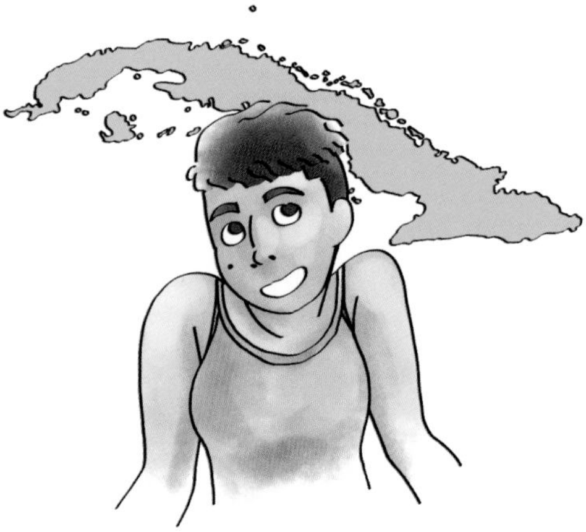

It's enough to know that there was more to my family than I originally believed.

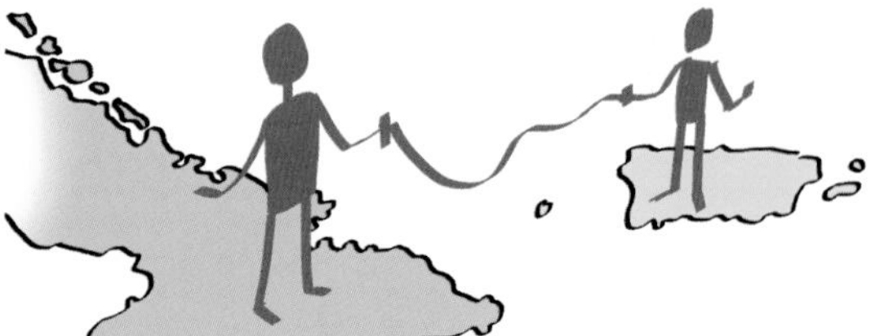

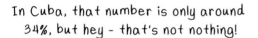

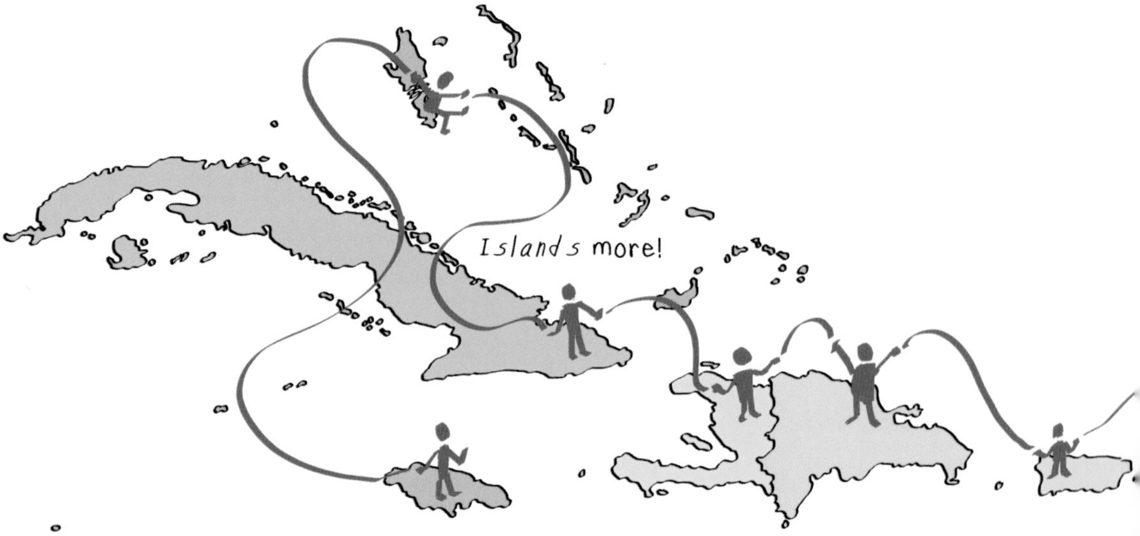
*Islands* more!

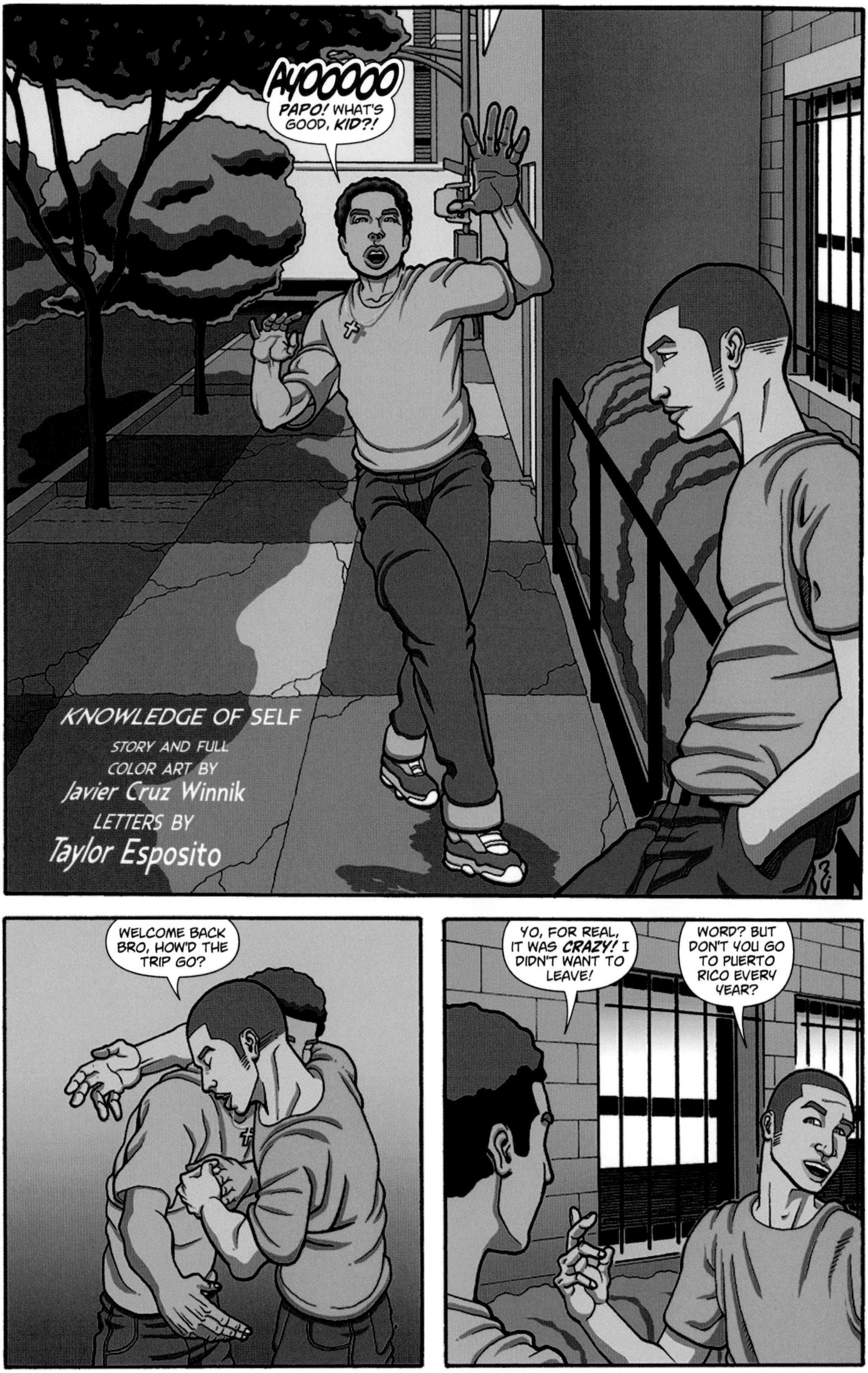
AYOOOOO
PAPO! WHAT'S GOOD, KID?!
KNOWLEDGE OF SELF
STORY AND FULL COLOR ART BY
Javier Cruz Winnik
LETTERS BY
Taylor Esposito
WELCOME BACK BRO, HOW'D THE TRIP GO?
YO, FOR REAL, IT WAS CRAZY! I DIDN'T WANT TO LEAVE!
WORD? BUT DON'T YOU GO TO PUERTO RICO EVERY YEAR?

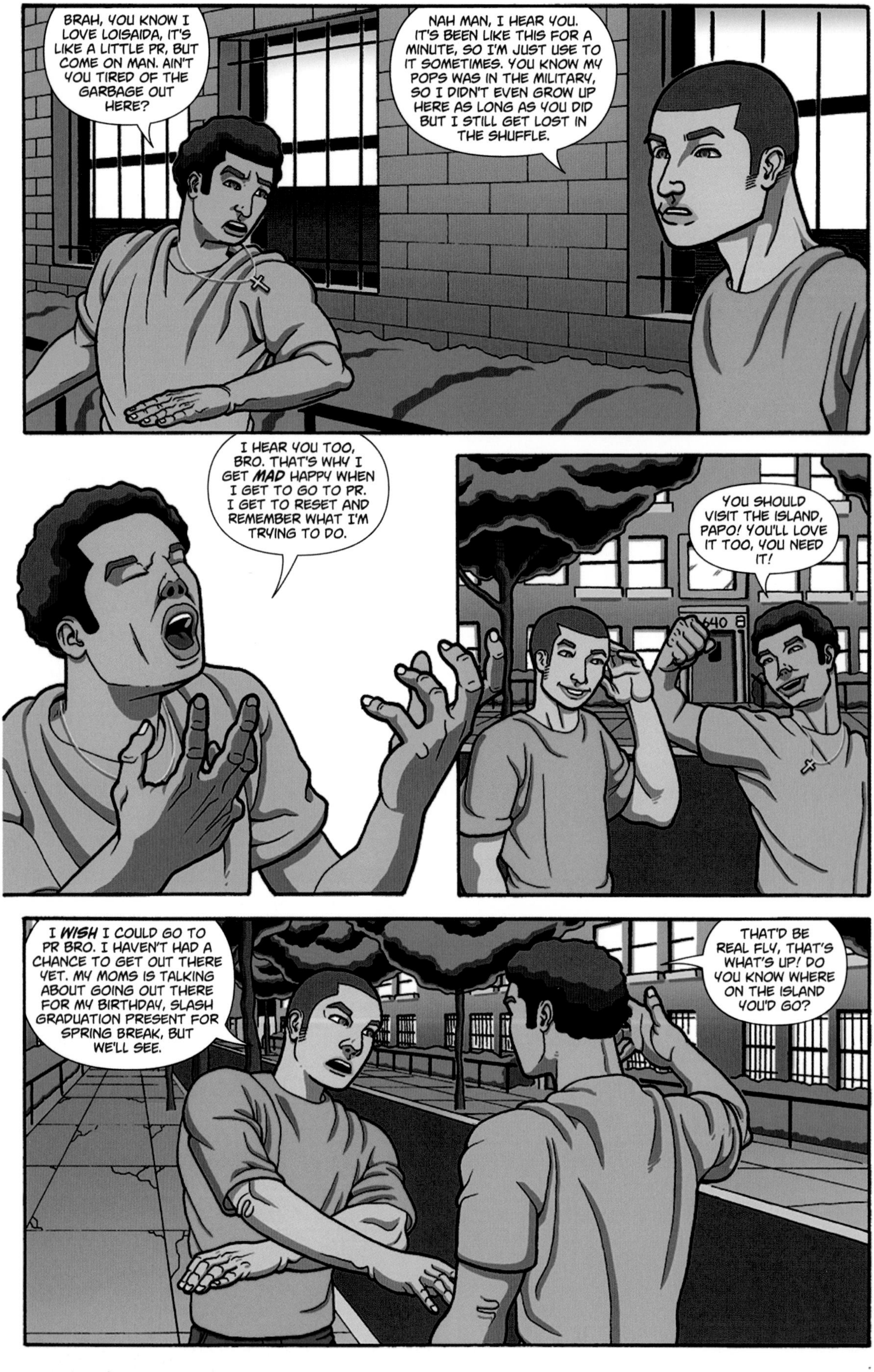
BRAH, YOU KNOW I LOVE LOISAIDA, IT'S LIKE A LITTLE PR, BUT COME ON MAN. AIN'T YOU TIRED OF THE GARBAGE OUT HERE?
NAH MAN, I HEAR YOU. IT'S BEEN LIKE THIS FOR A MINUTE, SO I'M JUST USE TO IT SOMETIMES. YOU KNOW MY POPS WAS IN THE MILITARY, SO I DIDN'T EVEN GROW UP HERE AS LONG AS YOU DID BUT I STILL GET LOST IN THE SHUFFLE.
I HEAR YOU TOO, BRO. THAT'S WHY I GET ***MAD*** HAPPY WHEN I GET TO GO TO PR. I GET TO RESET AND REMEMBER WHAT I'M TRYING TO DO.
YOU SHOULD VISIT THE ISLAND, PAPO! YOU'LL LOVE IT TOO, YOU NEED IT!
640
I ***WISH*** I COULD GO TO PR BRO. I HAVEN'T HAD A CHANCE TO GET OUT THERE YET. MY MOMS IS TALKING ABOUT GOING OUT THERE FOR MY BIRTHDAY, SLASH GRADUATION PRESENT FOR SPRING BREAK, BUT WE'LL SEE.
THAT'D BE REAL FLY, THAT'S WHAT'S UP! DO YOU KNOW WHERE ON THE ISLAND YOU'D GO?

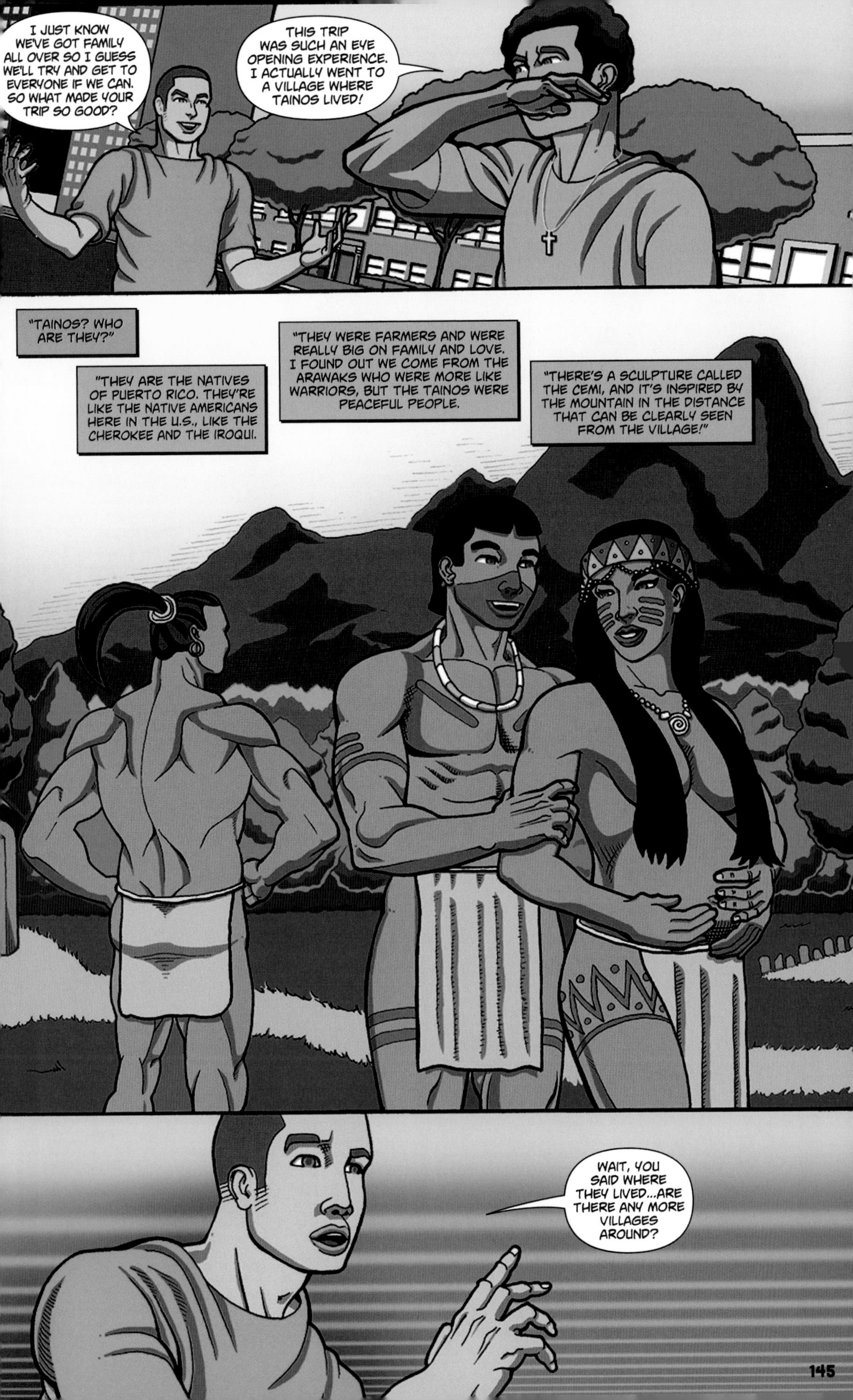
I JUST KNOW WE'VE GOT FAMILY ALL OVER SO I GUESS WE'LL TRY AND GET TO EVERYONE IF WE CAN. SO WHAT MADE YOUR TRIP SO GOOD?
THIS TRIP WAS SUCH AN EYE OPENING EXPERIENCE. I ACTUALLY WENT TO A VILLAGE WHERE TAINOS LIVED!
"TAINOS? WHO ARE THEY?"
"THEY ARE THE NATIVES OF PUERTO RICO. THEY'RE LIKE THE NATIVE AMERICANS HERE IN THE U.S., LIKE THE CHEROKEE AND THE IROQUI.
"THEY WERE FARMERS AND WERE REALLY BIG ON FAMILY AND LOVE. I FOUND OUT WE COME FROM THE ARAWAKS WHO WERE MORE LIKE WARRIORS, BUT THE TAINOS WERE PEACEFUL PEOPLE.
"THERE'S A SCULPTURE CALLED THE CEMI, AND IT'S INSPIRED BY THE MOUNTAIN IN THE DISTANCE THAT CAN BE CLEARLY SEEN FROM THE VILLAGE!"
WAIT, YOU SAID WHERE THEY LIVED...ARE THERE ANY MORE VILLAGES AROUND?

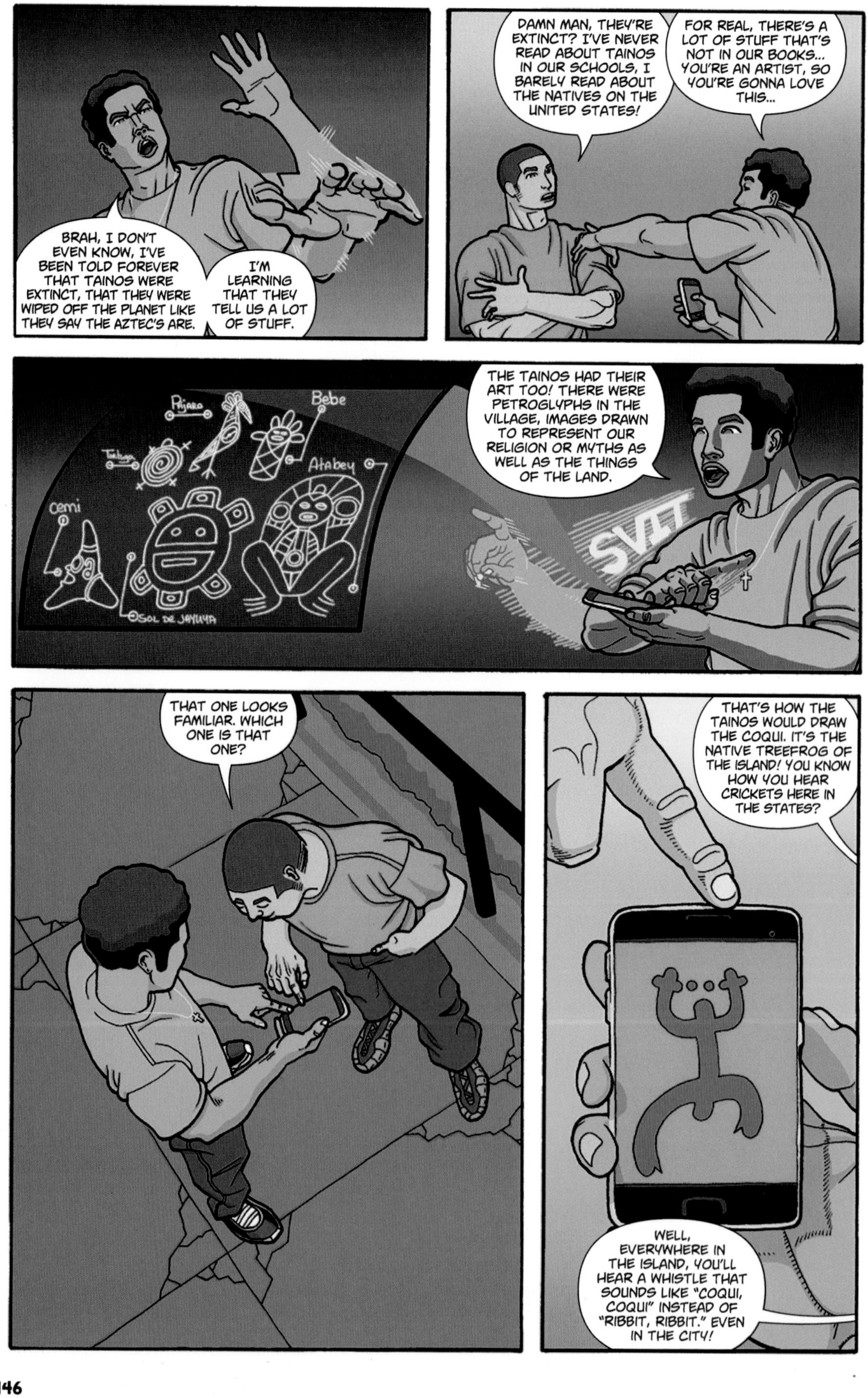
BRAH, I DON'T EVEN KNOW, I'VE BEEN TOLD FOREVER THAT TAINOS WERE EXTINCT, THAT THEY WERE WIPED OFF THE PLANET LIKE THEY SAY THE AZTEC'S ARE.
I'M LEARNING THAT THEY TELL US A LOT OF STUFF.
DAMN MAN, THEY'RE EXTINCT? I'VE NEVER READ ABOUT TAINOS IN OUR SCHOOLS, I BARELY READ ABOUT THE NATIVES ON THE UNITED STATES!
FOR REAL, THERE'S A LOT OF STUFF THAT'S NOT IN OUR BOOKS... YOU'RE AN ARTIST, SO YOU'RE GONNA LOVE THIS...
THE TAINOS HAD THEIR ART TOO! THERE WERE PETROGLYPHS IN THE VILLAGE, IMAGES DRAWN TO REPRESENT OUR RELIGION OR MYTHS AS WELL AS THE THINGS OF THE LAND.
Pájaro
Bebe
Atabey
cemi
SOL DE JAYUYA
SVIT
THAT ONE LOOKS FAMILIAR. WHICH ONE IS THAT ONE?
THAT'S HOW THE TAINOS WOULD DRAW THE COQUI. IT'S THE NATIVE TREEFROG OF THE ISLAND! YOU KNOW HOW YOU HEAR CRICKETS HERE IN THE STATES?
WELL, EVERYWHERE IN THE ISLAND, YOU'LL HEAR A WHISTLE THAT SOUNDS LIKE "COQUI, COQUI" INSTEAD OF "RIBBIT, RIBBIT." EVEN IN THE CITY!

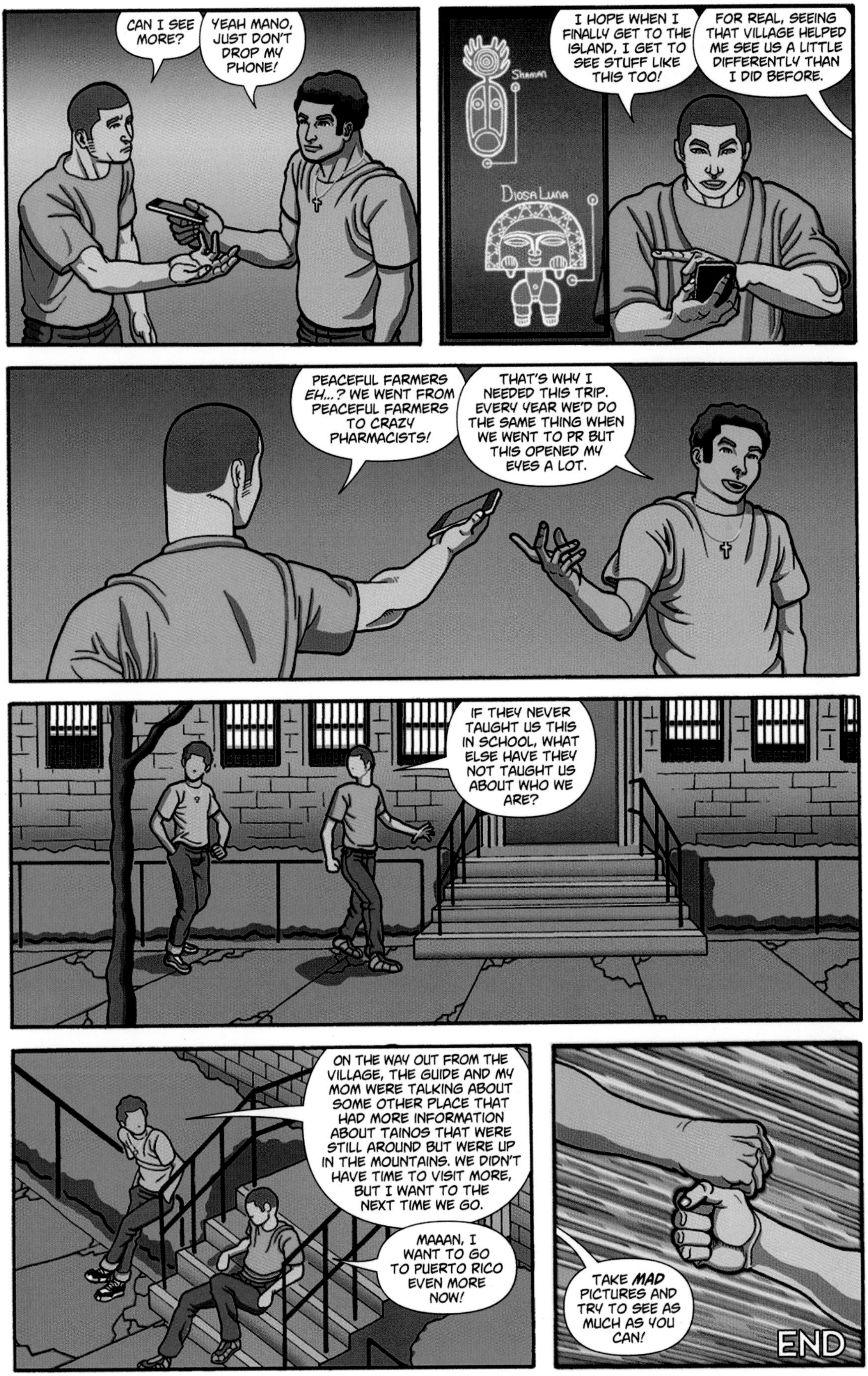

CAN I SEE MORE?
YEAH MANO, JUST DON'T DROP MY PHONE!
Shaman
Diosa Luna
I HOPE WHEN I FINALLY GET TO THE ISLAND, I GET TO SEE STUFF LIKE THIS TOO!
FOR REAL, SEEING THAT VILLAGE HELPED ME SEE US A LITTLE DIFFERENTLY THAN I DID BEFORE.
PEACEFUL FARMERS EH...? WE WENT FROM PEACEFUL FARMERS TO CRAZY PHARMACISTS!
THAT'S WHY I NEEDED THIS TRIP. EVERY YEAR WE'D DO THE SAME THING WHEN WE WENT TO PR BUT THIS OPENED MY EYES A LOT.
IF THEY NEVER TAUGHT US THIS IN SCHOOL, WHAT ELSE HAVE THEY NOT TAUGHT US ABOUT WHO WE ARE?
ON THE WAY OUT FROM THE VILLAGE, THE GUIDE AND MY MOM WERE TALKING ABOUT SOME OTHER PLACE THAT HAD MORE INFORMATION ABOUT TAINOS THAT WERE STILL AROUND BUT WERE UP IN THE MOUNTAINS. WE DIDN'T HAVE TIME TO VISIT MORE, BUT I WANT TO THE NEXT TIME WE GO.
MAAAN, I WANT TO GO TO PUERTO RICO EVEN MORE NOW!
TAKE MAD PICTURES AND TRY TO SEE AS MUCH AS YOU CAN!
END

## ***Blame It On 'Rico*** by Alberto 'Tito' Serrano

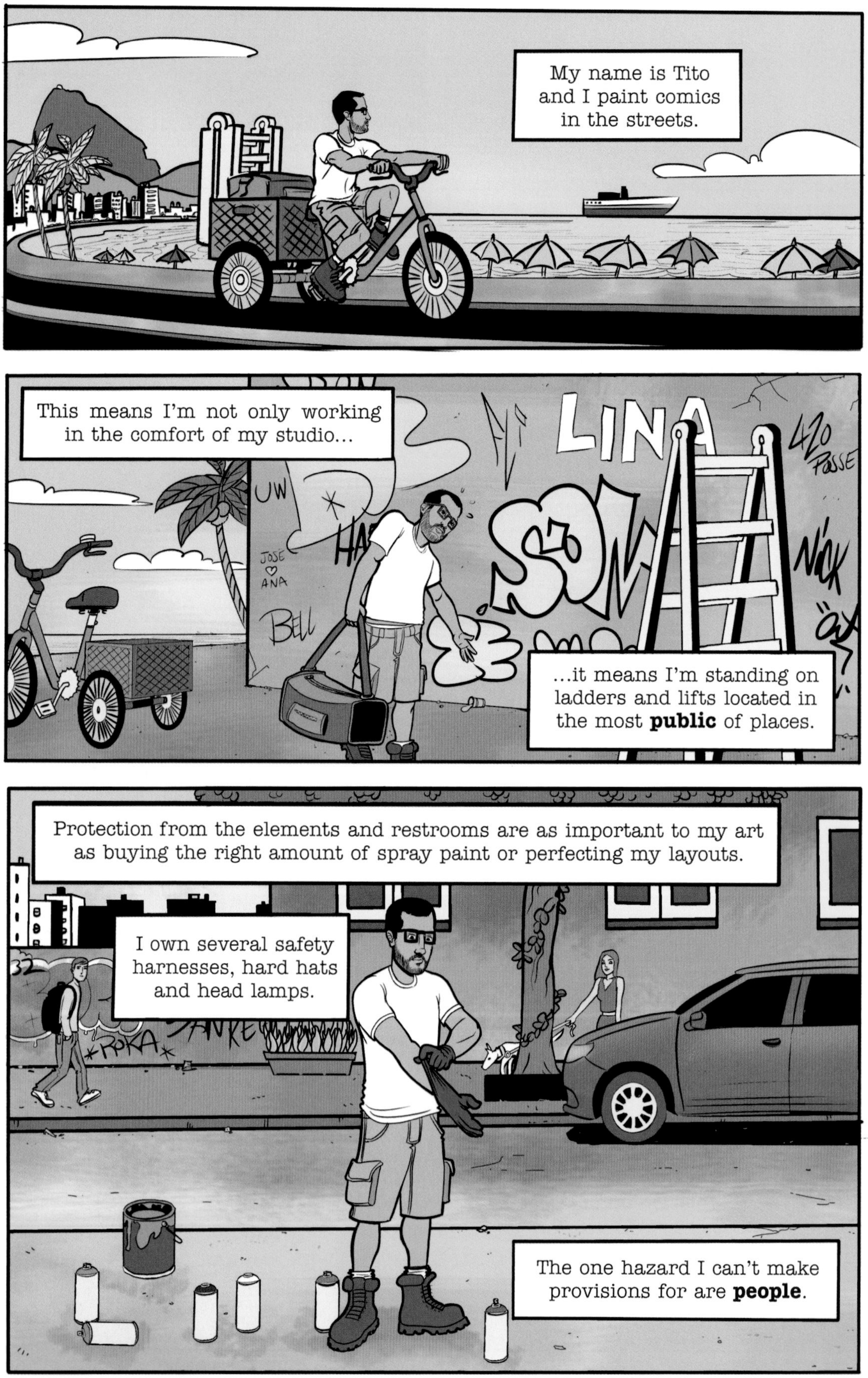

My name is Tito and I paint comics in the streets.
This means I'm not only working in the comfort of my studio...
LINA
...it means I'm standing on ladders and lifts located in the most **public** of places.
Protection from the elements and restrooms are as important to my art as buying the right amount of spray paint or perfecting my layouts.
I own several safety harnesses, hard hats and head lamps.
The one hazard I can't make provisions for are **people**.

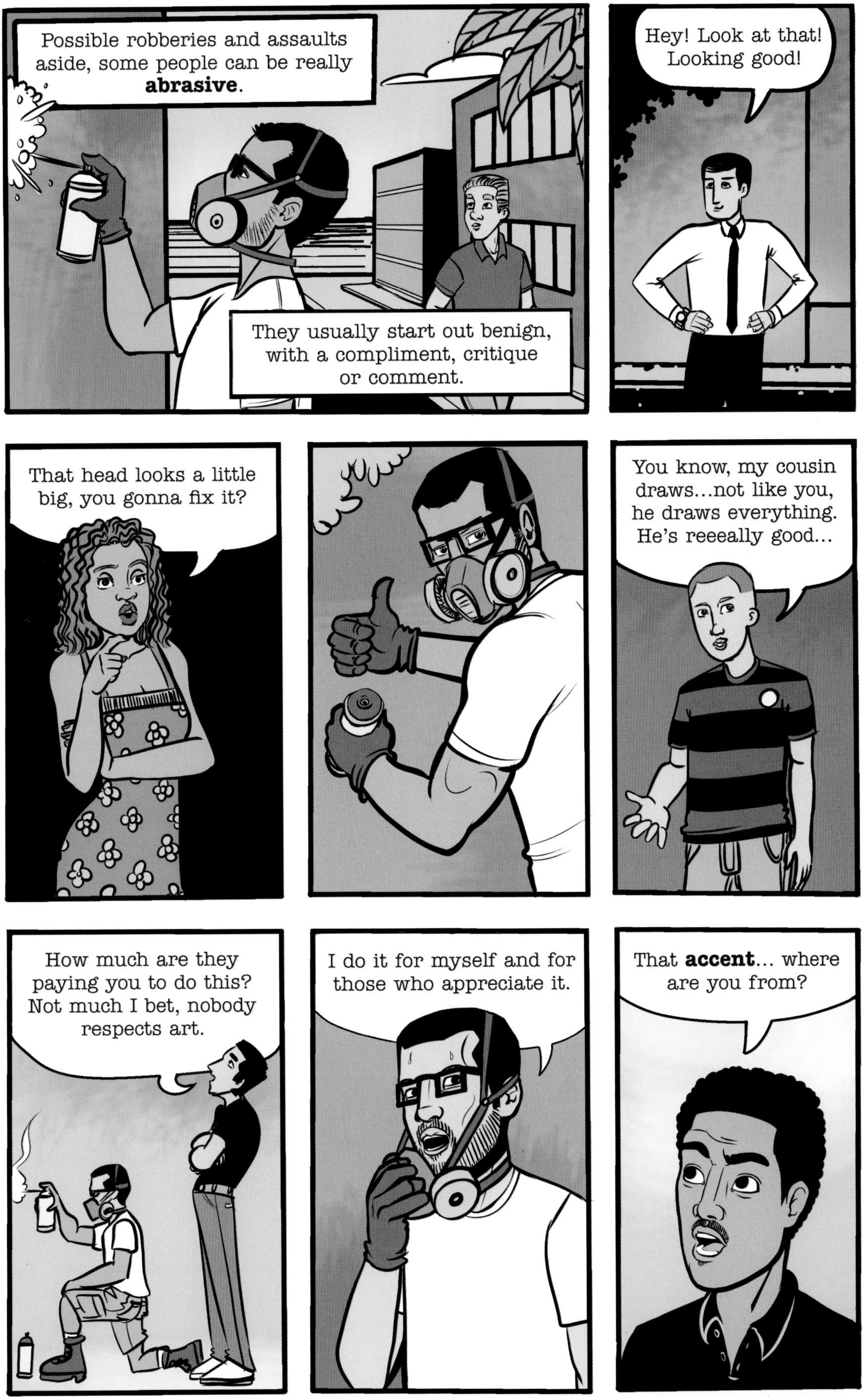
Possible robberies and assaults aside, some people can be really **abrasive**.
They usually start out benign, with a compliment, critique or comment.
Hey! Look at that! Looking good!
That head looks a little big, you gonna fix it?
You know, my cousin draws...not like you, he draws everything. He's reeeally good...
How much are they paying you to do this? Not much I bet, nobody respects art.
I do it for myself and for those who appreciate it.
That **accent**... where are you from?

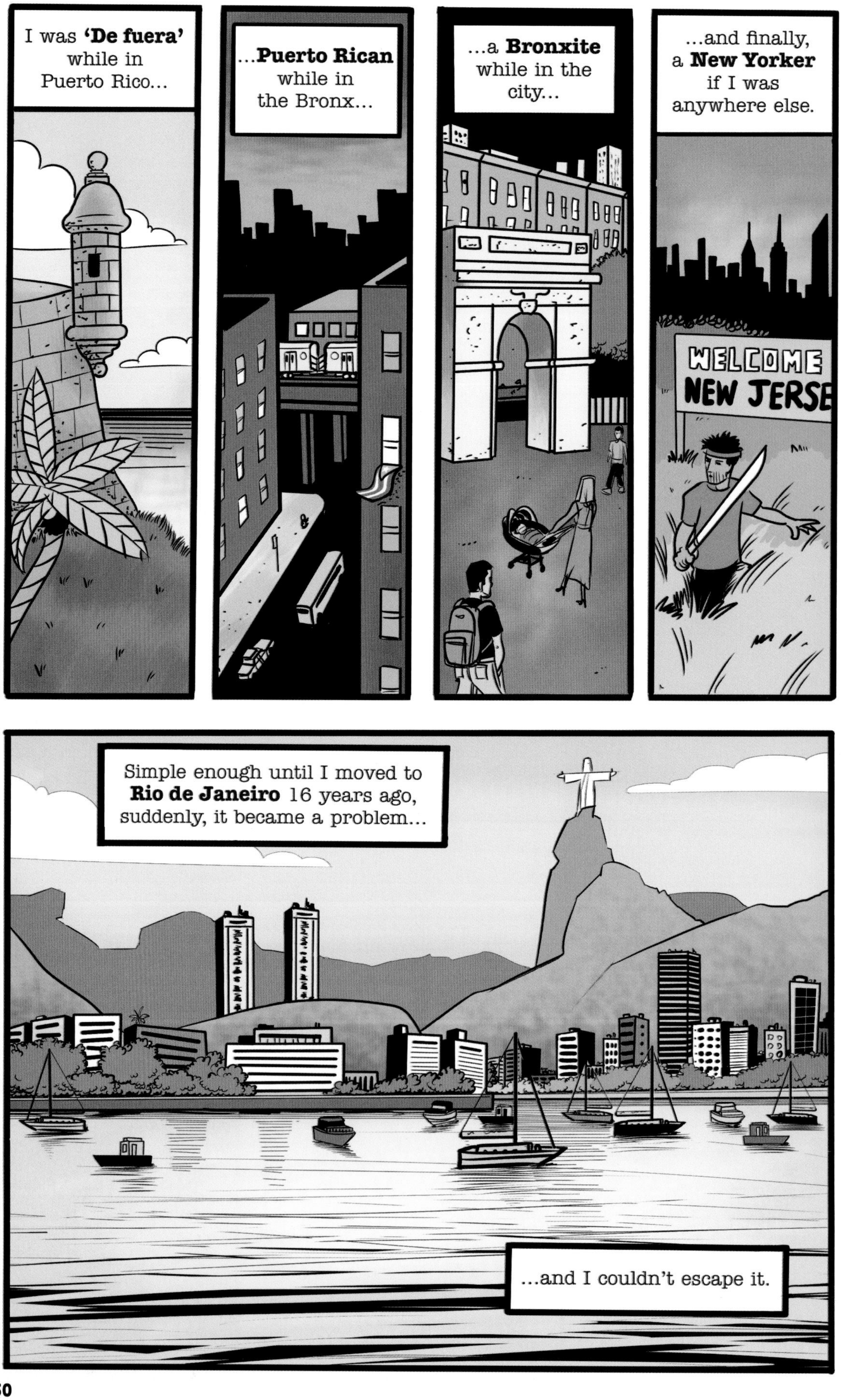
I was **'De fuera'** while in Puerto Rico...
...**Puerto Rican** while in the Bronx...
...a **Bronxite** while in the city...
...and finally, a **New Yorker** if I was anywhere else.
WELCOME NEW JERSE
Simple enough until I moved to **Rio de Janeiro** 16 years ago, suddenly, it became a problem...
...and I couldn't escape it.

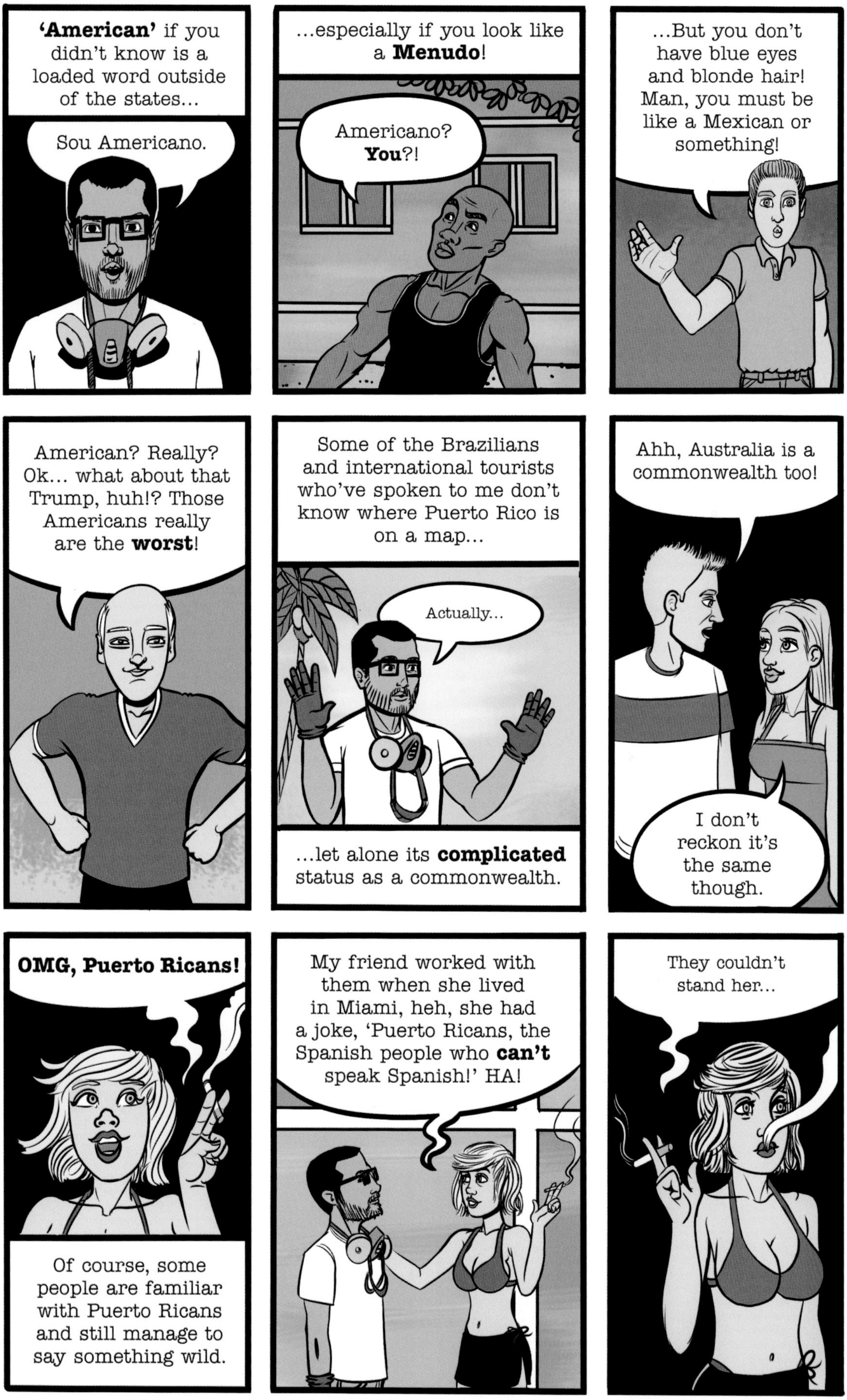

**'American'** if you didn't know is a loaded word outside of the states...
Sou Americano.
...especially if you look like a **Menudo**!
Americano? **You**?!
...But you don't have blue eyes and blonde hair! Man, you must be like a Mexican or something!
American? Really? Ok... what about that Trump, huh!? Those Americans really are the **worst**!
Some of the Brazilians and international tourists who've spoken to me don't know where Puerto Rico is on a map...
Actually...
...let alone its **complicated** status as a commonwealth.
Ahh, Australia is a commonwealth too!
I don't reckon it's the same though.
**OMG, Puerto Ricans!**
Of course, some people are familiar with Puerto Ricans and still manage to say something wild.
My friend worked with them when she lived in Miami, heh, she had a joke, 'Puerto Ricans, the Spanish people who **can't** speak Spanish!' HA!
They couldn't stand her...

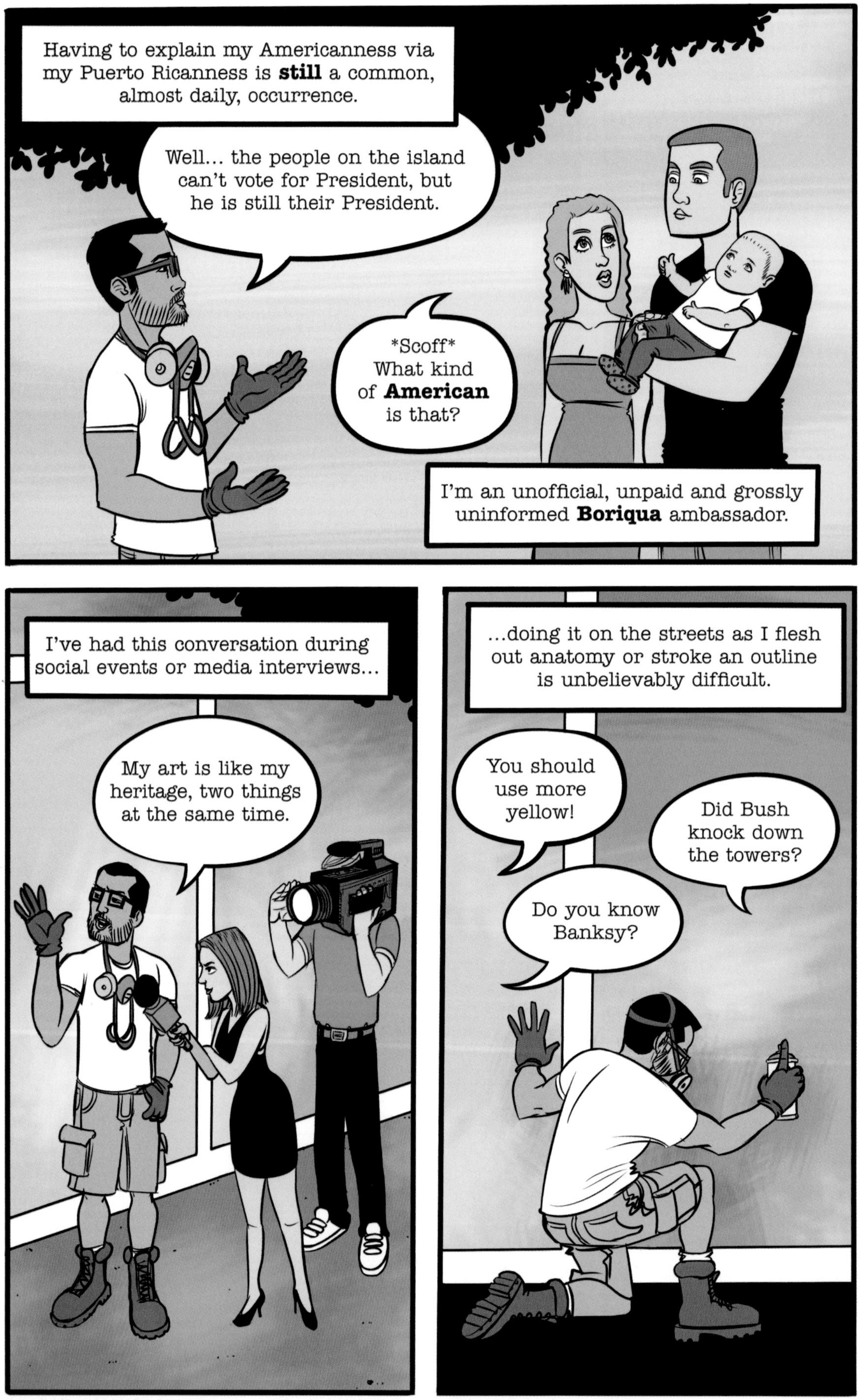
Having to explain my Americanness via my Puerto Ricanness is **still** a common, almost daily, occurrence.
Well... the people on the island can't vote for President, but he is still their President.
*Scoff* What kind of **American** is that?
I'm an unofficial, unpaid and grossly uninformed **Boriqua** ambassador.
I've had this conversation during social events or media interviews...
My art is like my heritage, two things at the same time.
...doing it on the streets as I flesh out anatomy or stroke an outline is unbelievably difficult.
You should use more yellow!
Did Bush knock down the towers?
Do you know Banksy?

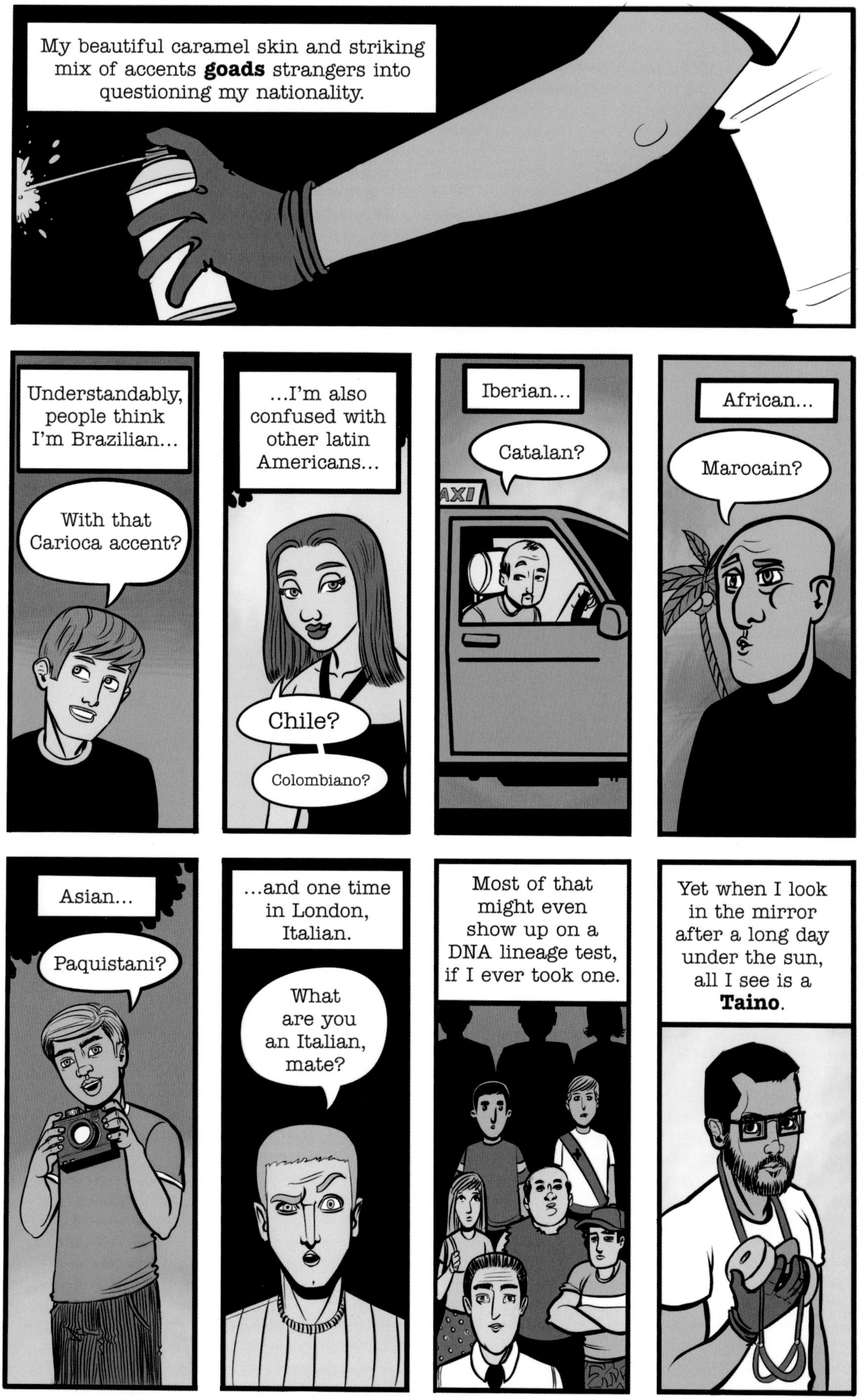

My beautiful caramel skin and striking mix of accents **goads** strangers into questioning my nationality.
Understandably, people think I'm Brazilian...
With that Carioca accent?
...I'm also confused with other latin Americans...
Chile?
Colombiano?
Iberian...
Catalan?
AXI
African...
Marocain?
Asian...
Paquistani?
...and one time in London, Italian.
What are you an Italian, mate?
Most of that might even show up on a DNA lineage test, if I ever took one.
Yet when I look in the mirror after a long day under the sun, all I see is a **Taino**.

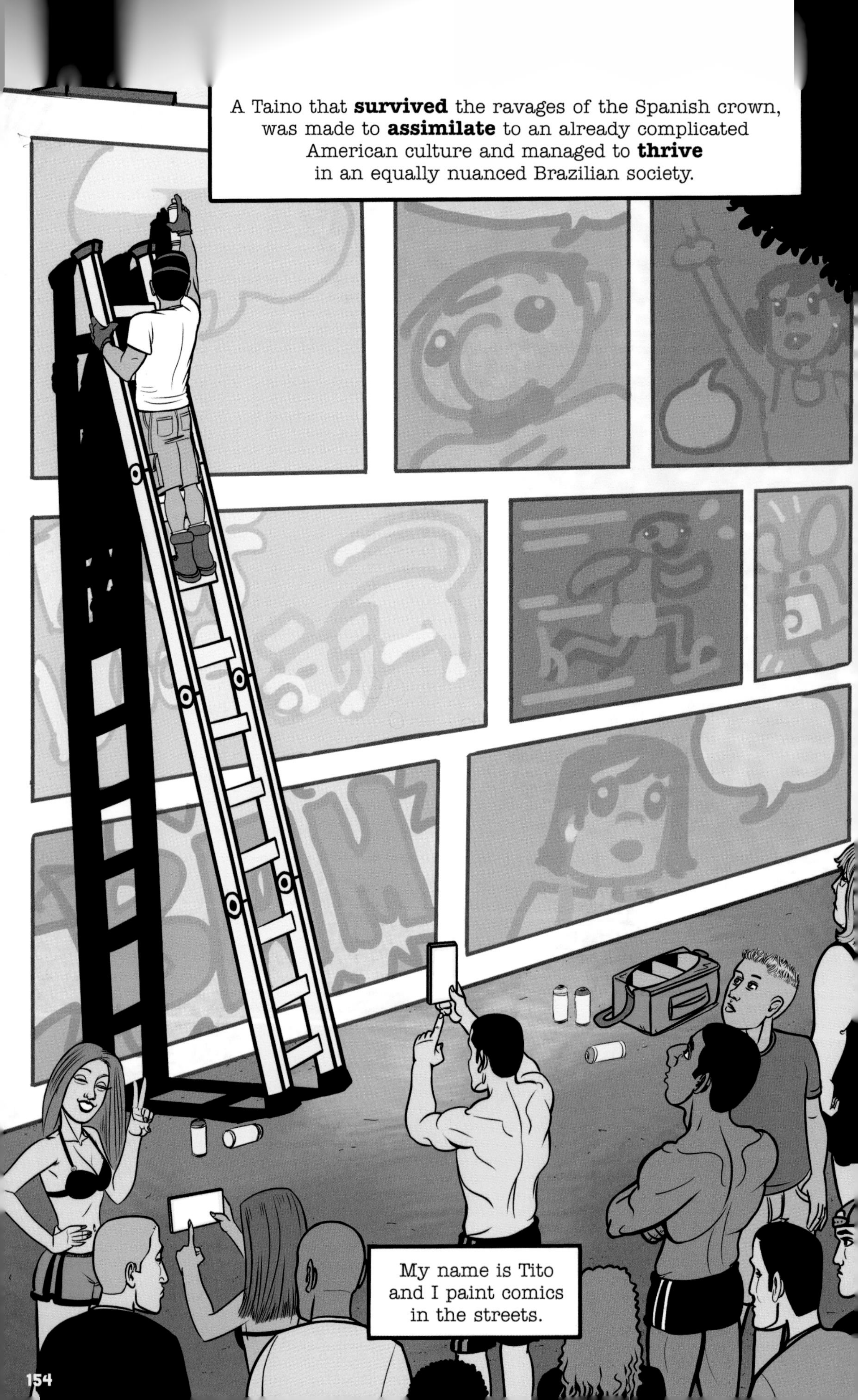
A Taino that **survived** the ravages of the Spanish crown, was made to **assimilate** to an already complicated American culture and managed to **thrive** in an equally nuanced Brazilian society.
My name is Tito and I paint comics in the streets.

# Macondo, Puerto Rico

WRITTEN BY JAVIER MORILLO ILLUSTRATED BY DAN MÉNDEZ MOORE

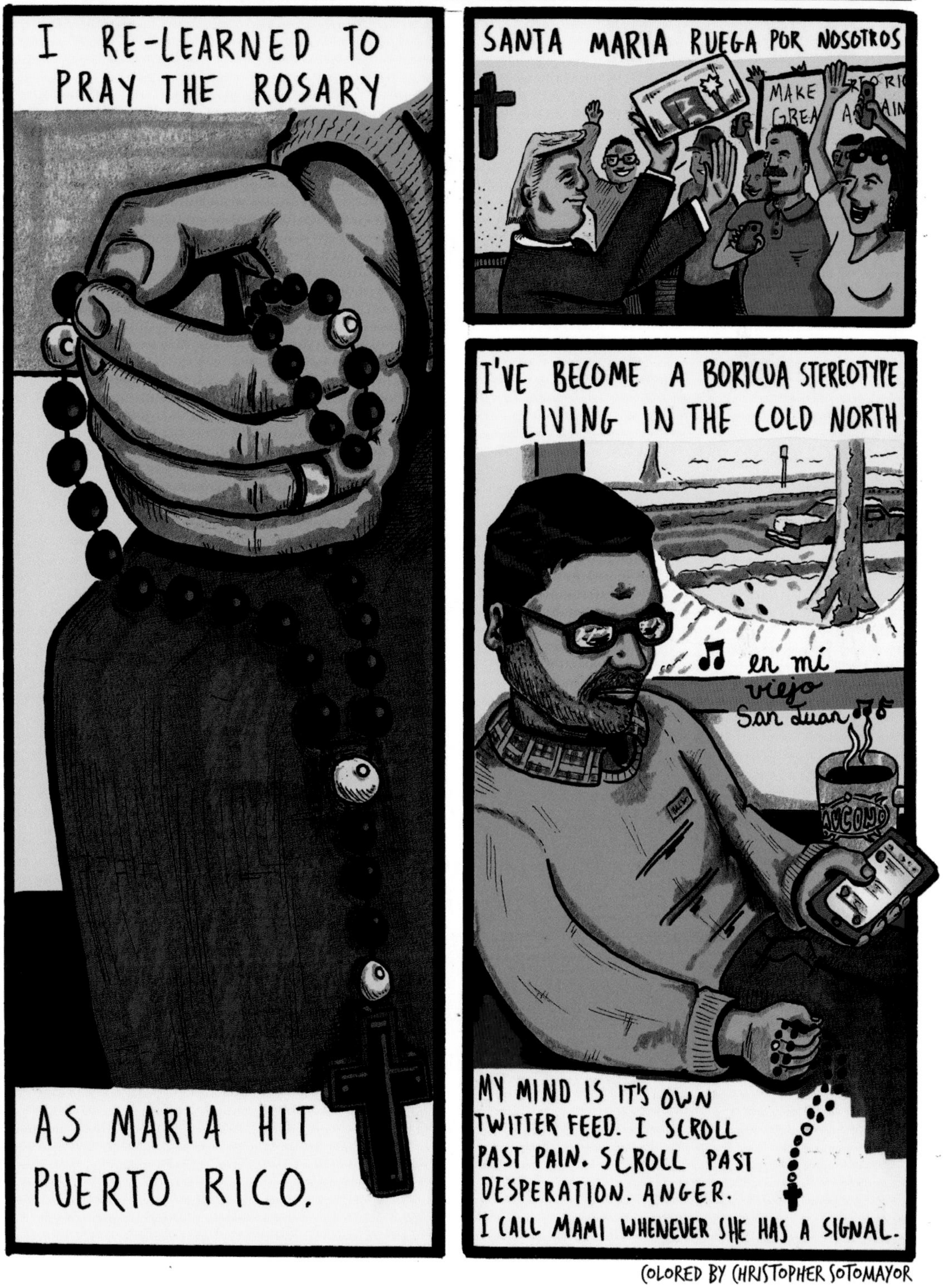

I RE-LEARNED TO PRAY THE ROSARY
AS MARIA HIT PUERTO RICO.
SANTA MARIA RUEGA POR NOSOTROS
MAKE
I'VE BECOME A BORICUA STEREOTYPE LIVING IN THE COLD NORTH
en mí viejo San Juan
MY MIND IS IT'S OWN TWITTER FEED. I SCROLL PAST PAIN. SCROLL PAST DESPERATION. ANGER.
I CALL MAMI WHENEVER SHE HAS A SIGNAL.


COLORED BY CHRISTOPHER SOTOMAYOR

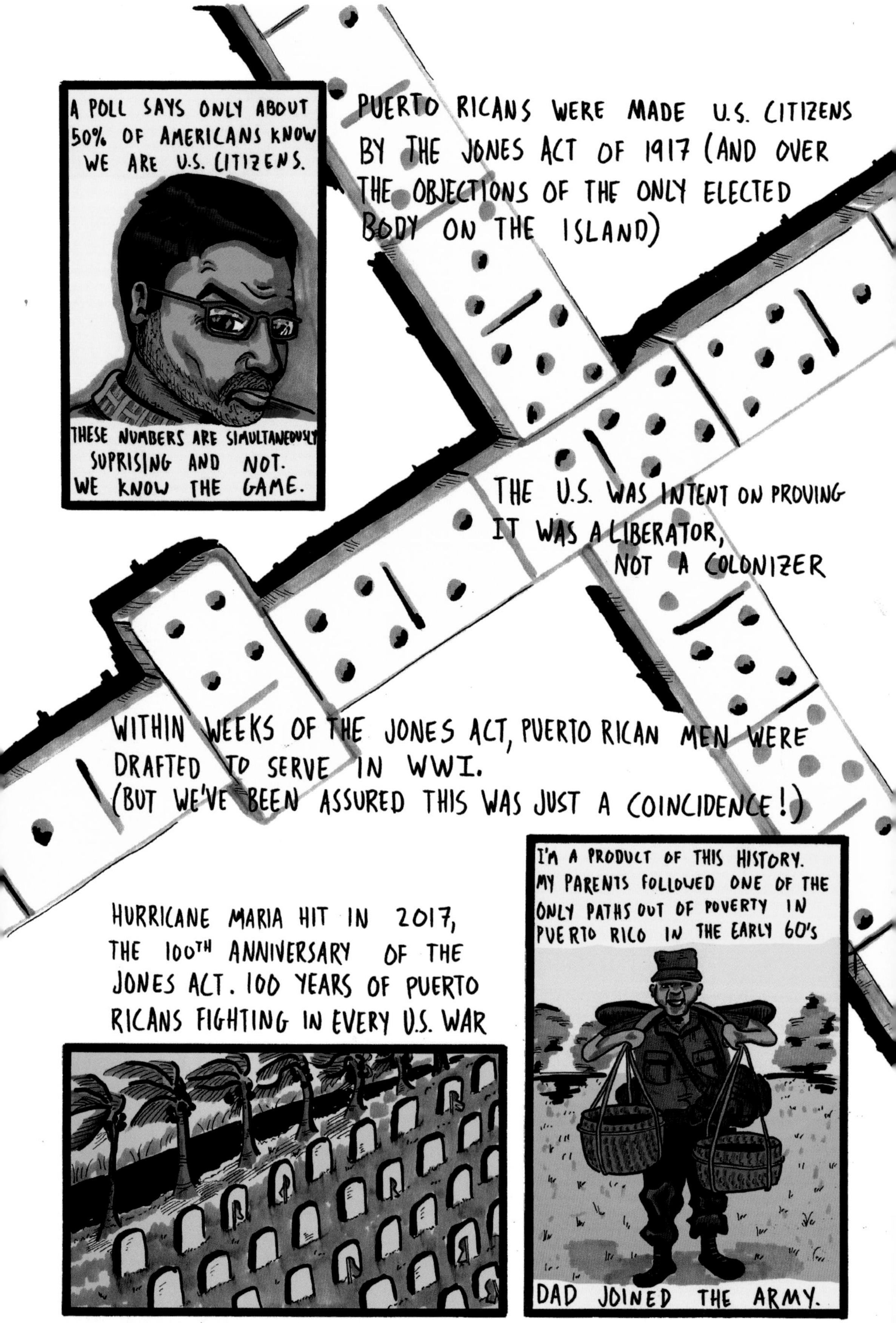
A POLL SAYS ONLY ABOUT 50% OF AMERICANS KNOW WE ARE U.S. CITIZENS.
THESE NUMBERS ARE SIMULTANEOUSLY SUPRISING AND NOT. WE KNOW THE GAME.
PUERTO RICANS WERE MADE U.S. CITIZENS BY THE JONES ACT OF 1917 (AND OVER THE OBJECTIONS OF THE ONLY ELECTED BODY ON THE ISLAND)
THE U.S. WAS INTENT ON PROVING IT WAS A LIBERATOR, NOT A COLONIZER
WITHIN WEEKS OF THE JONES ACT, PUERTO RICAN MEN WERE DRAFTED TO SERVE IN WWI.
(BUT WE'VE BEEN ASSURED THIS WAS JUST A COINCIDENCE!)
HURRICANE MARIA HIT IN 2017, THE 100TH ANNIVERSARY OF THE JONES ACT. 100 YEARS OF PUERTO RICANS FIGHTING IN EVERY U.S. WAR
I'M A PRODUCT OF THIS HISTORY. MY PARENTS FOLLOWED ONE OF THE ONLY PATHS OUT OF POVERTY IN PUERTO RICO IN THE EARLY 60'S
DAD JOINED THE ARMY.

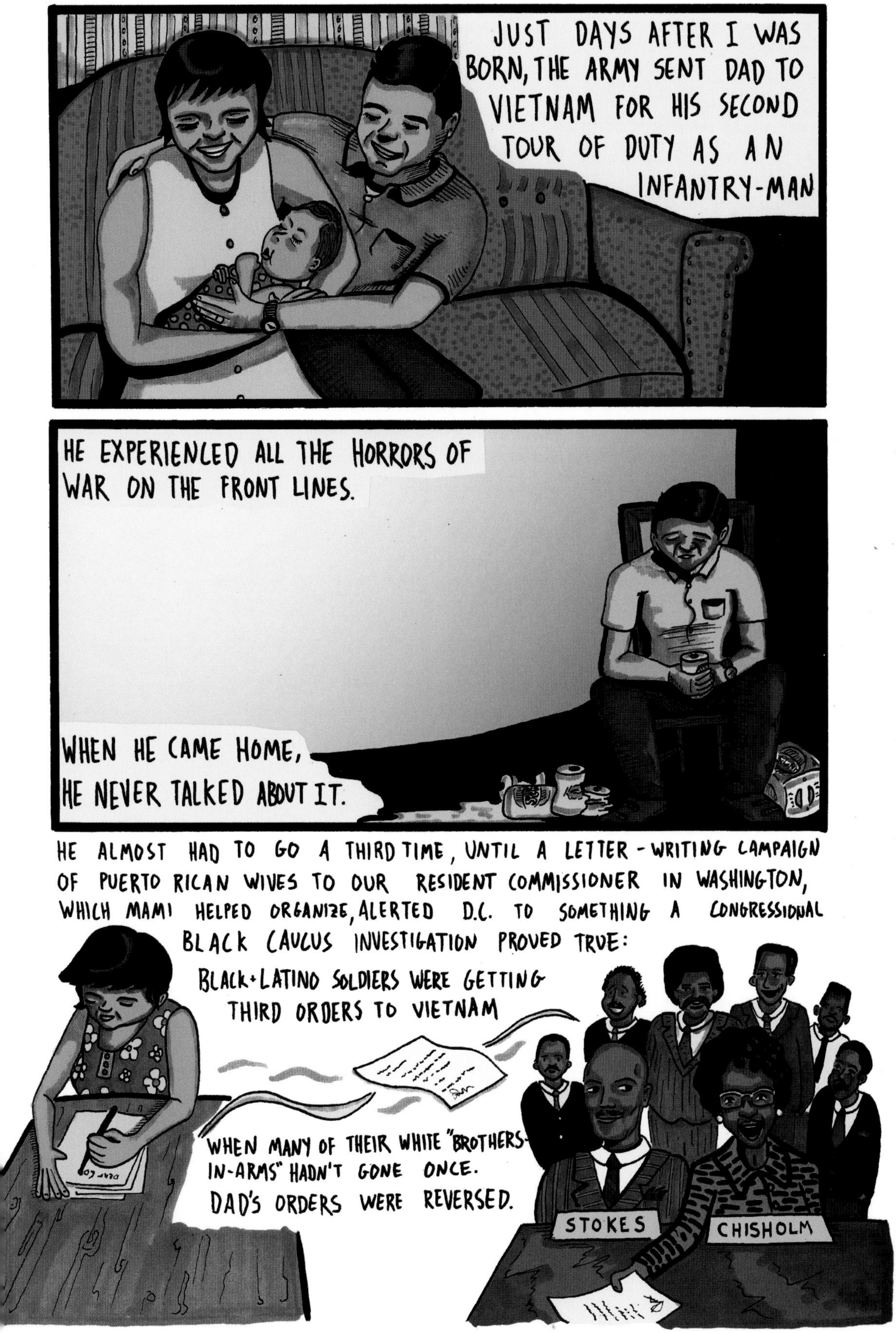
JUST DAYS AFTER I WAS BORN, THE ARMY SENT DAD TO VIETNAM FOR HIS SECOND TOUR OF DUTY AS AN INFANTRY-MAN
HE EXPERIENCED ALL THE HORRORS OF WAR ON THE FRONT LINES.
WHEN HE CAME HOME, HE NEVER TALKED ABOUT IT.
HE ALMOST HAD TO GO A THIRD TIME, UNTIL A LETTER-WRITING CAMPAIGN OF PUERTO RICAN WIVES TO OUR RESIDENT COMMISSIONER IN WASHINGTON, WHICH MAMI HELPED ORGANIZE, ALERTED D.C. TO SOMETHING A CONGRESSIONAL BLACK CAUCUS INVESTIGATION PROVED TRUE:
BLACK + LATINO SOLDIERS WERE GETTING THIRD ORDERS TO VIETNAM
WHEN MANY OF THEIR WHITE "BROTHERS-IN-ARMS" HADN'T GONE ONCE.
DAD'S ORDERS WERE REVERSED.
STOKES
CHISHOLM

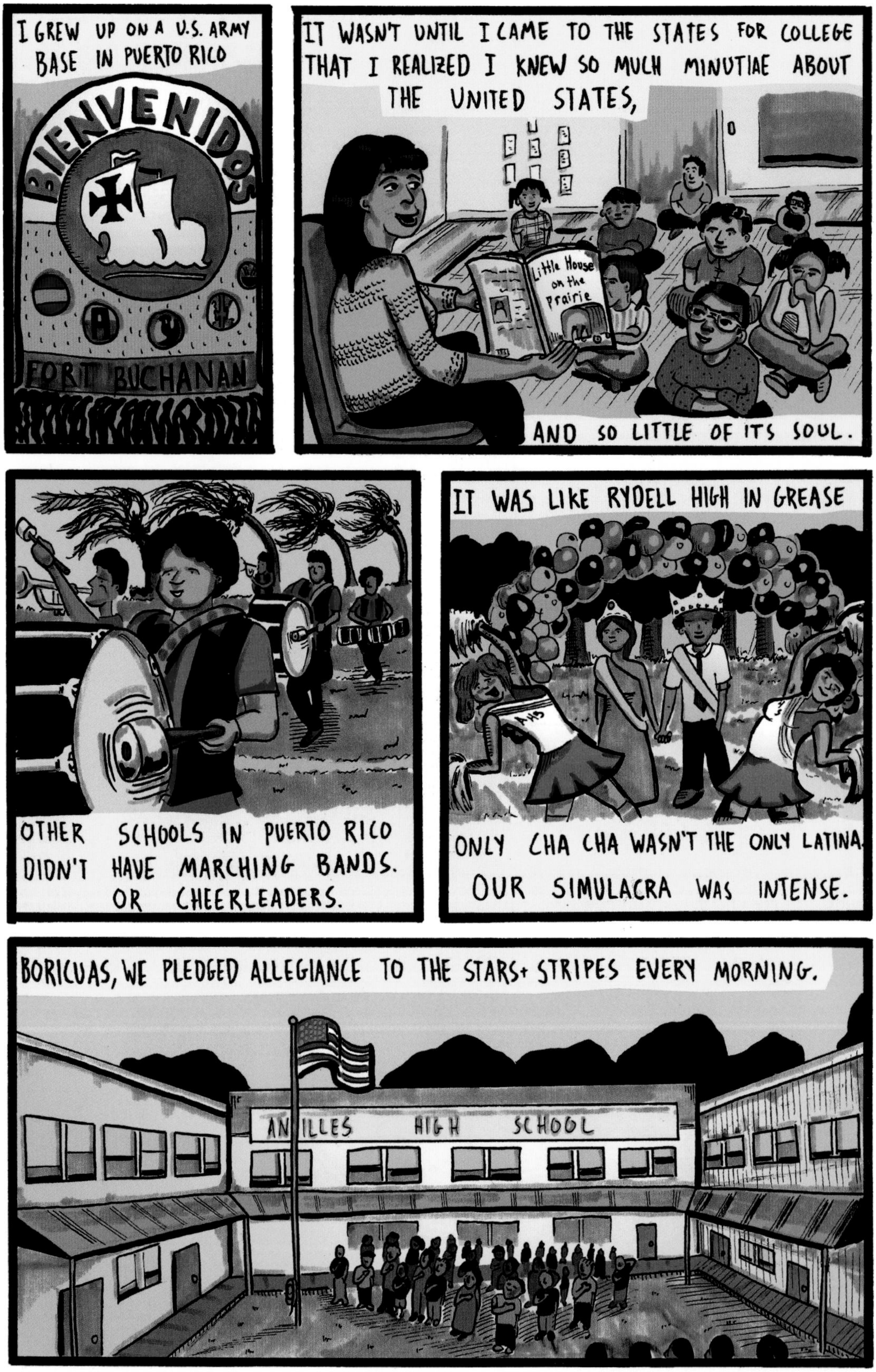
I GREW UP ON A U.S. ARMY BASE IN PUERTO RICO
BIENVENIDOS
FORT BUCHANAN
IT WASN'T UNTIL I CAME TO THE STATES FOR COLLEGE THAT I REALIZED I KNEW SO MUCH MINUTIAE ABOUT THE UNITED STATES,
Little House on the Prairie
AND SO LITTLE OF ITS SOUL.
OTHER SCHOOLS IN PUERTO RICO DIDN'T HAVE MARCHING BANDS. OR CHEERLEADERS.
IT WAS LIKE RYDELL HIGH IN GREASE
AHS
ONLY CHA CHA WASN'T THE ONLY LATINA.
OUR SIMULACRA WAS INTENSE.
BORICUAS, WE PLEDGED ALLEGIANCE TO THE STARS+ STRIPES EVERY MORNING.
AN ILLES HIGH SCHOOL

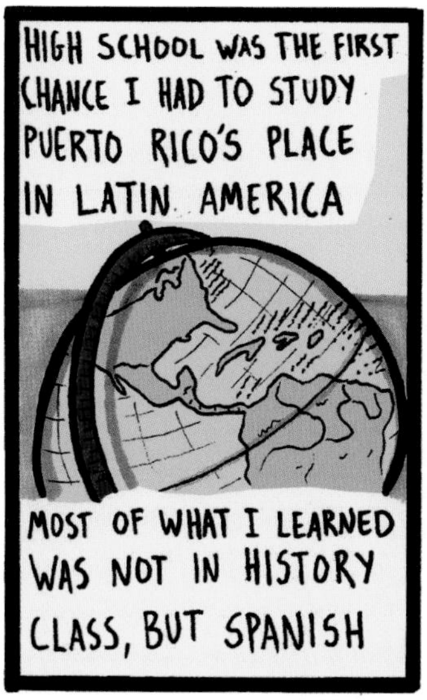
HIGH SCHOOL WAS THE FIRST CHANCE I HAD TO STUDY PUERTO RICO'S PLACE IN LATIN AMERICA
MOST OF WHAT I LEARNED WAS NOT IN HISTORY CLASS, BUT SPANISH

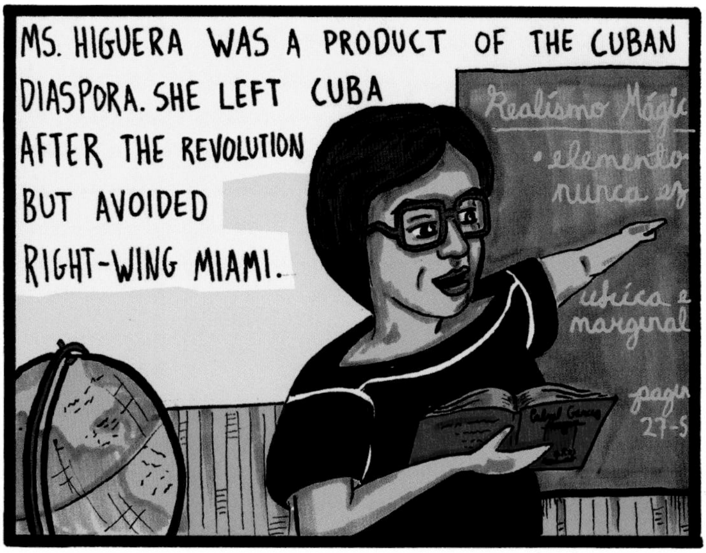
MS. HIGUERA WAS A PRODUCT OF THE CUBAN DIASPORA. SHE LEFT CUBA AFTER THE REVOLUTION BUT AVOIDED RIGHT-WING MIAMI.

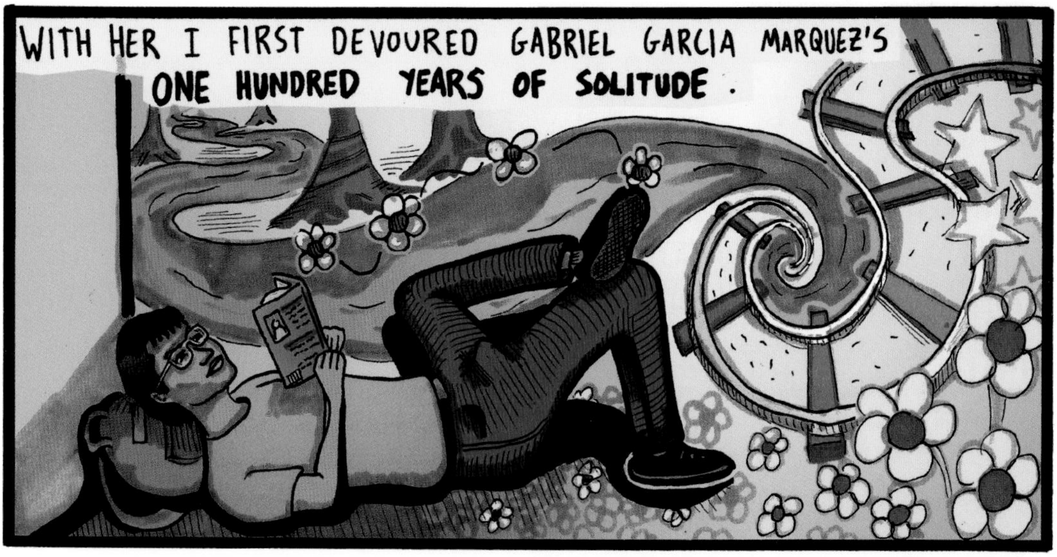
WITH HER I FIRST DEVOURED GABRIEL GARCIA MARQUEZ'S **ONE HUNDRED YEARS OF SOLITUDE**.

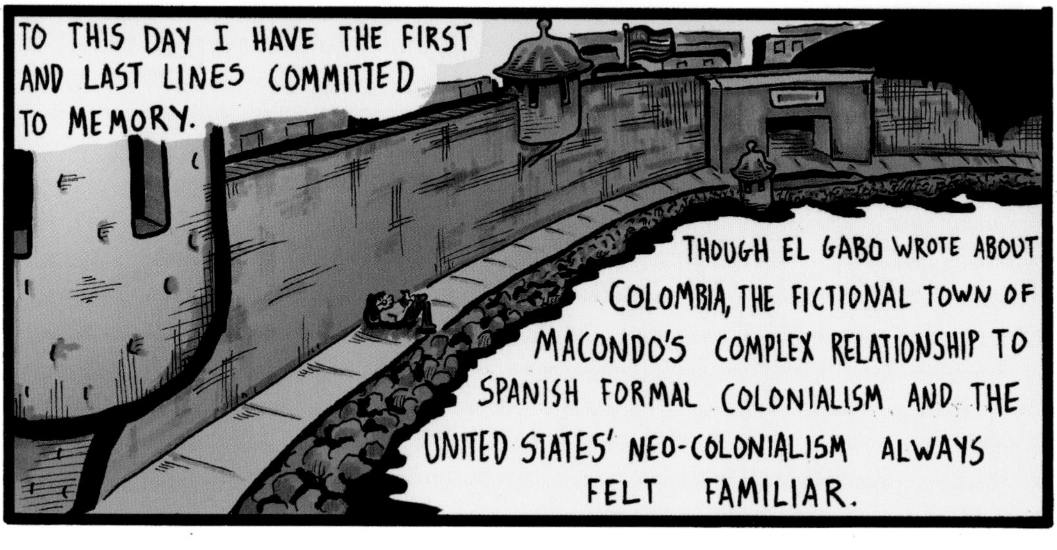
TO THIS DAY I HAVE THE FIRST AND LAST LINES COMMITTED TO MEMORY.
THOUGH EL GABO WROTE ABOUT COLOMBIA, THE FICTIONAL TOWN OF MACONDO'S COMPLEX RELATIONSHIP TO SPANISH FORMAL COLONIALISM AND THE UNITED STATES' NEO-COLONIALISM ALWAYS FELT FAMILIAR.

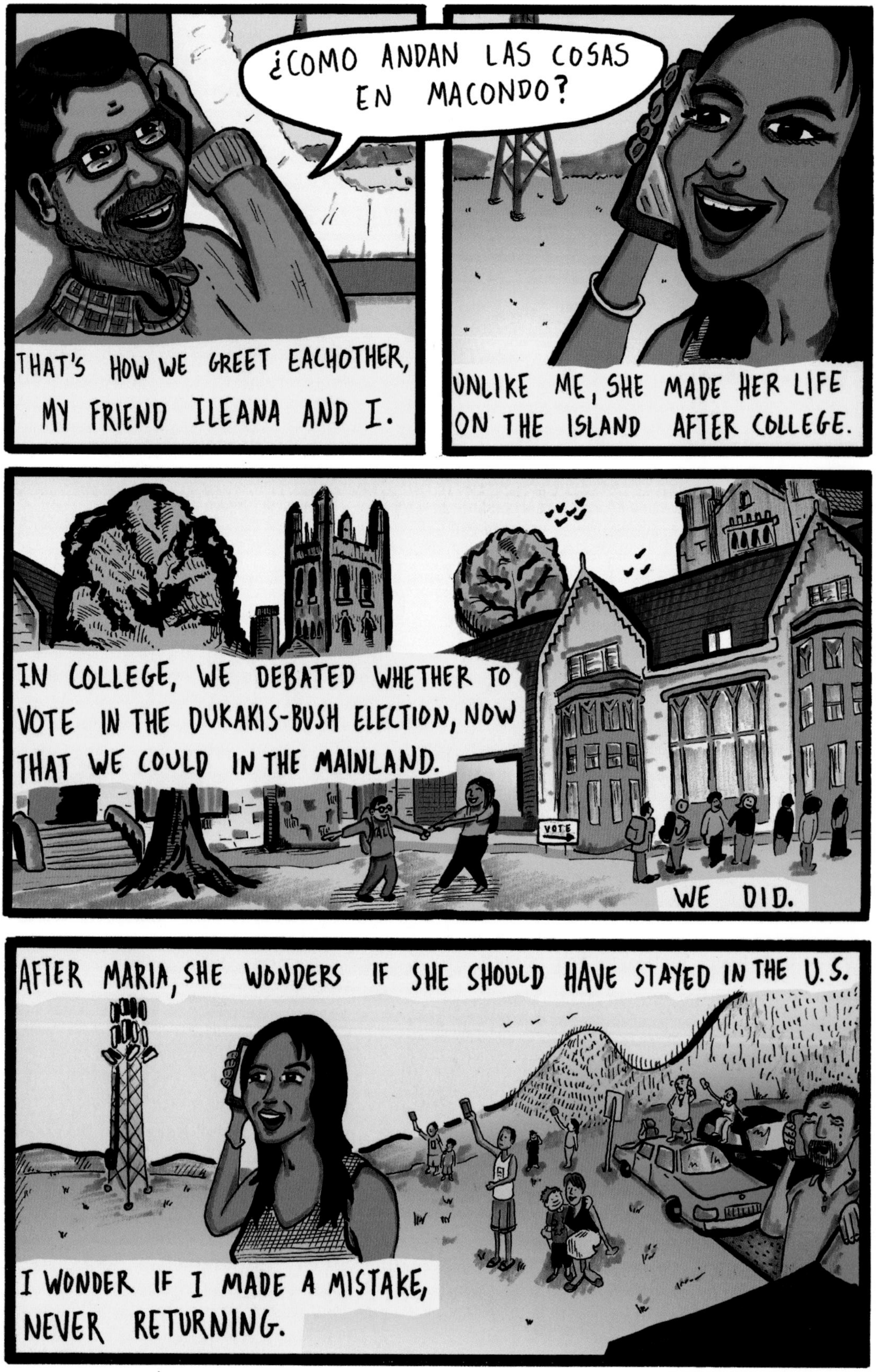
¿COMO ANDAN LAS COSAS EN MACONDO?
THAT'S HOW WE GREET EACHOTHER, MY FRIEND ILEANA AND I.
UNLIKE ME, SHE MADE HER LIFE ON THE ISLAND AFTER COLLEGE.
IN COLLEGE, WE DEBATED WHETHER TO VOTE IN THE DUKAKIS-BUSH ELECTION, NOW THAT WE COULD IN THE MAINLAND.
VOTE
WE DID.
AFTER MARIA, SHE WONDERS IF SHE SHOULD HAVE STAYED IN THE U.S.
I WONDER IF I MADE A MISTAKE, NEVER RETURNING.

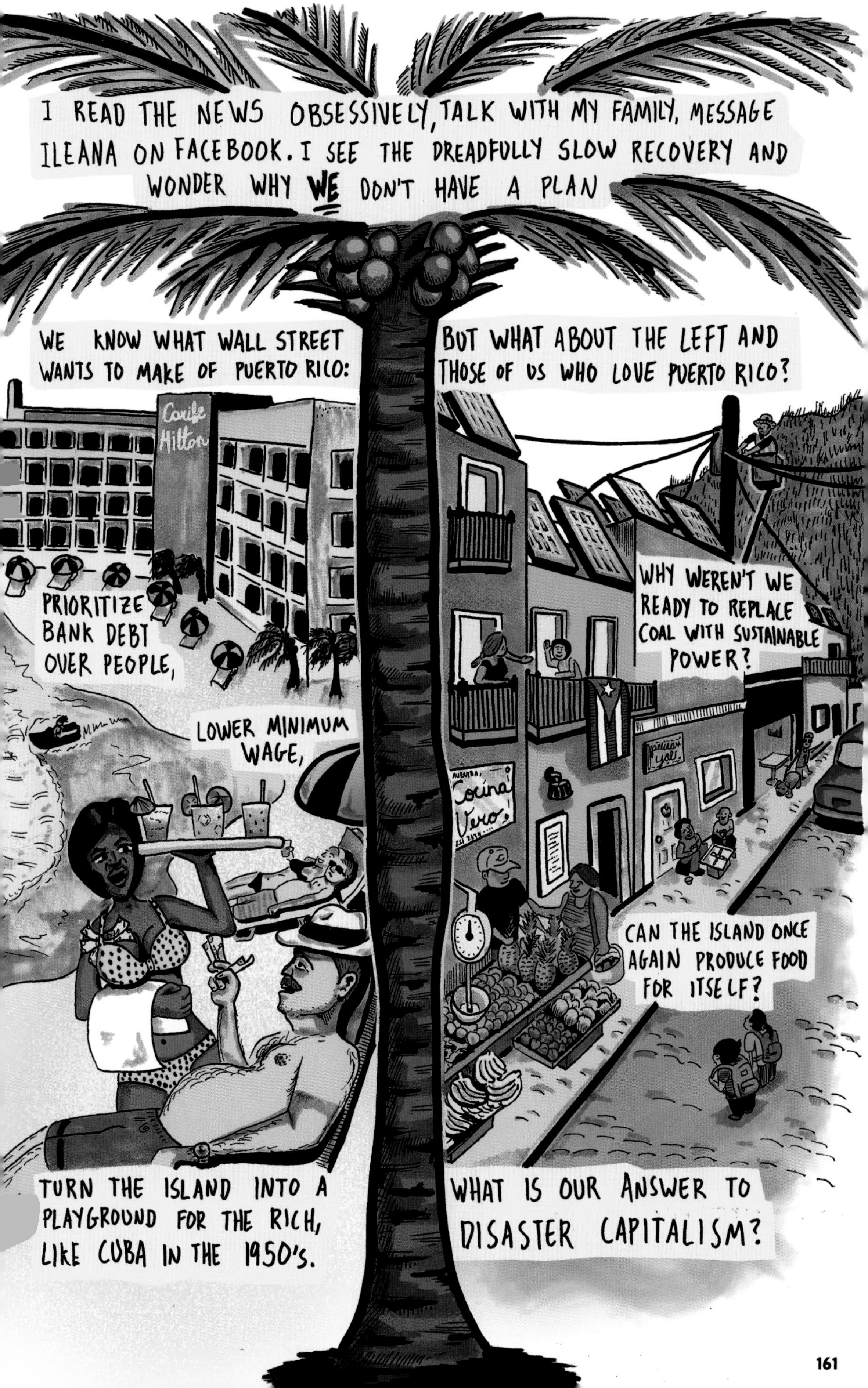
I READ THE NEWS OBSESSIVELY, TALK WITH MY FAMILY, MESSAGE ILEANA ON FACEBOOK. I SEE THE DREADFULLY SLOW RECOVERY AND WONDER WHY WE DON'T HAVE A PLAN
WE KNOW WHAT WALL STREET WANTS TO MAKE OF PUERTO RICO:
Caribe Hilton
PRIORITIZE BANK DEBT OVER PEOPLE,
LOWER MINIMUM WAGE,
TURN THE ISLAND INTO A PLAYGROUND FOR THE RICH, LIKE CUBA IN THE 1950'S.
BUT WHAT ABOUT THE LEFT AND THOSE OF US WHO LOVE PUERTO RICO?
WHY WEREN'T WE READY TO REPLACE COAL WITH SUSTAINABLE POWER?
Cocina Vero
CAN THE ISLAND ONCE AGAIN PRODUCE FOOD FOR ITSELF?
WHAT IS OUR ANSWER TO DISASTER CAPITALISM?

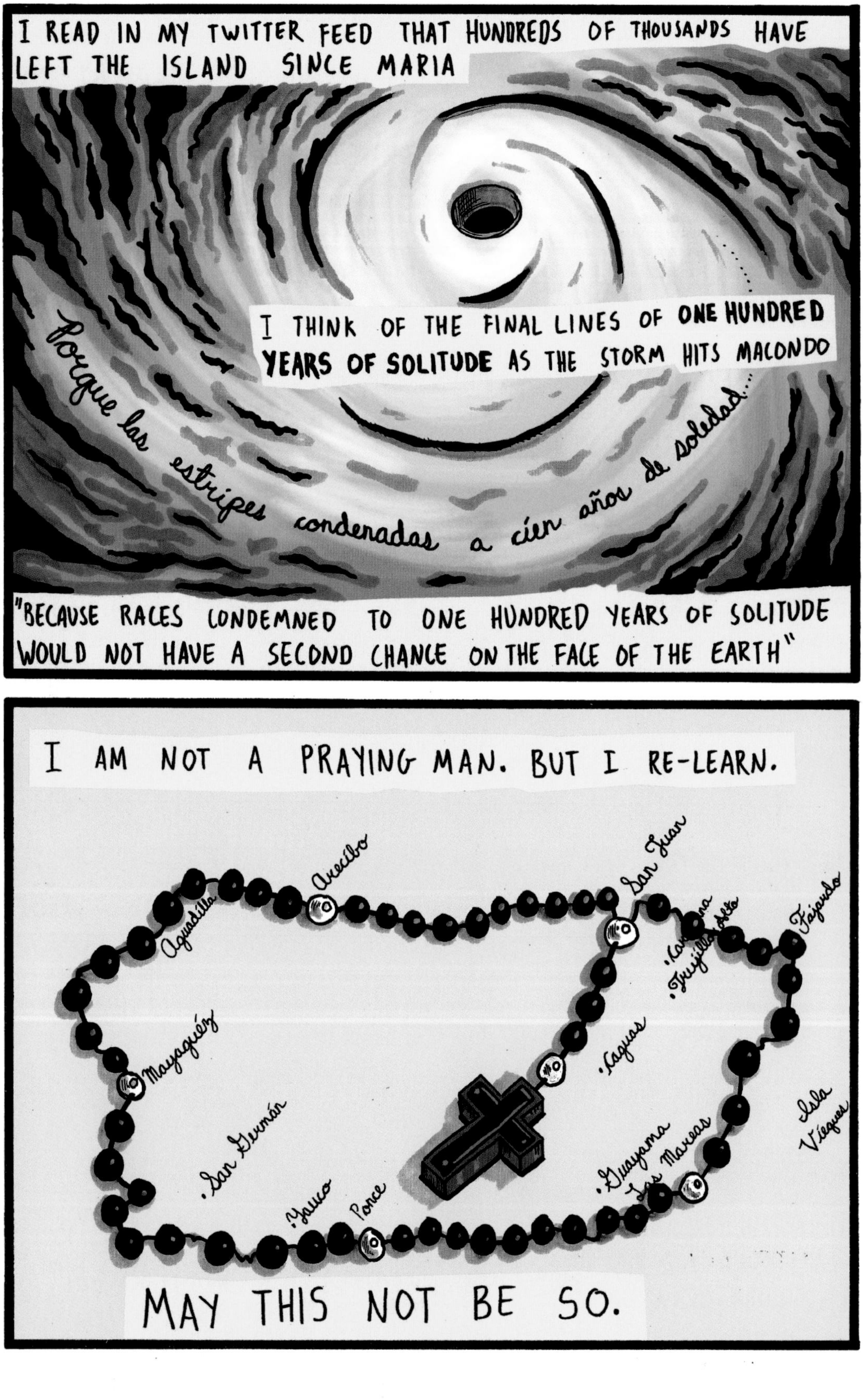
I READ IN MY TWITTER FEED THAT HUNDREDS OF THOUSANDS HAVE LEFT THE ISLAND SINCE MARIA
I THINK OF THE FINAL LINES OF ONE HUNDRED YEARS OF SOLITUDE AS THE STORM HITS MACONDO
Porque las estripes condenadas a cien años de soledad...
"BECAUSE RACES CONDEMNED TO ONE HUNDRED YEARS OF SOLITUDE WOULD NOT HAVE A SECOND CHANCE ON THE FACE OF THE EARTH"
I AM NOT A PRAYING MAN. BUT I RE-LEARN.
Aguadilla
Arecibo
San Juan
Fajardo
Mayagüez
Caguas
San Germán
Isla Vieques
Guayama
Las Mareas
Yauco
Ponce
MAY THIS NOT BE SO.

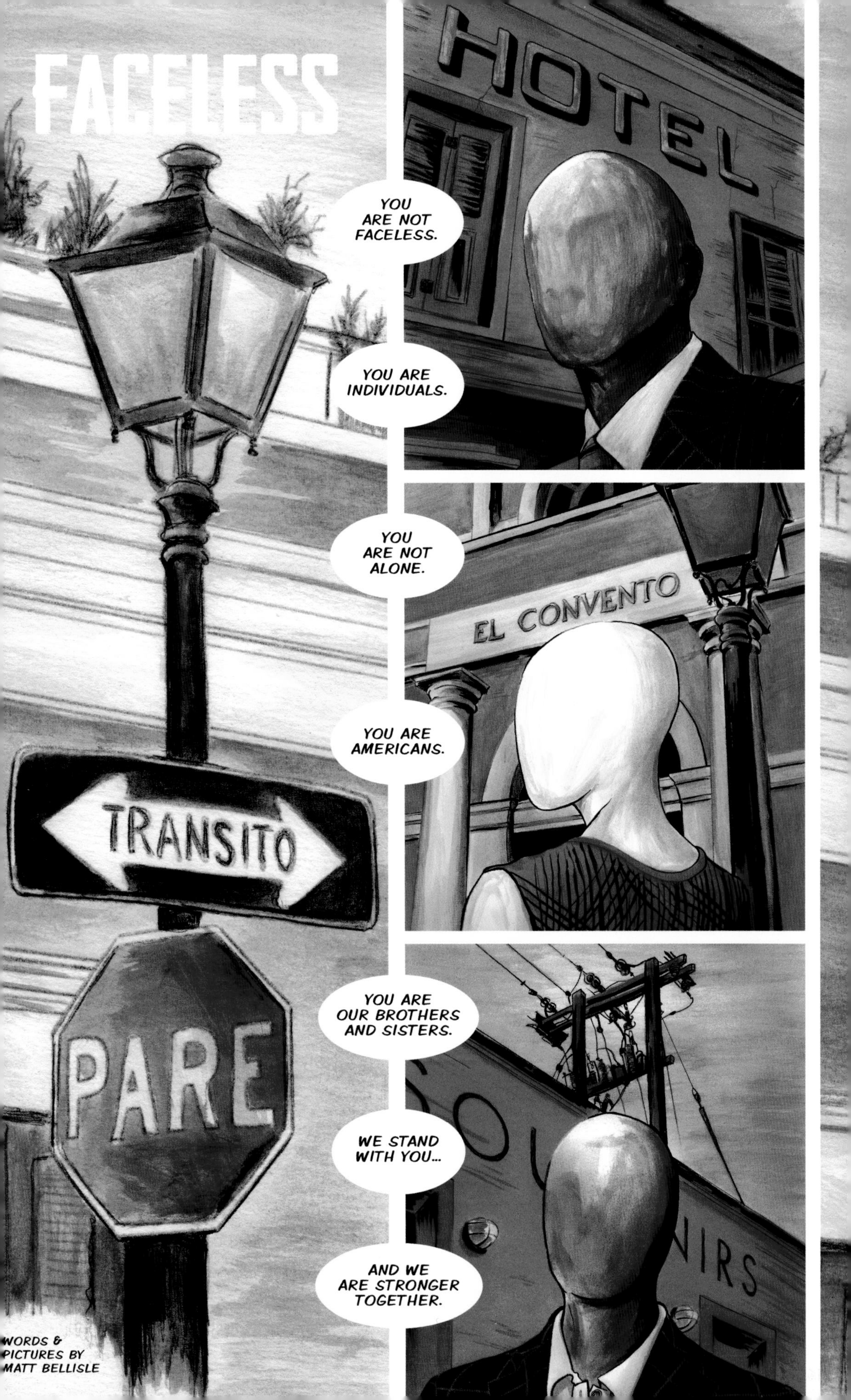
FACELESS
HOTEL
YOU ARE NOT FACELESS.
YOU ARE INDIVIDUALS.
YOU ARE NOT ALONE.
EL CONVENTO
YOU ARE AMERICANS.
TRANSITO
PARE
YOU ARE OUR BROTHERS AND SISTERS.
WE STAND WITH YOU...
AND WE ARE STRONGER TOGETHER.
WORDS & PICTURES BY MATT BELLISLE

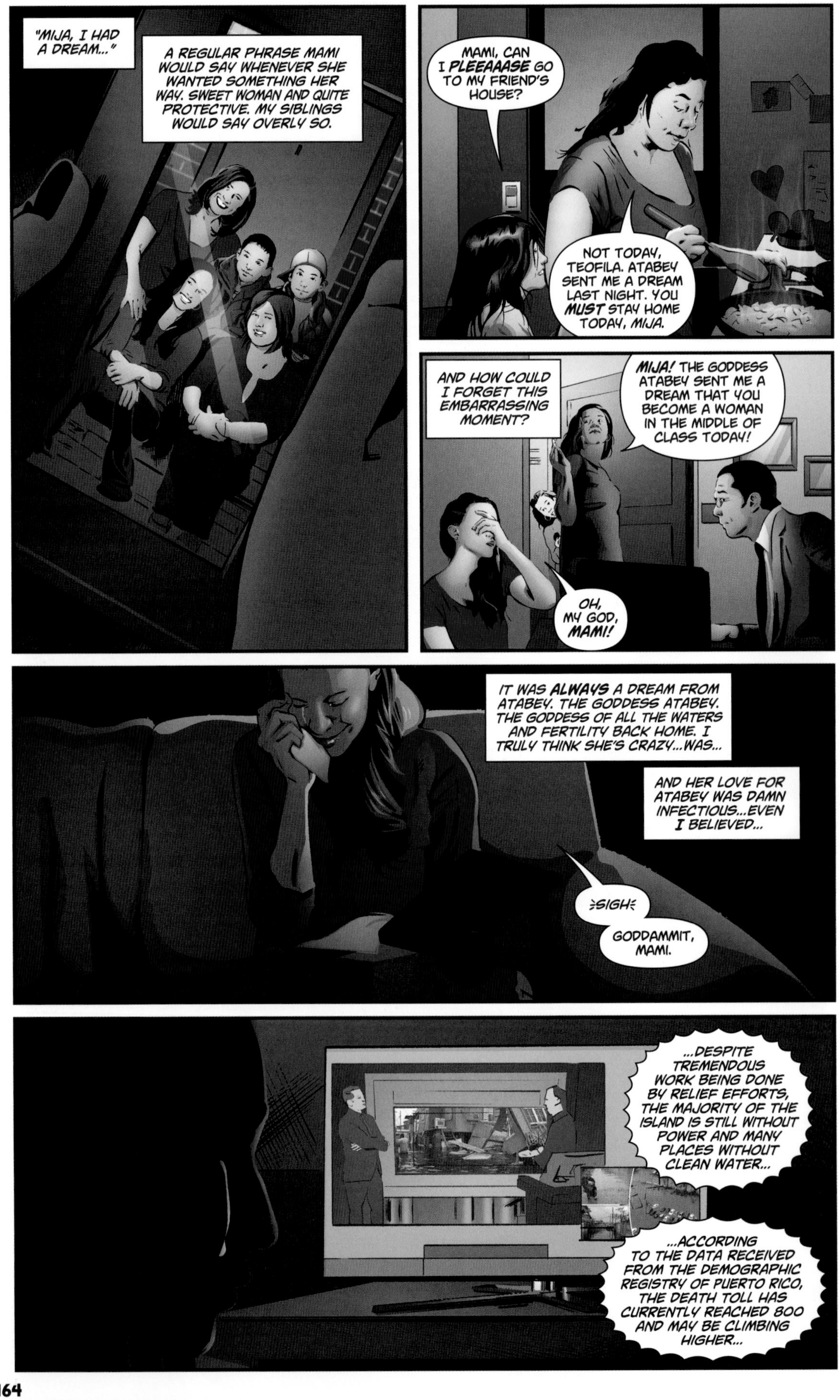
"MIJA, I HAD A DREAM..."
A REGULAR PHRASE MAMI WOULD SAY WHENEVER SHE WANTED SOMETHING HER WAY. SWEET WOMAN AND QUITE PROTECTIVE. MY SIBLINGS WOULD SAY OVERLY SO.
MAMI, CAN I PLEEAAASE GO TO MY FRIEND'S HOUSE?
NOT TODAY, TEOFILA. ATABEY SENT ME A DREAM LAST NIGHT. YOU MUST STAY HOME TODAY, MIJA.
AND HOW COULD I FORGET THIS EMBARRASSING MOMENT?
MIJA! THE GODDESS ATABEY SENT ME A DREAM THAT YOU BECOME A WOMAN IN THE MIDDLE OF CLASS TODAY!
OH, MY GOD, MAMI!
IT WAS ALWAYS A DREAM FROM ATABEY. THE GODDESS ATABEY. THE GODDESS OF ALL THE WATERS AND FERTILITY BACK HOME. I TRULY THINK SHE'S CRAZY...WAS...
AND HER LOVE FOR ATABEY WAS DAMN INFECTIOUS...EVEN I BELIEVED...
SIGH
GODDAMMIT, MAMI.
...DESPITE TREMENDOUS WORK BEING DONE BY RELIEF EFFORTS, THE MAJORITY OF THE ISLAND IS STILL WITHOUT POWER AND MANY PLACES WITHOUT CLEAN WATER...
...ACCORDING TO THE DATA RECEIVED FROM THE DEMOGRAPHIC REGISTRY OF PUERTO RICO, THE DEATH TOLL HAS CURRENTLY REACHED 800 AND MAY BE CLIMBING HIGHER...

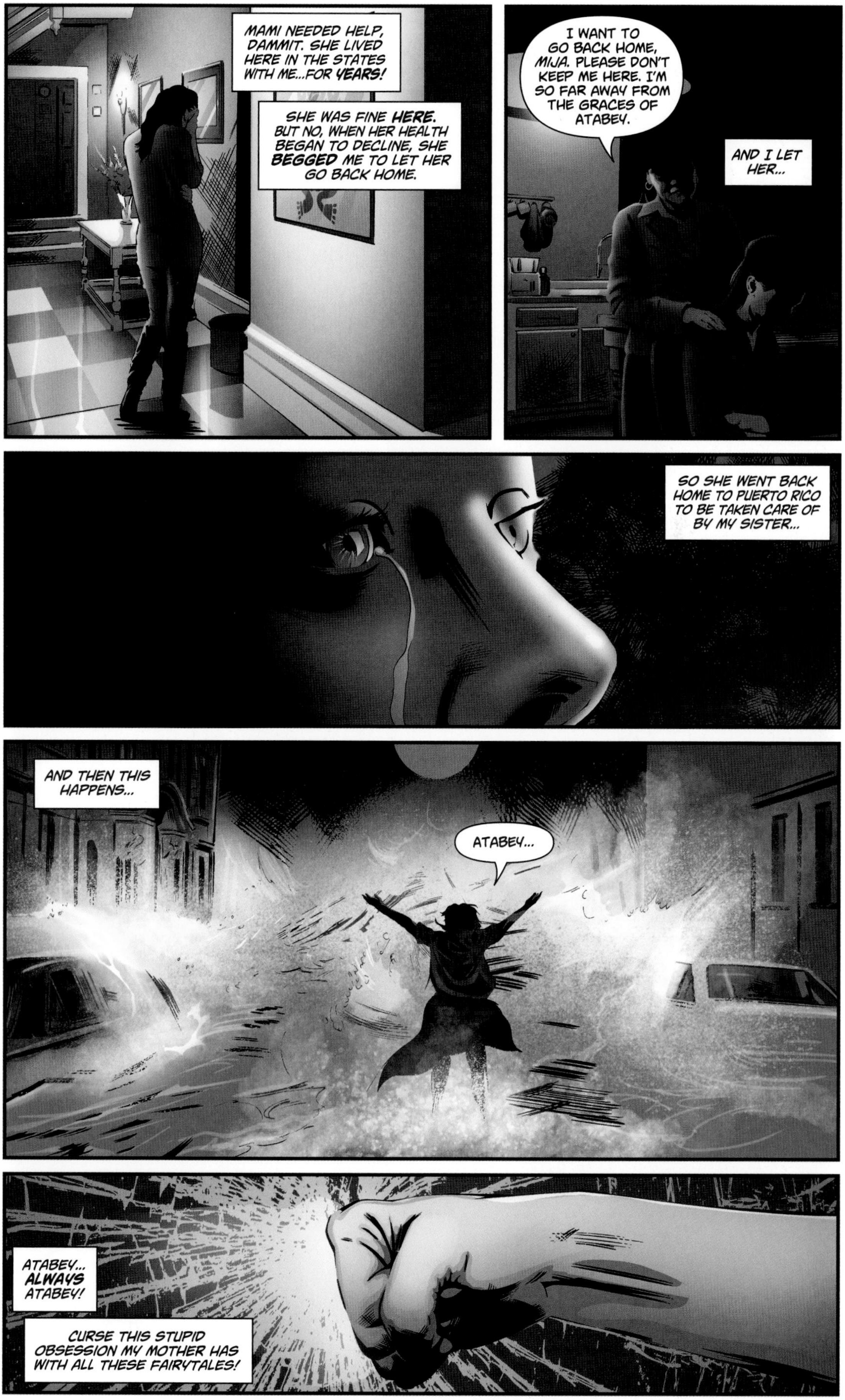
MAMI NEEDED HELP, DAMMIT. SHE LIVED HERE IN THE STATES WITH ME...FOR YEARS!
SHE WAS FINE HERE. BUT NO, WHEN HER HEALTH BEGAN TO DECLINE, SHE BEGGED ME TO LET HER GO BACK HOME.
I WANT TO GO BACK HOME, MIJA. PLEASE DON'T KEEP ME HERE. I'M SO FAR AWAY FROM THE GRACES OF ATABEY.
AND I LET HER...
SO SHE WENT BACK HOME TO PUERTO RICO TO BE TAKEN CARE OF BY MY SISTER...
AND THEN THIS HAPPENS...
ATABEY...
ATABEY... ALWAYS ATABEY!
CURSE THIS STUPID OBSESSION MY MOTHER HAS WITH ALL THESE FAIRYTALES!

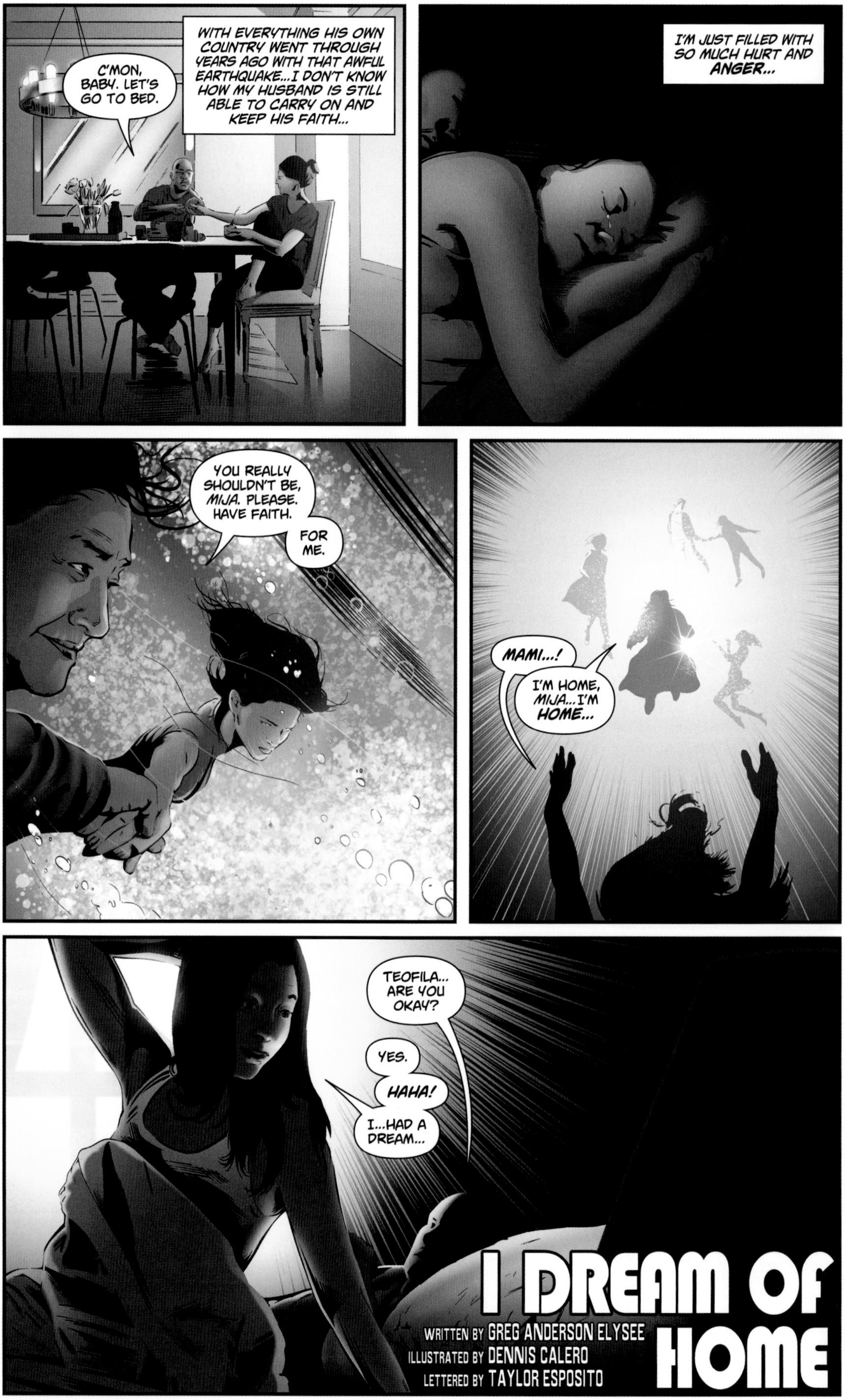
C'MON, BABY. LET'S GO TO BED.
WITH EVERYTHING HIS OWN COUNTRY WENT THROUGH YEARS AGO WITH THAT AWFUL EARTHQUAKE...I DON'T KNOW HOW MY HUSBAND IS STILL ABLE TO CARRY ON AND KEEP HIS FAITH...
I'M JUST FILLED WITH SO MUCH HURT AND ANGER...
YOU REALLY SHOULDN'T BE, MIJA. PLEASE. HAVE FAITH.
FOR ME.
MAMI...!
I'M HOME, MIJA...I'M HOME...
TEOFILA... ARE YOU OKAY?
YES.
HAHA!
I...HAD A DREAM...
I DREAM OF HOME
WRITTEN BY GREG ANDERSON ELYSEE
ILLUSTRATED BY DENNIS CALERO
LETTERED BY TAYLOR ESPOSITO

# HOPE

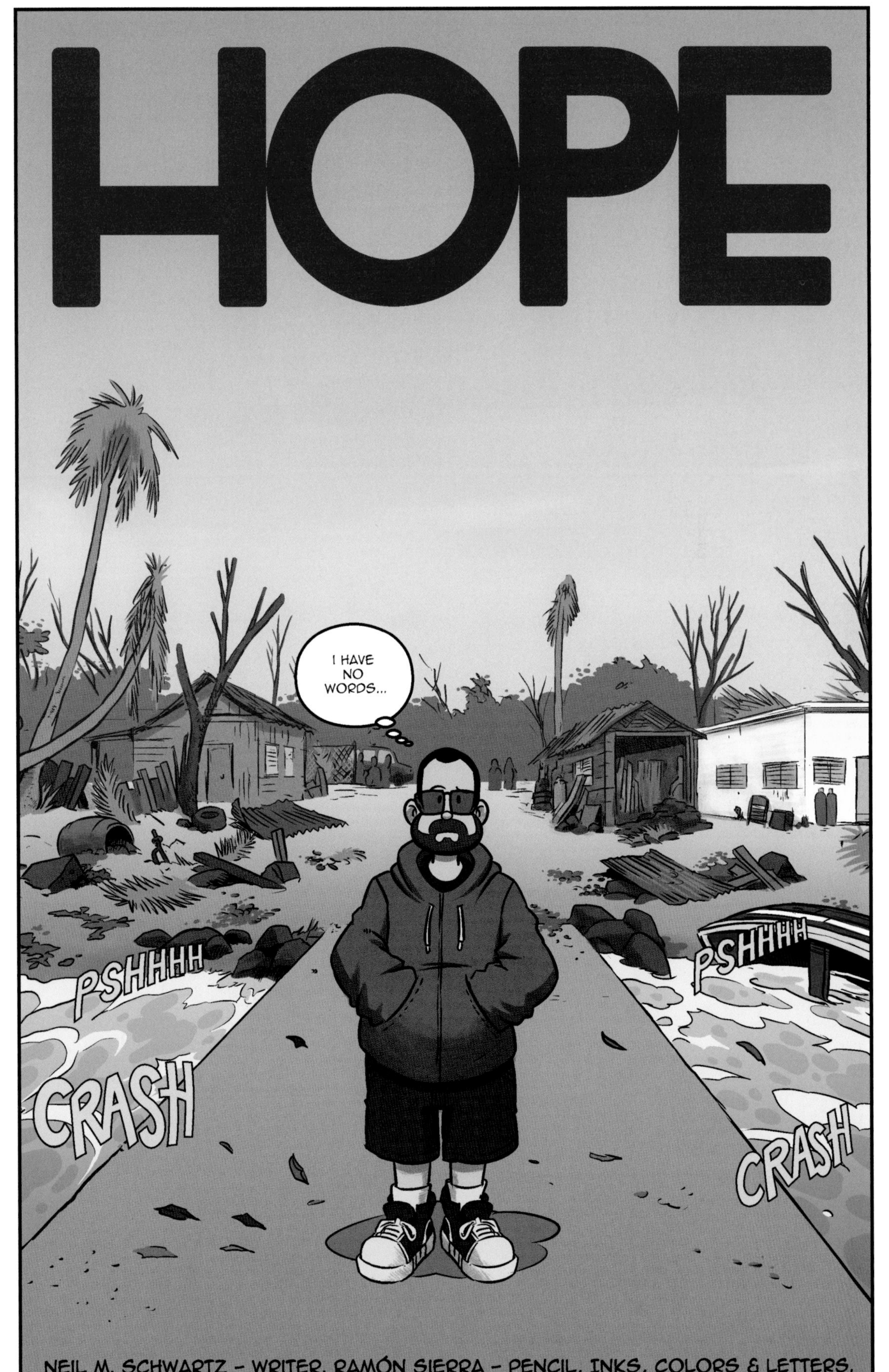
I HAVE NO WORDS...
PSHHHH
PSHHHH
CRASH
CRASH

NEIL M. SCHWARTZ - WRITER. RAMÓN SIERRA - PENCIL, INKS, COLORS & LETTERS.

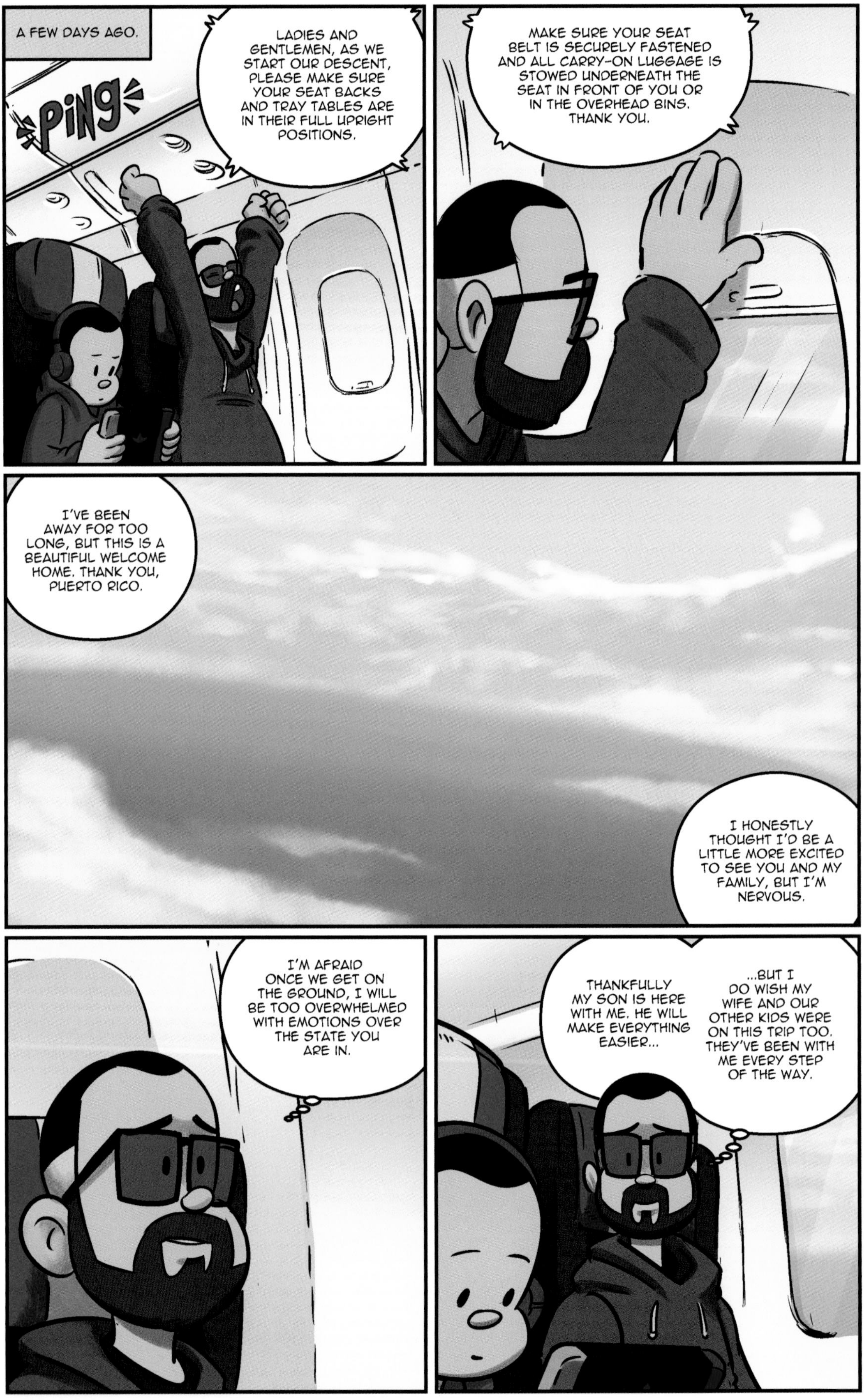

A FEW DAYS AGO.
LADIES AND GENTLEMEN, AS WE START OUR DESCENT, PLEASE MAKE SURE YOUR SEAT BACKS AND TRAY TABLES ARE IN THEIR FULL UPRIGHT POSITIONS.
PING
MAKE SURE YOUR SEAT BELT IS SECURELY FASTENED AND ALL CARRY-ON LUGGAGE IS STOWED UNDERNEATH THE SEAT IN FRONT OF YOU OR IN THE OVERHEAD BINS. THANK YOU.
I'VE BEEN AWAY FOR TOO LONG, BUT THIS IS A BEAUTIFUL WELCOME HOME. THANK YOU, PUERTO RICO.
I HONESTLY THOUGHT I'D BE A LITTLE MORE EXCITED TO SEE YOU AND MY FAMILY, BUT I'M NERVOUS.
I'M AFRAID ONCE WE GET ON THE GROUND, I WILL BE TOO OVERWHELMED WITH EMOTIONS OVER THE STATE YOU ARE IN.
THANKFULLY MY SON IS HERE WITH ME. HE WILL MAKE EVERYTHING EASIER...
...BUT I DO WISH MY WIFE AND OUR OTHER KIDS WERE ON THIS TRIP TOO. THEY'VE BEEN WITH ME EVERY STEP OF THE WAY.

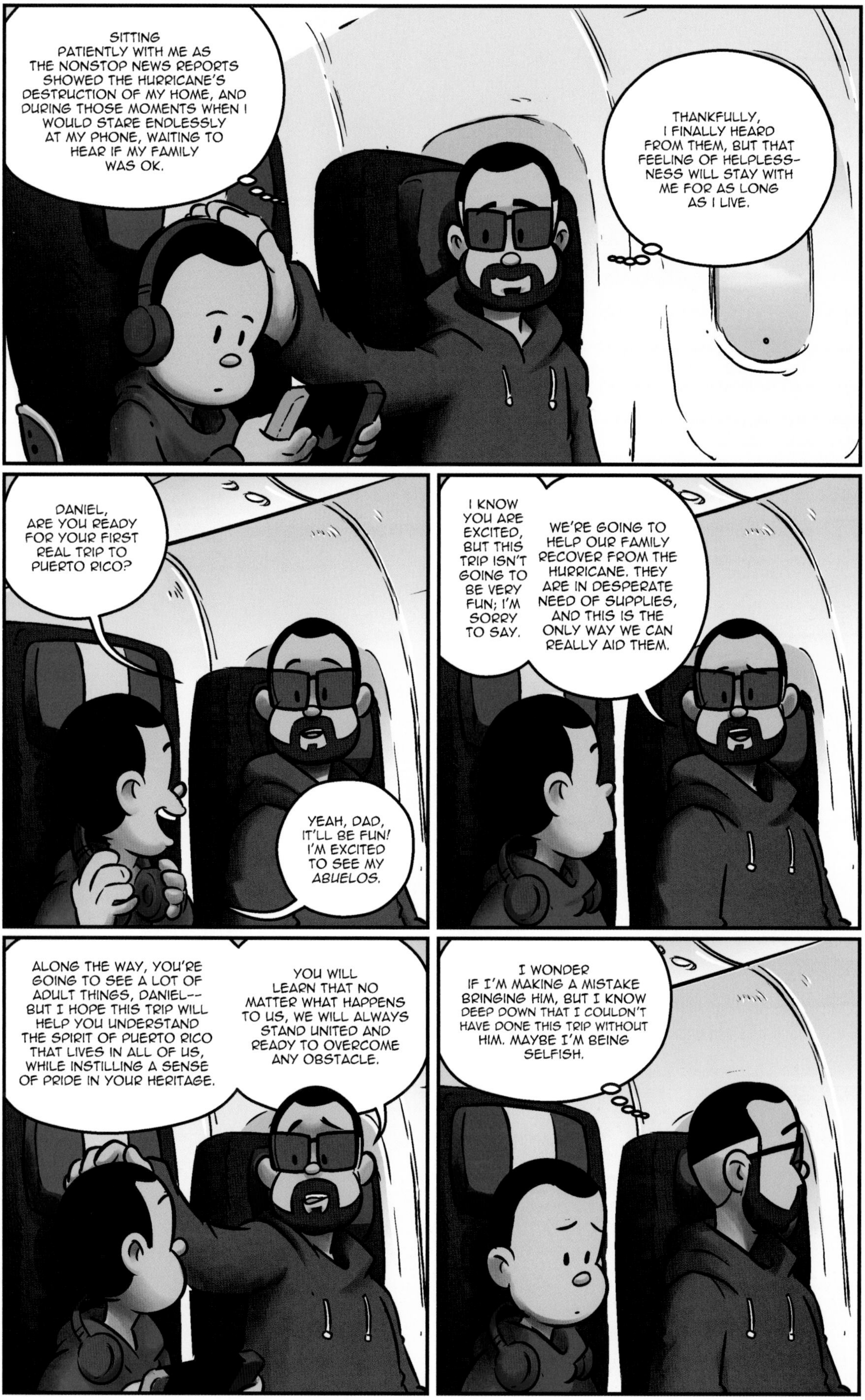
SITTING PATIENTLY WITH ME AS THE NONSTOP NEWS REPORTS SHOWED THE HURRICANE'S DESTRUCTION OF MY HOME, AND DURING THOSE MOMENTS WHEN I WOULD STARE ENDLESSLY AT MY PHONE, WAITING TO HEAR IF MY FAMILY WAS OK.
THANKFULLY, I FINALLY HEARD FROM THEM, BUT THAT FEELING OF HELPLESS-NESS WILL STAY WITH ME FOR AS LONG AS I LIVE.
DANIEL, ARE YOU READY FOR YOUR FIRST REAL TRIP TO PUERTO RICO?
YEAH, DAD, IT'LL BE FUN! I'M EXCITED TO SEE MY ABUELOS.
I KNOW YOU ARE EXCITED, BUT THIS TRIP ISN'T GOING TO BE VERY FUN; I'M SORRY TO SAY.
WE'RE GOING TO HELP OUR FAMILY RECOVER FROM THE HURRICANE. THEY ARE IN DESPERATE NEED OF SUPPLIES, AND THIS IS THE ONLY WAY WE CAN REALLY AID THEM.
ALONG THE WAY, YOU'RE GOING TO SEE A LOT OF ADULT THINGS, DANIEL-- BUT I HOPE THIS TRIP WILL HELP YOU UNDERSTAND THE SPIRIT OF PUERTO RICO THAT LIVES IN ALL OF US, WHILE INSTILLING A SENSE OF PRIDE IN YOUR HERITAGE.
YOU WILL LEARN THAT NO MATTER WHAT HAPPENS TO US, WE WILL ALWAYS STAND UNITED AND READY TO OVERCOME ANY OBSTACLE.
I WONDER IF I'M MAKING A MISTAKE BRINGING HIM, BUT I KNOW DEEP DOWN THAT I COULDN'T HAVE DONE THIS TRIP WITHOUT HIM. MAYBE I'M BEING SELFISH.

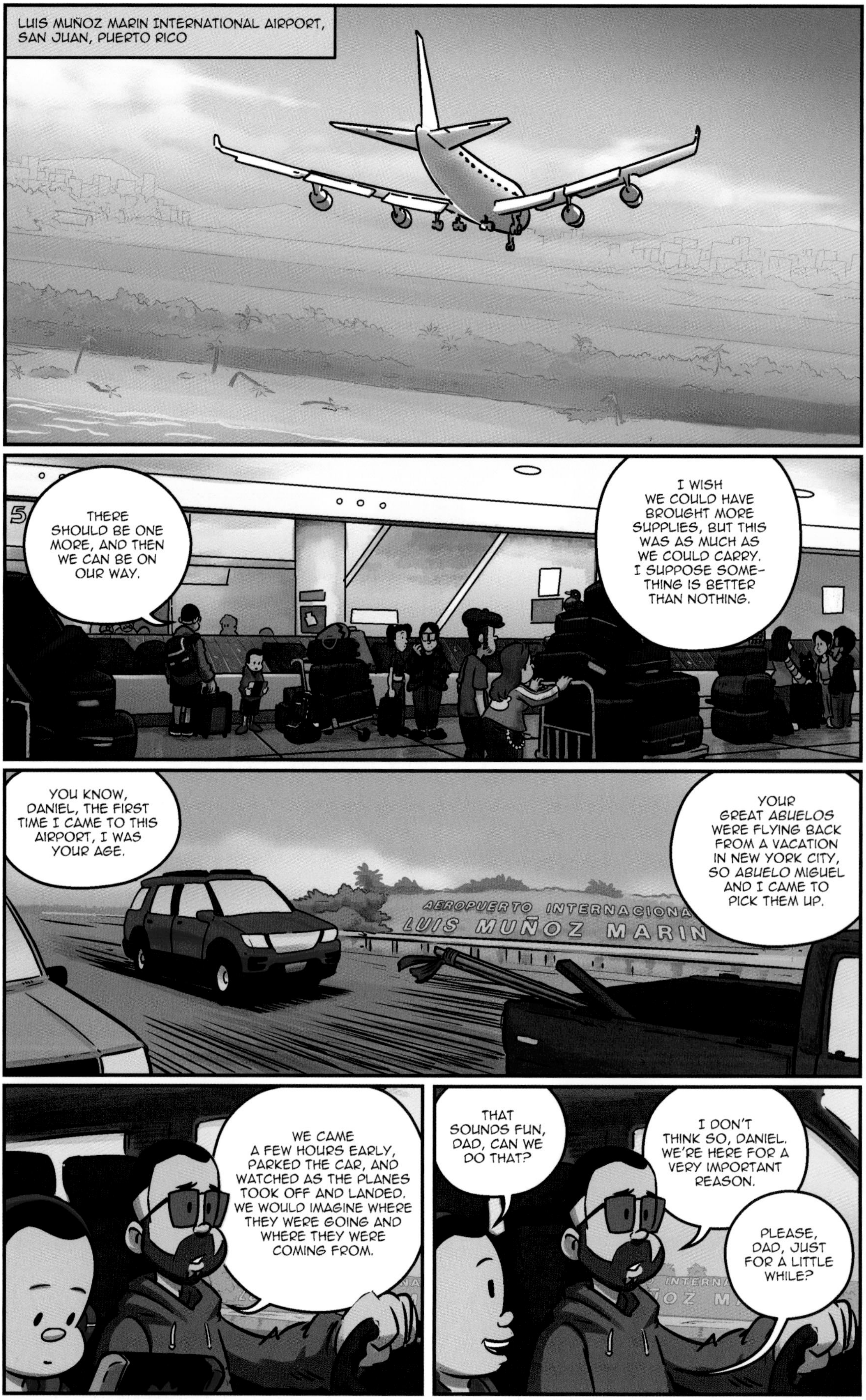
LUIS MUÑOZ MARIN INTERNATIONAL AIRPORT, SAN JUAN, PUERTO RICO
THERE SHOULD BE ONE MORE, AND THEN WE CAN BE ON OUR WAY.
I WISH WE COULD HAVE BROUGHT MORE SUPPLIES, BUT THIS WAS AS MUCH AS WE COULD CARRY. I SUPPOSE SOME-THING IS BETTER THAN NOTHING.
YOU KNOW, DANIEL, THE FIRST TIME I CAME TO THIS AIRPORT, I WAS YOUR AGE.
YOUR GREAT ABUELOS WERE FLYING BACK FROM A VACATION IN NEW YORK CITY, SO ABUELO MIGUEL AND I CAME TO PICK THEM UP.
AEROPUERTO INTERNACIONA
LUIS MUÑOZ MARIN
WE CAME A FEW HOURS EARLY, PARKED THE CAR, AND WATCHED AS THE PLANES TOOK OFF AND LANDED. WE WOULD IMAGINE WHERE THEY WERE GOING AND WHERE THEY WERE COMING FROM.
THAT SOUNDS FUN, DAD, CAN WE DO THAT?
I DON'T THINK SO, DANIEL. WE'RE HERE FOR A VERY IMPORTANT REASON.
PLEASE, DAD, JUST FOR A LITTLE WHILE?

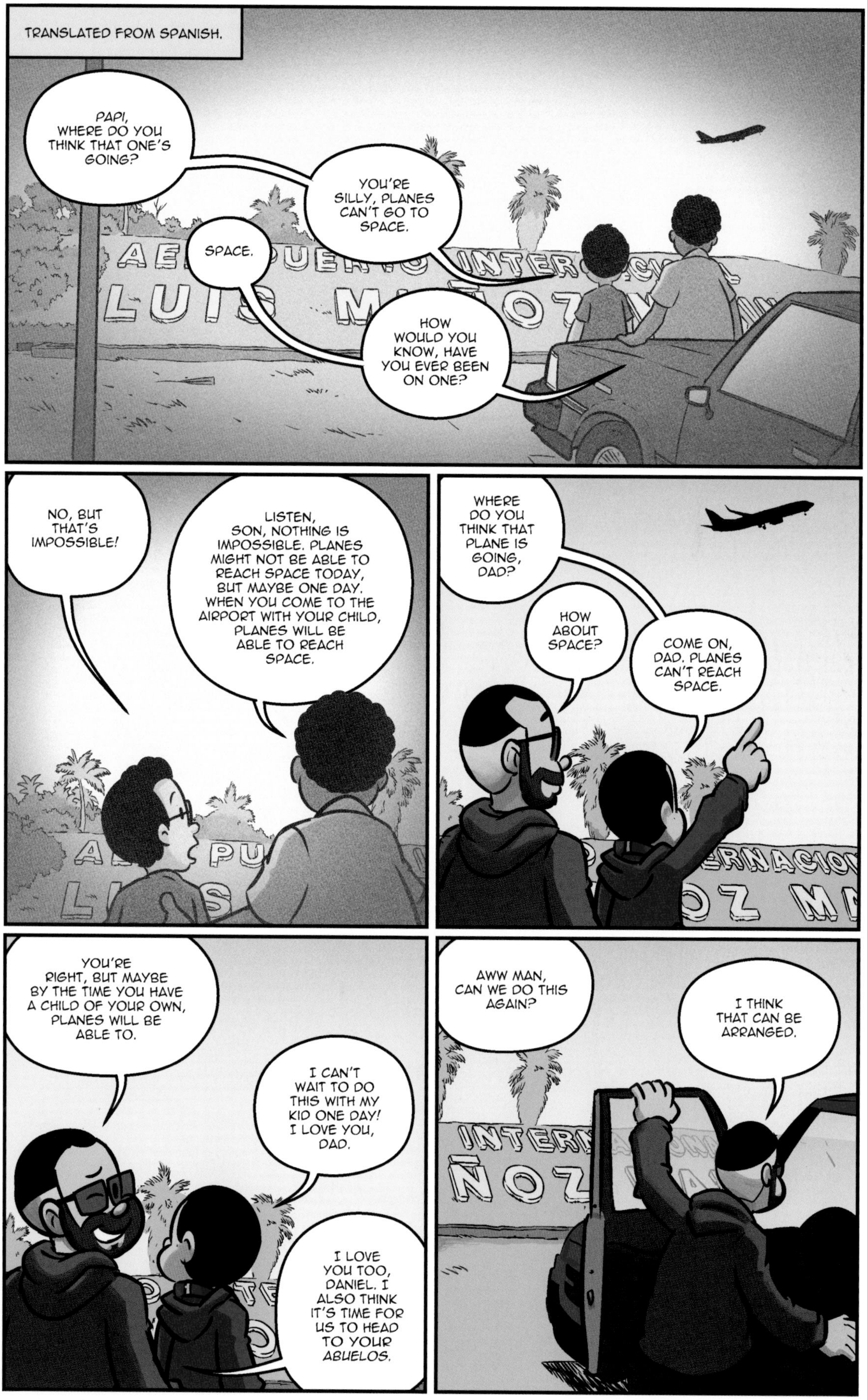
TRANSLATED FROM SPANISH.
PAPI, WHERE DO YOU THINK THAT ONE'S GOING?
SPACE.
YOU'RE SILLY, PLANES CAN'T GO TO SPACE.
HOW WOULD YOU KNOW, HAVE YOU EVER BEEN ON ONE?
NO, BUT THAT'S IMPOSSIBLE!
LISTEN, SON, NOTHING IS IMPOSSIBLE. PLANES MIGHT NOT BE ABLE TO REACH SPACE TODAY, BUT MAYBE ONE DAY. WHEN YOU COME TO THE AIRPORT WITH YOUR CHILD, PLANES WILL BE ABLE TO REACH SPACE.
WHERE DO YOU THINK THAT PLANE IS GOING, DAD?
HOW ABOUT SPACE?
COME ON, DAD. PLANES CAN'T REACH SPACE.
YOU'RE RIGHT, BUT MAYBE BY THE TIME YOU HAVE A CHILD OF YOUR OWN, PLANES WILL BE ABLE TO.
I CAN'T WAIT TO DO THIS WITH MY KID ONE DAY! I LOVE YOU, DAD.
I LOVE YOU TOO, DANIEL. I ALSO THINK IT'S TIME FOR US TO HEAD TO YOUR ABUELOS.
AWW MAN, CAN WE DO THIS AGAIN?
I THINK THAT CAN BE ARRANGED.

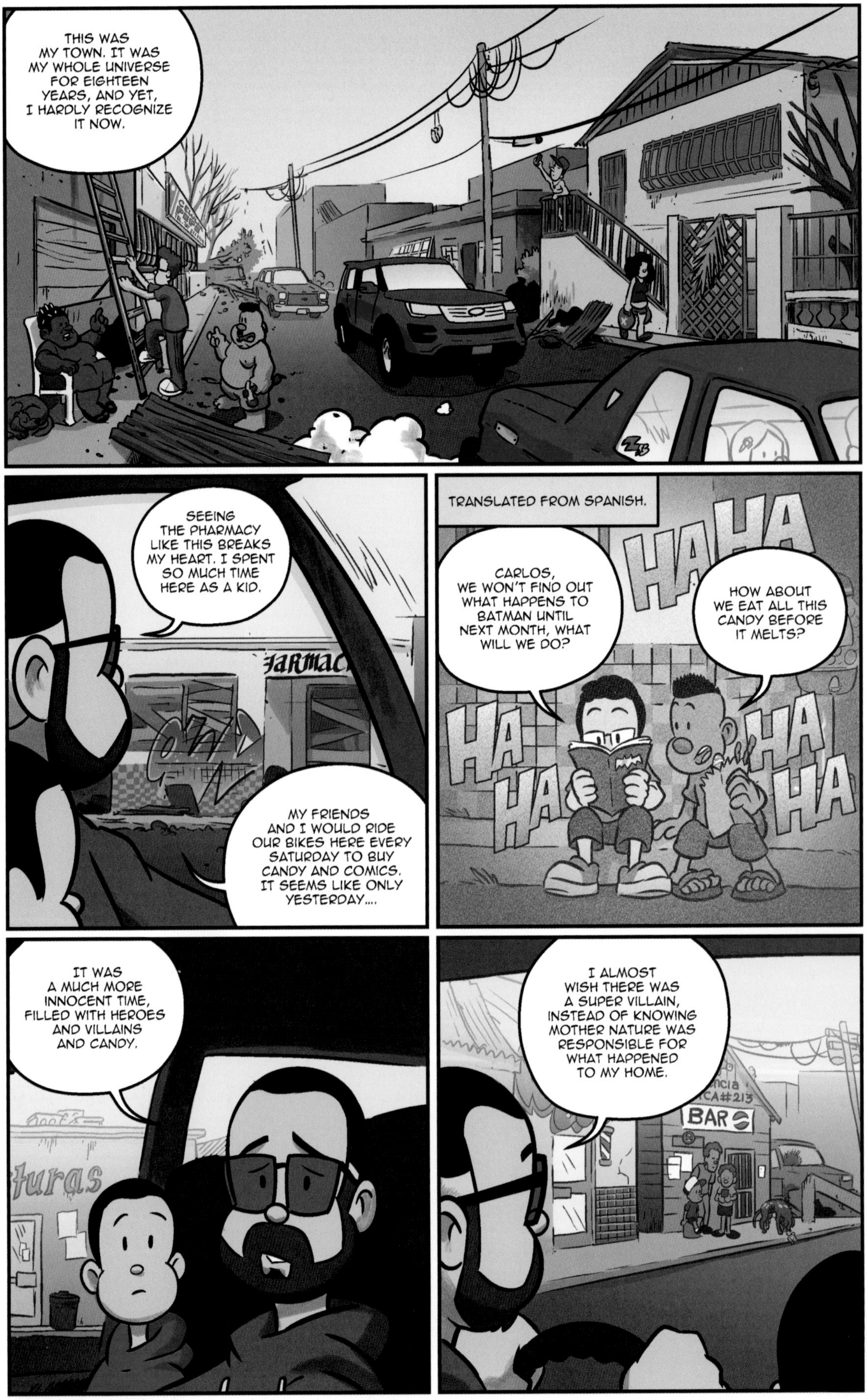
THIS WAS MY TOWN. IT WAS MY WHOLE UNIVERSE FOR EIGHTEEN YEARS, AND YET, I HARDLY RECOGNIZE IT NOW.
SEEING THE PHARMACY LIKE THIS BREAKS MY HEART. I SPENT SO MUCH TIME HERE AS A KID.
MY FRIENDS AND I WOULD RIDE OUR BIKES HERE EVERY SATURDAY TO BUY CANDY AND COMICS. IT SEEMS LIKE ONLY YESTERDAY....
TRANSLATED FROM SPANISH.
HAHA
CARLOS, WE WON'T FIND OUT WHAT HAPPENS TO BATMAN UNTIL NEXT MONTH, WHAT WILL WE DO?
HOW ABOUT WE EAT ALL THIS CANDY BEFORE IT MELTS?
HA HA
HA HA
IT WAS A MUCH MORE INNOCENT TIME, FILLED WITH HEROES AND VILLAINS AND CANDY.
I ALMOST WISH THERE WAS A SUPER VILLAIN, INSTEAD OF KNOWING MOTHER NATURE WAS RESPONSIBLE FOR WHAT HAPPENED TO MY HOME.
BAR

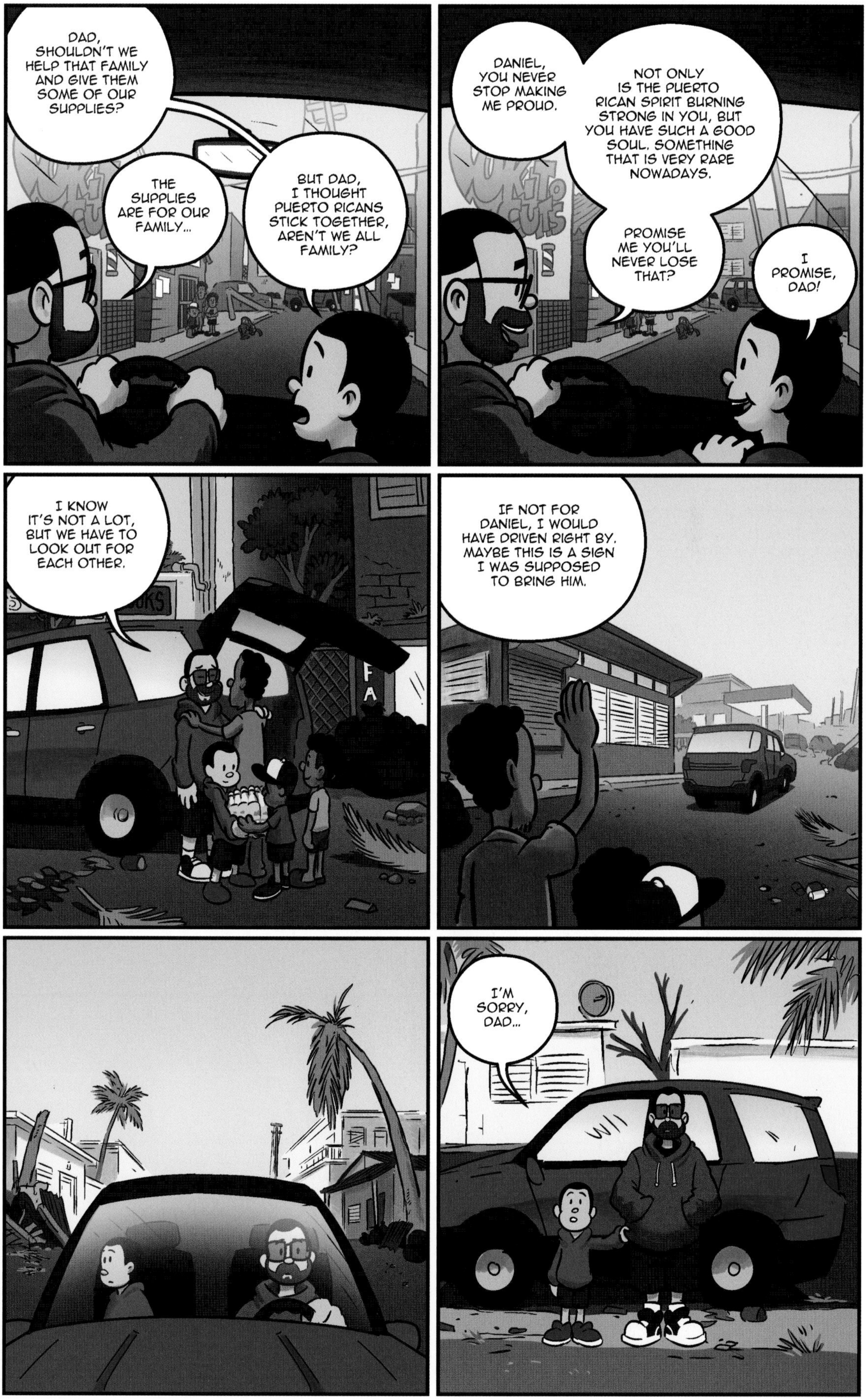
DAD, SHOULDN'T WE HELP THAT FAMILY AND GIVE THEM SOME OF OUR SUPPLIES?
THE SUPPLIES ARE FOR OUR FAMILY...
BUT DAD, I THOUGHT PUERTO RICANS STICK TOGETHER, AREN'T WE ALL FAMILY?
DANIEL, YOU NEVER STOP MAKING ME PROUD.
NOT ONLY IS THE PUERTO RICAN SPIRIT BURNING STRONG IN YOU, BUT YOU HAVE SUCH A GOOD SOUL. SOMETHING THAT IS VERY RARE NOWADAYS.
PROMISE ME YOU'LL NEVER LOSE THAT?
I PROMISE, DAD!
I KNOW IT'S NOT A LOT, BUT WE HAVE TO LOOK OUT FOR EACH OTHER.
IF NOT FOR DANIEL, I WOULD HAVE DRIVEN RIGHT BY. MAYBE THIS IS A SIGN I WAS SUPPOSED TO BRING HIM.
I'M SORRY, DAD...

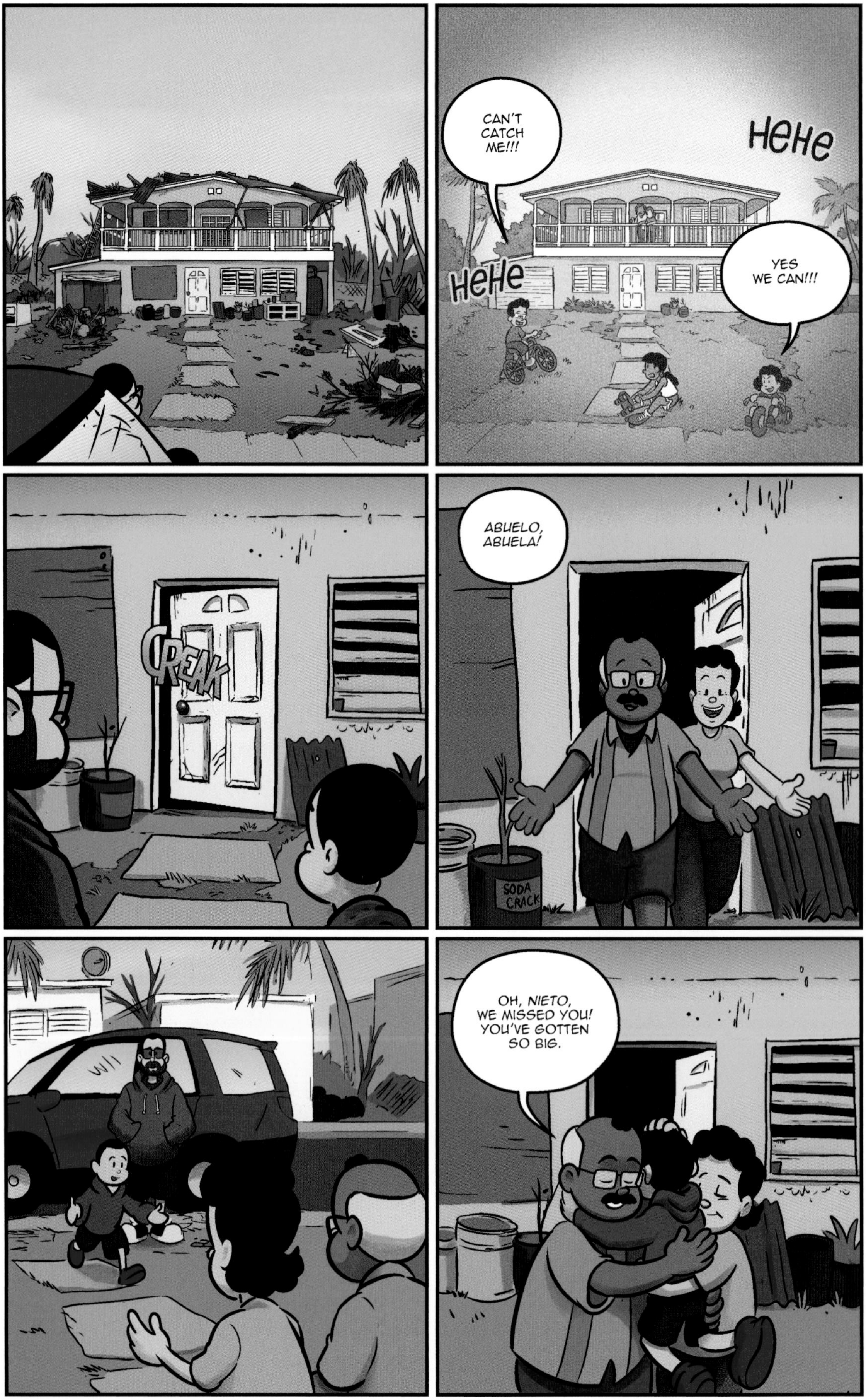
CAN'T CATCH ME!!!
HEHE
HEHE
YES WE CAN!!!
CREAK
ABUELO, ABUELA!
SODA CRACK
OH, NIETO, WE MISSED YOU! YOU'VE GOTTEN SO BIG.

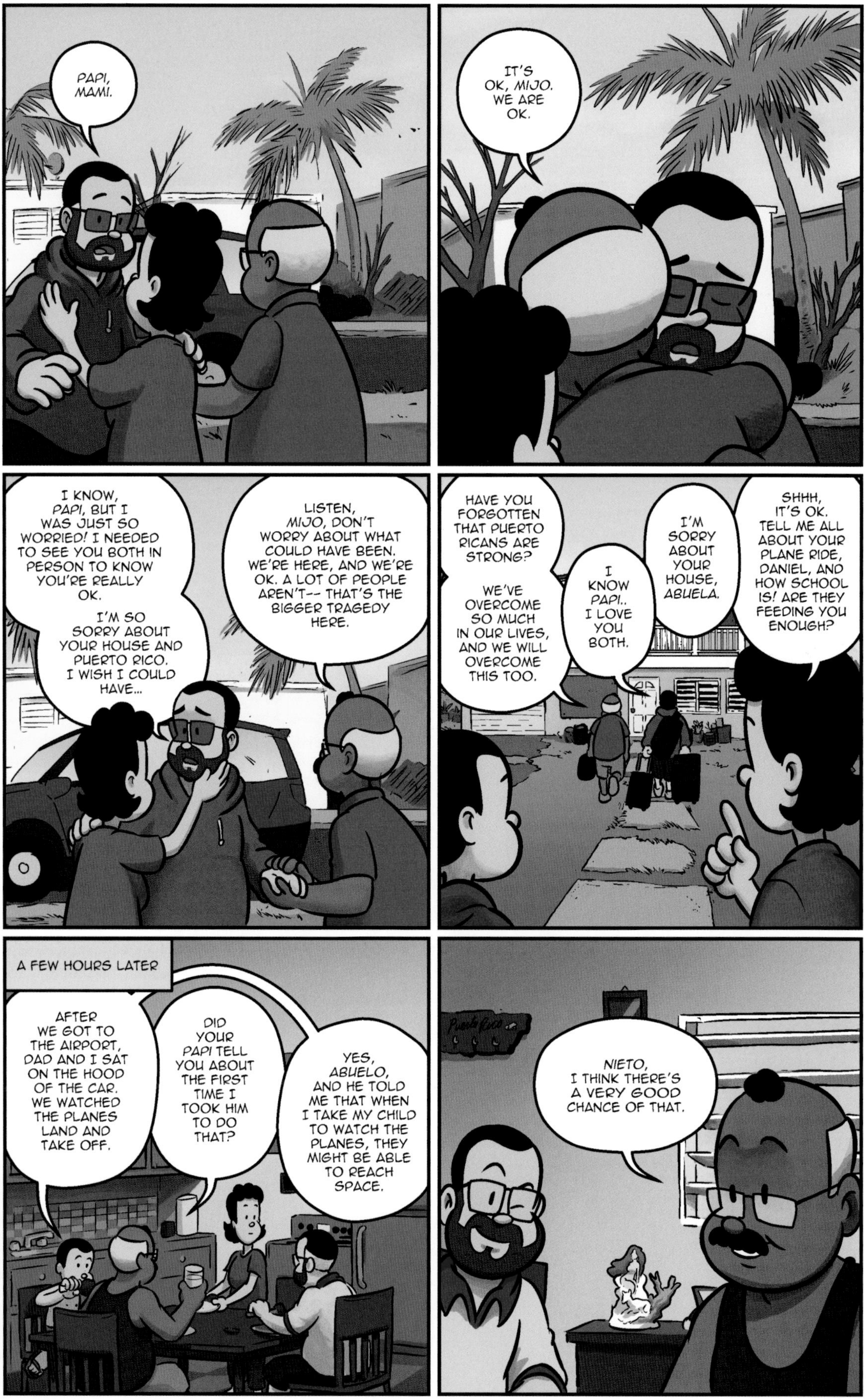
PAPI, MAMI.
IT'S OK, MIJO. WE ARE OK.
I KNOW, PAPI, BUT I WAS JUST SO WORRIED! I NEEDED TO SEE YOU BOTH IN PERSON TO KNOW YOU'RE REALLY OK.
I'M SO SORRY ABOUT YOUR HOUSE AND PUERTO RICO. I WISH I COULD HAVE...
LISTEN, MIJO, DON'T WORRY ABOUT WHAT COULD HAVE BEEN. WE'RE HERE, AND WE'RE OK. A LOT OF PEOPLE AREN'T-- THAT'S THE BIGGER TRAGEDY HERE.
HAVE YOU FORGOTTEN THAT PUERTO RICANS ARE STRONG?
WE'VE OVERCOME SO MUCH IN OUR LIVES, AND WE WILL OVERCOME THIS TOO.
I KNOW PAPI.. I LOVE YOU BOTH.
I'M SORRY ABOUT YOUR HOUSE, ABUELA.
SHHH, IT'S OK. TELL ME ALL ABOUT YOUR PLANE RIDE, DANIEL, AND HOW SCHOOL IS! ARE THEY FEEDING YOU ENOUGH?
A FEW HOURS LATER
AFTER WE GOT TO THE AIRPORT, DAD AND I SAT ON THE HOOD OF THE CAR. WE WATCHED THE PLANES LAND AND TAKE OFF.
DID YOUR PAPI TELL YOU ABOUT THE FIRST TIME I TOOK HIM TO DO THAT?
YES, ABUELO, AND HE TOLD ME THAT WHEN I TAKE MY CHILD TO WATCH THE PLANES, THEY MIGHT BE ABLE TO REACH SPACE.
NIETO, I THINK THERE'S A VERY GOOD CHANCE OF THAT.

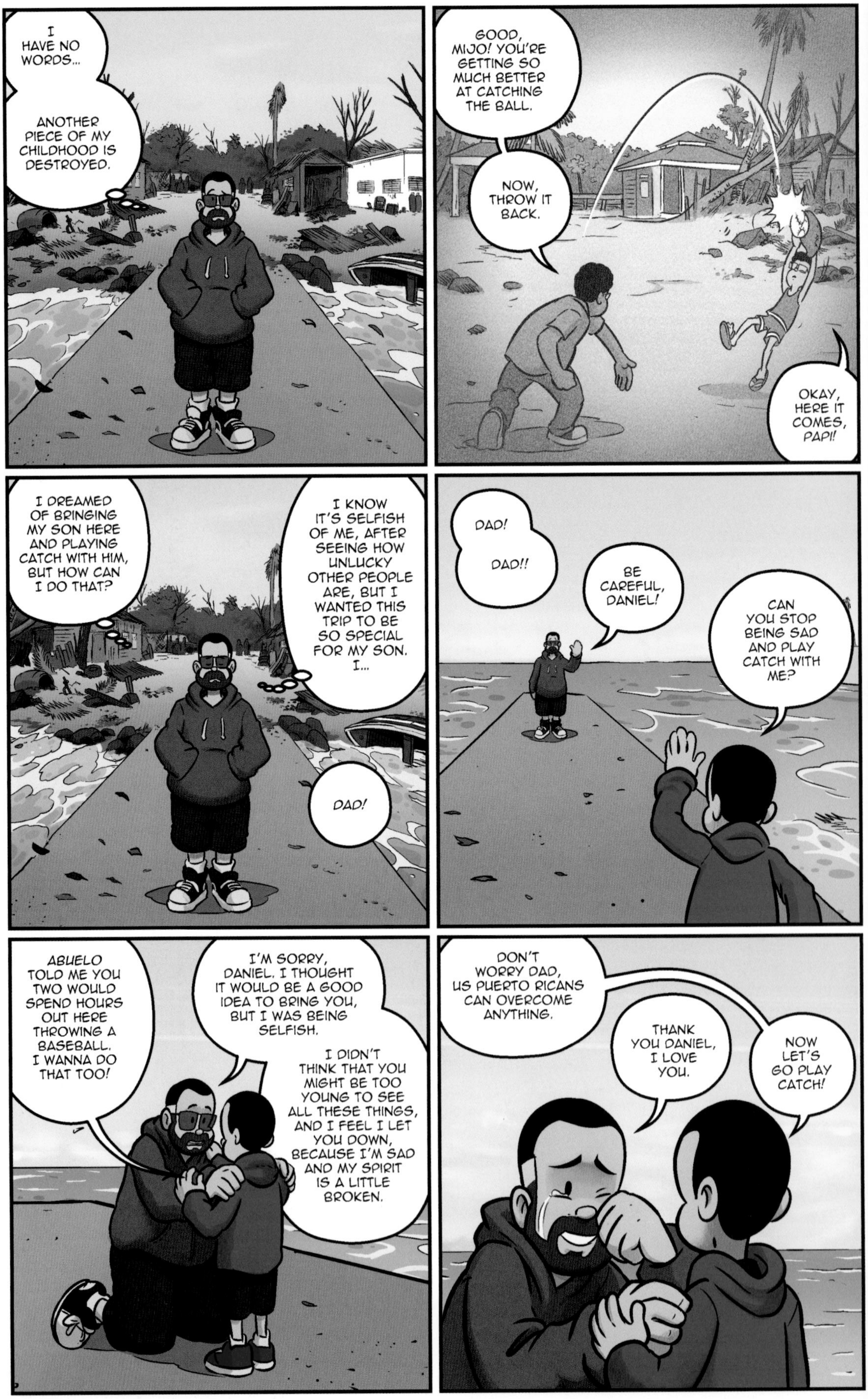
I HAVE NO WORDS...
ANOTHER PIECE OF MY CHILDHOOD IS DESTROYED.
GOOD, MIJO! YOU'RE GETTING SO MUCH BETTER AT CATCHING THE BALL.
NOW, THROW IT BACK.
OKAY, HERE IT COMES, PAPI!
I DREAMED OF BRINGING MY SON HERE AND PLAYING CATCH WITH HIM, BUT HOW CAN I DO THAT?
I KNOW IT'S SELFISH OF ME, AFTER SEEING HOW UNLUCKY OTHER PEOPLE ARE, BUT I WANTED THIS TRIP TO BE SO SPECIAL FOR MY SON. I...
DAD!
DAD!
DAD!!
BE CAREFUL, DANIEL!
CAN YOU STOP BEING SAD AND PLAY CATCH WITH ME?
ABUELO TOLD ME YOU TWO WOULD SPEND HOURS OUT HERE THROWING A BASEBALL. I WANNA DO THAT TOO!
I'M SORRY, DANIEL. I THOUGHT IT WOULD BE A GOOD IDEA TO BRING YOU, BUT I WAS BEING SELFISH.
I DIDN'T THINK THAT YOU MIGHT BE TOO YOUNG TO SEE ALL THESE THINGS, AND I FEEL I LET YOU DOWN, BECAUSE I'M SAD AND MY SPIRIT IS A LITTLE BROKEN.
DON'T WORRY DAD, US PUERTO RICANS CAN OVERCOME ANYTHING.
THANK YOU DANIEL, I LOVE YOU.
NOW LET'S GO PLAY CATCH!

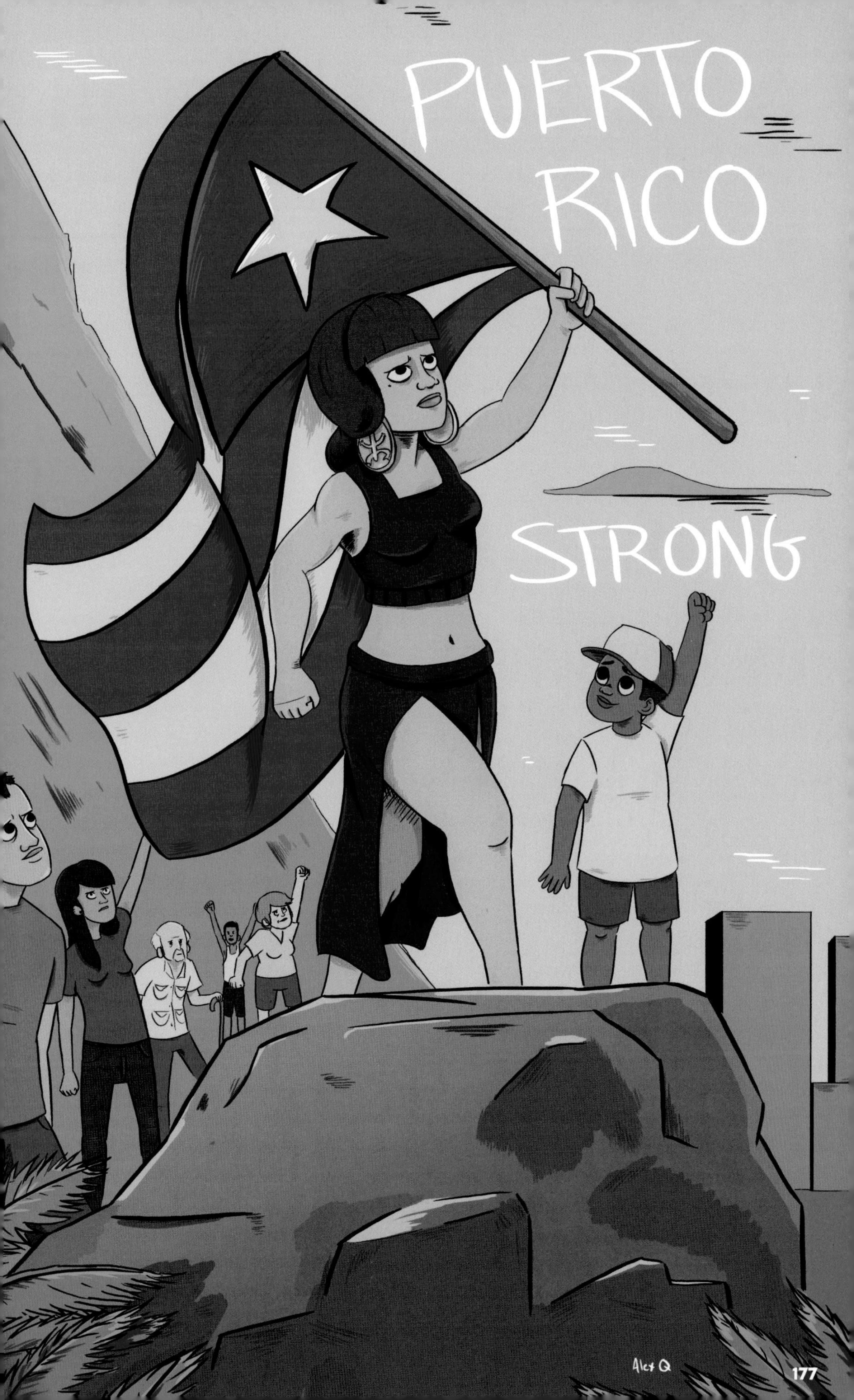
PUERTO
RICO
STRONG
Alex Q

# REALITY CHECK

BY TONY BEDARD & JOHN R HOLMES

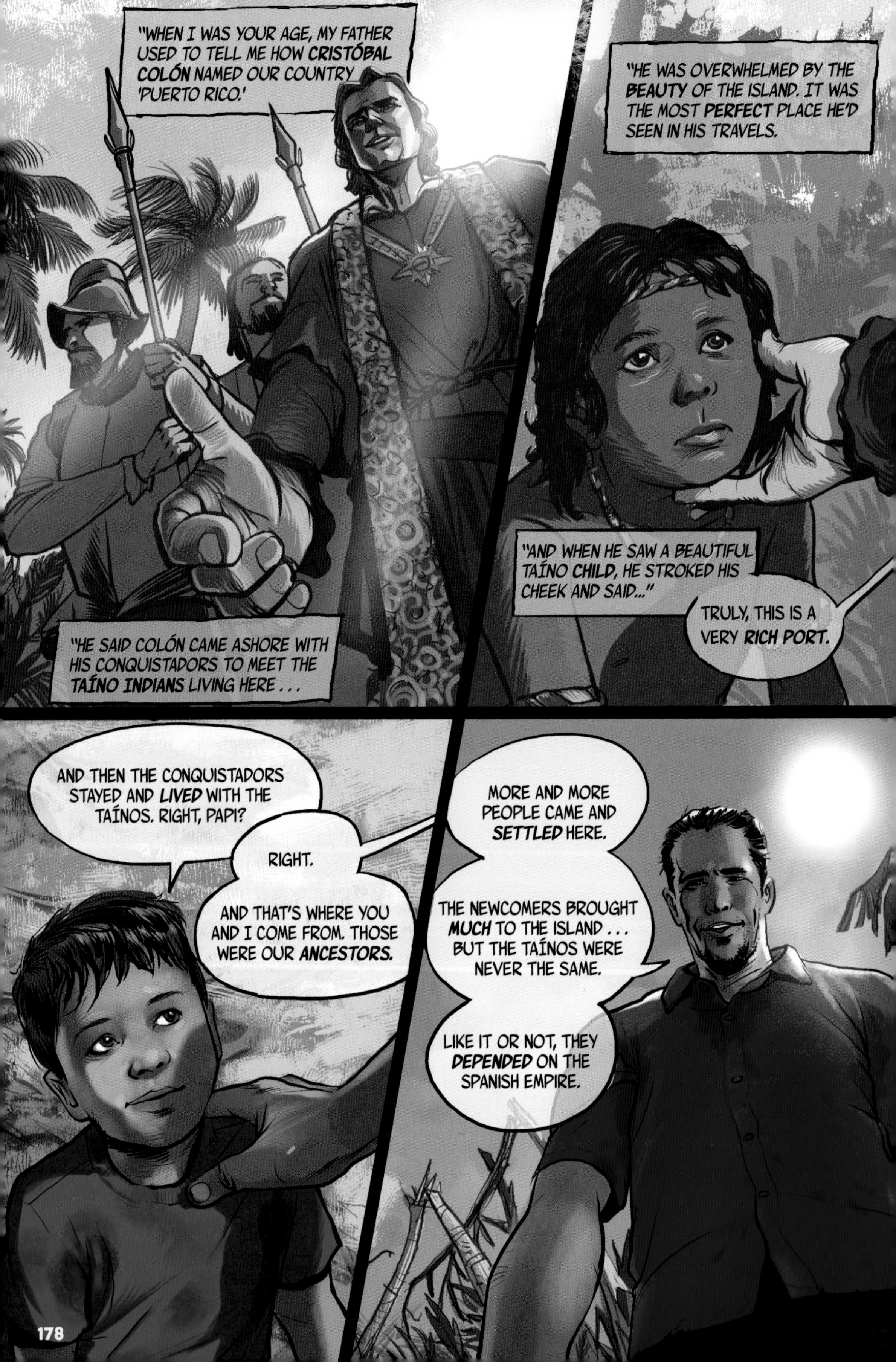
"WHEN I WAS YOUR AGE, MY FATHER USED TO TELL ME HOW CRISTÓBAL COLÓN NAMED OUR COUNTRY 'PUERTO RICO.'
"HE SAID COLÓN CAME ASHORE WITH HIS CONQUISTADORS TO MEET THE TAÍNO INDIANS LIVING HERE . . .
"HE WAS OVERWHELMED BY THE BEAUTY OF THE ISLAND. IT WAS THE MOST PERFECT PLACE HE'D SEEN IN HIS TRAVELS.
"AND WHEN HE SAW A BEAUTIFUL TAÍNO CHILD, HE STROKED HIS CHEEK AND SAID..."
TRULY, THIS IS A VERY RICH PORT.
AND THEN THE CONQUISTADORS STAYED AND LIVED WITH THE TAÍNOS. RIGHT, PAPI?
RIGHT.
AND THAT'S WHERE YOU AND I COME FROM. THOSE WERE OUR ANCESTORS.
MORE AND MORE PEOPLE CAME AND SETTLED HERE.
THE NEWCOMERS BROUGHT MUCH TO THE ISLAND . . . BUT THE TAÍNOS WERE NEVER THE SAME.
LIKE IT OR NOT, THEY DEPENDED ON THE SPANISH EMPIRE.

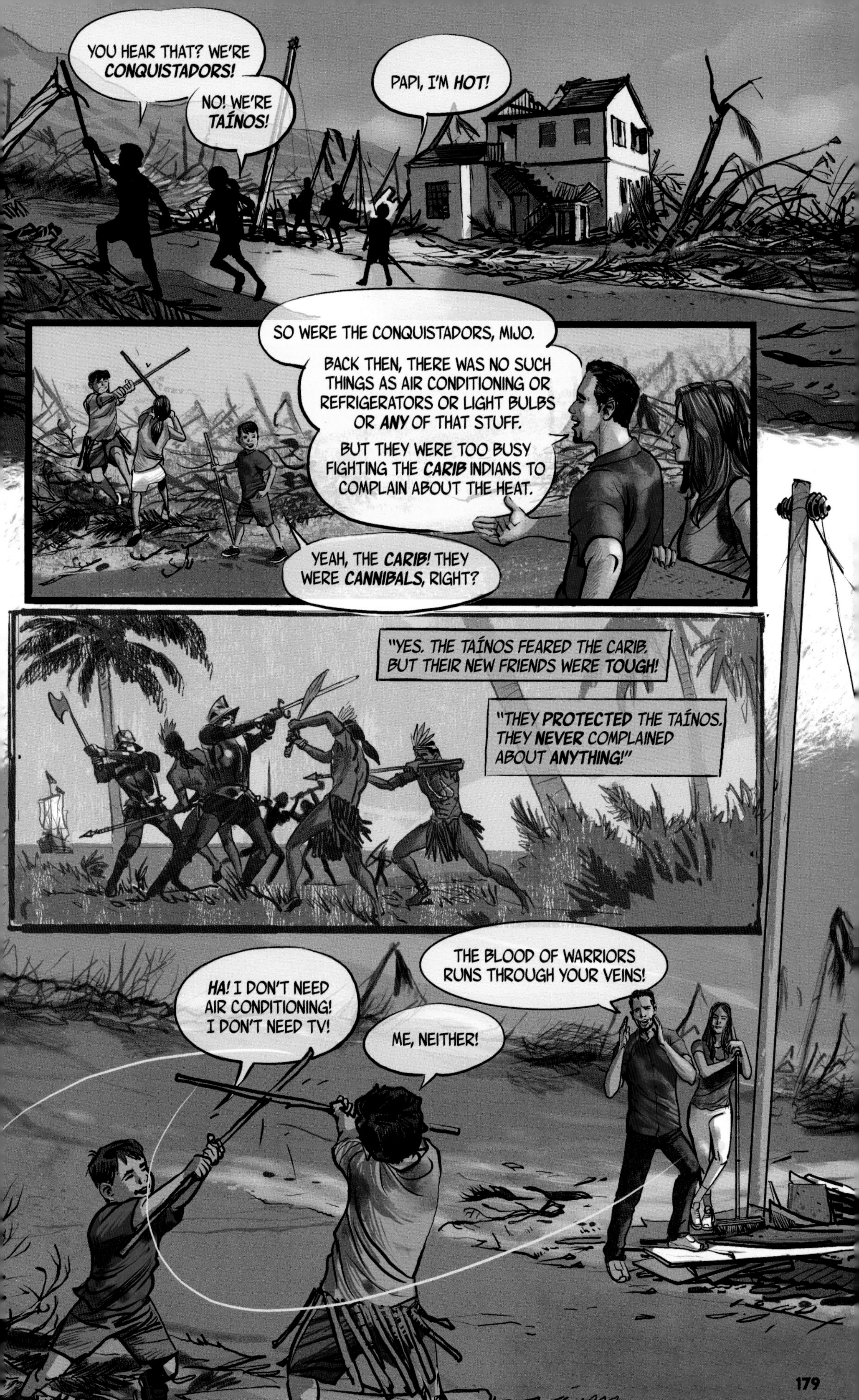
YOU HEAR THAT? WE'RE CONQUISTADORS!
NO! WE'RE TAÍNOS!
PAPI, I'M HOT!
SO WERE THE CONQUISTADORS, MIJO.
BACK THEN, THERE WAS NO SUCH THINGS AS AIR CONDITIONING OR REFRIGERATORS OR LIGHT BULBS OR ANY OF THAT STUFF.
BUT THEY WERE TOO BUSY FIGHTING THE CARIB INDIANS TO COMPLAIN ABOUT THE HEAT.
YEAH, THE CARIB! THEY WERE CANNIBALS, RIGHT?
"YES. THE TAÍNOS FEARED THE CARIB. BUT THEIR NEW FRIENDS WERE TOUGH!
"THEY PROTECTED THE TAÍNOS. THEY NEVER COMPLAINED ABOUT ANYTHING!"
THE BLOOD OF WARRIORS RUNS THROUGH YOUR VEINS!
HA! I DON'T NEED AIR CONDITIONING! I DON'T NEED TV!
ME, NEITHER!

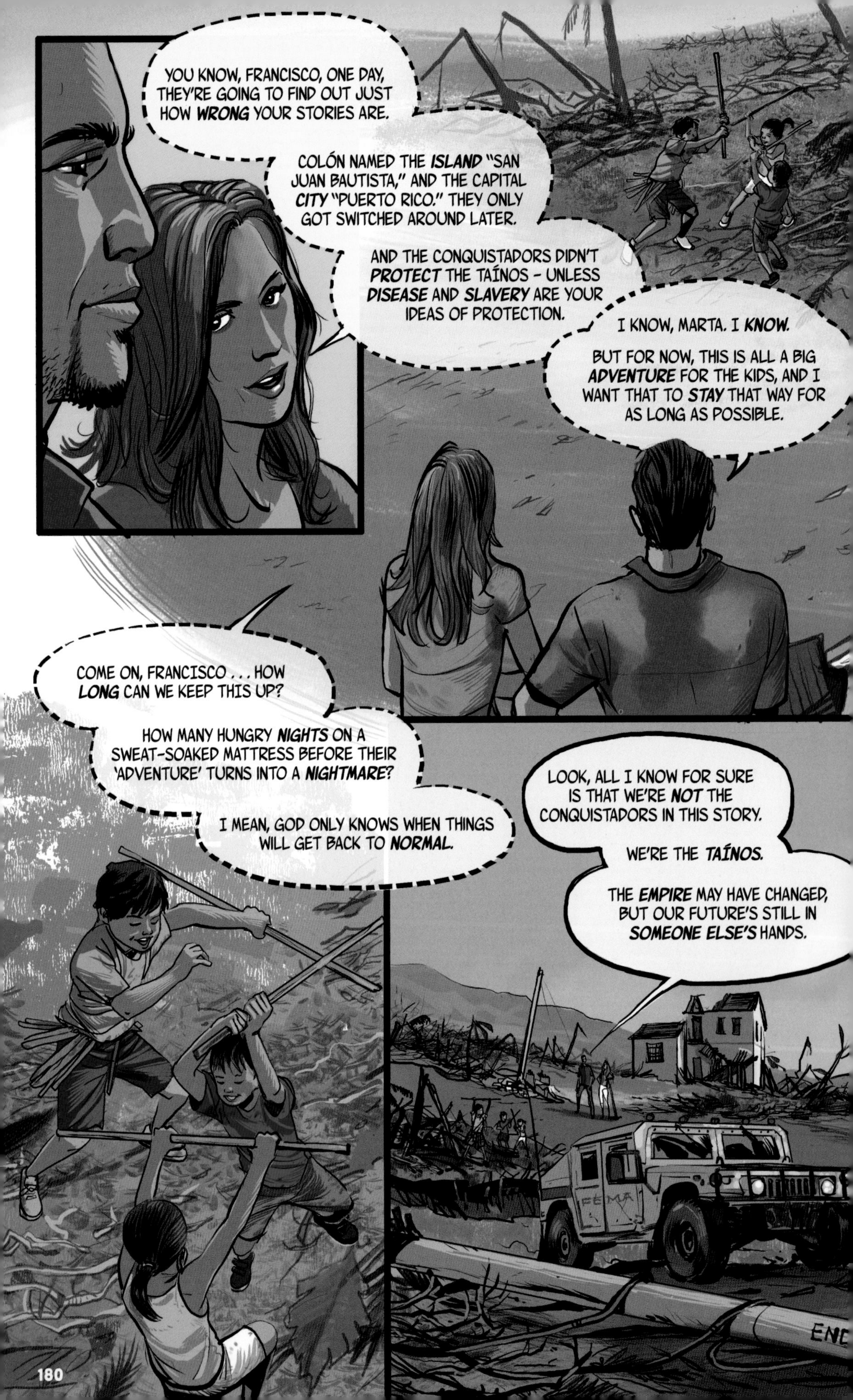
YOU KNOW, FRANCISCO, ONE DAY, THEY'RE GOING TO FIND OUT JUST HOW WRONG YOUR STORIES ARE.
COLÓN NAMED THE ISLAND "SAN JUAN BAUTISTA," AND THE CAPITAL CITY "PUERTO RICO." THEY ONLY GOT SWITCHED AROUND LATER.
AND THE CONQUISTADORS DIDN'T PROTECT THE TAÍNOS - UNLESS DISEASE AND SLAVERY ARE YOUR IDEAS OF PROTECTION.
I KNOW, MARTA. I KNOW.
BUT FOR NOW, THIS IS ALL A BIG ADVENTURE FOR THE KIDS, AND I WANT THAT TO STAY THAT WAY FOR AS LONG AS POSSIBLE.
COME ON, FRANCISCO . . . HOW LONG CAN WE KEEP THIS UP?
HOW MANY HUNGRY NIGHTS ON A SWEAT-SOAKED MATTRESS BEFORE THEIR 'ADVENTURE' TURNS INTO A NIGHTMARE?
I MEAN, GOD ONLY KNOWS WHEN THINGS WILL GET BACK TO NORMAL.
LOOK, ALL I KNOW FOR SURE IS THAT WE'RE NOT THE CONQUISTADORS IN THIS STORY.
WE'RE THE TAÍNOS.
THE EMPIRE MAY HAVE CHANGED, BUT OUR FUTURE'S STILL IN SOMEONE ELSE'S HANDS.
FEMA
END

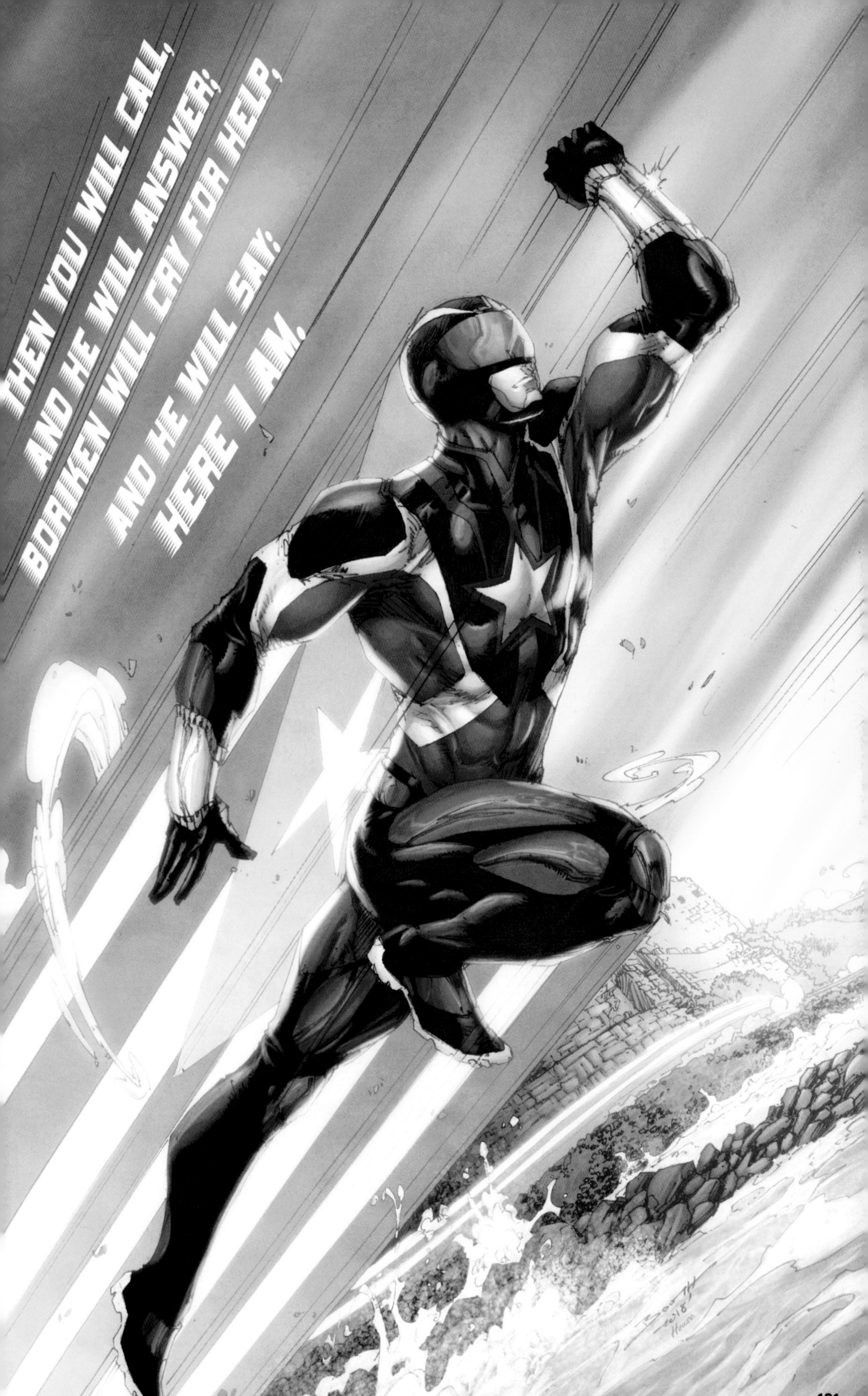
THEN YOU WILL CALL,
AND HE WILL ANSWER;
BORIKEN WILL CRY FOR HELP,
AND HE WILL SAY:
HERE I AM.

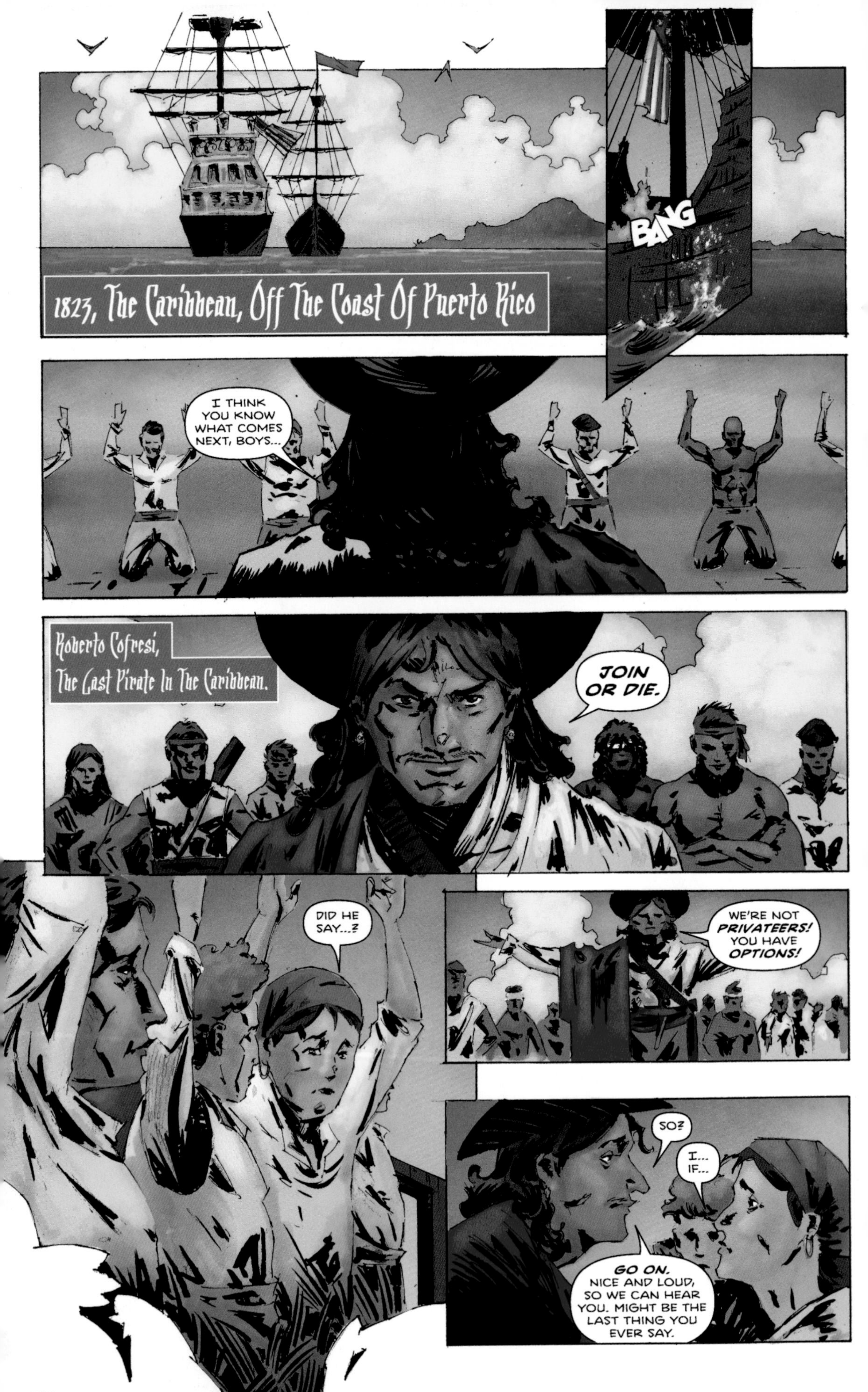
1823, The Caribbean, Off The Coast Of Puerto Rico
BANG
I THINK YOU KNOW WHAT COMES NEXT, BOYS...
Roberto Cofresi, The Last Pirate In The Caribbean.
JOIN OR DIE.
DID HE SAY...?
WE'RE NOT PRIVATEERS! YOU HAVE OPTIONS!
SO?
I... IF...
GO ON. NICE AND LOUD, SO WE CAN HEAR YOU. MIGHT BE THE LAST THING YOU EVER SAY.

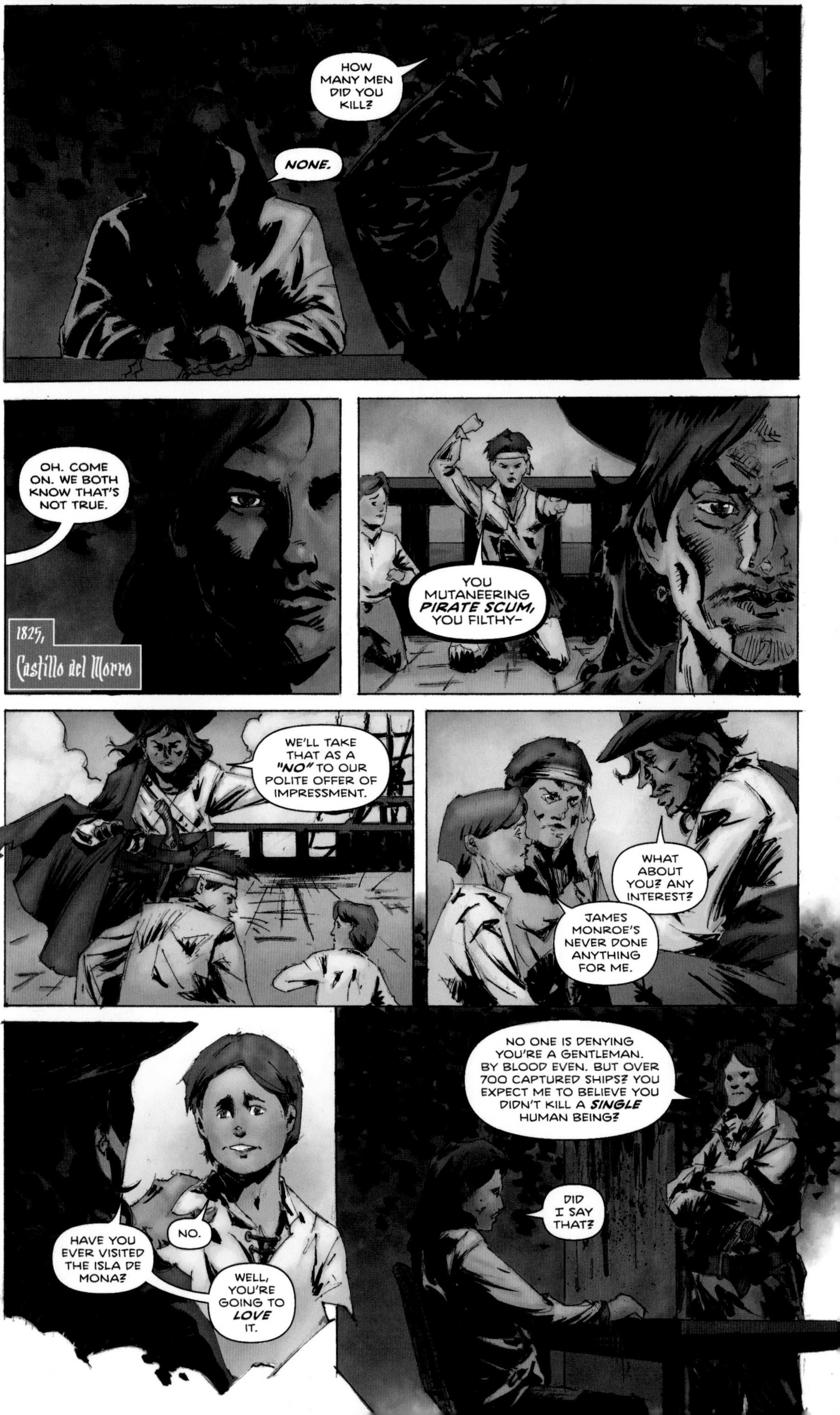
HOW MANY MEN DID YOU KILL?
NONE.
OH. COME ON. WE BOTH KNOW THAT'S NOT TRUE.
1825, Castillo del Morro
YOU MUTANEERING PIRATE SCUM, YOU FILTHY–
WE'LL TAKE THAT AS A "NO" TO OUR POLITE OFFER OF IMPRESSMENT.
WHAT ABOUT YOU? ANY INTEREST?
JAMES MONROE'S NEVER DONE ANYTHING FOR ME.
HAVE YOU EVER VISITED THE ISLA DE MONA?
NO.
WELL, YOU'RE GOING TO LOVE IT.
NO ONE IS DENYING YOU'RE A GENTLEMAN. BY BLOOD EVEN. BUT OVER 700 CAPTURED SHIPS? YOU EXPECT ME TO BELIEVE YOU DIDN'T KILL A SINGLE HUMAN BEING?
DID I SAY THAT?

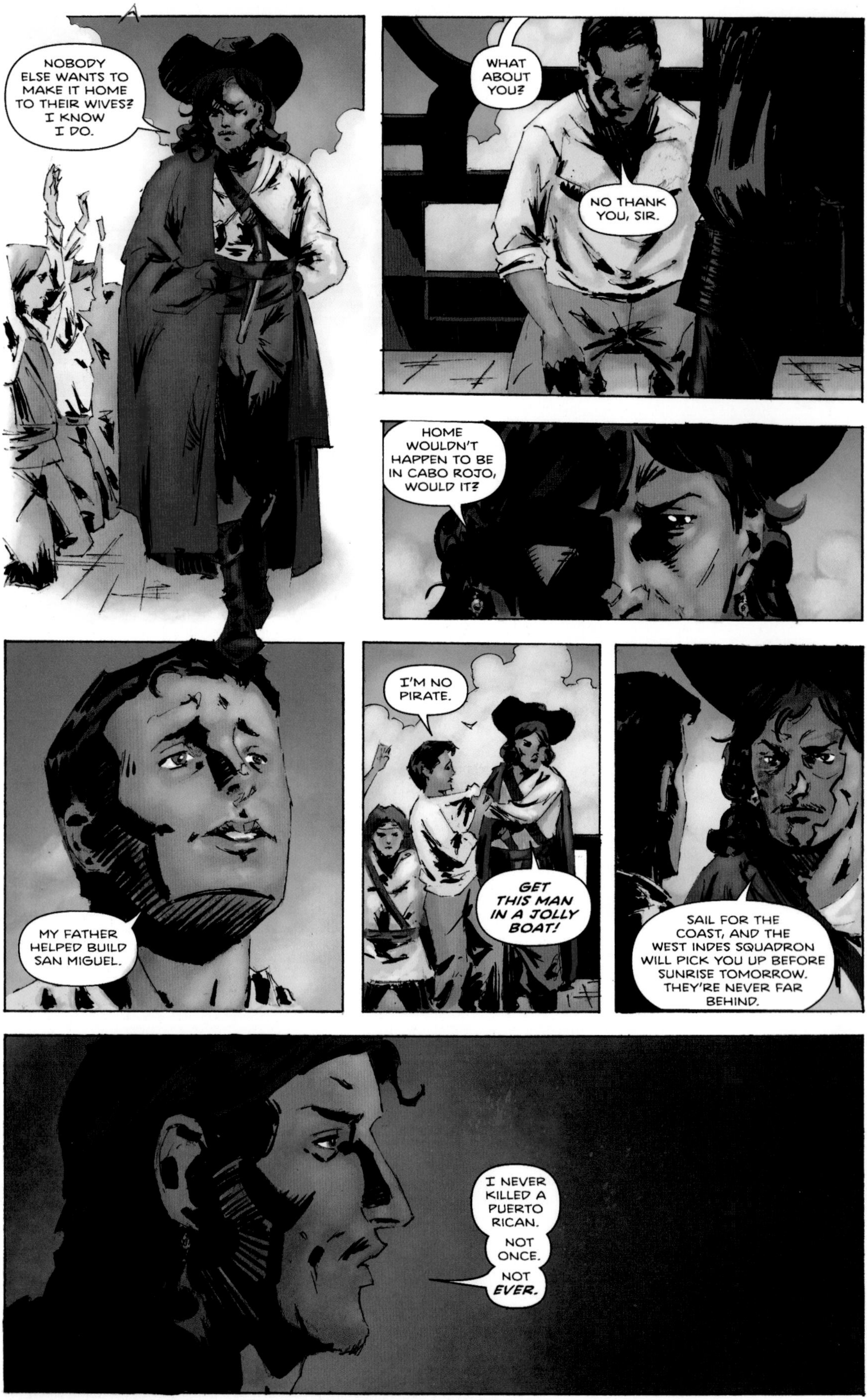
NOBODY ELSE WANTS TO MAKE IT HOME TO THEIR WIVES? I KNOW I DO.
WHAT ABOUT YOU?
NO THANK YOU, SIR.
HOME WOULDN'T HAPPEN TO BE IN CABO ROJO, WOULD IT?
MY FATHER HELPED BUILD SAN MIGUEL.
I'M NO PIRATE.
GET THIS MAN IN A JOLLY BOAT!
SAIL FOR THE COAST, AND THE WEST INDES SQUADRON WILL PICK YOU UP BEFORE SUNRISE TOMORROW. THEY'RE NEVER FAR BEHIND.
I NEVER KILLED A PUERTO RICAN.
NOT ONCE.
NOT EVER.

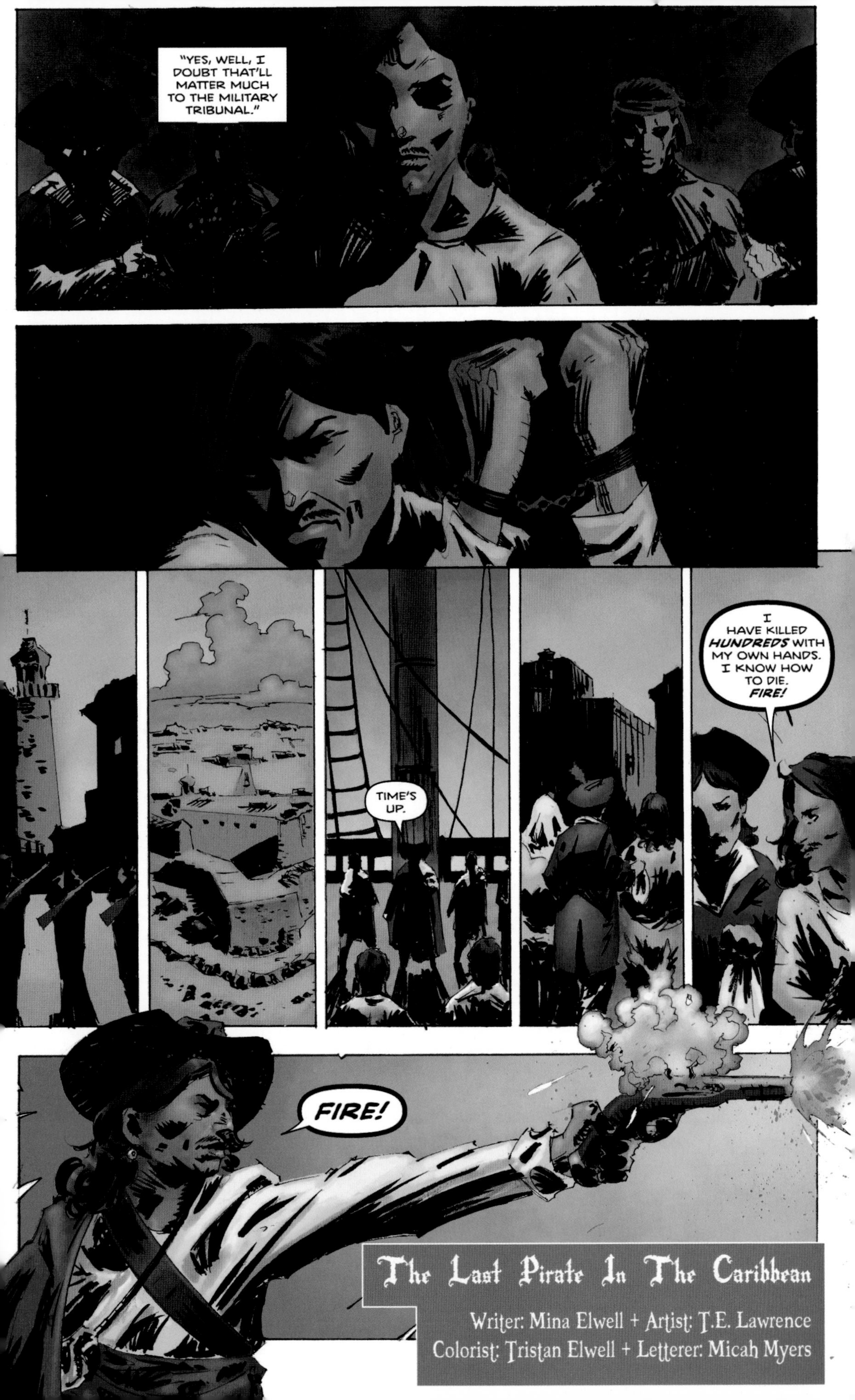
"YES, WELL, I DOUBT THAT'LL MATTER MUCH TO THE MILITARY TRIBUNAL."
TIME'S UP.
I HAVE KILLED HUNDREDS WITH MY OWN HANDS. I KNOW HOW TO DIE. FIRE!
FIRE!
The Last Pirate In The Caribbean
Writer: Mina Elwell + Artist: T.E. Lawrence
Colorist: Tristan Elwell + Letterer: Micah Myers

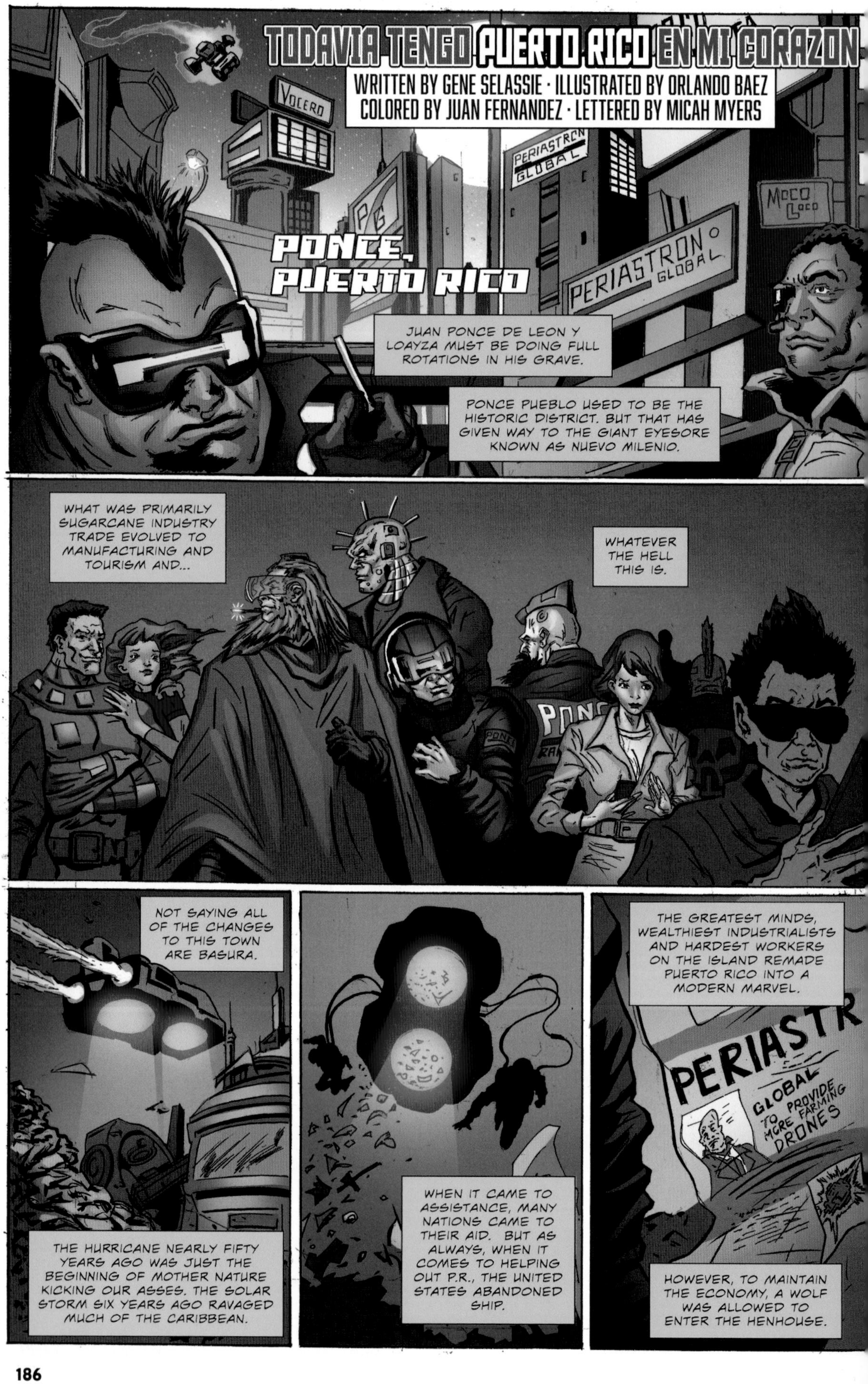
TODAVIA TENGO PUERTO RICO EN MI CORAZON
WRITTEN BY GENE SELASSIE · ILLUSTRATED BY ORLANDO BAEZ
COLORED BY JUAN FERNANDEZ · LETTERED BY MICAH MYERS
VOCERO
PERIASTRON GLOBAL
PONCE, PUERTO RICO
PERIASTRON GLOBAL
JUAN PONCE DE LEON Y LOAYZA MUST BE DOING FULL ROTATIONS IN HIS GRAVE.
PONCE PUEBLO USED TO BE THE HISTORIC DISTRICT. BUT THAT HAS GIVEN WAY TO THE GIANT EYESORE KNOWN AS NUEVO MILENIO.
WHAT WAS PRIMARILY SUGARCANE INDUSTRY TRADE EVOLVED TO MANUFACTURING AND TOURISM AND...
WHATEVER THE HELL THIS IS.
NOT SAYING ALL OF THE CHANGES TO THIS TOWN ARE BASURA.
THE HURRICANE NEARLY FIFTY YEARS AGO WAS JUST THE BEGINNING OF MOTHER NATURE KICKING OUR ASSES. THE SOLAR STORM SIX YEARS AGO RAVAGED MUCH OF THE CARIBBEAN.
WHEN IT CAME TO ASSISTANCE, MANY NATIONS CAME TO THEIR AID. BUT AS ALWAYS, WHEN IT COMES TO HELPING OUT P.R., THE UNITED STATES ABANDONED SHIP.
THE GREATEST MINDS, WEALTHIEST INDUSTRIALISTS AND HARDEST WORKERS ON THE ISLAND REMADE PUERTO RICO INTO A MODERN MARVEL.
PERIASTR
PERIAS
GLOBAL TO PROVIDE MORE FARMING DRONES
HOWEVER, TO MAINTAIN THE ECONOMY, A WOLF WAS ALLOWED TO ENTER THE HENHOUSE.

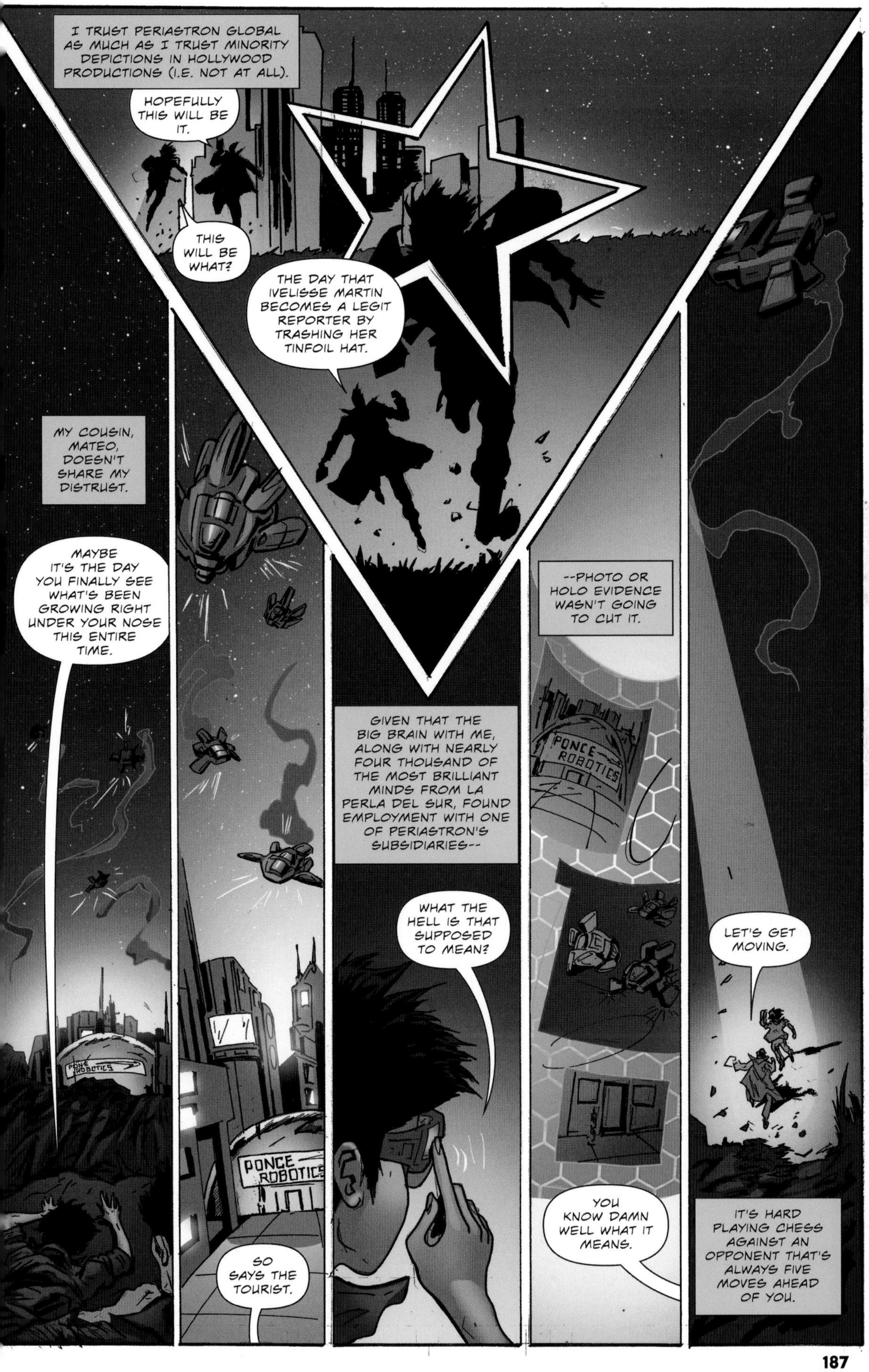
I TRUST PERIASTRON GLOBAL AS MUCH AS I TRUST MINORITY DEPICTIONS IN HOLLYWOOD PRODUCTIONS (I.E. NOT AT ALL).
HOPEFULLY THIS WILL BE IT.
THIS WILL BE WHAT?
THE DAY THAT IVELISSE MARTIN BECOMES A LEGIT REPORTER BY TRASHING HER TINFOIL HAT.
MY COUSIN, MATEO, DOESN'T SHARE MY DISTRUST.
MAYBE IT'S THE DAY YOU FINALLY SEE WHAT'S BEEN GROWING RIGHT UNDER YOUR NOSE THIS ENTIRE TIME.
PONCE ROBOTICS
PONCE ROBOTICS
SO SAYS THE TOURIST.
GIVEN THAT THE BIG BRAIN WITH ME, ALONG WITH NEARLY FOUR THOUSAND OF THE MOST BRILLIANT MINDS FROM LA PERLA DEL SUR, FOUND EMPLOYMENT WITH ONE OF PERIASTRON'S SUBSIDIARIES--
WHAT THE HELL IS THAT SUPPOSED TO MEAN?
--PHOTO OR HOLO EVIDENCE WASN'T GOING TO CUT IT.
PONCE ROBOTICS
YOU KNOW DAMN WELL WHAT IT MEANS.
LET'S GET MOVING.
IT'S HARD PLAYING CHESS AGAINST AN OPPONENT THAT'S ALWAYS FIVE MOVES AHEAD OF YOU.

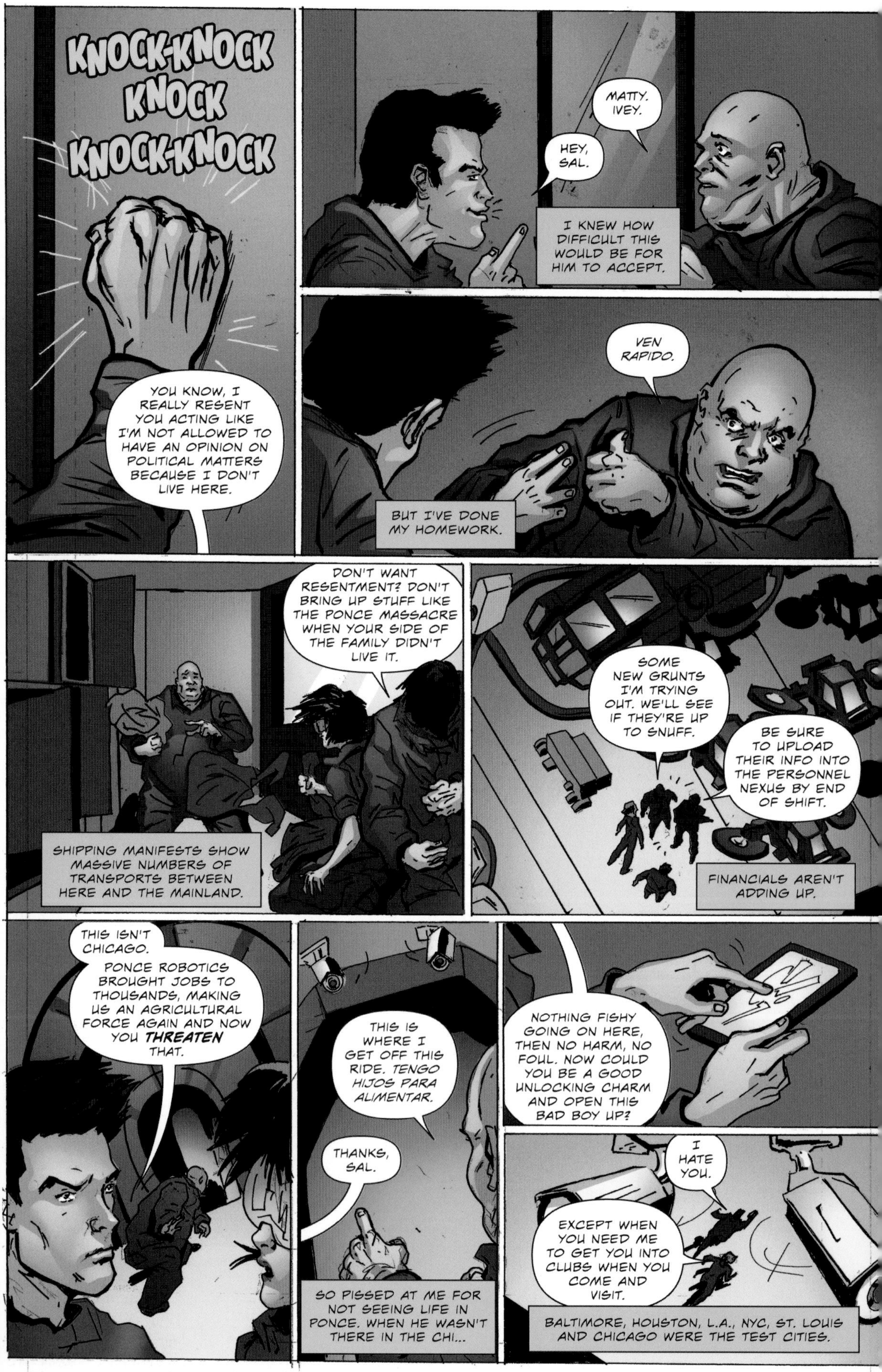
KNOCK-KNOCK KNOCK KNOCK-KNOCK
YOU KNOW, I REALLY RESENT YOU ACTING LIKE I'M NOT ALLOWED TO HAVE AN OPINION ON POLITICAL MATTERS BECAUSE I DON'T LIVE HERE.
MATTY. IVEY.
HEY, SAL.
I KNEW HOW DIFFICULT THIS WOULD BE FOR HIM TO ACCEPT.
VEN RAPIDO.
BUT I'VE DONE MY HOMEWORK.
DON'T WANT RESENTMENT? DON'T BRING UP STUFF LIKE THE PONCE MASSACRE WHEN YOUR SIDE OF THE FAMILY DIDN'T LIVE IT.
SHIPPING MANIFESTS SHOW MASSIVE NUMBERS OF TRANSPORTS BETWEEN HERE AND THE MAINLAND.
SOME NEW GRUNTS I'M TRYING OUT. WE'LL SEE IF THEY'RE UP TO SNUFF.
BE SURE TO UPLOAD THEIR INFO INTO THE PERSONNEL NEXUS BY END OF SHIFT.
FINANCIALS AREN'T ADDING UP.
THIS ISN'T CHICAGO.
PONCE ROBOTICS BROUGHT JOBS TO THOUSANDS, MAKING US AN AGRICULTURAL FORCE AGAIN AND NOW YOU **THREATEN** THAT.
THIS IS WHERE I GET OFF THIS RIDE. *TENGO HIJOS PARA ALIMENTAR.*
THANKS, SAL.
SO PISSED AT ME FOR NOT SEEING LIFE IN PONCE. WHEN HE WASN'T THERE IN THE CHI...
NOTHING FISHY GOING ON HERE, THEN NO HARM, NO FOUL. NOW COULD YOU BE A GOOD UNLOCKING CHARM AND OPEN THIS BAD BOY UP?
I HATE YOU.
EXCEPT WHEN YOU NEED ME TO GET YOU INTO CLUBS WHEN YOU COME AND VISIT.
BALTIMORE, HOUSTON, L.A., NYC, ST. LOUIS AND CHICAGO WERE THE TEST CITIES.

OPEN SESAME.

LAW ENFORCEMENT AGENCIES IN THESE "TROUBLED" CITIES BECAME PART OF A NEW INITIATIVE.

TO STEM THE RISING NUMBER OF EXCESSIVE FORCE CASES AND SHOOTINGS OF UNARMED PEOPLE OF COLOR, THIS INITIATIVE SOUGHT TO TAKE HUMAN EMOTION OUT OF THE EQUATION.

THEY WANTED TO CLEAN UP THE TAINTED IMAGE OF POLICE. THE SMALL NUMBER OF BAD ONES TAINTED THE WELL.

BUT IN TRYING TO STOP MONSTERS FROM GAINING BADGES, THEY CREATED A WHOLE NEW MONSTER.

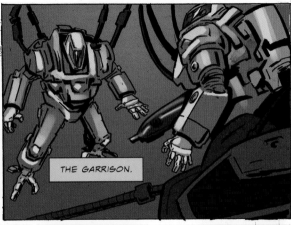

THE GARRISON.

IT'S...IT'S TRUE.

THESE MECHANIZED DRONES STARTED AS PEACEKEEPERS. BUT THEIR CREATORS WANTED QUICKER RESULTS.

SO THESE "HUMANITARIANS" PROGRAMMED THE GARRISON TO BECOME JUDGE, JURY AND EXECUTIONER.

I...I AM SO SORRY, IVEY.

APOLOGIES LATER. RIGHT NOW, WE'VE GOT TO GET AS MUCH EVIDENCE AND MAKE OUR--

ESCAPE?

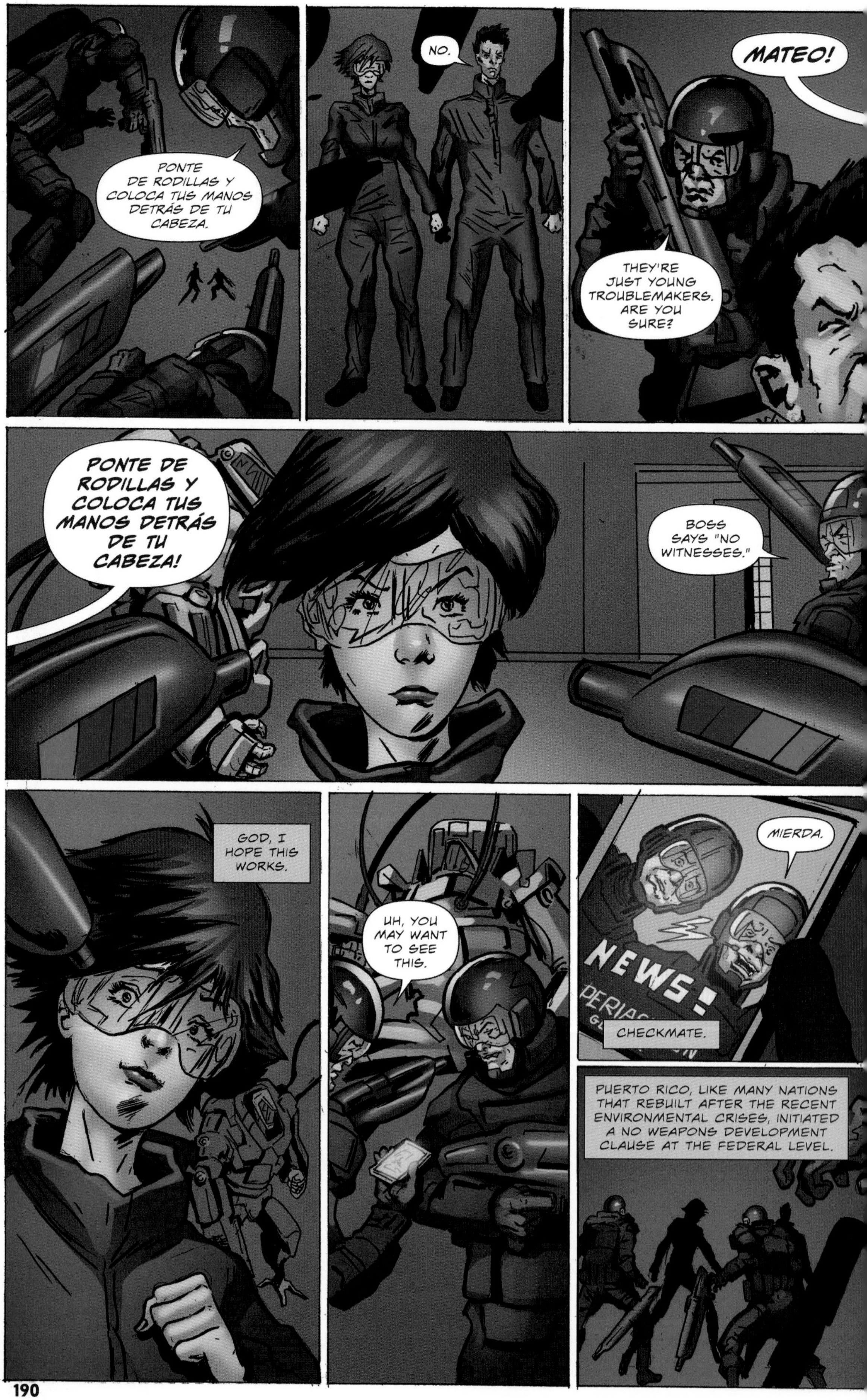
PONTE DE RODILLAS Y COLOCA TUS MANOS DETRÁS DE TU CABEZA.
NO.
MATEO!
THEY'RE JUST YOUNG TROUBLEMAKERS. ARE YOU SURE?
PONTE DE RODILLAS Y COLOCA TUS MANOS DETRÁS DE TU CABEZA!
BOSS SAYS "NO WITNESSES."
GOD, I HOPE THIS WORKS.
UH, YOU MAY WANT TO SEE THIS.
MIERDA.
NEWS!
CHECKMATE.
PUERTO RICO, LIKE MANY NATIONS THAT REBUILT AFTER THE RECENT ENVIRONMENTAL CRISES, INITIATED A NO WEAPONS DEVELOPMENT CLAUSE AT THE FEDERAL LEVEL.

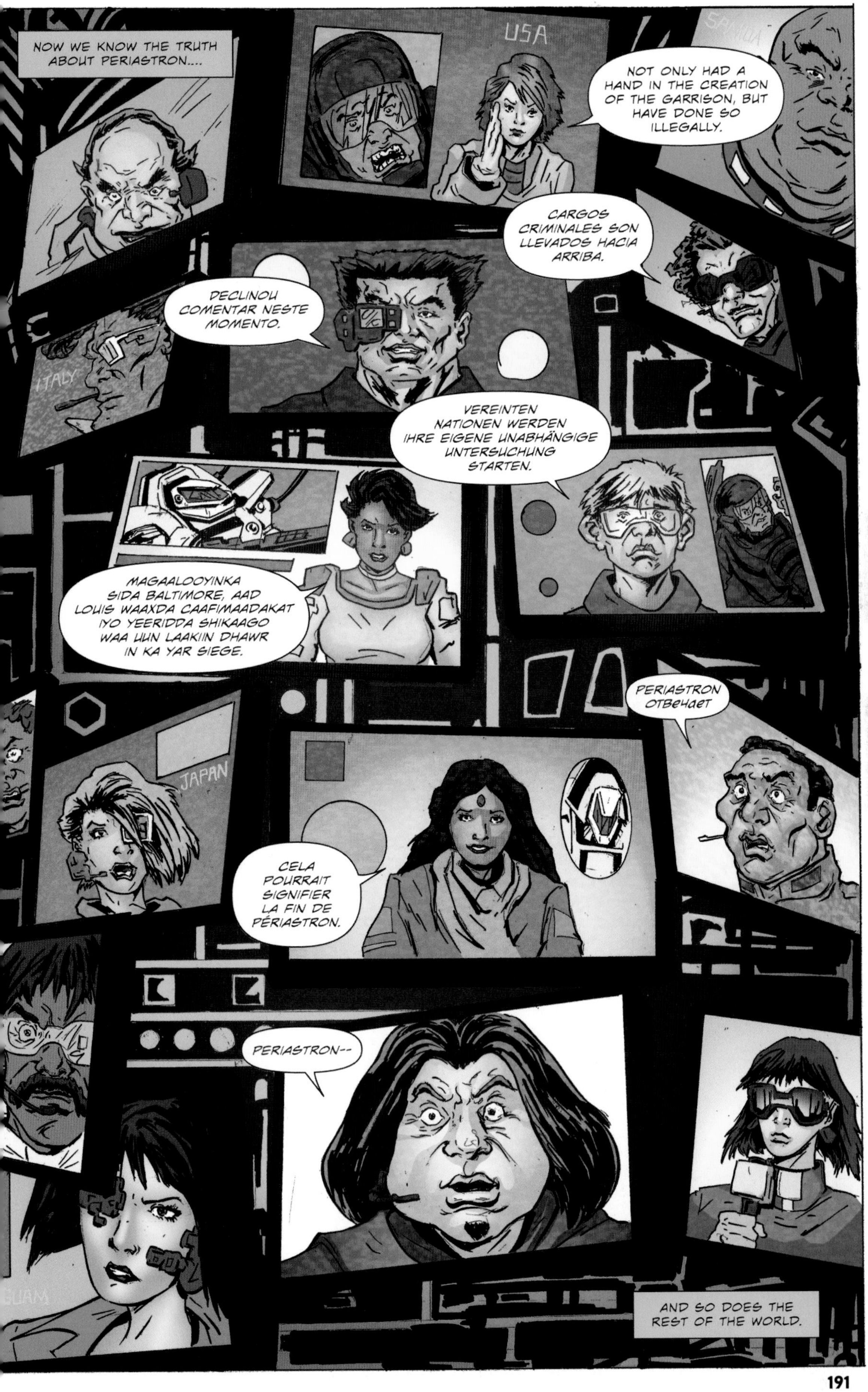
NOW WE KNOW THE TRUTH ABOUT PERIASTRON....
USA
NOT ONLY HAD A HAND IN THE CREATION OF THE GARRISON, BUT HAVE DONE SO ILLEGALLY.
CARGOS CRIMINALES SON LLEVADOS HACIA ARRIBA.
DECLINOU COMENTAR NESTE MOMENTO.
ITALY
VEREINTEN NATIONEN WERDEN IHRE EIGENE UNABHÄNGIGE UNTERSUCHUNG STARTEN.
MAGAALOOYINKA SIDA BALTIMORE, AAD LOUIS WAAXDA CAAFIMAADAKAT IYO YEERIDDA SHIKAAGO WAA UUN LAAKIIN DHAWR IN KA YAR SIEGE.
PERIASTRON ОТВечает
JAPAN
CELA POURRAIT SIGNIFIER LA FIN DE PÉRIASTRON.
PERIASTRON--
GUAM
AND SO DOES THE REST OF THE WORLD.

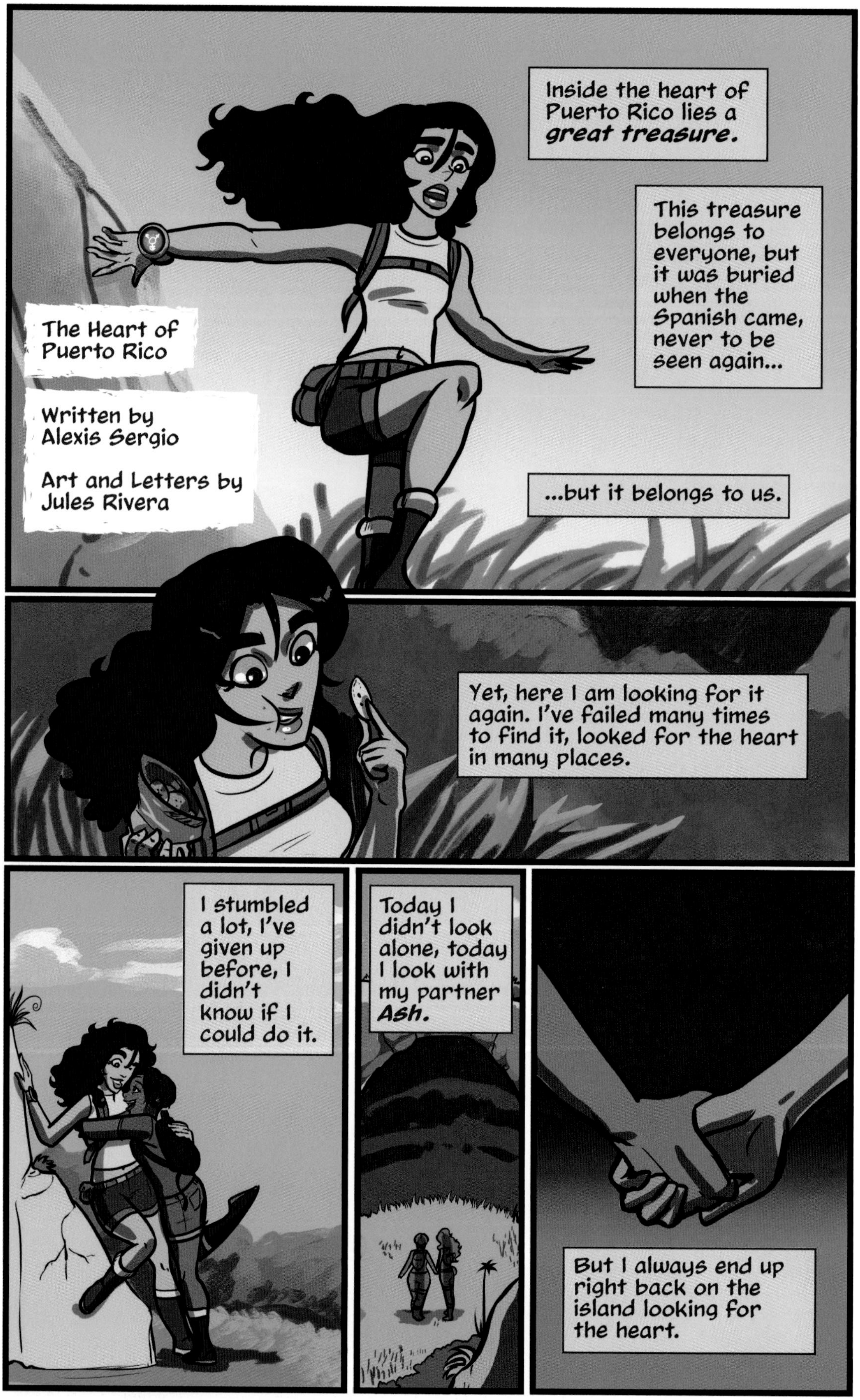

Inside the heart of Puerto Rico lies a ***great treasure.***
The Heart of Puerto Rico
Written by Alexis Sergio
Art and Letters by Jules Rivera
This treasure belongs to everyone, but it was buried when the Spanish came, never to be seen again...
...but it belongs to us.
Yet, here I am looking for it again. I've failed many times to find it, looked for the heart in many places.
I stumbled a lot, I've given up before, I didn't know if I could do it.
Today I didn't look alone, today I look with my partner ***Ash.***
But I always end up right back on the island looking for the heart.

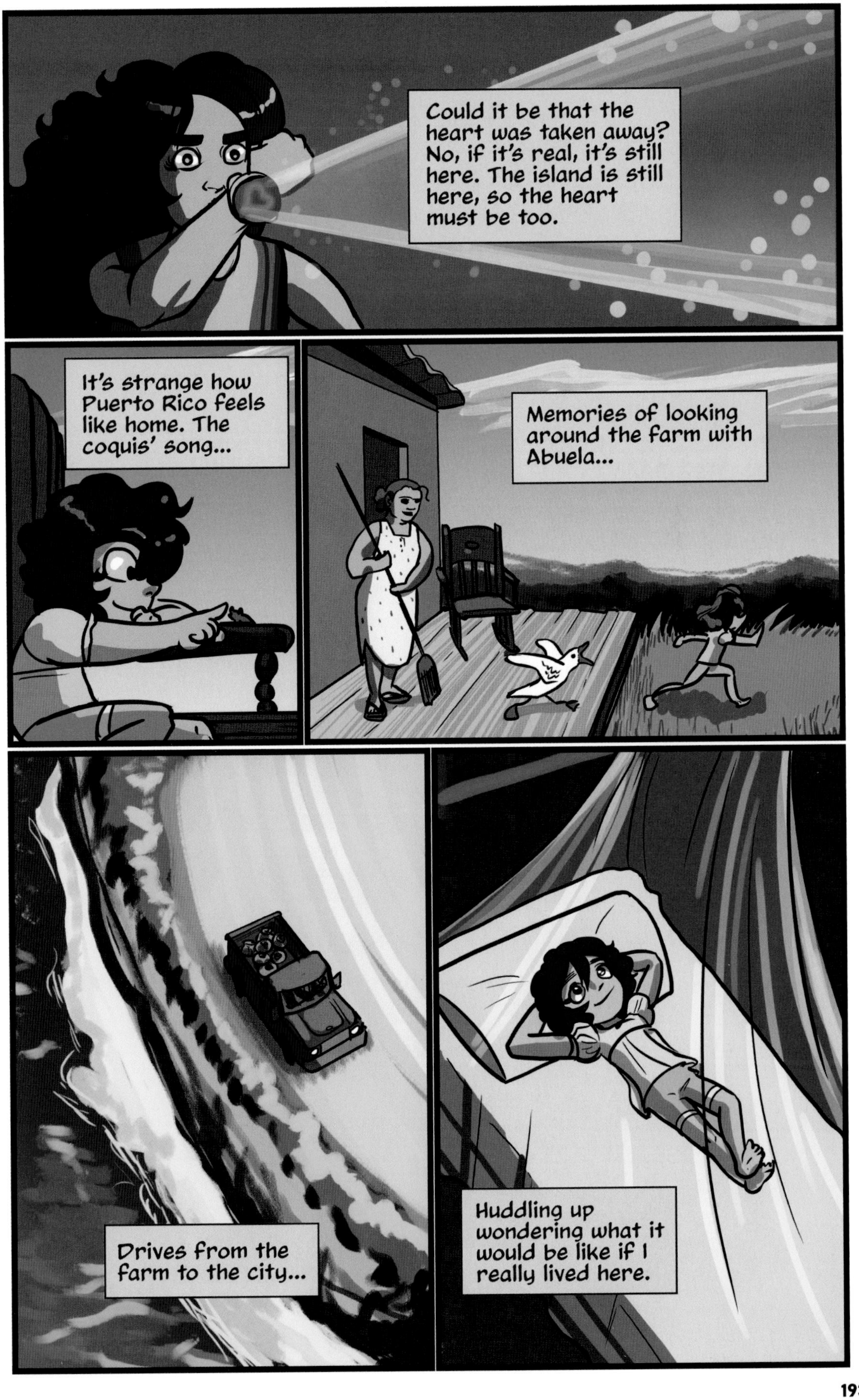
Could it be that the heart was taken away? No, if it's real, it's still here. The island is still here, so the heart must be too.
It's strange how Puerto Rico feels like home. The coquis' song...
Memories of looking around the farm with Abuela...
Drives from the farm to the city...
Huddling up wondering what it would be like if I really lived here.

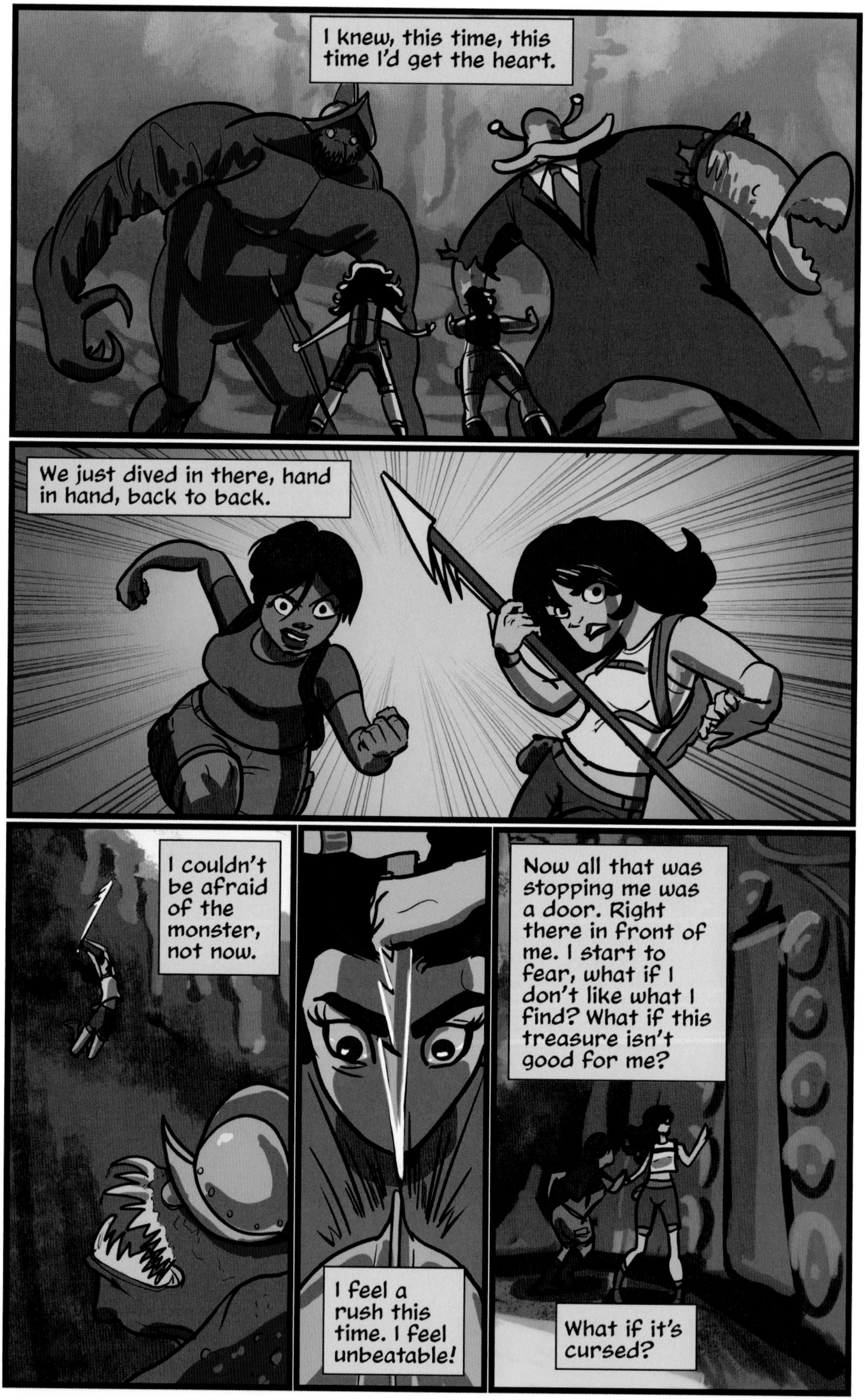

I knew, this time, this time I'd get the heart.
We just dived in there, hand in hand, back to back.
I couldn't be afraid of the monster, not now.
I feel a rush this time. I feel unbeatable!
Now all that was stopping me was a door. Right there in front of me. I start to fear, what if I don't like what I find? What if this treasure isn't good for me?
What if it's cursed?

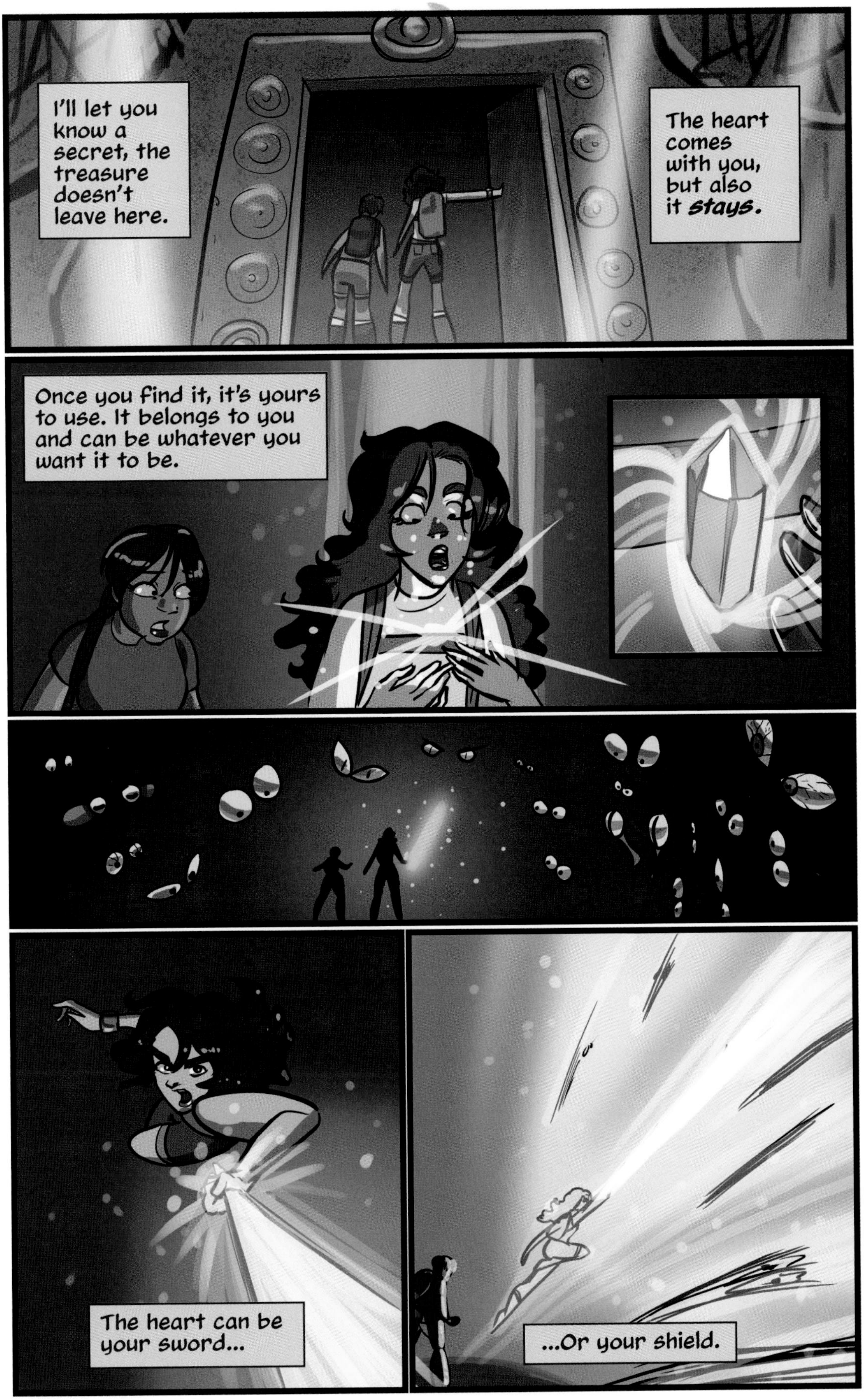
I'll let you know a secret, the treasure doesn't leave here.
The heart comes with you, but also it *stays.*
Once you find it, it's yours to use. It belongs to you and can be whatever you want it to be.
The heart can be your sword...
...Or your shield.

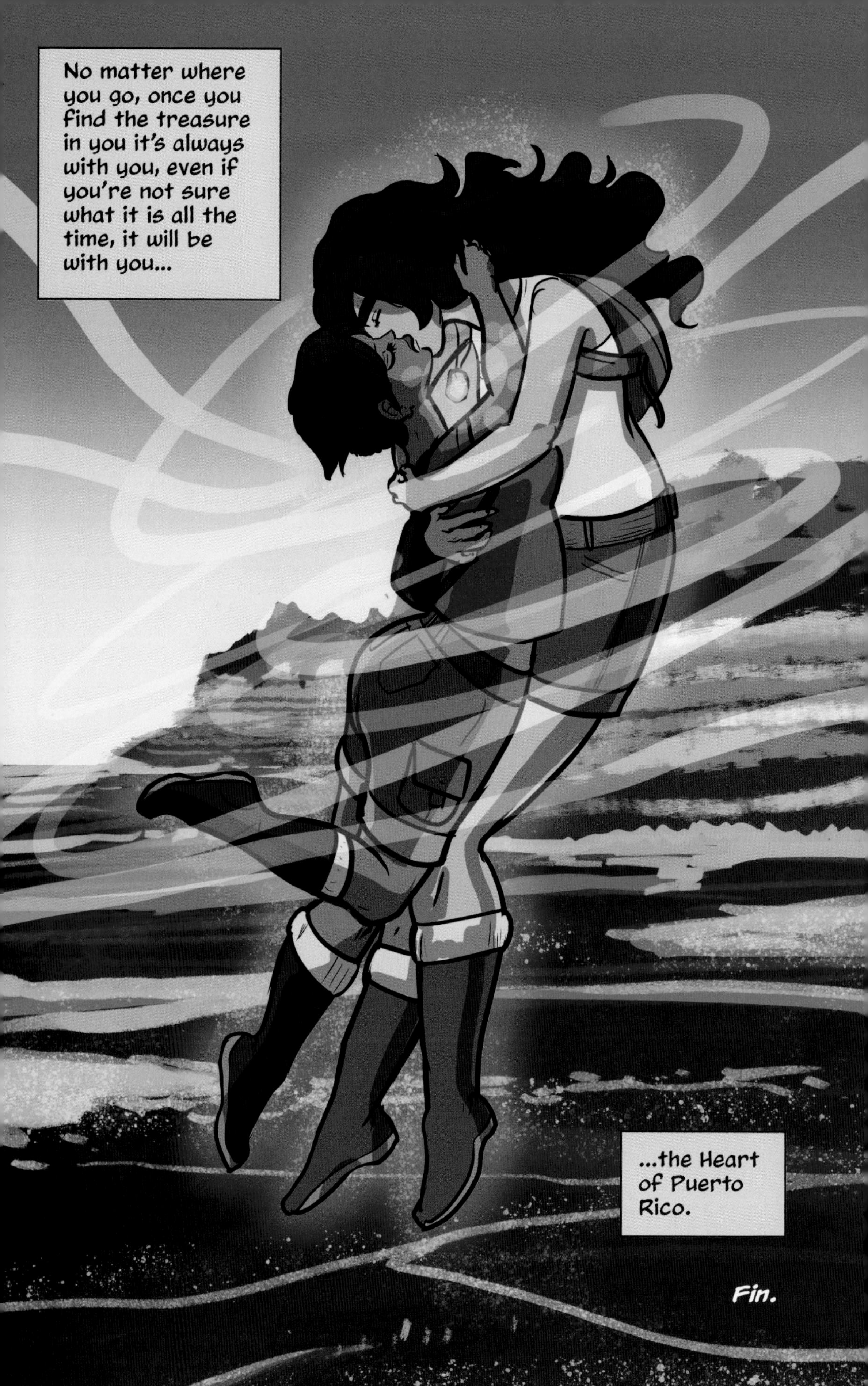
No matter where you go, once you find the treasure in you it's always with you, even if you're not sure what it is all the time, it will be with you...
...the Heart of Puerto Rico.
Fin.

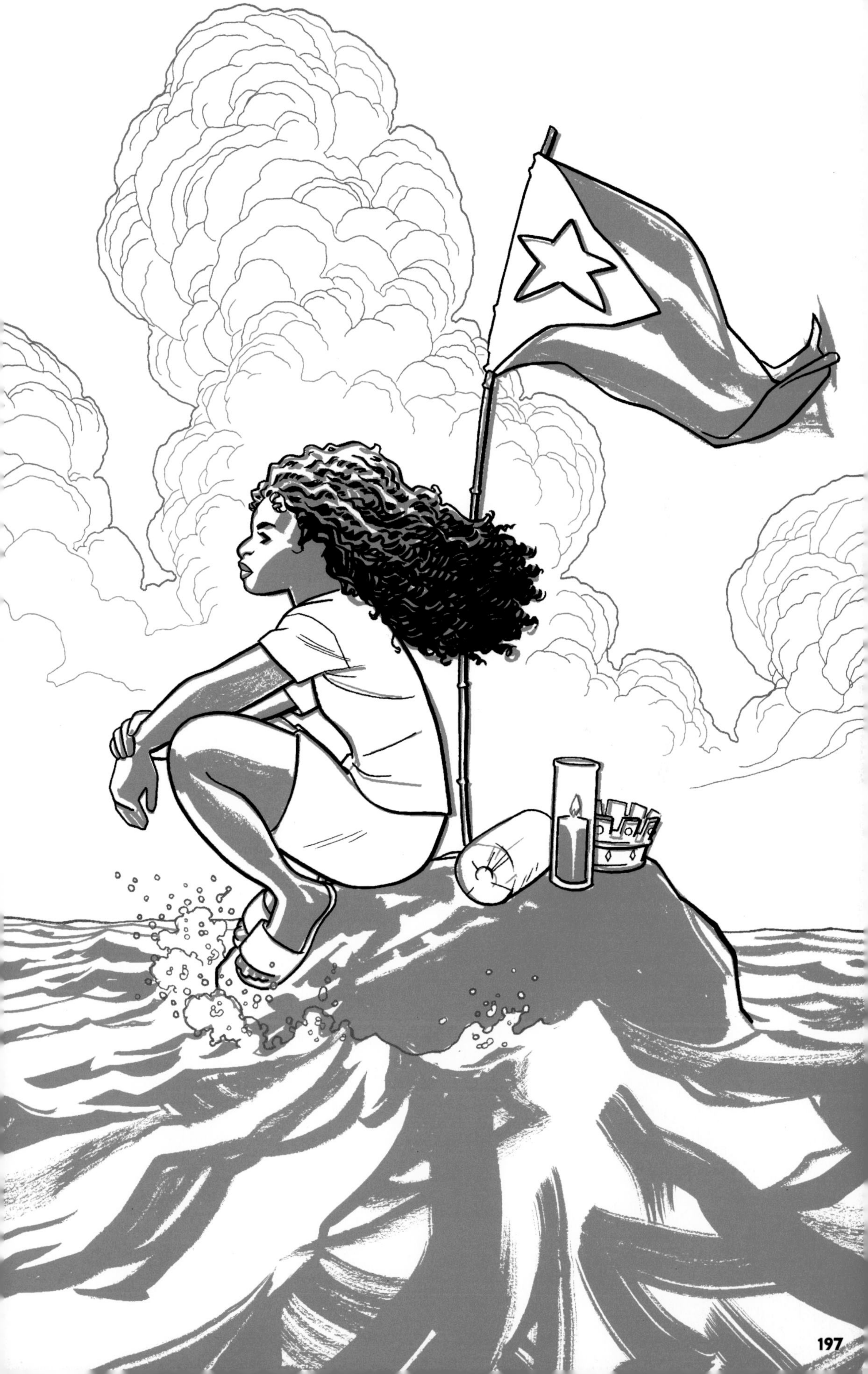

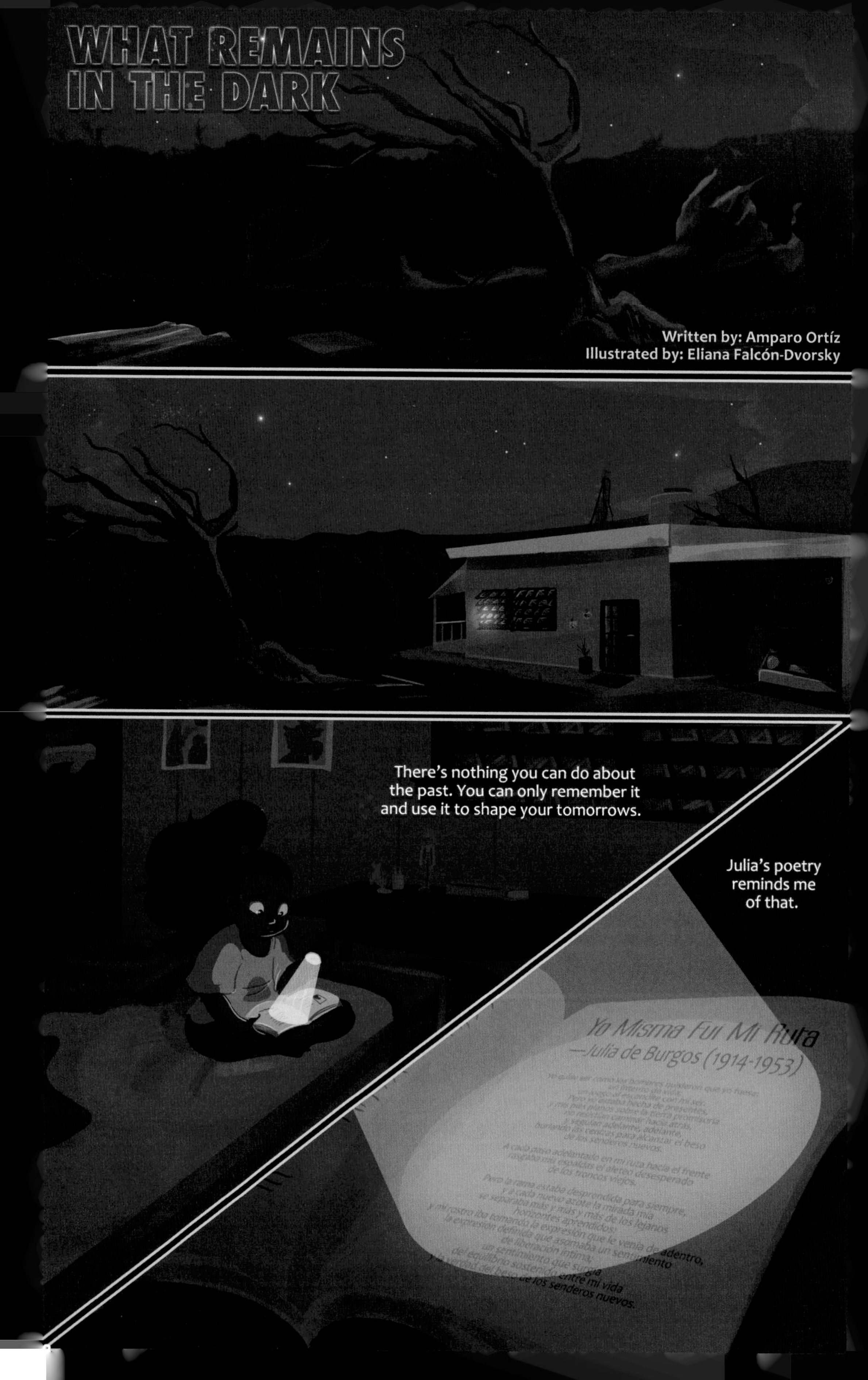

WHAT REMAINS IN THE DARK
Written by: Amparo Ortíz
Illustrated by: Eliana Falcón-Dvorsky
There's nothing you can do about the past. You can only remember it and use it to shape your tomorrows.
Julia's poetry reminds me of that.
Yo Misma Fui Mi Ruta
—Julia de Burgos (1914-1953)
Pero yo estaba hecha de presentes,
y mis pies planos sobre la tierra promisoria
no resistían caminar hacia atrás,
y seguían adelante, adelante,
burlando las cenizas para alcanzar el beso
de los senderos nuevos.
A cada paso adelantado en mi ruta hacia el frente
rasgaba mis espaldas el aleteo desesperado
de los troncos viejos.
Pero la rama estaba desprendida para siempre,
y a cada nuevo azote la mirada mía
se separaba más y más y más de los lejanos
horizontes aprendidos:
y mi rostro iba tomando la expresión que le venía de adentro,
la expresión definida que asomaba un sentimiento
de liberación íntima;
un sentimiento que surgía
del equilibrio sostenido entre mi vida
y la verdad del beso de los senderos nuevos.

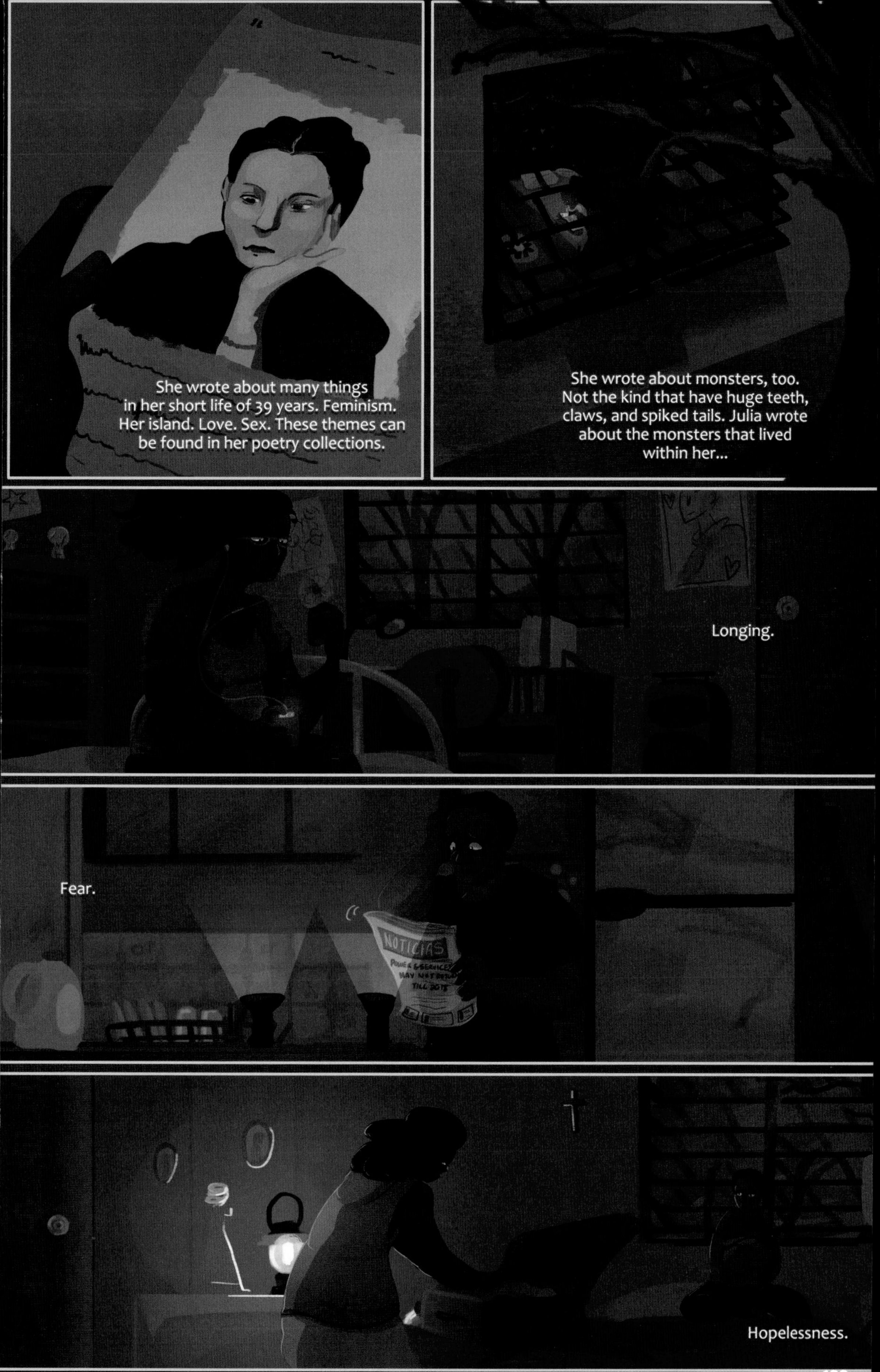
She wrote about many things in her short life of 39 years. Feminism. Her island. Love. Sex. These themes can be found in her poetry collections.
She wrote about monsters, too. Not the kind that have huge teeth, claws, and spiked tails. Julia wrote about the monsters that lived within her...
Longing.
Fear.
NOTICIAS
Hopelessness.

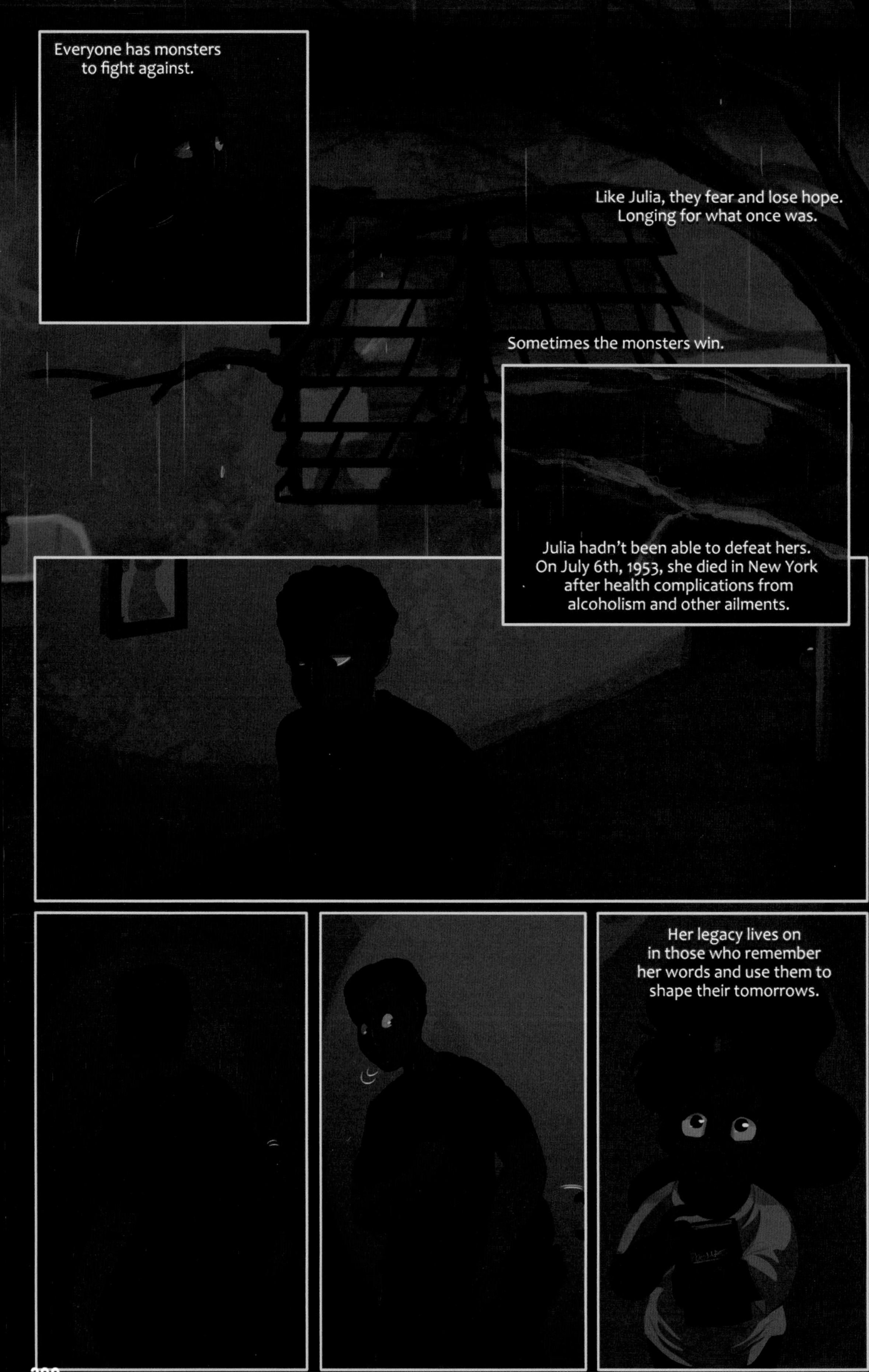
Everyone has monsters to fight against.
Like Julia, they fear and lose hope. Longing for what once was.
Sometimes the monsters win.
Julia hadn't been able to defeat hers. On July 6th, 1953, she died in New York after health complications from alcoholism and other ailments.
Her legacy lives on in those who remember her words and use them to shape their tomorrows.

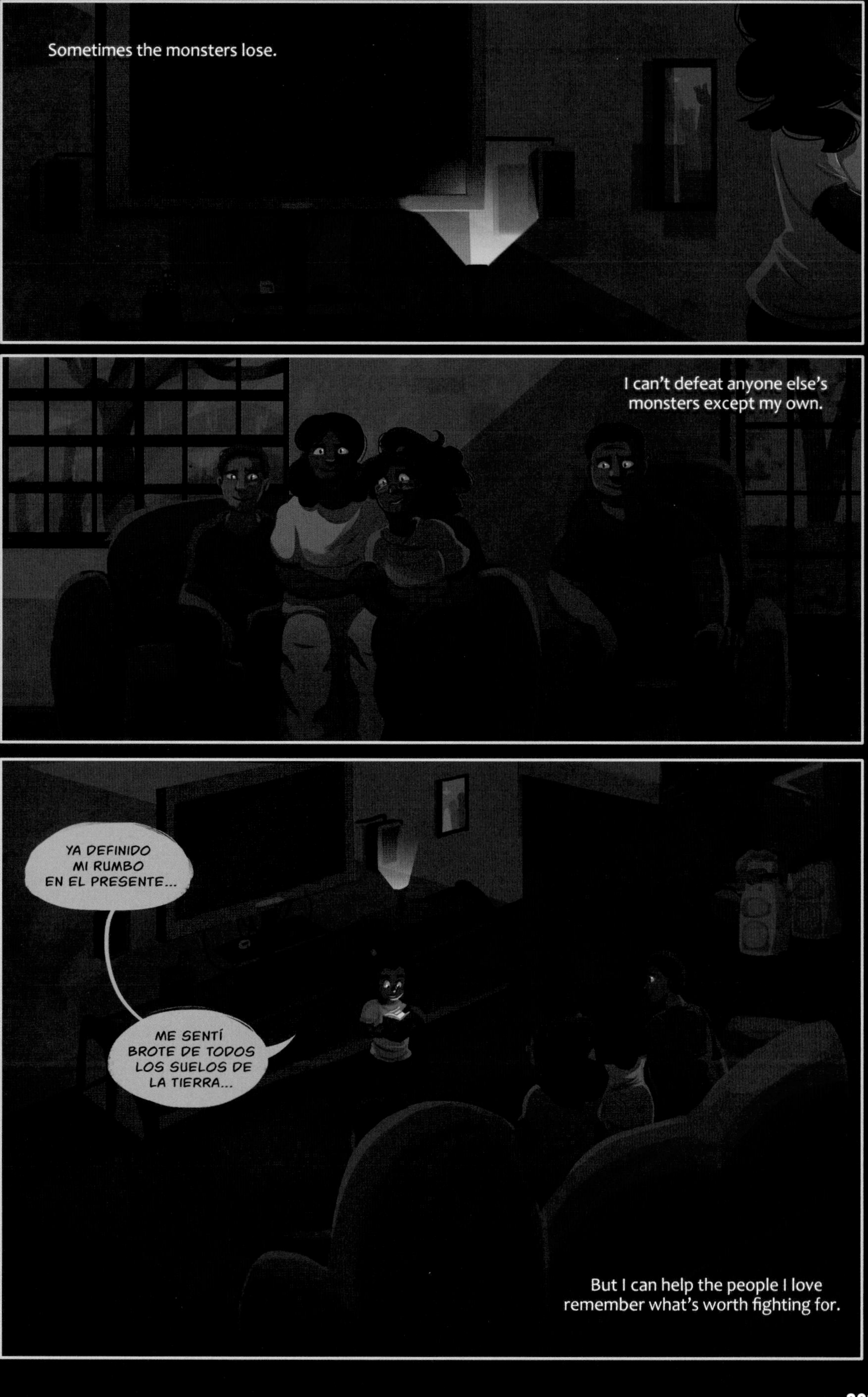
Sometimes the monsters lose.
I can't defeat anyone else's monsters except my own.
YA DEFINIDO MI RUMBO EN EL PRESENTE...
ME SENTÍ BROTE DE TODOS LOS SUELOS DE LA TIERRA...
But I can help the people I love remember what's worth fighting for.

# CONTRIBUTOR QUOTES

"Not only does this book give a voice to a group that is severely underrepresented in mainstream comics, but it is for a noble cause. I am honored to be a part of this project."

**GENE SELASSIE**, *writer of "Todavia Tengo Puerto Rico En Mi Corazon"*

"The meaning of this story to me is Puerto Rico in time will be moving ahead toward a greater future with new advances and technological things that can aid the Puerto Rican people to be protected against disastrous storms and life conditions."

**ORLANDO BAEZ**, *artist of "Todavia Tengo Puerto Rico En Mi Corazon"*

"This story allowed me to really share my feelings about the island, along with others who all have different perspectives. It's about sharing the feelings of all Puerto Ricans with all sorts of backgrounds with Puerto Rico to create a picture of what this place means."

**ALEXIS SERGIO**, *writer of "The Heart of the Island"*

"I was honored to participate in this *Puerto Rico Strong* anthology. Being that my family from my mother's side are from the island, it was my duty to be part of it. I sincerely had my grandparents in mind when I illustrated the last scene of 'La Casita of American Heroes.' They were my heroes and I miss them."

**CHARLES "OOGE" UGAS**, *artist of "La Casita of American Heroes"*

"I've had this dream to illustrate a story, a novel, a children's book, or create a painting about Puerto Rican culture, folklore, and mythology. My contribution to this anthology helped achieve part of this dream and I can't wait to take it to the next level. Thank you for allowing me to be a part of this."

**LEONARDO "LAGONZA" GONZALEZ**, *illustrator of "El Vampiro de Moca"*

"I am always glad for the chance to spread awareness and supportive messages through my art, and it is my hope that my work will be a positive influence on those experiencing it."

**ALLISON STREJAU**, *artist of "Family Ends with Me"*

"After living through such a harrowing experience, the amount of support Puerto Rico has received has been overwhelming. I am thankful for the opportunity to contribute in the rebuilding efforts through such a wonderful project."

**ROSA COLÓN,** *creator of "A Broken P.R.O.M.E.S.A."*

"Since Hurricane Maria, my heart has been broken for my island and my people. Putting feelings to words, and seeing those words turned into beautiful art, has been cathartic and healing— especially because this project is directly contributing to helping the people of Puerto Rico."

**JAVIER MORILLO,** *writer of "Macondo, Puerto Rico"*

"The story chosen was more of an uplifting and playful idea for the youth learning at school about the Taíno culture. It was perfect mix of the children's imagination of how the gods and natives were."

**ALEJANDRO ROSADO,** *artist of "A Taíno's Tale"*

"Maria's aftermath left me feeling powerless, what with living so far away from Puerto Rico and having no way of helping my loved ones. When I heard about this project, I knew I wanted to be part of it. Being able to use my artistic skills to help my people made me feel like I have done a small part in helping our little island back up."

**RAMÓN J. SIERRA SANTIAGO,** *artist of "Hope"*

"I believe in the magic of hope. Being a part of this anthology means helping the only home I've ever known using hope as the guiding light for a brighter tomorrow."

**AMPARO ORTIZ,** *author of "What Remains in the Dark"*

"For my mother, Maria de Lourdes Cedeño Albarano."

**VITO DELSANTE,** *author of "Cocinar"*

# CONTRIBUTOR QUOTES *cont.*

"It was my family who fostered my love for creating art, who taught me to take pride in our history and identity. I wanted to give back to them and others in our community the best way I knew how."

**VERONICA GARCIA,** *creator of "Here"*

"I am so proud that we can use our art to help the island of our ancestors and family! Being a part of this anthology, a book that is the first of its kind, all about us, is an extreme honor. As I continue to try and connect with our culture, this book is another piece of our journey to draw strength from! Vive Puerto Rico!"

**JAVIER CRUZ WINNIK,** *creator of "Knowledge of Self"*

"I am so proud to be a part of this anthology. It is amazing that this goofy talent that I have can be used to help others."

**MICAH MYERS,** *letterer of "The Last Pirate in the Caribbean"*

"I wanted to capture some of the beauty and strength of Puerto Rico and her people. It's in the land, the water, the plants, the arts, and most of all in her people's hearts."

**KRISTEN VAN DAM,** *illustrator of "Dreamer"*

"It is an honor to be involved. We did the same thing some years ago with "Renaissance," an anthology by Filipino artists who raised money for typhoon flooding. Together, we are strong. Thank you."

**ROD ESPINOSA,** *artist for "Breaking Bread"*

"My aunt lost her house in the storm. My uncle described the aftermath as 'straight out of *The Walking Dead*.' Thank you for buying *Puerto Rico Strong* and helping thousands like them in their time of need."

**TONY BEDARD,** *author of "Reality Check"*

"My contributions to *Puerto Rico Strong* were not only my small way of supporting Puerto Rico in the wake of the hurricane, but also a way to raise awareness about Puerto Rico itself and its relationship with the US. I knew little of the politics between them, an ignorance of which a lot of mainland US citizens like myself might be guilty; but through my research, I gained a deeper understanding of a history I never learned about in school or the media. I hope these comics bring that same understanding to a wider audience."

**ALLY SHWED,** *author of "La Operación"*

"I went to Puerto Rico every summer during my childhood and my experiences were a lot like Julian's in the comic. With the story Fabian and I wrote, I wanted to convey how scary it was, not only to be in a foreign environment, but to be subjected to the expectations of this father who was so much more masculine than I felt, whose skin was darker, whose interests were so far from my own. Those rare moments when we did connect, like over that comic book, I could feel my heritage. I could taste what it was like to be Puerto Rican and wanted to share that."

**JEFF GOMEZ,** *author of "The Dragon of Bayamón"*

"As a writer, you get to write about all kinds of characters mostly fictitious in nature, and for that reason working on this anthology was a true honor as it allowed me to write about the real heroes in my life. Heroes that a lot of the world sadly choose to forget or dismiss when we should only honor them. Thanks again for having me on this project, it was a true honor."

**ALAN C. MEDINA,** *author of "Helping Hands"*

"When I was asked if I wanted to participate in this anthology, I knew that I did. I had wanted to contribute to the Puerto Rican people in some way, but I didn't know how. And this made sense. So I took the opportunity to tell a true story about when my best buddy introduced me to his family and how much they all mean to me."

**GRANT ALTER,** *author of "Family"*

# CONTRIBUTOR QUOTES *cont.*

"Illustrating this piece gave me the chance to learn more about the people that inhabited Puerto Rico so long ago. The stories they told of powerful gods and forces of nature were incredible to read about. It was a great learning experience and I'm proud to be a part of *Puerto Rico Strong.*"

**SABRINA CINTRON,** *illustrator of "Gods of Borikén"*

"Contributing to *Puerto Rico Strong* was a way for me to honor the women and culture that shaped me as a person. I'm proud to be Puerto Rican and equally proud to have taken part in this project that's helping so many people."

**TARA MARTINEZ,** *author of "Breaking Bread"*

"Puerto Rico was never my home, but it is my heritage and my heart. I hope my story will remind those of Puerto Rican descent of the magic the island still holds, no matter what generation they might be."

**ADAM LANCE GARCIA,** *author of "Stories from My Father"*

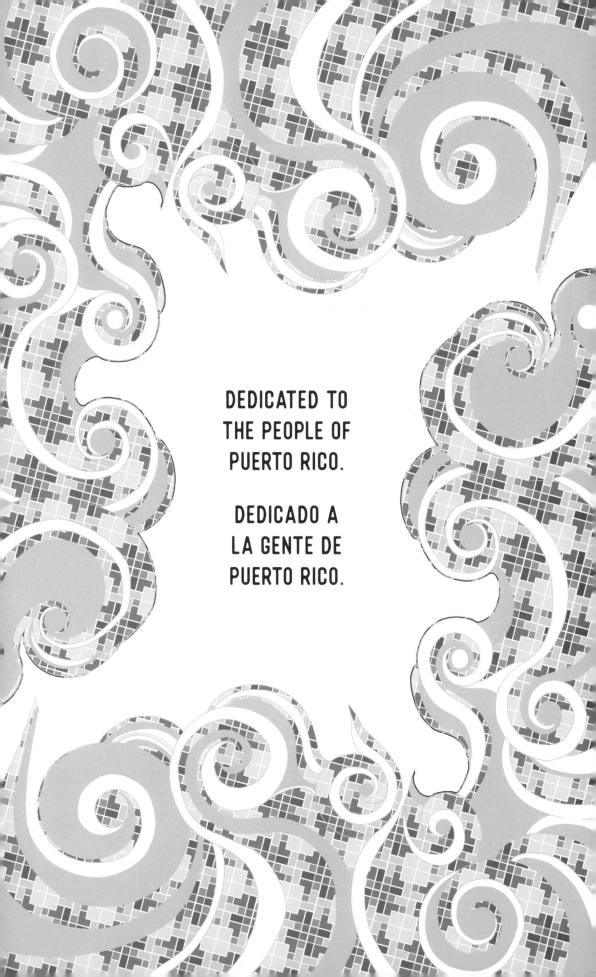

DEDICATED TO
THE PEOPLE OF
PUERTO RICO.

DEDICADO A
LA GENTE DE
PUERTO RICO.

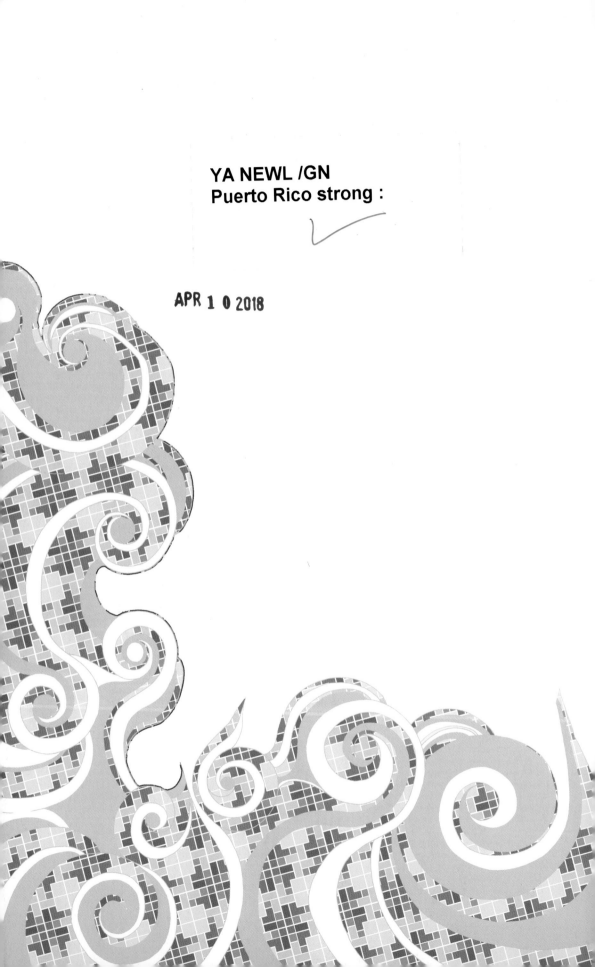